We Are All Migrants

In 2015, Germany agreed to accept a million Syrian refugees. The country had become an epicenter of global migration and one of Europe's most diverse countries. But was this influx of migration new to Germany? In this highly readable volume, Jan Plamper charts the groups and waves of post-1945 mobility to Germany. *We Are All Migrants* is the first narrative history of multicultural Germany told through life-stories. It explores the experiences of the 12.5 million German expellees from Eastern Europe who arrived at the end of the Second World War; the 14 million "guest workers" from Italy and Turkey who turned West Germany into an economic powerhouse; the GDR's Vietnamese labor migrants; and the 2.3 million Germans and 230,000 Jews who came from the Soviet Union after 1987. Without minimizing racism, *We Are All Migrants* shows that immigration is a success story – and that Germany has been, and is, one of the most fascinating laboratories on our planet in which multiple ways of belonging, and ethnic, national, and supranational identities, are hotly debated and messily lived.

Jan Plamper is Professor of History at the University of Limerick. He specializes in migration history, the history of emotions and the senses, and Russian history. His other books include *The Stalin Cult: A Study in the Alchemy of Power* (2012) and *The History of Emotions: An Introduction* (2015).

We Are All Migrants

A History of Multicultural Germany

Jan Plamper

University of Limerick

Shaftesbury Road, Cambridge CB2 8EA, United Kingdom

One Liberty Plaza, 20th Floor, New York, NY 10006, USA

477 Williamstown Road, Port Melbourne, VIC 3207, Australia

314–321, 3rd Floor, Plot 3, Splendor Forum, Jasola District Centre, New Delhi – 110025, India

103 Penang Road, #05–06/07, Visioncrest Commercial, Singapore 238467

Cambridge University Press is part of Cambridge University Press & Assessment, a department of the University of Cambridge.

We share the University's mission to contribute to society through the pursuit of education, learning and research at the highest international levels of excellence.

www.cambridge.org
Information on this title: www.cambridge.org/9781009242295

DOI: 10.1017/9781009242264

First published in English by Cambridge University Press & Assessment 2023 as *We Are All Migrants: A History of Multicultural Germany*

First published 2023

A catalogue record for this publication is available from the British Library.

A Cataloging-in-Publication data record for this book is available from the Library of Congress.

ISBN 978-1-009-24229-5 Hardback
ISBN 978-1-009-24225-7 Paperback

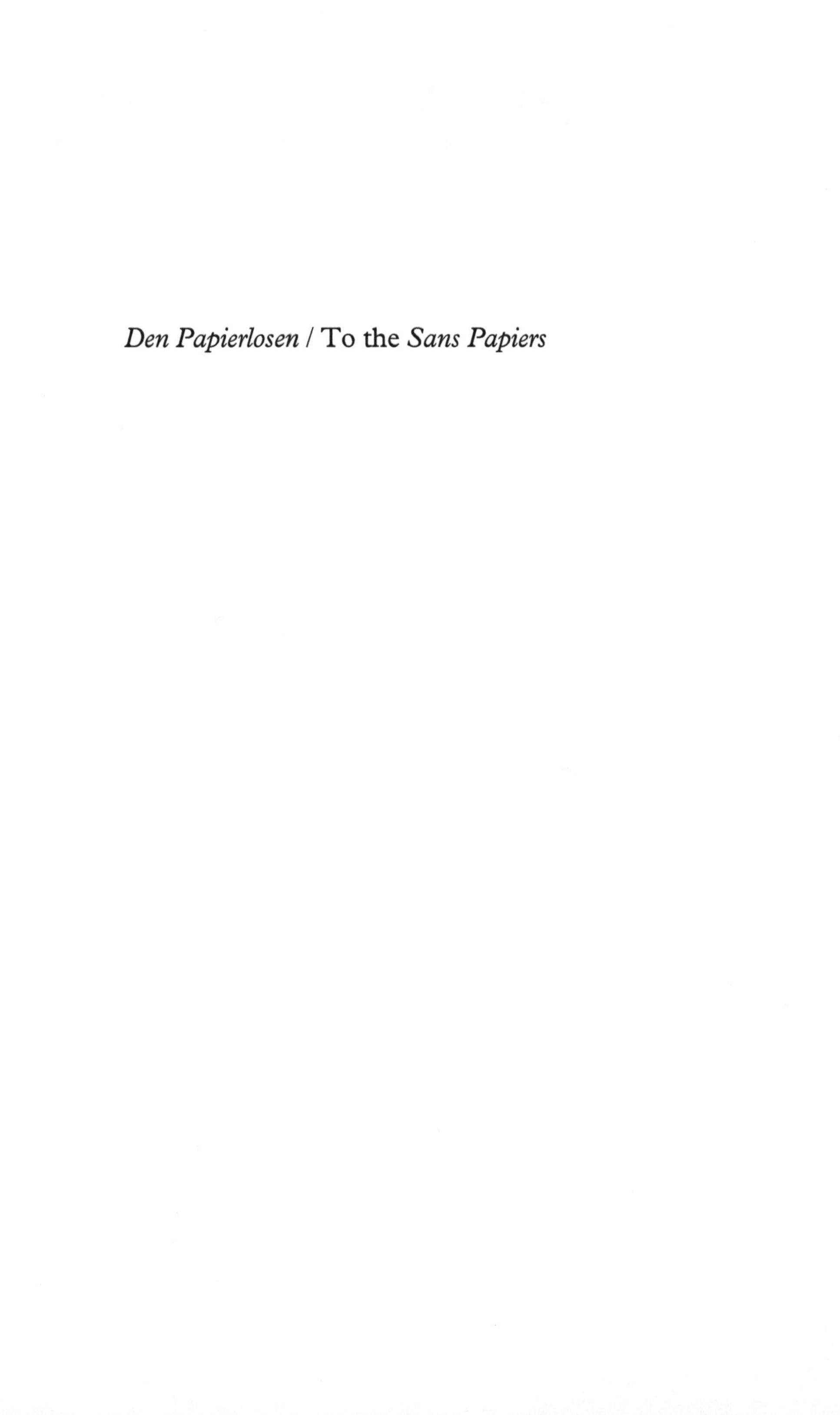

Den Papierlosen / To the *Sans Papiers*

Contents

Figures

Acknowledgments

The present volume is my own translation from the German of my book *Das neue Wir: Warum Migration dazugehört. Eine andere Geschichte der Deutschen*, published in 2019.

This book would hardly have materialized without the help of a great number of individuals and institutions. I owe an enormous debt to Elliot Beck, Dmitrij Belkin, Lisa Carter, Lorraine Daston, Belinda Davis, Irina Flige, Liz Friend-Smith, Evgenia Gostrer, Steven Holt, Tanja Hommen, Frank Jansen, Uffa Jensen, Lorenz Kähler, Heike Kleffner, Andrea Korte-Böger, Irina Kremenetskaia, Dieter Langewiesche, Margarita Mamontova, Kate McIntosh, Martina Müller-Wallraf, Philipp Nielsen, Alexandra Oberländer, Jannis Panagiotidis, Glenn Penny, Harald Plamper, Lisa Plamper, Olga Plamper, Paul Plamper, Anna Schäffler, Aslı Sevindim, Nina Sillem, Barbara Wenner, and Frank Wolff. I am most grateful to Alfried Krupp Wissenschaftskolleg Greifswald; Antifaschistisches Pressearchiv und Bildungszentrum (apabiz) Berlin; DOMiD – Dokumentationszentrum und Museum über die Migration in Deutschland; Ute Frevert's Center for the History of Emotions at Berlin's Max Planck Institute for Human Development; Historisches Archiv der Kreisstadt Siegburg; History Department, Goldsmiths, University of London; History Department, University of Limerick; Imre Kertész Kolleg Jena; Bettina Hitzer's and Paul Nolte's Kolloquium Vergleichs- und Verflechtungsgeschichte/Zeitgeschichte, Freie Universität Berlin; Memorial St. Petersburg; ReachOut Berlin; and Wissenschaftskolleg zu Berlin. Finally, I wish to dedicate the book to the loving memory of Hedwig Plamper (July 25, 1989–April 6, 2018).

Introduction

"And who are you?"

"A foreigner, of course!"

Speaking to my eleven-year-old daughter Olga at the end of the year 2000, this was the answer I received. I had asked her who she was, who she felt herself to be in terms of "nationality." We had moved to Berlin in the summer of that year, and she had never lived in Germany before. She was born in 1989 in St. Petersburg, then still known as Leningrad. I arrived on the scene when she was four, first as her mother's boyfriend, then her husband. In 1995 we moved to Berkeley, Northern California, for our studies and enrolled her in a school. In 1999 we left Berkeley to spend a year in Moscow. There we decided to move to Berlin. At first Russian was our family language, and Olga used the German word *Ausländer*, "foreigner," in a Russian sentence: Аусленденр, конечно!

I was shocked – after half a year in America she had described herself as American, despite holding only a Russian passport. By this point in Berlin she had German citizenship, but described herself as a foreigner.

Perhaps it was because German was her third identity after Russian and American. Or that we lived in America before 9/11 and long before Donald Trump, when immigrants were not yet viewed with general suspicion.

And yet something wasn't right. Olga attended a regular primary school in Berlin-Charlottenburg. Almost all her friends had at least one parent who came from another country and spoke a second language at home alongside German: Zhaabiz spoke Persian, Onur spoke Turkish, Ibrahim and Karim spoke Arabic, Amalia spoke Greek, and Yeon-hee spoke Korean.[1] Like Olga, Zhaabiz, Onur, Ibrahim, Karim, Amalia, and Yeon-hee had German citizenship. And yet they all called themselves "foreigners." In the United States, Onur, for example, would have described himself as Turkish American: the citizenship, American, as a noun, the parents' culture of origin, Turkish, as an adjective. Primarily American, then Turkish, and the two identities would have got along very well.

It was, as I said, the year 2000. The topics of migration and nationality had been on everyone's lips for over a year. Chancellor Gerhard Schröder's "Red–Green" government (a first-ever coalition at the federal level between the Social Democratic Party and the Green Party) had dusted off the German nationality law, which dated back to 1913. As of January 1, 2000, there were fewer obstacles to naturalization, and people aged up to 23 had the option of dual citizenship.

But there was resistance. In the Hesse state election of 1999, the conservative Christian Democratic Union's (CDU) top candidate, Roland Koch, won the vote with a signature campaign against dual passports. State elections followed in North Rhine-Westphalia in early 2000; with an eye on the green card introduced by the Red–Green coalition, CDU frontrunner Jürgen Rüttgers said: "We need our children at computers, not Indians."[2] His comments went down in history as the "Kinder statt Inder" (Children not Indians) election campaign. The "dominant culture" (*Leitkultur*) debate raged from October 2000, and continues to haunt the media. This debate was triggered by CDU politician Friedrich Merz, who called for immigrants to adapt to the "free democratic German dominant culture."[3]

So what was different about Berkeley? For one thing, in Berkeley there were not primarily demands, but offers – to engage, to feel you belonged to the country, to feel like you belonged at all. And the means were provided to do so. Shortly after our arrival late in the summer of 1995, Olga was assigned to an intensive "English as a Second Language" (ESL) class, which involved many hours of teaching per week. In Berlin, it was suggested she attend 45 minutes of remedial German lessons per week together with children with learning difficulties or dyslexia, a good dozen of them.

Clearly, Germany neglected to supply positive influences, either to teach the key techniques required to become a functioning member of society – particularly the German language – or to establish an emotional connection with Germany. Exclusion reigned on many levels: almost all the people shown in Olga's schoolbooks were white and blonde, the stories taken from a long-extinct world of family farms and fishing boats. And in day-to-day life, non-white Germans were asked how they had managed to learn such good German and when they would be "going home." Jewish Germans would be asked what nonsense their president had been talking now, usually meaning the Israeli Prime Minister, not the German Federal President. And all those who looked "different" – "visible minorities," as they are known in migration research – were described as foreigners.

That was the situation in the year 2000. In politics, a message to shed any additional cultural baggage and submit to the dominant culture. In real life, 45 minutes of remedial German for children experiencing very different problems with the language. And a great deal of exclusion.

More than 20 years have passed since then, and much has changed. My second daughter, Lisa, born in 2002, has never called herself a "foreigner." As soon as she was enrolled in school, she was entered in the statistics as a child with a "migration background."[4] In 2017 she was one of 19.3 million people, almost a quarter of the population, with a migration background.[5] This term has few fans – for good reason, as we will soon see – but, taken literally, it does allow a person to have a German passport in the foreground and migration experience in the background. The status of what the Germans call the "mega-topic" (*Megathema*) of migration has also changed since 2000. Since the 2015 refugee crisis, the whole of Germany has been talking – arguing – about asylum, immigration, integration. This was preceded by a decade and a half of continual development. While Germany dispelled the myth that it is not a country of immigration, and diversity became more natural, racism, xenophobia, Islamophobia, and antisemitism continued to spread, making their way onto the streets and into parliaments. But one thing has not changed in this time: what it means to be German remains a blank, is still missing something elementary – new terms, concepts, and stories.

This book is about migration, nation, and identity. It is a history of migration to Germany since 1945, inscribing into German history migrant groups that rarely appear within it. This history is both entangled with, and highly relevant to, the rest of the world. Germany, in other words, here serves as one European example that has wide implications for locales from Northern Africa to Turkey and Russia, from the Middle East to the United States and Canada, Latin America, South Asia, East Asia, and Australia.[6] The book narrates history based on people who have migrated to West and East Germany since the Second World War and who really do or did exist. The sum of their histories is the history of the Germans. Together they form a new collective, "the New We" (*Das neue Wir*, as in the original German title of this book).

For me, however, the New We means something else, something that goes beyond the sum of all Germans, including the immigrants ignored in the traditional historical narrative and thus historically invisible. The New We is a plea for a collective identity.

I work on the basic assumption that we all live countless identities and that these identities and how they relate to one another are constantly changing, depending on where and with whom we communicate and interact – and this is why I talk of "living" identities, rather than "possessing" or "having" identities.[7] In Germany these lived identities include Rhinelander, Leipziger, East German, the Märkisches Viertel district of Berlin, goth, soccer fan, queer, Catholic, trans woman, Alevi, Alawi, often simultaneously and in rapid flux depending on whether people are interacting with a boss or colleague, a mother or son, in the sauna or in the synagogue. Migration specialists Steven Vertovec and Mark Terkessidis have respectively called this highly complex, fluid, forever changing state of multiple attachments "super-diversity" and "interculture."[8]

One of these attachments is to a nation. Almost all of us have a citizenship, and some of us have more than one. Germany is one of the countries that defines attachment to a nation not just according to citizenship. Particularly in everyday life, which is why my daughter and her friends described themselves as "foreigners" despite holding German passports. There is a notion that one cannot be German and come from another country – German *or* Russian, but not both at the same time. Or that you need to have been in Germany a very long time to be "truly" German. Or that you need to be Christian. Or that you need to look a certain way – visible minorities are suspected of not being German.

This book aims to establish an understanding of "nation" in which belonging to the German nation and other attachments, including origins in another country, go together rather than ruling each other out. German plus Russian origins, German of Russian origin. Turkish Germans, not German Turks. German Turks would be Turkish citizens of German origin, for example if Angela Merkel were to migrate to Turkey, give up her German citizenship, and take Turkish citizenship.

In this book, I suggest a collective term for all German citizens with additional cultural baggage: "German plus" or the synonym "PlusGerman." They are German plus something else. This term is self-descriptive and has been coined by, among others, Cologne's SPD politician Tayfun Keltek and the President of Gießen University and the German Academic Exchange Service (DAAD), Joybrato Mukherjee, both German citizens. "I feel German, I was born here and grew up here, and I feel most at home in the German language," says Mukherjee. He also says: "My family has a strong Indian identity, and I am a member of the Hindu faith." He therefore calls himself "German plus."[9]

Each person can describe themselves however they want – "We don't want any labels lumping us together as foreign. We ourselves want to decide how we are described," says the "New German Organisations" (neue deutsche organisationen) network, a project of the New German Media Professionals association (Neue deutsche Medienmacher, NdM): "We, that is people with a migration background or foreground, migrants, bicultural people, cross-cultural people, Black Germans, People of Color, Turkogermans, German Kurds, and many, many more. Being German is complex. Ask us."[10] The three most common self-descriptive collective terms for German citizens plus are "New German" (*Neue Deutsche*), "hyphenated German" (*Bindestrich-deutsche*), and "post-migrant" (*Postmigranten*). "PlusGerman" has some advantages over these terms, which I will briefly explain.

The term "New German" emerged in the 2000s. NdM was set up in early 2009 to strengthen the position of migrant voices in the public sphere. At the same time, the term was taken up by the rapper Harris and migration scholar Naika Foroutan, followed by three journalists and later a series of migrant and anti-racism organizations. For all of these people, the term was an alternative to "foreigner," and they all had the same goal: to find a linguistic marker for the idea of belonging both to the German nation and to other cultures.[11] In 2016, Herfried and Marina Münkler adopted the term, no longer self-descriptively, for their book *Die neuen Deutschen* (*The New Germans*).[12]

"German plus" has the fundamental advantage that it is not a temporal term; it does not distinguish between "old" and "new" Germans. "Old" could be seen as having an unalterable quality; even in the year 2100, immigrated Syrian Germans who had fled the civil war in Syria, which started in 2011, and their descendants would still be described as "new Germans."

The self-descriptive term "hyphenated German" (*Bindestrichdeutsche*) makes no linguistic sense – after all, the German word *Türkeideutsche* (Turkish German) does not contain a hyphen. The term has been imported from English, "hyphenated Americans." Finally, the disadvantage of the self-description "post-migrant" is that it does not contain the word "German." The term reduces a person to their migrant status, linguistically excluding them from being German.

Compared with all these terms, "PlusGerman" has the additional advantage of openness: the number of plus-identities is unlimited, and the "plus" could even refer to a German federal state or region (such as Saxony or the Ruhr area). It could also refer to a migration that took place a long time ago (for example the Huguenots from France in the seventeenth century or the Poles who migrated to the Ruhr area from the late nineteenth century): "PlusGerman" signals that, at some time or other, we have all crossed borders, that all Germans were "New Germans" once upon a time. That, ultimately, we are all migrants.

As stated, "PlusGerman" or "German plus" is a self-descriptive term, and self-description is self-empowerment. But "migration background" is no self-descriptive term. It is an official term originating from research that was first applied by the Federal Statistical Office (Statistisches Bundesamt) in the 2005 micro census. Following the increase in naturalizations from 2000 onward, the aim was to find another way of recording multicultural backgrounds in statistics (the term "foreigner" was no longer considered suitable); this seemed important to generate meaningful data, for example for education policy. A person has a migration background "if they or at least one parent is not a German citizen by birth."[13] The term then made its way from statistics to society, where a few welcomed it as an alternative to "foreigner." However, most criticized the risk it entails of making a person's background something biological – you will never shake off your migration background, particularly if you belong to a visible minority.[14]

No term is actually required for those designated in scholarship as autochthonous Germans and colloquially described by some as "BioGermans" (*Biodeutsche*). Invoking biology and blood, this resonates with a notion of the true, authentic German. "Despite" their citizenship, all others would be considered artificial Germans (admittedly, some people use this term ironically, playing on the word for, say, organic yoghurt, *Biojoghurt*).

Another term that should be scrapped is "integration." Usually, integration means assimilation or acculturation – giving up all other attachments and total absorption in the unitary culture. In the United States, this is denoted with the "melting-pot" metaphor that prevailed into the 1950s: give up your Italian, Swedish, or German origins and blend with everyone else to form a homogeneous American identity. Here I am making the case for something resembling the model that has prevailed in the United States since the 1960s, the metaphor of the salad bowl – the bowl as the national collective identity with space for many identities of origin, the leaves in a colorful salad. Applied to Germany, the salad bowl model means that multicultural skills and multilingualism – the knowledge of other languages in addition to German, "German plus" – should be promoted by the state and symbolically valued.

This is not a call for multiculturalism – if you understand multiculturalism as the sole existence of particular identities without a collective identity or, to maintain this imagery, the various salad ingredients without a bowl. Multiculturalism in this sense has plenty of charm, but seems to me impractical for at least two reasons. First, society is too heterogeneous – just look at the media landscape. In the past, the whole nation would gather in front of the television at 8 pm to watch forum media like the evening news, which simply do not have the same unifying power as they did 30 years ago. Today we move in digital echo chambers; social media feeds bolster our existing, highly polarized opinions rather than confront us with opinions different from our own.

Second, the siren call of some countries from which "PlusGermans" originate is too loud. If Germany fails to offer alternatives to the attempted co-optation through ethnic/linguistic/cultural/religious propaganda (for example from Erdoğan's Turkey or Putin's Russia), if all national attachment to Germany has to offer is a blank space, then German society will be put under excessive strain.

We Are All Migrants aims to contribute to the current debate with historical arguments, as well as offering guidance by taking a look at society: what works, what errors should be avoided? I will illustrate abstract concepts by telling the stories of specific people while analyzing background information – specialists would describe this as actor-centered, narrative historiography, and this is what I shall try to provide.[15]

To do so, I draw primarily on migrant memory initiatives, attempts to make migrant voices audible from the past – first and foremost the oral history archive at Cologne's Documentation Center and Museum of Migration in Germany (Dokumentationszentrum und Museum über die Migration in Deutschland, DOMiD). I also use the many first-hand migrant reports recorded in books, in press, radio, and TV contributions, and in gray literature – "ego documents." Second, I draw on the social history migration research of Klaus J. Bade in particular and in general the Osnabrück Institute for Migration Research and Intercultural Studies (Osnabrücker Institut für Migrationsforschung und Interkulturelle Studien, IMIS), founded by Bade in 1991.

However, this is no "general" history of Germany supplemented with the aspect of migration. No special lens filter has been used to incorporate the topic of migration into key events and processes such as the building of the Berlin Wall, the peace movement, and European integration. That would be a different book examining the role migration has played in these events and processes, how migrants have contributed, and how they have been perceived. A book such as this would have chapter headings like "The 1970s and the Rise of Postindustrial Society" rather than "Labor Migration to West Germany"; it would be organized by period or topic, not according to the migrant groups with the greatest numbers.

A narrative such as this has yet to be produced; migrants play practically no role at all in the traditional syntheses of German history. Where migrants have surfaced in overviews of West and East German postwar history – the older produced by Heinrich-August Winkler and the newer by Eckart Conze – they have appeared on 1 of 742 pages (Winkler) or 10 of 1,071 pages (Conze).[16] There is simply no synthetic study of German history since the Second World War that consistently places migrants and migration at its center.[17]

If my book encourages others to write such a history, then it has fulfilled one of its purposes. If "PlusGerman" readers can identify with the people in the book and are happy that their story has finally been told for once, then it has fulfilled another. If other readers develop empathy for the people in the book despite the huge gulf in their lived experience – for example because they have been residing in Germany for a long time – then yet another has been fulfilled. These goals can be summarized in two words: empowerment and empathy.

However, I have deliberately chosen not to start the book with the topic of immigration. The first chapter is about the history of emigration from Germany. Before the twentieth century, Germany was a classic emigrant country – back then, German émigrés had similar experiences all over the world (primarily in the United States, Russia, and South America) to those of immigrants in Germany today.

This is followed by the first of two snapshots, outlining the image offered by Germany in 1945, when it became the hub of the largest migration movements of modern European times. The other snapshot comes later in the book and looks at 1989, the second major year of upheaval, when Germany opened up to Eastern European migration. These snapshots set the tone for the chapters that follow.

The first major migrant group after the Second World War was the expellees who arrived between 1944 and 1950. As the second chapter shows, they were initially far more excluded than the "myth of rapid integration" indicates.[18] In 1950, the Federal Republic's political sphere found an identity construct that would allow the expellees to maintain their Pomeranian or Sudeten German identity of origin and be recognized as "true" Germans. Many problems would have been avoided had this identity construct been extended to the "guest workers" (*Gastarbeiter*, the focus of Chapter 3) who arrived from 1955 as soon as it became clear that some of them would stay and adopt German citizenship. However, migrant workers moved not just to the Federal Republic, but also to the German Democratic Republic as "contract workers" (*Vertragsarbeiter*, the subject of Chapter 4). The fifth chapter turns back to West Germany, focusing on the asylum seekers of the 1980s through to the early 2000s and the debate about the German Basic Law (*Grundgesetz*) that in 1993 led to the "asylum compromise" (*Asylkompromiss*). Chapters follow on the Volga Germans, Polish and Romanian (late) resettlers (Chapter 6), and the Jewish quota refugees (*jüdische Kontingentflüchtlinge*, Chapter 7). These two migration movements from the former Eastern Bloc were set in motion by the fall of the Iron Curtain, captured in the snapshot of 1989.

The eighth and final chapter takes us from this point to the present day. By the time the book concludes, the migration questions that have occupied German politics and society since the turn of the millennium will, I hope, appear in a different light – particularly the "welcoming culture" (*Willkommenskultur*) of 2015. The book concludes with a plea for bringing together particularism and universalism, for radically diverse identities *and* a "New We."

1 We Are All Migrants, Almost Everywhere, Almost Always – Especially the Germans

Humans have been migrating since time immemorial. Humans migrate in the course of a day, in search of food, across their lifespan. They become sedentary for a while and then mobile again. They migrate alone or in groups, in "waves" or in "pushes," as the saying goes. They migrate because the place they are in has become intolerable, or because another place seems more promising, or because of both – scholars of migration speak of push and pull factors.[1] Humans have been migrating so much and for so long that one historian has called the earth a "planet of nomads." Another went so far as to rechristen the human person, homo sapiens, as "homo migrans."[2]

The Germans are typical humans. They too have been migrating since time immemorial. Let's take a brief look at German *Wanderlust* and *Wanderzwang*, pull and push, since, say, the Middle Ages. What about the peasantry, the absolute majority of the population? As serfs they migrated a lot more than the feudal system with its bondage to a specific plot of manorial land would lead us to assume. In German-speaking Europe this was especially true where there was primogeniture. When a father died, his first-born son inherited the farm; his brothers got nothing. Often they had no choice but to hit the road and try their luck as day laborers elsewhere. In doing so, they crossed the borders of principalities and kingdoms: they became migrants.

Craftsmen migrated. For journeymen migration was part of their training, for carpenters it is to this day. They can be seen in German cities in black corduroy bell-bottoms, sloppy hats, and an earring in their left ear. They take to the road for three years, at the end the earring goes. Merchants migrated when moving money and goods from one place to another. The elites were no less mobile: noblewomen married outside the borders of the German-speaking states and moved with their husbands to French-, Hungarian-, or English-speaking places. In the seventeenth century French became the nobility's lingua franca, which made migration easier, at least insofar as communication was concerned. In that regard monks and clergymen had a distinct advantage from the beginning, as Latin was their common language. This eased migration from monastery to monastery, parish to parish, diocese to diocese.

Borders became tighter in the seventeenth century when centralized states with standing armies formed. From then on it makes sense to speak of "internal migration," that is, migration within the borders of a country. The late-nineteenth-century migration of "Ruhr Poles" was such an internal migration. "Ruhr Poles" were Polish-speaking subjects of the German Empire, founded in 1871, who were recruited from the territories of contemporary Poland to work as miners in the booming Ruhr area. Another way of speaking of them would be as "internal labor migrants." Ernst Kuzorra, Sports Club Schalke 04's 1930s soccer star, was of Ruhr Polish descent, and the popular TV detective Horst Schimanski is modeled on a Ruhr Pole.

But Germans also took part in transatlantic migration from the very beginning. They crossed the Atlantic in the wake of Columbus in the early sixteenth century – as cartographers, as mercenaries in the military conquest of the Spaniards, or, coming from the Ore Mountains located between today's Czech Republic and Germany, as experts in order to mine silver in the south of the continent. In North America they were among the earliest European settlers. In 1607 the Breslau doctor and botanist Johannes Fleischer the Younger was the only non-Briton to make the passage from England across the Atlantic to establish the first British colony in Jamestown, Virginia. Two glassmakers from Hesse followed suit. Later entire groups immigrated, first in the thousands, later in the tens of thousands. Many did not survive the arduous ship passage across the Atlantic, which lasted for weeks. Yet they took the risk anyway: because they suffered persecution in Germanophone Europe as Lutheran religious minorities or as anti-Monarchist republicans, or because they were hurting economically. Or simply because they hoped for an improvement of their economic situation in America, much like today many of those disparagingly called "economic refugees" are not going hungry in their countries of origin, but hope for an improvement of their living standard: in Germany they, as a family of six, might be able to live in four instead of two rooms and perhaps be able to have a flatscreen TV instead of a single transistor radio for the entire family.

In the nineteenth century the United States became one of two destinations for mass emigration (Figure 1.1). Today Germans comprise the largest ethnic group there. In 2011, 49.8 million out of 310 million Americans, almost one-sixth, reported having German ancestors.[3] The other destination was Tsarist Russia, where German peasants and religious minorities, such as Mennonites, began migrating after 1763 to colonize the regions on the Volga and Black Sea.

Figure 1.1 Nineteenth-century mass emigration: German migrants board a steamer in Hamburg to travel to the United States. *From the Old to the New World*, wood engraving by E. G. Specht, 1876. DigitalVision Vectors / Getty Images.

The Riddle

When considering this mass emigration from Germany and, more broadly, the long history of German migration, it seems all the more mysterious that resistance to immigration in West and East Germany during the second half of the twentieth century was so fierce. Whence the reticence to define oneself as a country of immigrants when immigration on the ground was impossible to ignore?

Does it come down to how Germany formed as a nation?[4] The German nation-state came into being only in 1871; it is among the youngest nation-states in the Western world. In 1800 in the Holy Roman Empire of the German Nation there were roughly 300 German-speaking states, from the County of Rieneck to large kingdoms like Bohemia. Because they were latecomers to nationhood – this is the argument – the Germans phantasized themselves to be particularly homogeneous. Put differently, because their diversity was so patently obvious, they went to special ends to overwrite this diversity with a myth of homogeneity. Older nation-states like Britain or

France felt little need to do this. No wonder historians speak of two ideal-types of nationalism, Anglo-American–French civic nationalism and German ethnic nationalism.

But more recently scholars have pointed out that Germany looks like a latecomer to nationhood only if measured against the yardstick of Britain or France. Italians also lived in a multitude of states before the creation of their nation-state in 1861, and the Czechs were part of the Austro-Hungarian Empire until 1918. Belgium and Greece became independent only in 1830, and even Switzerland was not a nation-state until 1848. What is more, the clear-cut distinction between Anglo-American–French civic nationalism and German ethnonationalism no longer seems tenable.[5] So "the delayed nation" argument alone is no solution to the riddle.[6]

Is it because of a specifically German line of thought the philosopher Johann Gottfried Herder (1744–1803) came to embody? Herder was a product of his time, the eighteenth century, when 300-plus states existed. Precisely because Germany as a unified state did not exist, he defined the nation first and foremost via language and culture, not citizenship. He dreamed about the non-existent unified, single German state via criteria that united people across state borders: whether one belonged to the nation was not a question of passport, but of language and culture.

In the nineteenth century "race" entered the picture. With the rise of Darwinism, language and culture began to be imagined as something hereditary, Germanness as "descent." In other words, half a century after Herder's death his ideas were biologized. It was only then that talk about "German blood" began.

But variants of Herder's thinking about the nation and its biologizing later in the nineteenth century were present in other parts of the globe as well. In the United States nativists also defined the nation through language and culture and in contradistinction to immigrants – by the way, especially German immigrants since the middle of the nineteenth century, but also Irish Catholics and many others, such as Chinese immigrants from the 1870s onward. These ideas were biologized everywhere over the course of the nineteenth century. Nativists in the United States believed that Americans were an exceptional, superior "Anglo-Saxon race."[7] So the Herder tradition does not solve the riddle either.

And yet the fact remains that post-1945 Germany had even greater difficulty than other countries in coming to terms with diversity and extending symbolic forms of belonging to the civic nation to, for instance, visible minorities. Specialists continue to share this diagnosis, including in the most recent migration research, where we can read, for example, that "the remarkable stubbornness of viewing the complex issues of negotiating difference exclusively through the ethnocultural lens" is typically German. True, compared with other European states, Germany is not unique, "However, no other nation carries as much baggage from a fifty-year history of denial, and in no other country does the tonality of the narrative sound so unyielding."[8]

So the riddle remains. Most likely the solution lies in a confluence of a number of circumstances in the 1950s through 1980s and good explanations will be quite complex and context-specific. Here we need more research.

German "Parallel Society" in Pennsylvania, 1750

On March 20, 1751, Benjamin Franklin, printer, inventor, natural scientist, and one of the founding fathers of the United States, sat down at his desk and vented his anger in a letter to a colleague: "Instead of their Learning our Language, we must learn their's, or live as in a foreign Country. Already the English begin to quit particular Neighbourhoods surrounded by [Germans], being made uneasy by the Disagreeableness of disonant Manners."[9] A few years later he added insult to injury and wrote disparagingly about the German immigrants: "why should the Palatine Boors be suffered to swarm into our Settlements, and by herding together establish their Language and Manners to the Exclusion of ours?"[10]

Just a few years before, in 1747, Franklin had welcomed German immigration. The immigrants, "the brave and steady Germans," to him were true democrats who would fight alongside American republicans against the British Crown's colonial rule.[11] What had happened? Why did his attitude toward German immigrants change so radically in such a short period of time? How can we explain rapid swings in popular mood toward migration, as was to be observed in Germany in 2016, when the enthusiasm of the "welcoming culture" of summer 2015 gave way to skepticism?

In Benjamin Franklin's case the reason was that the German immigrants to him seemed disappointingly conciliatory toward the British in the North American colonies. But Franklin wasn't the only one to worry about the mores of the Germans in Pennsylvania in the 1750s. In 1751 there was a complaint in the Pennsylvania legislature about the German custom of celebrating the New Year by shooting into the air.[12] The German fireworks on New Year's Eve seemed very alien to the citizens of Pennsylvania, who for the most part hailed from Britain. Clinging to the German language also aroused a lot of resentment. German shop signs dominated some streets, German newspapers were on sale, and the children of many German immigrants went to German-language schools.

The houses of the Germans also differed from those of the British: they were surrounded by fences. In addition Germans settled compactly, so that entirely German neighborhoods came into being. The fear of a German "parallel society," a term right-wingers in contemporary Germany use with reference to parts of town where many people of Arab or Turkish descent live, was a red thread in the entire history of German immigration to the United States. In 1857 the landscape architect and journalist Frederick Law Olmsted published a report on his *Journey through Texas, or, A Saddle-Trip on the Southwestern Frontier*, in which he wrote about the German settlers: "They mingle little with the Americans, except for the necessary buying and selling."[13]

Strong feelings toward migrants, especially fears, are fertile soil for all kinds of phantasies. In Pennsylvania during the 1750s the fear was that the new German arrivals could spread unknown diseases. There were many proposals for legislation to contain through isolation and quarantine the epidemic the Germans would allegedly cause. Even an educated Enlightenment thinker like Benjamin Franklin slid down the slippery slope into phantasmatic thinking, where the German immigrants were concerned. He suddenly began to imagine them as "swarthy": "That the Number of purely white People in the World is proportionably very small. [...] And in Europe, the Spaniards, Italians, French, Russians and Swedes, are generally of what we call a swarthy Complexion; as are the Germans also, the Saxons only excepted, who with the English, make the principal Body of White People on the Face of the Earth. I could wish their Numbers were increased."[14] Franklin here emerges as an antecedent to racist thought, more than a century before the advent of vulgarized Darwinist pseudobiology.

On the question how to deal with these "parallel societies," which troubled him so deeply, Franklin found pragmatic answers. He is not known to have ever considered the capping of immigration, for example through limits on numbers, let alone forced deportation to Europe. His suggestion was to mingle people of German and British descent in the places where they lived.[15] To be sure, this was as futile as similar suggestions today. In a society with basic liberties and mobility, mingling according to ethnic criteria by way of top-down state order or even force is as difficult to put into practice as mingling according to economic criteria: rich people also prefer living among themselves, no one calls their self-isolation in neighborhoods with mansions or in gated communities a "parallel society."

As so often with migration, the febrile, dangerous phantasy didn't last long. In real life the criticized Germans were in the process of becoming Americans. Pamphlets like *Anleitung zur Englischen Sprache für Teutsche*

Neuankommende (*Instruction in the English Language for German New Arrivals*) of 1752 made assimilation easier. The German surname "Schmidt" became "Smith," the surname "Jäger" became "Jaeger," "Jager," "Yager," and "Hunter." But assimilation was not the only process taking place, there was also the commingling and hybridization of different cultures and languages. The dialect of Pennsylvania Deitsch emerged, a variant of Palatinate-inflected German with a lot of English elements. *Es hod sich besser ausgedreht* derived from "It has turned out better." Pennsylvania Deitsch also had a lot of terms directly borrowed from English: *leifinschuranz* (life insurance), *uf kors* (of course). Sounds familiar? Indeed, the Pennsylvania Deitsch of the eighteenth and nineteenth centuries was the ethnolect of today's PlusGermans, such as YouTube star İdil Baydar (alter ego Jilet Ayşe) or comedian Kaya Yanar (*Was guckst du?!*).[16]

On the Plight of German Tent Camps in London, on Human Traffickers and German Migrants as "White Slaves"

Pennsylvania was the exception among the American colonies. It had its own democratic constitution and largely cut its ties with the British Crown long before the War of Independence (1775–1783). The other colonies were linked to Britain much more closely. In many of them large-scale landowners ran the show. As a result, how the German immigrants were treated very much depended on the colony they ended up in. This applied even to the beginning of their migration – from the get-go.

In 1677, before ever setting foot on the American continent, William Penn recruited potential immigrants in the German states along the Rhine for a colony he planned to set up on the East Coast of North America. Penn needed tradespeople, merchants, and farmers. He looked for them wherever people were going hungry, paying exorbitant taxes, or doing serf labor for their lords. Or where they saw no professional future for themselves. Or suffered persecution as members of a protestant minority, such as Pietists, Moravians, Quakers, Mennonites, Labadists, Schwenkfelders, and Old German Baptist Brethren, who refused to serve in the military for religious reasons. Penn was careful to avoid Catholics – we will return to American prejudice vis-à-vis Catholics, which endured well into the twentieth century.

At the same time British agents were recruiting immigrants for other colonies. Private agents were also in the recruiting business – they were the equivalent of today's human traffickers. Like today, they lied and cheated, made false promises, capitalized on the misery of the migrants and didn't give a damn about the health and livelihood of their fellow human beings, women and children included. Like today, many of them had once been migrants themselves. "But that so many people emigrate to America, and particularly to Pennsylvania, is due to the deceptions and persuasions" of the agents, or rather, "men-thieves," Gottlieb Mittelberger, a Swabian Pastor and author of a widely circulated travelogue, warned in 1756.[17] Another Pastor noted in 1763 what the "cajolery" of the agents sounded like: "If you go as a vassal, you will become a lord, if you go as a maid, you will become a madam, as a farmer, a nobleman, as a bourgeois and craftsman, a baron."[18]

Today it is hard to fathom just how difficult travel in premodern times was, before the invention of cars, trains, motorboats, and airplanes. Migrants from the German states traveled to Rotterdam on the Rhine by boat. But Europe was divided up by countless borders, and the migrants ended up accumulating in Rotterdam, where they were confined in a tent camp. Hygiene was so catastrophic that the agent Dayrolle put out an ad in a Cologne newspaper: admissions freeze in Rotterdam camps! When that didn't help, the Dutch started putting up warning signs on the shores of the Rhine.

As is so often the case, the migration panic went away as suddenly as it had come. The Rotterdam camps of the early eighteenth century emptied as soon as another boat trip across the channel to England became available. There, however, the story was much the same as group after group of German transit migrants on their way to America arrived. As soon as the bed and breakfast rooms, inns, and even warehouses were full to the brim, tent camps were set up. While the Germans were waiting for permission to cross the Atlantic, the situation in the camps got rapidly worse. Many died of diseases, 320 men were so desperate that they signed up as mercenaries with the British military, and families sold 140 children as domestic helpers to British households. The local population came to stare at and to rant about the dirty, sick people who didn't do anything all day long and on top of that spoke in a foreign language. Others organized charity events and collected money for the migrants. Yet others, most of them poor and jealous of the donations the migrants were receiving from the rich, attacked the camps and beat up the migrants – once 2,000 Londoners were involved in such a mob.[19]

Inside the camps it often turned out that the migrants had been duped. The money they had paid the agents back home was not enough for the transatlantic voyage, or the money was gone – together with the agents. Many agreed to a credit system whereby they got an advance for the trip across the Atlantic and would pay it back through labor on American farms. They then had to work in that capacity for decades. There were uprisings and some immigrants called themselves "white slaves."[20]

Toward slaves from Africa the attitude of the Germans was surprisingly humane. Surprisingly? This is only surprising when telescoping the Nazi era onto the past and when imagining that racism has been part and parcel of German culture since time immemorial and merely "broke out" in the twentieth century. That is nonsense, there is no such thing as a German gene for racism. Racism can be learned – unfortunately. Racism can be unlearned – thank goodness.

The fact that many German immigrants belonged to Protestant minorities that preached non-violence and were conscientious objectors played a major positive role. Franz Pastorius, the co-founder of Germantown in Philadelphia, in 1688, together with other prominent Quakers, authored the first protest note against slavery: "Now tho they are black, we can not conceive there is more liberty to have them slaves, as it is to have other white ones. [. . .] we shall doe to all men licke as we will be done ourselves; macking no difference of what generation, descent or Colour they are. [. . .] In Europe there are many oppressed for Conscience sacke; and here there are those oppressed wch are of a Black Colour."[21] In the Civil War (1861–1865) the majority of German Americans sided with the Union. More than 200,000 fought with weapons against slavery.

Some of the German immigrants married African and Native Americans. Claus Heins, a baker from Hannover in Lower Saxony, and his African American wife Emma had five children who in the 1880 census were classified as "mulatto."[22] But there were also German slaveholders. A local study of Charleston in South Carolina showed that around 1860, of 281 German households 72 owned slaves, approximately 25 percent. True, that is much less than the 75 percent of English or French households, but it goes to show that absolute German opposition to slavery is a myth.[23]

Mass Emigration in the Nineteenth Century

Hardly had the European carnage of the Napoleonic Wars ended in 1815 than it was followed by the eruption of the Indonesian Mount Tambora volcano, causing an exceptionally wet and cold year of 1816. This "year without summer" in turn caused a famine. And the famine set off mass emigration to the United States. The years around 1855 and 1880 were the absolute peaks, but it should be said that in no year did more than 275,000 Germans emigrate to the United States.[24]

If forced to name a single cause – a single push factor – to explain why so many emigrated, it would have to be industrialization. When transforming from an agricultural into an industrial society, the population grew faster than it could be fed. Emigration was the key valve to ease population pressure.

But there were political causes as well: disappointed by the failed 1848 Revolution, many proponents of a republic left their German places of origin, where monarchs continued to rule. Quite a few of them were at risk of being jailed; they were political refugees. In the United States these immigrants were called the "Forty-Eighters." Carl Schurz (1829–1906) was the most famous of them. In the Civil War he led a Northern brigade in the battle against slavery, later he became US Secretary of the Interior. His wife, Margarethe Meyer-Schurz (1833–1876), in 1856 set up, influenced by the German educator Friedrich Fröbel, the first US childcare institution. To this day American children go to *kindergarten*.

The failure of the 1848 Revolution was doubly disappointing for one group: German Jews. They had fought not only for a democratic nation-state, but also for equality with Christians – for getting the same basic rights as citizens that had already been extended to French Jews after emancipation in 1791. At century's end, roughly a quarter million German Jews had emigrated to America. One of them was Löb Strauß, who was born in 1829 in Buttenheim in Franconia. In 1847 he followed his brothers to New York, where they had a dry goods store. In 1853 he let himself get infected by the Gold Rush and moved on to San Francisco. On his way to the West Coast, his premium fabrics were stolen; the thieves spared only his tent fabrics. When he heard that the gold-diggers were lacking durable working pants, he sewed pants from his tent fabrics, and later he used a blue-dyed cotton fabric: Löb's pants, the Levi Strauss Blue Jeans were born (Figure 1.2).

How did nineteenth-century mass emigration work? To be sure, economic, political, and religious problems were the push factors, but what were the pull factors? For one there was, quite simply, opportunity – the United States took in people without putting many obstacles in their way. Then there were the letters, pamphlets, and books that earlier émigrés had sent to their home country. They painted a picture of America as the land of milk and honey. Gottfried Duden's 1829 *Report of a Journey to the Western States of North America and a Stay of Several Years along the Missouri* was particularly influential. It contained sentences like these: "The great fertility of the soil, its immense area, the mild climate, the splendid river connections, the completely unhindered communication in an area of several thousand miles, the perfect safety of person and property, together with very low taxes – all these must be considered as the real foundations for the fortunate situation of Americans. In what other country is all this combined?"[25] An 1832 pamphlet stated: "A law-abiding, smart, and active man nowhere lives

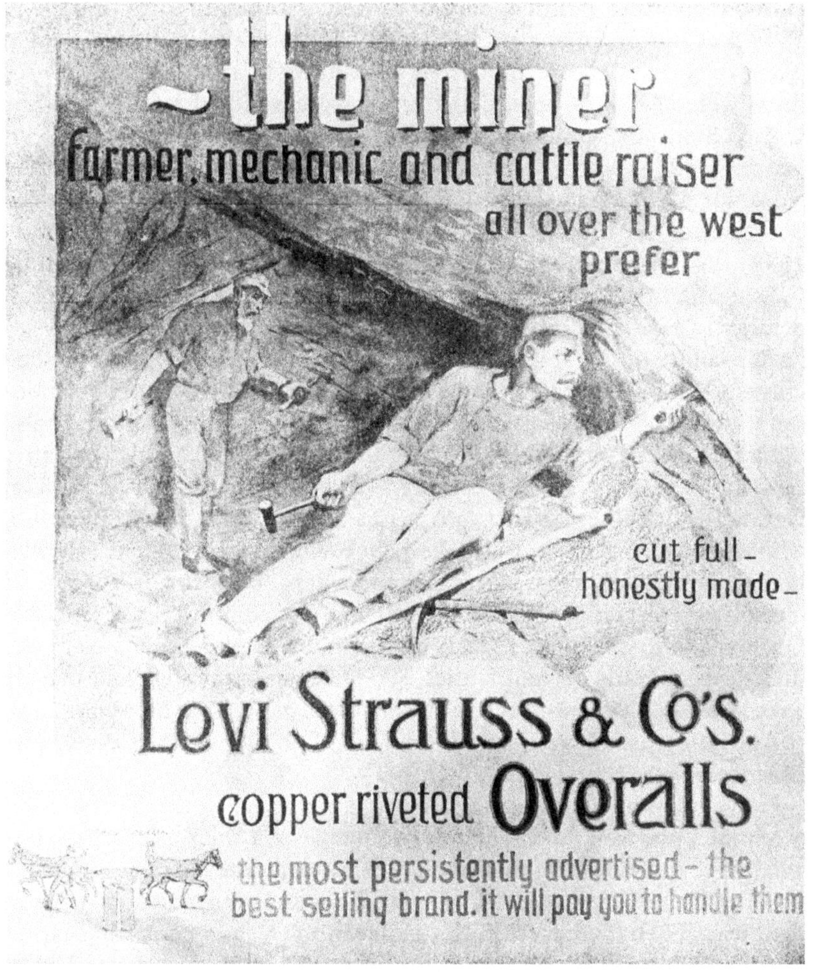

Figure 1.2 An advertisement for Levi Strauss overalls, *c.* 1875. Hackett / Archive Photos / Getty Images.

as well, freely, and happily as in America, the poorest man lives better than he who is considered two ranks higher than him in Europe."[26]

To take but one decade, in the 1840s alone more than 300 such "reports" or "instructions" were published. In addition, one historian has calculated that émigrés sent more than 100 million letters to their relatives and friends in Germany.[27] In the nineteenth century these letters took months to reach their addressees. Today's migrants send text and WhatsApp messages almost in real time, and the Facebook posts, Instagram images, and emails fulfill a similar function to the letters, pamphlets, and books of the nineteenth century. On September 10, 2015, refugees sent selfies with Angela Merkel from a Berlin branch of Germany's Federal Office for Migration and Refugees to their friends and relatives – and thus kindled dreams of being welcome, of refuge, and of a better life just like Gottfried Duden had done among his fellow Germans in the 1830s (see Figure 8.4).

As the nineteenth century progressed, German ports replaced English ones as the points of departure for the transatlantic passage. At first this was, most importantly, Bremerhaven, later Hamburg. In the second half of the century steamboats replaced sailing ships, which made the passage shorter and less dangerous. In North America the Germans began settling not just on the East Coast, but increasingly in the Midwest. Towns like Schaumburg in the State of Illinois or Bismarck in North Dakota are reminders of this.

The most American of American food goes back to German immigrants: hot dogs with frankfurter sausages, probably even hamburgers. Neither existed as such in Europe, they were invented in America and are hybrids that combined traditional German ingredients with new ones. Germany's contemporary signature national dish, the Döner (kebab, gyros, or shawarma in other countries), came into being the same way. It too didn't exist in this shape back in Turkey, it was created by Turkish immigrants in Germany, whether in Kadir Nurman's food stand at Berlin's Zoo train station in the early 1970s or as early as 1969 by Nevzat Salim in Swabian Reutlingen is a hotly contested issue.[28] The German immigrants brought another tradition to the United States: their clubs and societies, including republican, anti-monarchical ones, such as the gymnastics clubs and the choirs that began mushrooming, later also German-American clubs. From the 1870s socialists of German descent became active.

But there was resistance. At the midpoint of the century a right-wing populist movement formed that wanted to push back against the German 1848ers and especially Catholics, including growing numbers of Catholic arrivals from Ireland, through such measures as limits on immigration, higher obstacles for obtaining citizenship, and exclusion from public office. At first the right-wing populists acted clandestinely and became known as the *Know Nothing* movement – when they were caught during one of their violent attacks on a festival of gymnasts of German heritage, they claimed the movement didn't exist: "I know nothing." Later they began acting in the open and garnered almost 900,000 votes or 21.5 percent in the 1856 presidential elections.

As late as the fin-de-siècle, some of the cultural practices of the German, especially Catholic German, minority continued to raise eyebrows among the Protestant majority of British descent. Among these was the attitude toward alcohol. The German pubs and beer festivals, and the German practice of drinking in public, stood in marked contrast to the Puritan roots of the Anglo-Saxon immigrants. Indeed, today's major US breweries were all founded by Germans: Anheuser, Busch, Schlitz, and Pabst. Joseph Schlitz and Friedrich "Frederick" Pabst became millionaires, just like the hotel owner Johann Jakob Astor (of the Waldorf-Astoria in New York), the piano builder Henry E. Steinway (originally Heinrich Engelhard Steinweg), or the ketchup manufacturer Henry John Heinz.[29]

Only one group has left comparatively few traces in the historical record: those whose migration for whatever reason was unsuccessful, the remigrants. Remigrants were a sizable group number-wise – between 1899 and 1924, for instance, they made up 20 percent of all immigrants.[30] To this day we know hardly anything about those who come to Germany but leave fairly soon, either because they are disappointed and move on or back, or because they get forcefully deported.

No Place for Hyphens! How the First World War Changed Everything

In the evening of October 12, 1915, Theodore Roosevelt stepped up to the speaker's rostrum in New York's Carnegie Hall. The former President "was spurred on to his best effort by 2,500 enthusiastic men and women who cheered themselves hoarse when the national anthem was played," as the *New York Times* reported the following day. This was the second Columbus Day since the outbreak of the First World War in August 1914, and as always on this holiday the subject was the nation. Roosevelt's speech was no exception: "There is no place here for the hyphenated American," he began. "The one absolutely certain way of bringing this nation to ruin," he continued, "would be to permit it to become a tangle of squabbling nationalities, an intricate knot of German-Americans, Irish-Americans, English-Americans, French-Americans, Scandinavian-Americans, or Italian-Americans, each preserving its separate nationality, each at heart feeling more sympathy with Europeans of that nationality than with the other citizens of the American Republic."[31]

Whether they liked it or not, the possibility to live multiple identities at the same time, to feel multiple attachments, became narrower for the German immigrants in the early twentieth century. In the epoch of the world wars homogeneous concepts of nationhood were catching on. For the Americans of German extraction, no matter how differently they self-identified, this marked a break.

When in May 1915 a German submarine off the Irish coast sank the ocean liner *RMS Lusitania*, resulting in 123 American casualties, the attitude toward German immigrants in the United States grew more hostile. The situation became truly uncomfortable when the United States entered the war. Caricatures of Germans and German-Americans as bulldogs began to appear. *German measles*, so called because German doctors had discovered the virus that caused the disease, was renamed *liberty measles*, *sauerkraut* as *liberty cabbage*, and *German shepherd dog* became *Alsatian shepherd dog*.[32] A part of the German-Americans reacted with hyper-assimilation: they tried to shed the German aspects of their identity, to anglicize their names, and to blend into American culture as fully as possible. Another part retreated into safe, all-German ethnic communities and avoided contact with other Americans as much as possible.

And yet there were eruptions of physical, sometimes lethal, violence. On April 4, 1918, 300 angry, screaming men stormed a prison in Collinsville, Illinois, and dragged the 45-year-old German-American Robert Prager from his cell, where he had been brought to protect him from the mob. Prager had made, as the newspapers reported the following day, "disloyal utterances against the United States and President Wilson," which is why the mob wrapped him in an American flag and forced him to kiss it in the main street.[33] After he was dragged out of prison, the men hanged him on a tree on the outskirts of the city. Right before the lynching he was allowed a last prayer – in German.

Russia

May 27, 1915, afternoon. A hemisphere and exactly 8,434 kilometers aerial distance removed from Collinsville in Illinois, where Robert Prager will be lynched in three years time. Moscow, former and future capital of Russia, which, like the United States, fought with the Allied forces in the First World War against the German Empire. Furious workers of the Schrader Works, a textile factory that belonged to a man of German origin, forcefully entered the apartments of the managing director, Janson, and his neighbor Betti Engels, who had found refuge with Janson's wife Emilia and his 77-year-old aunt Emilia Stolle. Emilia Janson was beaten to death on the spot, Betti Engels drowned in a sewage duct, and Emilia Stolle died of her injuries in hospital. The apartments were set on fire, and when the firefighters arrived, they were beaten back by the angry mob. Similar scenes were taking place all over Moscow. The victims were Russians of German descent or German nationals.[34]

There had been Germans in Russia for ages. In Medieval times they were craftsmen, merchants, and doctors. In Moscow they made up the largest contingent among the non-Russians, so that the district for foreigners was called *nemetskaia sloboda*, the German settlement. Tsar Peter the Great, who ruled from 1682 until 1725, opened Russia to the West and had the new capital, St. Petersburg on the Baltic Sea, built as a "window to Europe." German engineers and builders were part of this from the start. The beginnings of Russian mathematics, geography, medicine, and many other sciences in the eighteenth century were all connected with German scholars.

Following a war with Sweden, the Baltics were also brought under Russian control during Peter the Great's reign. The nobility there had been conquered by the Teutonic Knights during the High Middle Ages and adopted their language. These noblemen, the Baltic Germans, soon climbed to the highest positions of power in politics and the army – Alexander von Benkendorff, who headed the infamous secret police, founded under Tsar Nicholas I in 1825, was one of them. The singer and Eurovision Song contest winner Lena Meyer-Landrut, born in 1991, and the writer Hermann Hesse also hailed from Baltic Germans; at birth Hesse even had dual German and Russian citizenship.

Yet mass immigration from German-speaking Central Europe began only in the second half of the eighteenth century. In 1762 a German was crowned tsarina: Sophia of Anhalt-Zerbst, who had grown up in Stettin, contemporary Polish Szczecin, and only came to Russia as a 15-year-old. Sophia learned Russian, converted to Russian Orthodoxy, and called herself Catherine II, later Catherine the Great. One year after her coronation she published in Germany a manifesto inviting immigration to Russia: "Inasmuch as the vast expanse of Our Empire's territories is fully known to Us, We perceive that, among other things, no small number of such regions still lie unimproved that could be employed with lucrative ease for a most productive settlement and occupation by mankind, most of which regions conceal within their depths an inexhaustible wealth of multifarious precious ores and metals; and since the selfsame [regions] are richly endowed with forests, rivers, seas, and oceans convenient for trade, so they are also exceptionally well adapted for the establishment and growth of many types of mills, factories, and various other plants."[35]

Along with this manifesto came a number of tangible promises, such as religious freedom and exemption from taxation, tributes, and compulsory labor for 30 years in uncultivated regions, for 5 years in cities. What is more, loans for houses, agricultural machinery, tools, and livestock with a repayment period of 10 years were made available. The immigrants were exempt from military service and from quartering soldiers in their homes. They got duty-free market days, their own local authority administrations, and churches. In return they were expected to take an oath of allegiance to the Tsarist Empire – we are talking about a time before the citizenship of the modern nation-state, before airport controls and biometric passports, a time when borders had yet to be secured by barbed wire and walls.

After the proclamation of the manifesto, tsarist agents took to the road and began recruiting in the German lands. By 1766, 23,000 people had already emigrated to Russia. Farmers in particular agreed to go eastward. Land shortage, bad soil quality, and high tributes to their lords were the decisive push factors, much like with those who emigrated westward to the United States.[36]

The most common route at first went from the port of Lübeck via the Baltic Sea to St. Petersburg, and from there via rivers southward to the Volga, specifically the Lower Volga region, around Saratov, a Russian city of currently 800,000 inhabitants.[37] The tsarist government had assigned the Volga region to the Germans because it had fertile soil on which the farmers were expected to apply their superior agricultural techniques. But it also had rebellious, hard-to-govern ethnic minorities like the Kalmyks, whom the Germans were expected to bring under control. Like in the United States, the settlement of German immigrants was always coupled with expansionist, colonizing, and civilizing missions, here of the Tsarist Empire. In the United States, however, the Germans were but one of many immigrant groups who were tasked with expanding the frontier, colonizing the land, and "civilizing" indigenous peoples. In Russia the Germans embodied this program like no other group.

In the early nineteenth century destinations for settlements in what today is Ukraine were added. The Germans, many of them Mennonites, settled as colonists around contemporary Odesa on the Black Sea. Moreover, German farmer-colonists, most of them from Württemberg and many Pietists, settled in Transcaucasian places that today are in Georgia and Azerbaijan – village and town names, such as Annenfeld, Helenendorf, and Georgsfeld in Azerbaijan bear witness. The last phase of immigration from Germany started in the 1860s, but the support on the part of the tsars had already waned. In this phase Germans from Pomerania and Silesia emigrated to Volhynia, which was Russian at the time and is in western Ukraine today.

In Russian culture a specific image of the Germans formed, in a word, a stereotype. This was because they colonized and civilized, settled compactly and kept their language and idiosyncrasies, because many of the (not uniformly popular) tsarinas were German, because Baltic Germans were hugely overrepresented in the highest echelons of state and military, and not least because German farmers had many advantages over Russian serfs. The "father of Russian socialism," the writer Alexander Herzen – his mother was from Stuttgart in German Württemberg, his father a Russian nobleman – caustically remarked in 1859: "German bureaucratism was enriched by Byzantine servility, the Tatar knout nicely supplemented the German gauntlets. There were Germans on the throne, Germans around the throne, Germans as military leaders, Germans as foreign ministers, Germans as bakers, Germans as pharmacists, Germans ad nauseam."[38]

That same year, 1859, saw the publication of Ivan Goncharov's *Oblomov*. Like no other, this novel cemented the stereotypical juxtaposition of the rational, ambitious German and the emotional, lazy Russian. Oblomov is a nobleman, who spends his idle St. Petersburg life in bed or on his divan, while his serfs work for him on his estate in the countryside. He is a good-natured person, but afflicted with a lethargy *sans pareil*: for pages Goncharov follows the meandering thoughts of his (anti)hero, who, in bed, ponders, whether to stick out his toe from underneath the duvet in order to test the room temperature and decide whether to get up or not – which, of course, never happens, so that at the end of the day it becomes clear that he has spent it prostrate again. His boyhood friend and antipode is a German-Russian, Andrei Stolz, not a nobleman, but a successful businessman, full of energy, calculating, clever, and the epitome of self-discipline. In short, not a very lovable figure.

Oblomov breaks out of his sloth only once, when falling in love with young Olga, whom Stolz has introduced to him. But soon he lapses into his old state, his energy vanishes: his friend Stolz marries Olga and Oblomov marries his housekeeper of many years, Agafya, of course without holding a grudge against his friend. "Oblomovism" or "Oblomovitis" became in many languages, including Russian (*oblomovshchina*), a synonym for parasitic idleness, whereas "Stolz" was the incarnation of the hard-working, law-abiding, ambitious (but not very likeable) German.

That is but one example of nineteenth-century cultural transfer and stereotyping – Russian literature is awash with Germans, they populate all the famous novels by Dostoevsky and Tolstoy. One could also point to the many Russian words borrowed from German. At the same time, a lot of Russian infiltrated the German of the ethnic Germans in Russia. The journalist Klaus Mehnert, born in 1906 in Moscow and raised there until emigration in 1914, remembers: "I grew up bilingually and learned to keep the two languages separate, even if many Russian words – some slightly modified – entered our spoken everyday German."[39]

Mehnert is typical of the tsar's subjects of German stock. In the first empire-wide census of 1897 as many as 18.9 percent of the Volga Germans under the age of 10 had reading knowledge of Russian, among Black Sea Germans the number was 42 percent.[40] (The census counted a total of about 1.8 million Germans in the Russian Empire.) How did linguistic assimilation come about? If the Germans had formed a "parallel society" before that, what triggered assimilation?

Become Russians! Serve in the Army! The 1870s as Break

The German Empire was founded in 1871. This not only signified the entrance on the scene of a great power that might one day compete with the other great powers – France, Britain, Austria-Hungary, and Russia – no matter how related the Hohenzollern and Romanov dynasties might have been. It also meant that a new nation-state had entered, which seriously put in doubt the loyalty of the ethnic Germans toward tsar and empire, for this new German nation-state defined itself not solely qua citizenship, but also qua language, culture, and even "blood." We are talking here about loyalties in a time that became more nervous by the year about the plural, about multiple identities and multiple attachments.

At the same time Russian nationalism was on the rise in the multinational tsarist empire. Part of it was Pan-Slavism, which saw as belonging to Russia people who were not Russian subjects and lived outside its state borders. Nationalism put pressure on the minorities of the vast empire: they were now expected to learn Russian, shed cultural idiosyncrasies, in short, to assimilate. This was called "Russification." In June 1871 Tsar Alexander II revoked the privileges (exemption from taxation, cheap loans) of the ethnic Germans. The only privilege that remained was exemption from military service.

But how is the classic modern nation constructed, how do loyalties get produced – beyond the confines of village, town, region? For one thing, there are standardized paths of transport and communication: streets, the railways, newspapers. Then there are institutions: schools, the army. And so universal conscription, introduced by Alexander II in 1874, also applied to Russia's Volga Germans. From now on they were expected to serve in the army for six years and as reservists for another nine.[41] That was not just a considerable hardship, it was also at loggerheads with the pacifism of religious minorities like the Mennonites, who had already clashed with the rulers of the German principalities, as their desire to conscript them into the army had been one of their main reasons to emigrate to Russia (or America).

A red line had been crossed, especially in the eyes of religious immigrants. They migrated once more – to Canada, the United States, and to South America. For those who stayed, the situation became increasingly uncomfortable. Thus the Moscow pogrom on May 27, 1915, did not emerge out of nowhere. The murder of Emilia Janson, Emilia Stolle, and

Betti Engels at the hands of the mob was preceded by four decades of anti-German propaganda.

On to South America

The Gaßmann family arrived in Brazil via Bremerhaven and the Atlantic Ocean in 1876 after a long and dangerous voyage that originated in Saratov. The new mass conscription law had pushed them to emigration. After their arrival in Brazil, they continued on to Argentina. There they founded in 1878, together with 202 other resettlers, the village Valle María, after Mariental, the original name of the German-founded Volga village which, following the Russian Revolution of 1917, became Sovetskoye and today is called Saratov.[42] Argentina, Brazil, Canada, the United States, but also Australia, those were the countries to which many Germans who had emigrated to Russia for religious reasons moved on when the tsarist empire too began to violate their religious freedoms. Perhaps this form of migration should be termed serial migration for religious reasons.

Alongside this late nineteenth-century migration, there were also 20,000 people who emigrated directly from Germany to Brazil. Many of them came because there was work on the coffee plantations in the state of São Paulo. The port of Santos, where they landed, became infamous because many of the new arrivals died of yellow fever. In order to get enough labor from Europe nonetheless, the regional administration started paying for the transatlantic passage. Many poor German families accepted, and the same was true for Italians. The local authorities began administering the first medical exam to passengers while they were still on board. After landing in Santos, they were then brought to the Hospederia de Imigrantes, the immigrants' station, from where they traveled via two railway lines to the plantations. Between 1875 and 1929 the state of São Paulo was the world's number one producer of coffee, with a global market share of about 70 percent. That was possible only with a great number of cheap laborers. When Brazil upended 400 years of slavery in 1888, it did so less out of humanitarian concerns and more because of economic reasons: since the European labor migrants cost hardly anything by way of transportation and accommodation, they were cheaper than slaves.[43]

Thus migration movements and migration routes are always entangled in countless ways, they are multidirectional; there is rarely an arrow that points in a single direction. They much rather resemble a tightly woven net. When movement stalls in one place because visa regulations get tougher or fences are built, it continues elsewhere. When the Austro-Hungarian and Russian Empires made it more difficult for Germans to immigrate in the 1820s, the United States gained in attractiveness as a destination. To take another example, Bremerhaven and Hamburg were the main transit ports on the way to the United States for Jews, who fled the Russian Empire from the 1880s in the wake of antisemitic pogroms. However, the passage from the North German ports was prohibitively expensive, and so a part of them remained stranded in Germany. The Scheunenviertel district in Berlin-Mitte became their home. And when the Balkan or Central Mediterranean route gets sealed off today, the number of those who escape through the Western Mediterranean route from Morocco to Spain via the Strait of Gibraltar goes up.

Conclusion

Migration, as should have become clear, has always been part of what it means to be human – homo sapiens truly is a homo migrans. This is particularly true for the Germans, who for centuries were the most active émigrés to North America and Russia. The Germans migrated so much that they explained their *Wanderlust* or *Wanderzwang*, enforced wandering, to themselves by invoking the "character of what it means to be German." In the middle of the nineteenth century, when people liked to think in categories of "blood," "national character," and "essence," the Berlin Society for the Centralization of German Emigration and Colonization (founded in 1849) traced German hypermigration to "the ease in the character of the German with which he gives up his fatherland and subordinates himself to other nationalities, together with his inherent drive to wander [*Wandertriebe*]."[44]

On the eve of the First World War in 1914, following a century of mass emigration first from a multitude of German states, then after 1871 from the German nation-state, 7 million Germans had emigrated to North and South America alone.[45] But these are bare numbers. They say nothing about what it really means to leave your familiar surroundings and start anew in a foreign place. At home German émigrés suffered religious and political persecution, but most of all they hoped for economic advantages from emigration. They were duped by traffickers, and many became ill during the voyage and died. In transit countries they had to live in muddy refugee tent camps and were stared at because of their foreign looks and foreign language; sometimes they were physically attacked, but they also received help out of human solidarity. The most outrageous rumors were ascribed to them, phantasy went into overdrive, they were linked with epidemics and crimes. Upon arrival in their country of destination, they preferred to stick to themselves, lived in their own quarters, and preserved the German language and their cultural peculiarities. Many locals were not amused; they hated the "parallel societies" and phantasy production continued. As time went by, most immigrants assimilated, their own language and culture mixed with that of the receiving country. Some immigrants became fabulously successful and attained greater wealth and fame than they would ever have attained in their country of origin. Things got difficult in the late nineteenth century when aggressive forms of nationalism started spreading and the receiving countries began striving for homogeneity. The space for diversity and admixture became successively smaller, often the immigrants were left with a choice between retreating into their ethnic communities and all-out assimilation, the renunciation of everything German.

Does this sound familiar from the current migration debate across the world, including in Germany?

That's the point.

1945

Berlin, May 2, 1945. Three soldiers and a photographer climb onto the roof of the Reichstag and attach a Soviet flag with hammer and sickle. Bombed-out Berlin is in the background, there is smoke above the ruins. This photograph will travel around the world and go on to become an iconic, in fact, *the* iconic image of the victory over Nazi Germany.

The three Red Army soldiers were Meliton Kantariya, Mikhail Yegorov, and Konstantin Samsonov. After their return to the USSR they would receive Hero of the Soviet Union medals, the highest honor Stalin's empire had to hand out.

In truth, the story was completely different. Almost everything. Days before May 2, Red Army soldiers had climbed the Reichstag and attached Soviet flags, only there was no photographer, perhaps because the lighting conditions were too bad for taking pictures. On May 2 the well-known photographer Yevgeny Khaldei arrived at the Reichstag in order to re-stage the scene. In his luggage he had a flag that a tailor had sewn from red tablecloths. Khaldei asked three random Red Army soldiers if they could help him out. The three of them put up the flag on the top of the Reichstag building, Khaldei pressed click. Later the smoke on the negative was retouched in darker colors to give the image a more dramatic touch. A wristwatch on the right arm of one of the soldiers was retouched away – he had wristwatches on both arms, which could easily have given the impression that he had stolen them by looting from the German population. The three soldiers who posed for Khaldei were not the ones awarded Hero of the Soviet Union medals. Stalin had chosen those according to ethnic criteria: like Stalin himself, Kantariya belonged to the Georgian minority, while Yegorov and Samsonov were ethnic Russians and thus represented the largest Soviet ethnicity and the dominant ethnic group. The actual soldiers on the photograph all belonged to non-Russian minorities: Aleksei Kovalev was Ukrainian, Leonid Gorichev was Belorusian, and Abdulkhakim Ismailov was a Kumyk, a member of an ethnic group from the Caucasus who speak a Turkic language. Khaldei himself was Jewish. On his way westward with the Red Army he had documented the horrors of the Holocaust, although these photographs never saw the light of day in Soviet times: they did not fit into the propaganda of the heroic Great Patriotic War.[1]

All of them, Khaldei and the flag raisers, the real and the fake ones, counted among the 3 million members of the Soviet Armed Forces who were then on the territory of the decimated German Reich. In addition there were the soldiers of the other victorious allied powers: 1.5 million Americans, 1 million Britons, and 150,000 French soldiers.

This was only a fraction of the many, many people on the move. Millions of German expellees had moved westward in their flight from the Red Army and were now looking for a place to settle in what remained of the German Reich. There were also the millions of Wehrmacht soldiers who had survived the war and who had, especially if they had been on the Eastern Front, blood on their hands. Then there were 10 million Displaced Persons (DPs), among them millions of forced laborers, prisoners of war (POWs), and survivors of the extermination camps – many of these people wanted to move on, to get as far as possible as fast as possible from the land of the perpetrators, away from their murderers. And there were the 9 million German city-dwellers who had been evacuated to the countryside when the bombing of urban areas started. Finally, there were the first remigrants, returning Jewish and other émigrés who had been forced to flee Nazi Germany.

Perpetrators, victims, hunger, epidemics; parts of walls left in the rubble with thousands of handwritten notes looking for missing persons; robberies, lootings, rapes, murder, suicide; families breaking apart because the wife had stood her ground for years and was hardly able to recognize her disheveled, amputated husband; children who failed to recognize their fathers; "uncles," that is, *ersatz* fathers, who would prefer not to recognize the biological fathers of the children; chaos, chaos, chaos – and everyone, everything, on the move: that was what was left of Germany in 1945, a gigantic merry-go-round of the greatest European migration movement in modern times.

***

"I like this goddam country, you know that? That's right. [. . .] You know what the hell I learned? That a nigger ain't no different from nobody else. I had to come over here to learn that. [. . .] They don't teach that stuff back in the land of the free."[2] These are the words of the African American writer William Gardner Smith. In January 1946 he had been drafted and sent to Berlin, where he worked in an office job in the US Army barracks. In 1948, at age 21, he published his novel *Last of the Conquerors* about his experience in Berlin. The greatest surprise for him in Berlin right after the Second World War was that for the first time in his life he felt equal – in Germany of all places, in the country that under Hitler had murdered the Jews, Sinti, and Roma, and had forcibly sterilized the "Rhineland bastards," the children of German women and French African colonial soldiers, who had been stationed in the Rhineland between 1918 and 1930.[3] For once he was not a second-class citizen, as was the case in the United States and the US Army, with its Jim Crow segregation that endured unchanged until the civil rights movement of the 1960s. Historians have cast doubt on German "color-blindness" toward African-American soldiers, and yet it is true: it is his truth. It is the subjective truth of William Gardner Smith, one of tens of thousands of Black American GIs who served in the US occupation zone after 1945.

***

Right before the war's end 19-year-old Mechthild Ewers married a marine, when he was called to duty. She and her husband agreed to reunite, should they survive, on the island of Hiddensee in the Baltic Sea. Then one day a Red Army truck pulled up. Ewers got scared, terrible rumors about "the Russians" were circulating. And yet: "To my great surprise my husband jumped off this truck. I mean, somehow, I was totally surprised, the situation was totally surprising. We ran toward each other, lay in each other's arms, were completely flabbergasted and just looked at these Russians, it was one of those moments, you know, totally confusing!"[4] After the dissolution of his Wehrmacht unit, her husband had been picked up by the Red Army soldiers and taken along to Hiddensee. Their treatment of him was beyond reproach – impeccable.

***

For weeks Lieutenant Jack E. Westbrook Martin had been fighting with his anti-tank defense unit for the capture of Munich. On April 29 the 21-year-old and the other soldiers in his unit closed in on the Bavarian capital. Right before the city border, they had to pass through a town called Dachau, today a suburb of Munich. There they came upon a concentration camp. None of the soldiers was prepared for what awaited them. When the soldiers entered the camp, they were greeted by emaciated figures who begged for food. Many of the GIs fathomed that human beings who had turned into skeletons of no more than 40 kilograms would have to get used to water and food gradually. But they found what they saw too hard to take. Martin gave his high-caloric US Army rations away among the survivors: "My initial reaction was to give the two or three K-Rations in my pocket." The consequences were devastating. "Later, as I passed that point coming back, I saw one inmate regurgitate – the food was just too rich for him. Another inmate picked up his vomit. But I do not remember if he ate it."[5]

Similar scenes took place in all of the extermination, concentration, and labor camps that the Allied forces liberated. Many of the emaciated survivors died because their bodies were unable to tolerate the first real food intake in a long time.

After liberation the survivors were housed in yet further camps, although the United Nations Relief and Rehabilitation Administration (UNRRA) saw to it that no one had to stay in the camp where they had been imprisoned. Slowly the former inmates came back to life. After a while most of them returned to their countries of origin or went on to make a home elsewhere – in the United States, Britain, or Israel after its establishment in 1948. Yet some stayed on – many of them were from Poland, where there were anti-Jewish pogroms right after the Second World War: the largest on July 4, 1946, in Kielce, after rumors about an abducted Christian boy had been spread. The pogrom left forty-two people dead, eighty injured. Tens of thousands of Jews left the country, many went to West Germany. It was they who rebuilt Jewish communities in Germany. Prior to the arrival of the Jewish quota refugees (*Kontingentflüchtlinge*) from 1990 onward, most of the 30,000 Jews officially registered in communities hailed from these former Polish Jews. Take Salomon Korn, the renowned architect and longstanding chairperson of Frankfurt am Main's Jewish community. Korn was born in 1943 in the Jewish ghetto in Lublin. After the war his parents ended up in the Frankfurt-Zeilsheim camp for DPs. They planned to emigrate to Israel or the United States – originally hardly any Jews wanted to settle in the land of their murderers. Until the 1980s they lived on "packed suitcases," as the saying went among West German Jews.

So Jewish West Germans were originally immigrants from Poland. Not German Jews: they had emigrated to other countries or had been killed. The Polish Jews in turn were originally immigrants from Germany: they, the Ashkenazim, spoke Yiddish, a language derived from German with elements of Hebrew and often Slavic languages, and had fled the Medieval persecutions in German-speaking lands.

On that April 29, Lieutenant Martin saw, however, not just the shocking misery of the inmates. When stepping outside the camp in the afternoon, he saw citizens of Dachau loitering at the fence: "Yes, and the civilians, residents of Dachau, riding bicycles down the streets outside the camp – rags tied over their noses and mouths to keep out the stench," he noted in his memoirs, recorded a year later. "Probably some of those very same people later told us that they did not know what was going on in the camp." Martin himself broke down when accompanying his officer boss who was "viewing the bodies stacked in a boxcar – some like cordwood, some in disarray": "my resistance gave way. I vomited." Only late on this penultimate day of the month of April did he gauge the full significance of what he had seen: "as I returned to my jeep, it continued to sink in – the enormity, the bestiality, the tragedy of what was happening here – of man's inhumanity to man."[6]

***

The mobility of the DPs was limited, the Jewish survivors of the camps and death marches were not allowed to move freely in Germany. They had to check out of the DP camps when they wanted to go into town. Yet non-Jewish Germans were allowed to move without restrictions. Many DPs were surprised how many private cars were still being driven in the streets of destroyed Germany. They, the victims, became bitter about the astonishingly high standard of living of the perpetrators. True, in cities like Berlin there was quite a bit of hardship: "No doubt the children loitering in railway stations or on the roads suffer cruelly at the approach of winter from a total lack of food and clothing." But outside the major cities there were "swarms of strapping, lively, cheerful children. . . . Probably not a town, not a village in the rest of ravaged Europe can show so many children in such good condition."[7]

***

"On May 30, 1945, I was expelled by the Czechs, we had to leave within 15 minutes. We had no time, not even to gather bare necessities. From our apartment we had to walk with the children for one night and one entire day to the camp. When we passed the city border they also took our alarm clock, scissors, knives, and other things away. Already in the first camp I witnessed with my own eyes how mothers had to bury their small children themselves. The entire way they beat us with rubber batons. Today I only have one of my three children. My youngest child is interred in a mass grave in Lower Austria."[8]

This quotation is from the time of the "wild" expulsions, when ethnic Germans were expelled without legal basis from Poland, Czechoslovakia, and other countries – out of rage and revenge for what the Germans had done to people in the occupied countries during the war.

The quotation is by a woman. That is typical: women and children bore the brunt of the expulsions, whereas men were still retreating with the Wehrmacht, missing in action, captured as POWs, or fallen. And the quotation is anonymous. That too is typical: the largest share of what women went through during the expulsions was unspeakable and never found its way into the historical record. In the part that made it into the record, the women usually preferred to remain anonymous.

According to conservative estimates, a minimum of 860,000 German women of different ages, from prepubescent girls to women aged over 60, were raped at the end of the war and in its immediate aftermath. (Boys and men were also raped, but the silence surrounding them in the sources is even more deafening.) The raping was done by the soldiers of the Allied powers. And not just one of the Allied powers, but all of them – in alphabetical order: Britain, France, the United States, and the USSR. Until recently the conventional wisdom was that only "the Russians" did the raping.[9] Soldiers raped for a variety of reasons: because the Germans had committed horrific crimes; because German soldiers had raped the wives, mothers, and daughters of others; because in wars men always use women's bodies in order to seek revenge, humiliate, and intimidate.

Refugee women from Eastern Europe, expelled ethnic German women, were hardest hit.

As a historian I am torn regarding whether to quote from a first-person report here. On the one hand, it could function like violent pornography and once more do violence to the victim, decades later. On the other hand, silence also hurts the victim – their suffering needs to be given space and a voice. So here goes.

Breslau, contemporary Wrocław in southwestern Poland. Early 1945. The Red Army has encircled the city. The following happens to 15-year-old Leonie Biallas with a Red Army soldier:

> Now he is grabbing me and pulling me toward a door. I am trying to wrestle free, am fighting back desperately. Mom wants to rush to help me and pull me away from him. But he pushes her away and opens a door. It leads to the bathroom. Mom tries to follow. He shuts the door and locks it. He is out of his mind and trying to pull down my pants, but can't open them. Now he's got a knife in his hand. I'm screaming: now he's going to stab me to death, I'm thinking. Mom is banging on the door from outside and screaming. The soldier cuts the fabric belt and tears apart the pants and underpants. Then he throws me onto the stone floor. My head hits the floor. He throws himself onto me. It's as though I'm paralyzed, and I'm no longer screaming. But all along mom is wailing behind the door. I don't think it took very long. He gets up and without saying a word leaves the bathroom and the house. I'm cowering on the cold floor and would like the ground to open up and swallow me. Mom enters, takes me into her arms, and comforts me; we're both crying.[10]

Venereal diseases, dangerous abortions, unwanted children, suicides, and, apart from shame, an overwhelming mood of fear, those were but some of the corollaries of the countless rapes.

Yet after everything they had been through, these expelled women and their children were not at all welcomed with open arms in Germany. "A truck brought us from Lingen to Gersten," began a young boy's school essay about his arrival in rural Lower Saxony after expulsion from Silesia.

"There we were rounded up in the school yard. The farmers appraised us like livestock. The farmers took only those who were able to work. In the end only my little brother and me and my mom were left standing there. A farmer found use for my older brother."[11]

In the countryside there was fierce competition for scarce resources – housing, food, and much more – between expellees and urbanites whose houses had been bombed. Expellees were abused as "refugee pigs, Polacks, rucksack Germans, 40 kilogram Gypsies."[12] They were considered alien and exotic, the racism of the Nazi era was applied to them. In Flensburg a District Administrator wrote about the expellees that "we ... Schleswig-Holsteiners have our own way of life that in no way wants to be conquered by the mulatto race [*Mulattenzucht*] that the East Prussian, it must be said, created in his mixing of peoples."[13] Tage Mortensen, a journalist and representative of the Danish minority in Schleswig-Holstein, in a brochure on the expellees described a stereotypical East Prussian "Frau Schiddrigkeit": "Frau Schiddrigkeit's hair oscillates between black and dark brown, her eyes are greenish, her cheekbones broad and her fingers strong and diminutive like those of the Polish girls who in the olden times used to work on the southern isles of Denmark during the turnip harvest. The Southern Schleswigers call the East Prussian mass of refugees a mulatto race. 'Mongrels,' mongrel race. In terms of her looks Margaretha Schiddrigkeit is a typical 'mongrel,' a descendant of many races and nations."[14] The tramline to Stuttgart-Rot, where many expelled ethnic Germans from Hungary, Yugoslavia, and Romania lived, was called the "garlic express" by local Swabians.[15] And of course expellees were accused of spreading epidemics, plagues of vermin in agriculture, and venereal diseases – the same production of rumors and phantasies that we always see in connection with immigrants, like in Chapter 1 on the Germans who were housed in refugee camps in London in the eighteenth century or came to Philadelphia.[16]

The expellees were perceived as fundamentally Other, as looking, speaking, and smelling differently. Their barrack quarters were colloquially called Barackingen, New Poland, Bolshevikia, and Little Moscow.[17] There was even a theoretical superstructure – much of it still very familiar from the recent Nazi era: "It is a big question," wrote a teacher, "whether we get entirely racially polluted [*überfremdet*] or if it is good for us to get fresh blood through the refugees. The real issue is whether this blood is pure. The influx of refugees harbors the danger that the original character of our traditions [*Volkstum*] will lose its authenticity through admixture with a character from another land and of an alien nature."[18]

***

July 1945. A boy or young man in three-quarter view, hands rested on his hips, is standing with his back toward the viewer. He is looking at a photo poster on a tripod in Bad Mergentheim in Baden-Württemberg. On the poster one can discern piles of corpses, mass graves, and concentration camps. The heading reads: "These atrocities: you are guilty!" The sun is shining and reflecting its rays on the Bad Mergentheim cobblestone.[19]

This photo documents an exception. Perhaps it is posed, because most Germans wouldn't even stop in front of the photo posters that had been put up everywhere – "and when they did stop, then only with a quick, furtive sideway glance," as a 1946 journal noted.[20] The concentration camp survivor Eugen Kogon wrote about the photo posters that they elicited "at most surprise or head-shaking in disbelief."[21]

The most common reactions of the Germans – when confronted with the crimes they committed or that were committed in their name – were: claiming to have known nothing about it; equating one's own suffering (bombardments, expulsion, hunger) with the suffering of the Jews and other victims of Nazism; skepticism and disbelief, rumors about lies and falsifications; avoiding personal responsibility, blaming others (Hitler, the SS).

***

"We were liberated by the Britons. I still remember how excited the inmates were: they ran toward the liberators over the trampled-down barbed wire, fell to their knees, and kissed their hands. For 14 days before the liberation we had been given nothing to eat and drink. Thousands perished. The rain saved us from dying of thirst. Famished inmates ate tree bark, old grass, and acorns – many died. We were so starved that Red Cross workers could not determine our gender and therefore asked: 'Man? Woman?' In my file card they noted: 'Russian female, approximately this old. Muscle mass or fat layers non-existent. Height 169 centimeters. Weight 38 kilograms.'"[22]

This quotation is from Lydia Gavrilova, born in 1924. She was one of millions of *Ostarbeiter* from the Soviet Union who did forced labor in Germany. After the Wehrmacht entered her south Russian city of Taganrog in the summer of 1942, Gavrilova was deported to the Ruhr region, where she had to work in mining. From Taganrog alone, which then had slightly fewer than 200,000 inhabitants, 13,930 *Ostarbeiter* were sent to Germany in June–July 1942.[23] To gauge the dimensions of this slave labor, in August 1944, 8.3 million people, most of them from Eastern Europe, were doing forced labor in the Reich – *Ostarbeiter*, POWs, concentration camp inmates. That amounted to a staggering third of the people working. They comprised the majority of the 10 to 12 million DPs after the War.[24]

Gavrilova was liberated from a concentration camp where she was serving a sentence – she had attempted escape from her forced labor camp several times. *Ostarbeiter* were not only occupied in mining or industry, many worked on family farms. This part of history has largely been forgotten. But when Germans do some digging, it often turns out that, during the war years, "Maria from Poland" or "a couple of Ukrainians" lived with the family and did the labor of the fathers and brothers who were serving in the Wehrmacht.

For Gavrilova the British Allied forces arranged a job as a kindergarten worker in London, from where she returned to the Soviet Union in 1948. Out of homesickness. First she was interned in a "filtration camp," because everyone who had been an *Ostarbeiter* or POW in Germany was suspected of treason, checked, and often ended up in Stalin's Gulag, usually without having committed any wrongdoing in Germany. "From the filtration camp they took me to the NKVD secret service headquarters," remembers Gavrilova. "For eight days they interrogated me and every day forced me to write down my biography anew. All the while they were telling me: 'We don't believe a word.' I was beside myself: 'The Germans humiliated us, I can understand that, they were our enemies. But how can you, Russians, mistreat a fellow Russian?'"[25]

In the Soviet Union *Ostarbeit* stuck to people such as Gavrilova like a mark of Cain. To protect themselves they kept secret their years in Germany even in front of their spouses. It was during Gorbachev's Perestroika that the veil of secrecy slowly began to lift. Rehabilitation came only in 1994 under President Yeltsin.

***

Five-year-old August Heinz Limpe and his parents had lost their home because of the bombardments and were evacuated from Dortmund to the countryside. But they didn't manage to find any accommodation there either: "And so we slept in the fields and in ditches – until American soldiers came. Suddenly they were standing in front of us with submachine guns. They thought we were Poles because there had been looting. And when they heard that we were Germans, they even gave us a ten kilometer lift on their truck, they weren't allowed to drive any further, they had their orders. My dad was very ill. They must have beaten his back to pieces, the Gestapo. He was denounced for allegedly having listened to a British radio station."[26]

Disheartened, the family started on their way back from the countryside into the rubble chaos that was Dortmund. They found refuge in the cellar of a bombed house: "That was really just a hole. The windows were blocked up with rubble. But we took away the rubble from inside, and after that they were free. Then we hung cloth in front of the cellar windows. There was a constant draft. And then we made sure to sleep always right in the corner so that we didn't get so much draft. My father was the worst off. He had to prove that he was working. He had to claim that I was working. Otherwise we wouldn't have gotten our residence permit. In truth his only work was 'guarding' a construction site at night. All he'd do is sit there, and then he might receive a couple of Reichsmarks, yes. But at least we had permission to live in Dortmund again."[27]

The family lived like this for a year and a half. Then they were allocated a real room: "From that moment on, when we got that room, all my father did was lie in bed. It was over with him. He was done for, he was exhausted. So he lay there in bed, and I sat in front at the table. And he always answered my questions when I didn't know the answer for homework. Suddenly I no longer got any answer. Then I went to his bed. I said, 'dad.' He was gone. Dead. It's like he died answering my homework questions."[28]

***

Everything is on the move, everyone is on the move. Almost everyone is on the move by foot, people are walking, wading, hobbling, crouching, falling, getting up again. They are dragging and pulling – household items and firewood. Old people, babies, and sick people. Through lunar landscapes that were once cities. Through rivers over which there were once bridges. Hardly any transportation is working – cars, buses, trains. Hardly anything is as it used to be.

2 Twelve-and-a-Half Million in Six Years

My father retired in 2011. He managed to stomach half a year of retirement, then he registered as a volunteer with Catholic Women Social Services, one of the best-functioning, he felt, social service providers in his hometown Frechen outside Cologne. The supervisor in the volunteer department assigned him a refugee father and one of his daughters from the Palestinian refugee camp Yarmuk near Damascus in Syria. My father taught them German, accompanied him and his wife, who arrived later with three more children via Egypt, the Mediterranean, and Italy in bureaucratic dealings with the authorities, and helped the children with homework. My father gets enthused easily – but there is more.

The plight of the refugees touches him because he remembers the stories about the expulsion of his own family. Born in April 1945 in Kaaden, today's Kadaň in the Czech Republic, he was expelled with his parents and three siblings in April 1946. When he started at Catholic Women Social Services in 2012, there were eight volunteers. In 2019 there were ninety. Many of them are from expellee families and got involved for similar reasons to my father. The same pattern applies to older refugee helpers all over Germany: in 2015, when confronted with the images of bombed cities and tent camps with refugees, of displaced children, memories of the flight of their own families from East-Central Europe came back.

The expulsions of the Germans from the eastern territories of the German Reich and of ethnic German minorities from Eastern Europe at the end of the Second World War were "the largest forced population transfer – and perhaps the greatest single movement of peoples – in human history. [...] Altogether, the expulsion operation permanently displaced at least 12 million people, and perhaps as many as 14 million. Most of these were women and children under the age of 16; the smallest cohort of those affected were adult males."[1]

The expulsions were rooted in the aggressive expansionist politics of the Nazis well before the Second World War. Among these was the 1938 annexation of the Sudetenland – it belonged to Czechoslovakia, and the

Sudeten ethnic German minority was "brought back into the Reich [*heim ins Reich*]," in the rhetoric of the time. During the Second World War the Nazis resettled ethnic Germans (*Volksdeutsche*) from the Baltics, Bessarabia, and other places – also "back into the Reich." In addition they deported particular population groups in large numbers within the conquered territories. Thus, in the framework of what the SS called a "racial purification [*rassische Flurbereinigung*]" drive, many Poles were expropriated, enslaved as forced laborers, murdered, or died during the ordeal of forced resettlement to eastern Poland. When it became clear in 1942–1943 that Germany would lose the war, and as the Red Army inexorably advanced westward, the first "wild expulsions" of German minorities started: as revenge for the brutal actions of the Nazi occupiers, but often the Germans also fled on their own initiative because they feared the revenge of the advancing Soviet troops.

Toward the end of the war these "wild expulsions" were legitimized after the fact by the Allied powers in treaties and laws. More expulsions followed, this time officially planned, and they all had the same goal, namely to solve the "minority problem" once and for all and to create Eastern European nation-states, in which people (*Staatsvolk*) and territory (*Staatsgebiet*) were as congruent, as "pure," as possible, that is, without minorities. On taking stock 5 years after the end of the war, about 12.5 million Germans had been expelled. About 8 million of them ended up in West Germany, 4.5 million in East Germany. As for the highly politicized question of the death toll – at stake here is not only the condemnation of Soviet-style communism, but also how focusing on German suffering can end up relativizing German crimes – the historian Mathias Beer writes, summarizing the state of research: "It is seemingly clearly under a million, although we will probably never be able to determine the exact figure."[2]

On top of that there were numerous rapes, and many Germans were deported to the Soviet Union for forced labor. There was also a lot of disease, and epidemics spread. The expellees who made it to what was left of Hitler's Germany were seldom welcomed with open arms. The encountered a "cold *Heimat*," as the historian Andreas Kossert has written.[3] They competed with the locals for food and housing and were abused as "refugee scum." They were considered deeply alien – an "integration bulletin" directed at the local Swabian population by the Commissar for Refugees in South West Germany read: "The expellees are from a foreign country, their habits and ideas are different from ours, their clothing is different as is their way of cooking, some of their working methods differ from ours. Their dialect is different from ours."[4] The integration of the expellees into society became "Germany's Question Number 1," as a newspaper put it in a 1949 headline.[5]

That this integration would eventually work was far from certain. A 1948 poll revealed that 90 percent of the expellees wanted to return to where they came from, and in 1961 that figure was still more than half of all canvased.[6]

There has been a long-standing perception among Germans that a taboo was attached to expulsion in both West and East Germany. This is a myth. That said, it is true that in postwar Germany there was little public space for what the expellees had gone through. Germans, expellees or not, were busy surviving and building a new life. Later, with the student movement in the 1960s, the suffering of expulsion was compared with the crimes that the Germans had committed against Poles, Czechs, Jews, and citizens of the Soviet Union. What have you done? – sons and daughters asked their father, not their mother: what was done to you during your expulsion? If at first "the Nazis" and the SS were the main target, in the 1990s the image of the "clean Wehrmacht" began crumbling, and now ordinary soldiers' and some expellees' participation in Nazi crimes came into focus.

In the GDR too the media reported on the "resettlement" (*Umsiedelung*), as the expulsions were called in official terminology. Only they were never questioned; after all, the "big brother" USSR had executed them.

In unified Germany the subject has become ever more central since the 2000s: at least two generations of Germans, those who themselves went through displacement and expulsion as children and their own children born around 1968, increasingly see themselves as second- or third-generation victims. For their self-definition as victims they avail themselves of trauma research and speak of inherited traumas. Meanwhile the New Right has jumped on the bandwagon. We can already discern the contours of a New Right social movement in which masculinist men's rights activists, anti-feminists, Pegida (Patriotic Europeans Against the Islamization of the Occident) demonstrators, members of the right-wing populist party Alternative for Germany (AfD), and expellees, who want "their" land in the East back, come together and increasingly orient themselves toward Putin's Russia, as paradoxical as this may sound. We'll get to this at the end of the chapter.

Yet things could be very different. If the expulsions were seen, first and foremost, as one of many forms of migration and fit into a new self-understanding of the Germans as a nation of migrants. If German expellees became one of many immigrant groups, not more important than or superior to immigrants from Eritrea, Spain, Turkey, or Kazakhstan,

Germany would be a lot better off. After all, their story after arrival in Germany is similar to that of many other immigrants: initially cold reception, then slow ascent through hard work, and today successful. What such a history of the German expellees as migrants might look like is the topic of this chapter.

What Happened? Historical Overview

For many centuries the German lands were a place of outmigration. A large portion of this outmigration went eastward, and as a result substantial German minority populations in East-Central and Southeastern Europe as well as in Russia came into being. Before modernity these German minorities lived more or less peacefully alongside other groups in the Austro-Hungarian and Russian empires. Trouble began with the rise of the modern nation-state in the later eighteenth century. As soon as national armies, based on universal conscription, replaced premodern armies of mercenaries, as soon as the unity of territory and people and "purity" became ideals, minority turned into a *question*, like the "social question" or "women's question" in an age of questions. Where would the loyalties lie of, for example, the German minority in case of war between the Russian empire, where they resided, and the German empire, whose territories they originally hailed from? Would they remain loyal to the Russian empire? The further the eighteenth and then the nineteenth centuries progressed, the more often the minority question got reduced to two, and only two, solutions: either complete assimilation in the dominant culture or their displacement – violent displacement, if need be.[7]

The First World War became the first great laboratory for the mass displacement of ethnic minorities. If one wished to establish the zero hour of displacement legitimated by international law, this would have to be the 1923 Treaty of Lausanne. It codified the population exchange of 1.2 million Orthodox Greeks and 400,000 Muslim Turks between Greece and Turkey. Many later displacements, including that of the Germans at the end of the Second World War, invoked Lausanne.

It bears emphasizing, however, that the displacement of the Germans at the end of the Second World War was preceded by the displacement of others (including Germans themselves) at the hand of the Germans. To run through key dates, from 1938 the Germans displaced Czechs from the annexed Sudetenland. In 1939 the Germans attacked Poland and displaced Germans to western Poland and Poles to eastern Poland, which after the Hitler–Stalin Pact of August 1939 became part of the Soviet Union. After that Poles were also deported to Siberian Gulag camps. Here is Adolf Hitler in a Reichstag speech on October 6, 1939: "... for the east and south of

Europe is to a large extent filled with splinters of the German nationality [. . .]. In this age of the principle of nationalities and of racial ideals it is utopian to believe that members of a highly developed people can be assimilated without trouble. It is therefore essential for a far-sighted ordering of the life of Europe that a resettlement should be undertaken here so as to remove at least part of the material for European conflict."[8] That was soft for the Nazis, comparatively speaking. In truth resettlement was an early stage in their hypernationalism, based on pseudobiological phantasies of purity. The final stage was industrial mass extermination in Auschwitz.

The "repatriation of ethnic Germans [*Volksdeutsche*]," couched in slogans like "lose the homeland to recoup the fatherland" and "back into the Reich," went hand in hand with the "elimination of damaging influences by segments of the population who are alien to the Volk [*volksfremd*]" and "resettlement [*Umvolkung*] of racially fit persons, deportation of racially indigestible persons, special treatment of destructive elements, and new settlement of the resulting free space with fresh German blood."[9] In other words, the expulsions were part and parcel of Nazi racist and expansionist policies.

The Second World War made possible ever more and ever more radical displacements. Ion Antonescu, the Prime Minister of Nazi Germany's ally Romania, in July 1941 said: "I don't know how many centuries will pass before the Romanian people meet again with such total liberty of action, such opportunity for ethnic cleansing and national revision. This is a time when we are masters of our land."[10]

The governments in exile of the states conquered by the Germans, such as Czechoslovakia and Poland, and the Allied powers, the United States, USSR, Britain, and France, also saw expulsion as a legitimate means. Expulsion was the best route to a peaceful postwar order, they believed. In December 1944 the British Prime Minister Winston Churchill proposed in parliament "the total expulsion of the Germans – from the area to be acquired by Poland in the west and the north. For expulsion is the method which, so far as we have been able to see, will be the most satisfactory and lasting. There will be no mixture of populations to cause endless trouble [. . .]. A clean sweep will be made."[11]

A clean sweep was made indeed – "from below." As soon as the German occupying power retreated and the Red Army came in, the old majority population, or the part of it that comprised the dominant people of the (future) nation-state, expelled the Germans – at first without any legal basis. Or the German occupying power issued an evacuation order to the local German population when it realized that a territory could not be held and that it was about to fall to the advancing Red Army. Or the German occupiers ran off, whereupon the left-behind Germans fled out of fear of the Red Army. Evacuation, eviction, flight, expulsion, displacement, resettlement, deportation, ethnic cleansing, population transfer, forced migration – the boundaries between the processes that these terms signified were fluid, and the same person was often subjected to several of them, (almost) simultaneously or in succession.

"Wild" expulsions were followed by "orderly" expulsions. The Allied forces created the legal foundations at the three major wartime conferences, in November 1943 in Teheran, in February 1945 in Yalta, and in July 1945 in Potsdam.

What an "orderly" expulsion concretely looked like is evidenced by a poster from summer 1945 from Bad Salzbrunn (today's Szczawno-Zdrój) in Lower Silesia, the birthplace of the playwright and Nobel Prize laureate Gerhart Hauptmann: "Special Order for the German population of the town of Bad Salzbrunn, including Sandberg district. The Polish Government orders: 1. On July 14 from 6 until 9 o'clock the German population will be resettled. 2. The German population will be resettled in the region west of the Neisse River. 3. Every German may bring a maximum of 20 kilograms of luggage. 4. No transport (vehicles, oxen, horses, cows, etc.) is allowed. 5. The entire living and non-living inventory will remain in undamaged condition as property of the Polish Government. [. . .] 7. Failure to follow this order will be sanctioned most severely, including with use of firearms. [. . .] 11. All residences in the town must be left open with the key in the outside lock. Bad Salzbrunn, July 14, 1945, 6 o'clock. District Commander Zinkowski, Lieutenant Colonel."[12]

Yet the actual execution of the expulsions was a lot more chaotic and violent than such a document suggests. Some Germans preempted expulsion with suicide – the prospect of losing overnight the house they had been living in and the field their family had been tilling for centuries was too painful, the fear of the unknown too great. The Red Army displaced others violently, rapes and murder were a common corollary. But the vast majority of Germans took to the road on their own, particularly women and children, but also the elderly (Figure 2.1). Men were less commonly present. If they were of fighting age, they were either on the frontline or in captivity as POWs, or they had fallen in combat. The enormous treks mostly used remote westward roads because the larger roads were used by the armies. Time and again the columns of expellees were shot up by low-flying aircraft. Weaker people often died during flight, either of diseases or of hunger and overexertion – their corpses lined the sides of the roads. When the treks moved through territory occupied by the Germans, they sometimes encountered emaciated concentration camp inmates on their death marches, after they had hastily been rounded up and forced out by

Figure 2.1 Germans leave the Sudetenland. © Hulton-Deutsch Collection / CORBIS / Corbis via Getty Images.

SS officers before the arrival of the Red Army. When the Red Army caught up with the treks of expellees, there were outbreaks of violence, rapes, and deportations to the Soviet Union for forced labor, but sometimes also gestures of humanity.

In broad brushstrokes, the course of the expulsions looked as follows: in January 1945 the Red Army began a general offensive and advanced westward through East Prussia, Pomerania, and Silesia. Soon cities like Danzig and Breslau were encircled and captured, following bombardments. After that there was only one corridor for escape, the Baltic Sea via ship. But these ships were also bombed by the Allies – the sinking of the *Wilhelm Gustloff* on January 30, 1945, and the attendant death of 9,000 expellees on board, many of them children, is the best-known case.

Generally speaking, the displacement movements usually went to the closest places in the Reich. That is why most of those expelled from East Prussia, Silesia, and Pomerania went to eastern and northern Germany. Most of the Sudeten and Carpathian Germans expelled from Czechoslovakia as well as the majority of Transylvanian Saxons and Banat Swabians, as well as other minorities known by the collective term Danube Swabians, expelled from Hungary and Yugoslavia, ended up in Bavaria. The Allied forces also had some say – France wanted to take in as few as possible in its zone and prevailed with this, so that disproportionate numbers ended up in the Soviet, American, and British zones.

At Home in Postwar Germany. At Home?

My father and his family of six arrived in a cattle wagon by train in Bavaria on April 23, 1946. They took along the permitted 25 kilograms per person, no money, no valuables. Right at the border they were deloused and then interned in Wülzburg fortress near Bavarian Weißenburg for six weeks. After that the family was quartered with a war widow who lived with her son on a farm in Übermatzhofen, a poor village in the Franconian Jura. The widow was hostile at first, but soon a cordial relationship formed, which was also due to the fact that the family's labor on the farm proved useful.

In February 1951 the Plampers were transferred to Nuremberg's Valka camp, a DP camp for as many as 4,000 from the Soviet Union and its conquered territories (the Baltics, Poland, Czechoslovakia, Hungary, Yugoslavia). In one of the barracks my father's oldest sister opened a grocery store. For a while my grandfather considered moving on to Argentina – the Argentinian immigration agency was recruiting among the refugees in the camp, just like the Canadian, American, and Australian agencies. He liked the idea of getting a large plot of land to cultivate, but in the end he felt too old for such a fundamental change.[13] The family moved out of the camp, started building houses, and so on: an unspectacular West German family story from the time of the West German economic miracle.

The story of my paternal family is quite typical. What is untypical is that the family stayed so unscathed. My grandfather survived, and so did my grandmother and all of their children, and everyone managed to stay together. Other families searched for their relatives for years, if not decades. "Lost children are looking for their parents," search posters read in 1947, and in the Soviet zone the weekly newsreels shown in cinemas featured films with children who were looking for their parents.[14]

Never before in modern history had so many refugees been absorbed in such a short period of time, let alone in a country that was administered by four different Allied powers. The logistical problems were staggering. At first the ghost that the expulsions were meant to banish seemed to reappear: the minority question. In some municipalities expellees came close to constituting a majority. In 1950 they made up, for instance, 44.3 percent of Mecklenburg-Vorpommern's population.[15] The Allied forces were not amused – here's Military Governor Lucius Clay in 1947:

"If it continues as at present, you will be establishing a minority group fostering hatred and hostility for years."[16]

On top of that, housing and food were extremely scarce. A quarter of available housing had been destroyed or damaged in the war. The temporary camps became a permanent fixture. In 1955, 3,008 war-related camps continued to exist, housing roughly a quarter million expellees, half of them since 1947. Unemployment was another major problem. According to the Federal Republic's unemployment statistics of December 31, 1949, 58.5 percent of the jobless in Lower Saxony were expellees.[17]

German society reacted to the expellees with fears, demands, confessional discrimination, and racism. The newspaper *Rhein-Neckar-Zeitung* in 1949 summarized the prejudices that were circulating about the expellees as follows: "The refugees are generally dirty. They are fundamentally primitive, even fundamentally dishonest. It hardly bears mentioning that they are lazy and would much rather dupe an honest local than help him with his work. Needless to say, they are also the most cantankerous people walking around in our streets and alleys. And you will never hear a word of gratitude for all the good things people do for them. That is what you will hear in ninety of a hundred conversations about refugees."[18] The expellees were abused in "prayers":

> Our Father in heaven, see our plight,
> we farmers have no grease and no bread.
> Refugees are stuffing themselves fat and fatter
> and steal from us our last bed.
> We are starving and hurting, I say,
> Lord, send the riffraff away.
> Send them back to Czechoslovakia, yee,
> Father, from the riffraff set us free.[19]

There was talk of an "imminent war between old and new citizens," of all the signs of "ethnic strife [*Nationalitätenkampf*]."[20] Some spoke of "Palestinian circumstances."[21] Even at the very top, Konrad Adenauer, a Christian Democrat and the Federal Republic's first chancellor, in 1946 expressed concerns about the expellees, "lest they implant the Prussian spirit in our Rhineland youth." He stressed the need to "assimilate the expellees and adapt them to our mentality."[22] West Germany, in short, feared that the situation might get out of hand and that the Federal Republic would never come together as a nation.

The GDR, by contrast, simply acted as if there were no problem. After all, the "resettlement" (as it was euphemistically called) by the Red army was justified, not an injustice committed by the class enemy, as was the

West German viewpoint. That is why blending into society was the order of the day. In 1952–1953 the resettlement problem was declared solved, the "former resettlers," as they were called from 1950 onward, became the "tacit four million."[23] And it worked, the combination of positive legitimation of expulsion, assimilation, silencing, and repression. Among other things, this was due to the fact that many unhappy "resettlers" went to West Germany until the wall was built in 1961 – expellees were over-represented among the "deserters of the republic," the GDR term for refugees.

And in West Germany? Why did things turn out alright after all, the many prejudices and problems notwithstanding? Why was integration ultimately successful? To be sure, the "economic miracle" starting up was a major factor, but here we have a bit of a chicken or the egg situation: which was cause, which effect? Did the booming economy facilitate the integration of the expellees? Or did the economy benefit from the expellees' great potential as workers, housebuilders, and entrepreneurs, driven by a self-made rags to riches mentality? One thing is certain: politics helped – with clever incentives, such as in redistribution programs to spread expellees more fairly among the various German *Bundesländer* (federal states); with the 1952 *Lastenausgleichsgesetz*, a law designed to distribute state expenditures for expellees more justly among the regions and especially to take into account the pre-expulsion living situations of expellees; and with "camp closure programs," in the wake of which Nuremberg's Valka camp, where my father's family had lived, was closed in 1960.

The Cold War and East–West confrontation certainly also played a role. It was in the West's interest to make sure the wound of the lost German eastern territories and the displacement from Eastern Europe would fester, for it proved the "Eastern Bloc's" moral-historical depravity. The 1950 Stuttgart Charter of Expellees codified the demand for the restitution of the German territories in the east just like the right to return to, for example, the Sudetenland in Czechoslovakia. At the same time the German government, at the behest of the Allied powers, began to grant expellees the same rights as locals, and increasingly they were now spoken of as "new citizens [*Neubürger*]."[24] This paradox of reserving the right to return to their place of origin in Eastern Europe while at the same time integrating in the Federal Republic was encapsulated in a 1959 sentence that perfectly captures the contradiction: "Therefore integration is also the precondition for a return."[25]

The Allied powers had ordered a ban on political parties and coalitions so that the expellees would not form their own political groups and instead had to blend in with the locals. Then the thinking changed and the ban was lifted, precisely to ease the equality and integration of the expellees as "new citizens." And sure enough, in Schleswig-Holstein, for instance, the League of Expellees and Those Deprived of Rights (BHE) in the 1950 state elections instantly garnered 23.4 percent of the vote. In the 1950s the first lobby organizations of expellees were founded, uniting in 1957 under the umbrella organization the Federation of Expellees (BdV).

The Federal Law on Refugees and Exiles (BVFG) of May 1953 codified the special position of expellees, including federally funded research on, and sponsorship of, their cultures of origin. Thus the original postwar policy of insisting on the complete melting in with the culture of the receiving society gave way to a new approach: integration alongside the preservation of their specific cultural baggage. That was a shift of enormous proportions. It foreshadowed the 1960s shift in the United States from the concept of a melting-pot to a salad bowl. It was in this new approach that the key to the successful solution of the expellee problem lay.

Remembering Expulsion: An Alternative to the Fashionable Theory of "Inherited Trauma"

Directly after the Second World War the expellees viewed themselves as victims – of the policies of the Hitler regime and the "Allied injustice of Potsdam."[26] This self-perception began showing cracks in the 1960s. This was because of the children, the so-called 68ers, who started pressing their parents – what did *you* do in the "Third Reich"? Even if they had not committed any crimes, their fate as expellees paled in comparison with that of the targets of Nazi crimes. In the 1990s the children of the expellees, who were now retired 68ers, began to take an interest in their family histories. The journalist Helga Hirsch put it like this: "Yes, it is probably first and foremost our problem, the problem of the second generation, that we stigmatized our parents during the 1960s and 1970s as political die-hards and enemies of détente. We, who no longer wanted to hear about their tragic experiences because we immediately assumed that they instrumentalized them for a politics of revanchism. It's true, we want to make up for forcing our parents into silence or small circles in which they shut themselves up, instead of opening up."[27]

In the 2000s there was another shift.[28] Today it is not just the children of the expellees who show an interest in the expulsions, but also their grandchildren. Expulsion is seen as something so horrific that it cannot be processed cognitively and has been lurking in the subconsciousness ever since. And allegedly to this day a taboo is active with regard to the expulsions and the attendant violence, so that it has been impossible to speak openly about rapes, shootings, and harassment. All of which supposedly exacerbated the trauma and its passing on to following generations. The excesses of the 68ers – their 1970s descent into communist fringe groups and ultimately the terrorist Red Army Fraction – were the consequences of the unprocessed, traumatic past of their parents and grandparents. The same goes for the way in which the 68ers brought up their children – the focus on individual fulfillment, the divorces, the anti-authoritarian childcare centers or *Kinderläden*, and the pedosex. All of this is purportedly why anxiety and depression are rampant among those born around 1968, the third generation. Inheritors of deep trauma, that generation refuses to procreate, which is what has caused Germany's demographic crisis, or so the argument goes.

This shift in memory of the expulsions is embedded in a second, larger shift that the historian Norbert Frei in 2005 called a "recoding of the past": if in the collective German memory during the 1980s and 1990s the Germans thought of themselves primarily as perpetrators, in the 2000s a new "master memory" of the "Germans as victims" took shape.[29]

Indeed, 60 years after the end of the Second World War there were a lot of signs of such a recoding. In 2002 Jörg Friedrich published *The Fire: The Bombing of Germany, 1940–1945.*[30] A broad debate ensued, including in the yellow press. Terms like "bombing holocaust" (coined by Jürgen Gansel of the neo-Nazi National Democratic Party of Germany, NPD) began to circulate.[31] Also in 2002 the Nobel Prize-winning writer Günter Grass published *Crabwalk*, a novella about the Soviet torpedoing of the ship *Wilhelm Gustloff*. And 2003 saw the reprinting of a forgotten eyewitness account of a woman ("Anonyma") in Berlin in 1945 after the entry of the Russians, which focused on the rapes by Red Army soldiers; in 2008 the book was made into a movie. In 2007 at the latest, with the two-part TV drama *Die Flucht* (*March of Millions*), the suffering of the Germans during the expulsions had definitively become mainstream and moved to the center of attention.[32]

Suffering and victim status now were also psychologized. In psychotherapy with older clients it became commonplace to ask about expulsion, experience of aerial bombings, rapes, or orphaning. Here the writings of the psychoanalyst and gerontologist Hartmut Radebold were most influential. Radebold attributed a large number of mental health issues to trauma caused by expulsion and other experiences of war, and not only among those old enough to have been perpetrators, but also among their children.[33]

Therapists started going to Radebold's seminars and learned to bring back into consciousness in family constellations, an increasingly popular form of group therapy in which participants impersonate a client's extended family, including the deceased and even those who had been aborted, the family members killed during the expulsions.[34] Radebold's approach was then extended to the next generation of the so-called war grandchildren (*Kriegsenkel*) and became common knowledge through bestsellers by such journalists as Sabine Bode and Anne-Ev Ustorf, the latter born in 1974 and therefore as a "sufferer" (*Betroffene*) the first mouthpiece of her generation.[35] An internet platform appeared (www.forumkriegsenkel.de) and even a countrywide grassroots movement of "regular gatherings of war grandchildren" (*Kriegsenkel-Stammtische*), where on any given night across Germany members of the third generation meet in pubs and elsewhere to discuss their "trauma."

The initially left-wing psychoanalytic discourse became – among other things – a conservative, sometimes right-wing extremist cause. One can already see the seeds for this in Sabine Bode's writings. She explains divorce rates, childlessness, and demographic change in terms of the lack of mourning of the horrors the war generation had to go through: "We Germans have internalized that we must not see ourselves as victims of Nazism and therefore also must not mourn."[36] Gabriele Baring, a psychotherapist and, like her husband Arnulf during his lifetime (he died in 2019), often cast as the conservative voice in TV talk shows, agrees and has no doubt who is to blame for "this 'historical correctness'": "Many 68ers were among the fiercest apologists of the ban on mourning [*Trauerverbot*]."[37]

Baring goes even further. Having recourse to epigenetics, she describes "depressions, a tendency toward violence, and commitment phobia" as hard, scientifically proven long-term consequences of the omitted mourning in the third generation, Germans born around 1968.[38] "A genetically inherited traumatization is indeed the rule," she writes.[39] What is to be done? Therapy and family constellations – one female war grandchild's clotted ovaries open as soon as she learns to accept her father, whose shame about his own father, a Nazi, is revealed during a family constellation: "The client's body became capable of conception as soon as she could give herself, as it were, inner permission for this."[40] Sabine Bode summarizes the tragedy of the children of the 68ers: "People born in the 1960s who only managed to become independent from their parents quite late in their lives [...]. These war grandchildren have all the intellectual requirements to lead successful lives, but with the majority you get the impression that they are emotionally blocked, in their private and professional lives they are stunted."[41] Germany is "on the brink of self-destruction," says Baring.[42]

There is now even a first interpretation of the 2015 "welcoming culture" for refugees as a social movement led by *Wiedergutmacher*, a play on the words of naïve social justice warriors (*Gutmenschen*) and atonement for the Holocaust (*Wiedergutmachung*), who supposedly never worked through their transgenerational traumas and hence risk destroying Germany.[43] This variant of psychotherapeutic-conservative collective memory has merged with New Right social movements, such as the "anti-feminist men's rights movement."[44] The psychotherapist Astrid von Friesen is one of the protagonists of this movement. The Second World War made Germany fatherless, the feminists of the 1970s perpetuated this fatherlessness by glorifying single motherhood and demonizing everything eternally male through gender mainstreaming, all of which produced commitment-phobic, depressed divorce boys, plagued by German angst – this is von Friesen's chain of reasoning.[45]

So what do we make of this? Simple questions falsify most of the arguments – why, for instance, is Italy as childless as Germany? A more fundamental critique, however, needs to revisit the concept of trauma deployed. Historian of science Ruth Leys has shown how after the Vietnam War a specific understanding of trauma won out, a concept in which the traumatic event is thought to exist outside language and consciousness and hence escapes representation, which makes it free-floating – and ultimately compatible with the Right.[46] This concept of trauma, which today gets neurobiological support from psychiatrists like Bessel A. van der Kolk and was encapsulated in a specific reading of the diagnosis of posttraumatic stress disorder (PTSD), allows the making of feasible (pointing from war to psychological disorders among those who today are in their eighties) and unfeasible (pointing from war to childlessness among those who today are in their forties) causal connections. These causal connections can neither be proven, nor can they be falsified.

A dangerous mix has formed since the noughties, and the theory of expulsion as inherited trauma is part of the mixture. The ingredients of the cocktail are: expellee activists, the New Right and AfD, followers of the Norwegian right-wing terrorist Anders Breivik, anti-feminist men's rights activists, who are fighting "Feminazis" and advocating "national motherhood," "concerned parents," who are fighting sex education and gender mainstreaming in schools, homophobes, evangelical Christians, ultraconservative Catholics, and, last but not least, proponents of transgenerational trauma theory. At this point the borders are still fluid, but you can already discern the contours of a Psycho Right. For a few years now they have been orienting themselves to Putin's Russia as the purported last bastion of traditional family values. They meet, for instance, at the World Congress of Families, an annual convention of Christian homophobic activists, right-wing populists, right-wing extremists, and others – the eighth World

Congress was supposed to take place in Moscow for the first time in September 2014 and was canceled only because of the Crimean crisis, the ninth Congress took place in Utah in the United States, and in 2017 it met in Viktor Orbán's Budapest.[47] Very important are also the conventions of the New Right, pro-Kremlin Jürgen Elsässer, who edits the right-wing populist magazine *Compact*, which has become the mouthpiece of the AfD.[48]

I am not saying we should forget the suffering of the expellees. But it would help to remember it together with the perpetration of Nazi crimes, rather than offsetting perpetration against victimhood. It would also help to remember expulsion as migration and arrival in Germany as a success, a success that materialized not least because the Germans found the most workable model of national identity: the salad bowl model. That would be a real alternative to the fashionable theory of the transgenerational inheritance of trauma.

Conclusion

Every fifth person in Germany is from a family of expellees.[49] The immigration of the twelve-and-a-half million expellees in only 6 years radically shaped West Germany: politically, socially, culturally, linguistically. Even the confessional map was redrawn: in places where previously Lutheranism had prevailed there were now also a lot of Catholics. And vice versa. In 1950 the historian Eugen Lemberg described the formation of the Federal Republic as the "formation of a new people of internal Germans [*Binnendeutsche*] and expellees from the east."[50] The same could have been said about the GDR.

All of Europe changed fundamentally as a result of the Second World War and its consequences, including the expulsions. Never in its history had Eastern Europe been this monoethnic: never had the nation-state's people and territory been this congruent. The seemingly intractable minority question seemed to have been "answered" once and for all.

After 1945, Germany for a while became the world's largest switching yard. Masses of expellees encountered members of the Red Army that had expelled them and was now the occupying Allied power in Eastern Germany. They encountered collaborators from the Soviet Union (Ukraine, Belorusia, the Baltics) and Eastern Europe, who had fled to the West to escape the revenge of the Red Army. They encountered surviving Soviet POWs and forced laborers, who after years in Nazi Germany were on their way to their homes in the East. They encountered Jewish and other survivors of the extermination and concentration camps. They encountered those who had been bombed out of their apartments in the cities and were now on the move to the countryside – internal migration.

They competed with all of these groups for scarce housing and food. The locals looked upon the new arrivals with a range of attitudes and emotions, from skepticism to rejection, and in so doing integrated elements of Nazi racism – thus expellees were called "mulatto race" and likened to "potato beetles."[51] In other respects too their experience was that of migrants: gritting one's teeth, getting ahead through hard work, having to be twice as good, slow, piecemeal acceptance, and finally arrival and blending into dominant society. "Expellee migration background" would perhaps be an apt term, if one were looking for one.

The basis for arrival, at least in West Germany, was, as I have tried to show, the migration politics that crystallized around 1950: promotion of the arrivals' heritage culture with express invitation into collective culture – the American salad bowl model that in the United States only superseded the melting-pot model in the 1960s. Only no one called this approach migration politics because the expulsions were not seen as migration. Instead contemporaries constructed an ethnobiological connection and acted as though Germans had returned to being Germans.

It is high time to recast this narrative and to forge a different memory. As extravagant as it may sound, the state-sponsored expellee cultural sponsorship (*Brauchtumspflege*) with its folklore evenings, *Heimat* festivities, traditional costumes, and folk dancing with simultaneous invitation under the roof of a German Federal Republican national identity was ahead of its time: it was progressive. The Germans already had the right model, but unfortunately they forgot it and did not treat everyone alike according to this model, not the asylum seekers, the Volga Germans, Jewish quota refugees, and not the *Gastarbeiter*, the subject of the next chapter. They have finally excavated this model and will now apply it to everyone: all's well that ends well, that is how the expulsions could be remembered one day.

3 Labor Migration to West Germany

"The unhappiest people in the world were the foreigners [*Ausländer*], the first generation," says Ioannis Petridis, who came to West Germany from Greece in 1961. They had planned to save up some money and then go back. But in the end it was often too late, they had grown roots. The *Gastarbeiter* were "actually tragic figures."[1]

Ayşe Özkan's parents belonged to this first generation: her father arrived from Turkey in 1973, her mother in 1975. She was born three years later in Cologne. Özkan represents the second generation. "Has Germany become your home now?," the interviewer wants to know from her. "Kind of like a second home. It's just that the annoying thing is that here we're foreigners, we remain foreigners, but in Turkey we're also foreigners."[2] Alev Yildirim, born in Berlin in 1971 and also second generation, in 1997 as rapper Aziza A. with her song *Es ist Zeit* (*It's Time*) landed the first hit with German lyrics and a Turkish refrain. Her album came out the same year, the cover says "Oriental Hip Hop." Some songs are in Turkish, others in German, and some are mixed. Aziza A. became a newcomer star and got asked "stupid questions like, well, what are you actually?" and "how many percent are you Turkish, how many percent German?" Her response: "Yeah, sure, I'm a cheese, 60 percent of me is fat, the rest is German and the rest is Turkish, or what do you mean?"[3] (Figure 3.1).

A group of girls with Moroccan, Turkish, Somali, and Palestinian backgrounds got interviewed in 2004. They were all born around 1990 and therefore teenagers at the time of the interview: generation three. They speak of themselves as "foreigners." One of them says: "When you move, for example, you have to apply for the new apartment, and if you apply it takes two months, but then a German family applies, and for them it only takes two weeks. That's unfair. Frankly, it's shit." When the girls get asked, "Do you like it here?," the answers are very different. One says: "You've got more rights here than in Morocco, for example, or in Turkey, actually any place. Women too. There are more cultures here than in my own country, in my own country you only know your own culture, you don't see any other

Figure 3.1 Aziza A., *Es ist Zeit: Oriental Hip Hop.* © Anna Neumann, Label OX, a label of Orient Express Wolfgang Galler, Ulrich Sackenreuter, Andreas Spieß, Ünal Yüksel GbR, 1997. Galler Musikverlag.

countries."[4] The fact that PlusGerman teenagers in the early twenty-first century perceive Germany as multicultural, but their countries of origin as culturally homogeneous, is the result of a decades-long process of migration, especially labor migration.

After the Second World War the West German economy boomed and workers were in high demand. In 1955 the government of Chancellor Konrad Adenauer concluded an agreement with Italy and the first labor migrants started arriving. In 1966–1967 there was an economic crisis and growing unemployment, in 1973 the recruitment of foreign labor migrants came to a halt. The vast majority of labor migrants – 11 million – returned to their countries of origin, as planned. Three million stayed. The Green Party politician Cem Özdemir, the actress Sibel Kekilli, the film director Fatih Akin, the rapper Lady "Bitch" Ray, the news anchorwoman Linda Zervakis, and one of the world's most famous soccer players of the 2010s, Mesut Özil, are their descendants.

They all have to live with the consequences of a birth defect. When their parents and grandparents were brought to Germany, the idea was that they would leave after a few years. But life is more complicated than the legalese of the recruitment agreements. People make friends, fall in love, and have kids who later go to kindergarten and school. So a part stayed. It's only that the laws weren't adapted. Let alone Germany's concept of nationhood. The term used for them reflects the whole dilemma. At first they were called "guest workers" (*Gastarbeiter*). But guests don't work, guests don't stay. Then they were called "foreigners" (*Ausländer*), or, more charitably, "foreign fellow citizens" (*ausländische Mitbürger*). But the second and third generations were born in Germany. There is nothing foreign about them, they are *Inländer*. What is more, as soon as the new citizenship law went into effect in 2000, they often became citizens. It will hinge on a new concept of nationhood, in which the German plus several other identities can easily go together, that the feeling of sitting between two stools or being torn, so palpable with Ayşe Özkan, Alev Yildirim, and the group of girls mentioned above, will diminish.

What Was *Gastarbeit*?

Carlos Pérez is 35 years old in summer 1972 when stepping into the coal mine's iron elevator cage for the first time and traveling 1 kilometer underground. So far he has worked as an installer for heating systems in Andalusian Córdoba, before that he served in the Spanish Army – all above ground. His family had migrated once before, to Córdoba from the village of Espejo, where his father, a farmhand, died when Carlos was 6. To pay for its move from the countryside to the city, the family sold its olive trees. In the city they lived in a poor quarter with other village migrants. Carlos attended school for 5 years, then he, the oldest of three brothers, had to give his single mother a hand and started working as a mason on construction sites.

The iron cage rattles. The pressure on the ears is enormous, it gets hotter and hotter, the air is stuffy. Downward is tolerable because the lift is traveling at reduced speed, but the trip upward at the end of the shift is at regular speed: one of the Spanish colleagues, who, like Pérez, is covered with black coal dust, gets so sick that he gives up during the first week and moves on, from the German Ruhr region to France, where he starts working in a car factory. Carlos Pérez stays and works underground in the tough job for 4 years.[5]

Ana Maria Ferreira Silva is 16 when arriving in 1969 in Bonn to work in a hospital cafeteria. She was born in 1953 in Braga in the north of Portugal. Her mother died at Ana Maria's birth, her father worked as a shoemaker. Ana Maria wanted to marry, but as the youngest of four children in a dirt poor family she could not hope for a dowry and therefore not for a marriage any time soon.

There is a cause for every labor migration, a push factor. And there is a pull factor for every labor migration, a demand in the labor market of another country. With Ana Maria Ferreira Silva the cause was poverty, that is, certain knowledge that the prospects of making it in Portugal, of marrying and founding a family, were next to nil. With Carlos Pérez it was also poverty and in addition a conflict with his employer. After the conflict only his wife, a nanny, was officially earning a salary; he himself worked illegally in a bakery. With other guest workers from Southern Europe political motives were decisive in pushing them to leave their countries: Portugal and Greece were military dictatorships until 1974, and in Spain the fascist dictator Franco ruled with an iron hand until his death in 1975. For Spanish and Portuguese labor migrants, nearby France was the logical choice of emigration. If that didn't work out, they tried the booming European industrial countries further north, such as Germany.

Carlos Pérez went to the recruitment agency in Córdoba and entered his name in a list of job seekers. He ended up in the Essen coalmine because this happened to be the only place that was looking for workers at the time. Ana Maria Silva had a sister who was already working in Germany. She arranged for the Bonn hospital to directly ask for Ana Maria. Such connections through family members or friends were typical – often entire Andalusian or Sicilian villages were depopulated and the migrants then worked in the same region or in a single North Rhine-Westphalian or Baden-Württemberg company rather than across all of West Germany. Employment contracts, whether arranged anonymously via lists as in Carlos Pérez's case or via existing networks as in Ana Maria Silva's case, were almost always signed at the recruitment office in the closest city. Uncontrolled migration rarely took place. This would have been exceedingly difficult in a Europe of border controls and different national currencies – after all, the process of European unification had only just begun.

Next came the health exam. It has left a deep imprint in the long-term memory of most labor migrants. The Ribeiro couple, both from farming families, underwent the first test in the closest city. "After we got the blood and urine results," says Camila Clara Ribeiro, "we traveled to Lisbon for an entire week. There a German doctor examined us. He tested if all our extremities were in good condition, he closely examined our legs, perhaps he was looking for varicose veins, and he examined our teeth really closely. My cousin had warned me about the teeth. She said we would be turned down if our teeth were in bad shape. So before the exam I went to the dentist; I had to borrow money for that."[6] For many the health exam was a humiliating experience: "With every one of us he put a finger in our underpants and pulled them down [...] You're ashamed. Because there are women in the room – female doctors," recalls Muzaffer Y. about his health exam in Ankara.[7] Giacomo Maturi, who came from Italy to Heidelberg for doctoral study and in the 1960s became first a "foreigner representative" at Ford Motors in Cologne, then the leading radio and press expert on the labor migrants from a "foreigner's perspective," looked into the health exam from the other side, the state's side: "I visited the [...] recruitment agencies, the commissions, both in Naples and Athens but also in Istanbul, and there I saw masses of candidates who were crowding together and who were of course incredibly disappointed or even despondent when they were rejected for whatever reasons. Because they had, I don't know, rotten teeth, or were too short or too tall, or whatever [...] It's gotta be said, there was such a thing as – I don't want to use this nasty [Nazi] word, but still – 'selection.'"[8]

Rotraud Herwig worked in medical services in Istanbul in the early 1970s. Hundreds of thousands left for Germany at the time. She remembers attempted frauds in which urine bottles were exchanged.[9] One job recruiter recalls about the early 1970s: "If you told the Yugoslavs, we need twenty bricklayers, they got a bricklayer's certificate, and if you told them, but we don't need any bricklayers, we need steel fixers, then they received a steel fixer certificate the next day."[10] The recruiters then devised tests to examine specialized technical skills. Attempts to bribe the recruiters and medics were also quite common.[11]

Carlos Pérez underwent a total of three medical examinations. He remembers these exams as tougher than those for entering the Spanish army, and yet he was the only one of thirty-three tested who passed. He finally held a work contract and a passport in his hands. Usually there were 2 weeks between medical exam and departure for Germany. If more than 4 weeks elapsed, women had to pass the mandatory pregnancy test for a second time.[12]

Chartered trains brought the migrants to Germany. The trains got longer and longer on their way to the north, because in every city new coaches with guest workers were attached. The seats were made of hard wood, "you can't sit for a long time, you can't sleep."[13] "The doors remained shut until the train reached the Greek border," remembers a Turkish worker. "That's how one treats animals, not humans."[14] Men and women were transported separately: "They put the women in the last coach. They separated it from ours with a chain because we weren't supposed to enter it," recounts another Turkish worker.[15] Later entire trains were designated for women only. Especially in

Turkey, "the fathers [. . .] were very worried about their daughters."[16] Later yet there were direct flights, particularly from Turkey.

Once the trains arrived at their final destinations, the labor migrants were either picked up by the companies that had recruited them or put on trains to other German towns. Munich, or, more precisely, the old air raid shelter next to the main train station's platform 11, was the most important distribution point. At peak times more than 1,000 *Gastarbeiter* a day passed through this node, amounting to a total of 1.8 million between 1960 and 1973.[17] "We were then," says a Turkish labor migrant about arrival in Munich, "led into a subterranean room that was huge, as large as a soccer field. [. . .] We continued to eat what we had brought along from Istanbul. [. . .] The administrators read out our names in the alphabetical order of the cities we were going to. They let everyone get on their trains and sent them off."[18]

The next destination was the factory dormitories – *Heim* is one of the first German words guest workers remember hearing (Figure 3.2). Sometimes barracks from the camps that had until recently housed DPs or expellees were used.[19] When organizing housing, the country of origin was ignored and migrants from Italy, Greece, and Turkey were mixed together. The

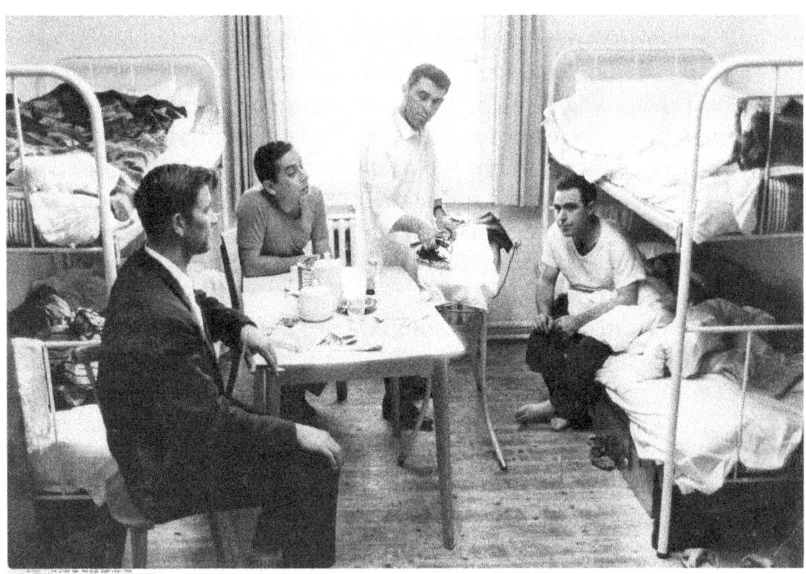

Figure 3.2 Labor migrant *Heim* in West Berlin, 1965. Ullstein bild / Getty Images.

migrants had to share rooms and prepared their meals in common kitchens. Many lived very frugally because their overriding goal was to send back home as much of their earnings as possible. As time went by, and the further their country of origin became removed mentally, this goal often became less pressing, so that in the end they lost sight of it. People slowly began to grow roots and spent money on rent, clothes, and leisure activities.

Most jobs were low-skilled work for which it was hard to tap into the domestic workforce – at conveyer belts, on construction sites, or in coal mines, as in Carlos Pérez's case. These were particularly dirty jobs or jobs in which one had to work particularly fast: one was paid for output, not according to the time worked. And they were jobs in which workers got injured easily or generally endangered their health. In the workplace one often only met Germans incarnated as bosses – they were the foremen in the factory or the overseers on the construction site. "I worked with a lot of Turks at Ford. There were also Italians and Greeks, but very few Germans among us," a Turkish *Gastarbeiter* recalls.[20] Correspondingly little German was spoken – or picked up. In larger companies there were interpreters. Language more generally was a touchy subject. German native speakers often used a specific kind of German with many infinitives and without articles, which they considered easier to understand: "At the aliens department the clerks are so unfriendly, they say: 'if not find new apartment, back Turkey.' Why do they speak like that with us? It's 'back to Turkey,' not 'back Turkey.'"[21] What is more, they enunciated this broken, simplified German not only especially clearly, but also especially loudly, in the belief that it might be more intelligible. Many guest workers felt as though they were constantly being yelled at.

Unfair wage differentials were common, and women suffered dual discrimination, both on the basis of their national origin and because of their gender. Aynur A., who came with two little daughters from Turkey in 1971, reports: "The money I earned at Siemens wasn't sufficient, and so there were times in which I worked two or three jobs at the same time. [. . .] After my eight-hour shift I went cleaning homes. And even later I did the household chores. I often fell asleep in the streetcar."[22]

As time went by, more and more *Gastarbeiter* organized in unions and got involved in politics, some in organizations according to country of origin, others in German trade unions like IG Metall. For *Gastarbeiter* from Greece, Portugal, and Spain, all of which were dictatorships until the mid-1970s, but equally from socialist Yugoslavia or Turkey after the 1980 military coup, trade union and political organizing was a particularly sensitive subject. The German recruitment agencies often tolerated the involvement of the respective secret services and had politically suspect, in the case of Spain, Portugal, and Greece above all communist, applicants weeded out in advance, whereas others were sent to Germany on purpose so as get rid of them as troublemakers at home. In Germany proper there were networks of informers who did the surveillance work among fellow *Gastarbeiter* for foreign secret services. For example, Spanish Franco supporters spied on Spanish communists.[23] In the German trade unions *Gastarbeiter* were involved in all the major industrial actions, such as the famous Ford strike of 1973.[24] Despite the wage differentials that led to this involvement, earnings not just helped support numerous relatives, but in the end did indeed enable many to buy their own house in their country of origin. The contribution of labor migrants to the economies of the countries they came from and to which the vast majority returned cannot be underestimated, just as their contribution to the German economic miracle cannot be underestimated.

When we remember the guest workers today, we think of men in boiler suits in factories or with safety helmets and soot-blackened faces in mines. Yet a large percentage of the labor migrant workforce was female. Ana Maria Ferreira Silva from Portugal, who worked at the Bonn hospital, was but one of 750,000.[25] Many groups of women labor migrants have been largely forgotten, such as the 18,000 South Korean nurses who were recruited between 1963 and 1977 or the several thousand nurses from the Philippines.[26] Caretaking is "emotional labor," to use the sociologist Arlie Russell Hochschild's term. Hochschild speaks of "a South-to-North 'heart transplant'": "A growing number of care workers leave the young and elderly of their families and communities in the poor South to take up paid jobs 'giving their hearts to' the young and elderly in families and communities in the affluent North."[27] Apart from this emotional guest labor, there are two other types of migrant labor that are predominantly female, invisible, and to this day poorly paid: assembly-line work and cleaning work.

Many women came as spouses, sometimes they married male guest workers while the latter were on home leave, sometimes they were already married when their husbands left for Germany to earn money. These husbands then often had their wives join them so that they could earn as well. If they had children, they frequently left them at home – there is an entire generation of so-called suitcase children who grew up with their grandparents or other relatives and sometimes became estranged from their parents.[28] Ivan Ikić and his wife, both Croats, left two children back in Bosnia with the grandparents: "It wasn't easy to live here without the kids. [...] They knew us as their parents, but their real-life parents were grandma and grandpa. They would have preferred if we hadn't visited them. Especially our boy. When we came they had to follow our rules, and the grandparents were different, more lenient."[29] Hayriye E. also left her children behind, in Turkey: "My younger son Hasan was 5 years old at the time. Together with the five sons of my brother he stayed at my mother's. [. . .] Before I left for Germany, I waited until Hasan fell asleep. [. . .] When Hasan woke the next morning, they told him, I heard: 'Your mother is not here, she went to Germany.' I heard he even looked for me under the sofa. [. . .] Eight months later, when I went on vacation, I saw my children again for the first time."[30]

Most parents reunited with their children in Germany at some point. At the latest, this was when they moved from their dormitory to a rental apartment.[31] All labor migrants remember how difficult it was to find an apartment on the tight housing market. Even those who spoke perfect German ended up at the very bottom of the pecking-order of apartment-hunters when they first mentioned their last name over the phone. What remained were apartments that no one else wanted – it's important to remember this when right-wingers today reproach migrants for self-ghettoizing in "parallel societies." Later networks developed in which migrants from one country or region brokered apartments for other migrants from their country or region. By 1972 approximately half of all Turkish guest workers lived in a rental apartment, in 1980 the number had gone up to 90 percent (Figure 3.3).[32]

As time went by, an entire infrastructure of ethnic stores, restaurants, and sports clubs developed, without which contemporary Germany is hard to imagine. And of course also religious institutions: Greek-Orthodox churches, Portuguese-speaking Catholic parishes, Turkish Millî Görüş mosques, Turkish Alevi societies, Muslim cemeteries. Muslim *Gastarbeiter* who observed dietary restrictions remember a time when this infrastructure had yet to come into being. "Buying meat was difficult," says a guest worker from Morocco. "We didn't dare go to German butchers. So we went to Jewish ones, who butcher their livestock the same way as us Muslims."[33] "We ate chicken most of the time," according to a woman guest worker from Turkey.[34]

Insofar as *Gastarbeiter* and members of the German society that had after all recruited them met, with generation one this happened in the workplace and with generation two, the children, in school – these were the two major sites of encounter. True, there was no state-sponsored segregation as in the GDR, where *Gastarbeiter*, or *Vertragsarbeiter*, as they were called there, were expressly prohibited to mingle with the locals, and where the dormitories often resembled prisons. And yet in West Germany too the entire system was not geared toward interaction and exchange and certainly not toward growing roots. With labor migrants from Turkey a kind of rotation system was used at first, whereby they weren't allowed to stay in Germany for more than 2 years, but this rule was soon (in 1964) abandoned.[35] The overriding goal from the

Figure 3.3 Turkish *Gastarbeiter* family in Essen, 1978. Ullstein bild / Getty Images.

perspective of the state was to benefit from *Gastarbeiter* labor for a few years and then send them back to their countries of origin. The goal of the *Gastarbeiter* was to earn money for a few years and with this money then live their dream of a family home or car back home.

A lot could be said about the kinds of encounters with German society that took place after all. Suffice it to say that the whole spectrum of attitudes toward the *Gastarbeiter* was on display – sometimes by a single individual in the course of a single day: solidarity and top-down domination; satisfaction that someone else was now doing the "dirty work" and one could get better jobs and generally move up in one's company; kindness and racism, from verbal (*Spagettifresser*, *Kümmeltürke*, *Kanake*) to physical violence down to murder; paternalism but also openness and true care up to friendship and love.

Staying On

To reiterate, the vast majority of labor migrants, 11 out of 14 million, returned to the countries they had come from. This cannot be said often enough, since the myth that all *Gastarbeiter* came in order to stay is hard to dispel. What kinds of impressions they took back home from their time in West Germany, with what kind of mental baggage they went on to shape their societies of origin, is worth discussing at greater length than can be done here. It was certainly not the case that the *Gastarbeiter* returnees neatly filled the gaps they had created with their departure. They themselves had changed, but people's attitudes toward them had also changed. They were now often seen as alien, envied because of their money, or called "Germans," for example *Almancı* in Turkey. A feeling of dislocation and fundamental homelessness took over: many of them never felt at home in Germany, but in their home country they did not feel at home either.

Those who stayed did so, first and foremost, because it was possible: it was legal. In 1965 West Germany passed a new Aliens Law that replaced the old 1938 law, the *Ausländerpolizeiverordnung*. This new law was complex, but what is important here is that it had a paradoxical effect: permanent residency in Germany was now on a legal footing. The temporary residence permits *Gastarbeiter* had been issued until 1965 were integrated into a European legal system and thus lost their arbitrariness. That doesn't mean that these temporary permits could easily be converted into permanent residence permits. And not at all that they led to naturalization: the greatest contradiction until the new citizenship law of 2000 was that Germany extended residence until life's end to the largest labor migrant group in Europe, but did not offer citizenship. Put differently, a residence permit grounded in arbitrariness became law and thereby acquired settledness, and could be extended over and over again until it was permanent. The same went for the welfare systems. A portion of the guest workers' salary was paid into the social welfare system, and if they got injured or fell ill, the German health and care system took care of them. Retirement benefits were the same: because they had contributed to the retirement plans, they had a right to get a pension, irrespective of whether they lived in their countries of origin or in Germany. In other words, the logic of the law became operative – *Gastarbeiter* were entitled to health and retirement benefits, and if these rights were curtailed in everyday life, which frequently happened, they could sue.

The halt to recruitment on November 23, 1973, marked, it seems at first glance, the end of an epoch – the epoch of *Gastarbeit* which had begun with the first recruitment agreement with Italy in 1955. Therefore for a long time 1973 was remembered as a watershed, a real break. The German politicians in charge cited the world economic crisis as the cause for the halt to recruitment. The Organization of the Petroleum

Exporting Countries (OPEC) had curtailed its crude oil production, triggering a steep rise in prices, the "oil price shock." The oil-based economies of Western industrial states collapsed, and the Federal Republic's long boom, its economic miracle, came to an end.

Historians today tell a different story.[36] Doubts about the usefulness of labor migration arose as early as in the late 1960s. In 1966 and 1967 there was an economic downturn and a right-wing party, the NPD, garnered 7.9 percent of the vote in Hesse state elections. Cost–benefit analyses began to figure more frequently in political discourse: do the social and political costs (a rise in unemployment among migrants from 137,200 in 1967 to 1.37 million in 1973, xenophobia, the rise of the NPD) justify the economic benefits?[37] Was *Gastarbeit* profitable in the long term? For a while scholars saw 1973 as the endpoint of a longer process rather than a sudden rupture.

But there are problems with this interpretation as well, for labor migration to Germany by no means ended in 1973. Many guest workers quickly brought over their families before this possibility was taken away from them – "family reunion" was the legal term. The result was a short-term rise in immigration numbers. Statistics always require interpretation, but here the numbers are unambiguous: while the number of foreign employees declined from 2.6 million in 1973 to 1.8 million in 1978, the number of foreigners living in Germany rose during the same period from 3.97 million in 1973 to 4.14 million in 1979. This rise reflected the influx of spouses and children.[38]

After the halt to recruitment the Federal Republic's politics toward the *Gastarbeiter* who stayed were ambiguous, or, more precisely, continued to be paradoxical. On the one hand, the mantra was that all *Gastarbeiter* should return because Germany was no immigration country. "If the federal government," said the new CDU (conservative) member of parliament Jürgen Todenhöfer in 1974, "fails to find means of limiting the swelling stream of *Gastarbeiter*, we will have difficult social conflicts that will endanger the inner peace of the Federal Republic."[39] On the other hand, Germany's social welfare systems were in the process of "integrating" *Gastarbeiter*, who were endowed with rights, into the working world, the school system, the healthcare system, the trade unions, and the professional associations. Moreover, *Gastarbeiter* definitively became objects of social-scientific inquiry, especially in educational studies. Social workers and social pedagogues discussed the "*Gastarbeiter* question" or the "*Gastarbeiter* problem," devised strategies to improve the situation, and put these into practice. Put cynically, entire social service professions owed their very existence to the labor migrants and the non-disappearance of their "problem." Put more charitably, social workers and social pedagogues attended to a significant segment of the population, who had initially been seen as manpower only, not as human beings with rights and needs – "euroslaves" was a term a competition organized by the WDR (a public broadcaster based in Cologne) came up with in the 1970s as an alternative to *Gastarbeiter*.[40]

But there was also a trend in politics to accept that some guest workers would stay and to think seriously about "integration." This trend became more pronounced throughout the 1970s, which had to do with the social democratic SPD–FDP coalition governments from 1969 to 1982. In addition to politicians and the social workers, there was civil society – with numerous neighborhood community groups, citizens' initiatives, and church actions. In 1979 it looked like the trend toward integration had won: Heinz Kühn, a former social democratic minister president of North Rhine-Westphalia, became the first countrywide Commissioner of Foreigners (*Ausländerbeauftragte*) and immediately criticized the misguided policies of the past. He spoke of labor migration as an "irreversible development": *Gastarbeiter* had become permanent immigrants. Kühn called for an end to discrimination and proposed a host of integration measures. And yet, from a historical perspective we should register a word of caution, for we do not want to create an impression that there had been a linear process by which a labor migration that had been imagined as temporary ultimately found everyone's approval as permanent immigration. It was not only conservatives who voiced criticisms of immigration after 1973; often the trade unions close to the SPD did so as well, fearing for the jobs of their members with German citizenship in economically rough times.

Many who ended up staying had hitherto found themselves stuck in limbo for many years. "At the *Heim* women friends said they would work for two years, save up this much money, and then go home," as was commonly heard.[41] "After we had our second child in 1967 we still thought we would return 'next year,'" says Metin K. "My father-in-law also insisted on this. He wanted us to return to Turkey. Even if we constantly spoke of 'return,' we weren't ready for it; the ideas in our heads hadn't matured yet. What was return supposed to do for us? Here we felt good, at AG Weser we were like one big family. There we would have depended on my father-in-law. My wife was with me anyway. The kids had grown and entered school. It was clear that they had more possibilities here than in Turkey. And so, with the idea 'we couldn't avail ourselves of any higher education, but our children should have a chance to do so,' we stayed here."[42] But often there wasn't enough money to put into practice one's dreams. Sometimes earnings were barely enough to get by in Germany: "That was the real reason why we weren't hopeful about a return any time soon. There were even times when we took out loans before we went to Turkey for vacation."[43]

The children suffered the most from this state of uncertainty. Many of the "suitcase children" were "commuter children" – a summer with the parents in their home country, half a school year in Germany, a year and a half with grandparents in the home country without seeing the parents at all, and so on. Emotional attachment to the parents became tenuous, "they will not call their mother 'mom.'" There was a rampant sense of abandonment, first by the parents and later, when they brought their children to Germany, by the grandparents.[44] This had a psychological price. Parents and children, siblings, of whom one grew up in the country of origin with relatives, the other in Germany with the parents, all were unfamiliar with each other: "Since the point wasn't," says 41-year-old Dilek in hindsight, "to win the affection and attention of my parents – after all these people did not feel like parents to me – there was practically no reason to be jealous of my sister. We would have only had sibling rivalry if we had both loved our parents. Back then this strange woman was to me merely the mother of a little girl who herself seemed like a total stranger. For example, I told my sister: please tell your mother to unlock the door of the outdoor toilet."[45] Some psychologists believe the overambition and overachievement of second-generation "poster immigrants" is an attempt to get in their professions the love and approval they never got from their parents when they were children.[46] The back-and-forth between country of origin and Germany sometimes lasted for decades: "Like many children, Dilek heard from her parents every year that they would return to their home country next year. Dilek's parents kept saying this for twenty years."[47] Other *Gastarbeiter* literally forbade themselves to sing "the song of return": "After that," in Nedret P.'s words, "I never again sang the song 'next year we shall return,' that so many of my compatriots sing all the time."[48]

They had come to work, and the workplace was the place with the most interaction with Germans, provided their colleagues weren't all *Gastarbeiter* like themselves. "In this textile factory we had a good relationship with some of the German colleagues," remembers one Turkish woman guest worker. "We communicated via hand signs. But there were some who looked down upon us because we were from Turkey. Back then we were new here, almost like guests. We didn't understand the language; but you can read the gestures. We felt in their glances that they looked down on us."[49] Often *Gastarbeiter* failed to conform to the images and expectations the Germans had of them. Especially when they moved from cities in their home countries to rural Germany. In the early years of Turkish labor migration, for instance, most were from Istanbul and it was only later that *Gastarbeiter* from rural Anatolia became more prevalent.[50] Aliye B. remembers: "I arrived in Bad Schwalbach. There a chauffeur, the main nurse, and three female staff members of the employment agency met me. These ladies recognized me from my paperwork. Apparently they were expecting an old Turkish woman in harem pants. I was 40 at the time but came across as younger because I was quite slim. Plus I was wearing a fashionable skirt and a long coat. I had make-up on and was well-manicured. While they were looking for a woman in harem pants, they met a woman who was trying to communicate in a mixture of German, English, and Turkish. They were very irritated. Later I heard that they looked at my make-up and painted fingernails and said: 'She's not the type who will work!' So they didn't give me work for four days."[51] Conversely, the urban *Gastarbeiter* were shocked by the low standard of living in the inner city districts, into whose rental apartments they moved from the dormitories. Filiz Y. felt that the apartments in Berlin-Kreuzberg were "often worse than the Istanbul '*Gecenkondus*' [Turkish for 'built overnight']."[52] Shared toilets, coal stoves in the apartments – in Turkey people had had a different image of Germany. Yet to others Germany did indeed seem like a land overflowing with milk and honey.

On all sides there was a tendency to generalize and to think in national and ethnic stereotypes – "the Greek," "the Italian per se," but also "the German." His "character," his "mentality," and invariably in the third person singular, masculine. Eduard Keintzel, who had been sent to Turkey for the Federation of Ruhr Mining Enterprises reported: "The Turk is reportedly extremely frugal and rarely initiates anything on his own. Apparently the peculiar climate influences his attitude to work; negatively when there are southern winds, positively when there are northern winds. The emotion of jealousy is, according to many, unknown to the Turk. He is used to being directed by an iron hand."[53] Dr. Giacomo Maturi explained to the readers of the newspaper *Die Welt* and the tabloid *Bild*, where his column "Nix Amore" ("No *Amore*") appeared in 1966, the different cultures of "Southerners" versus the Germans. Southerners were allegedly passionate and personal, Germans reserved and cold. Southerners were always late, Germans the opposite. Southern men were attractive and fiery, German men reliable but boring.[54] Selvi Gül, a homemaker of Turkish descent, explicated, "the Germans are cold people," whereas Mustafa Tekinez, a teacher of Turkish descent, thought that "the Germans are honest people."[55] To this day stereotyping dominates a lot of thinking, and people are finding it difficult to acknowledge and accept diversity, not least within groups.

Most of this thinking in generalizations was and continues to be hostile. Entire books could be written about prejudice, stereotyping, resentment, and racism, in fact the entire history of immigration to Germany West and East since 1945 could be framed this way. I too will come back to this many times, but suffice it to quote here this multilayered description by Nedret P.: "In those years many Germans asked questions and tried to make fun of me. In truth they knew neither Turks nor Turkey. I answered the question 'Are there telephones in Turkey?' by responding, 'no! We communicate through very long pipes.' [. . .] Apart from these questions, which stemmed from ignorance, I did not experience any serious discrimination. Actually, there was one word at the time: 'Caraway Turks' (*Kümmeltürken*). To hear this word was unbearable for me. Every time I heard it I talked back. *Kümmeltürke* came up in the 1960s when Turks began moving here. After a while we retaliated by using the term 'Potato Germans' (*Kartoffeldeutsche*)."[56]

As these examples make plain, the touchstone of hostile thinking and speaking was often food – in addition to the body, smells, and sexuality. Food in general is a key subject in the migration experience. After the end of the economic boom in the early 1970s, *Gastarbeiter* began opening restaurants in which they offered the cuisine of their countries of origin. That amounted to nothing less than a culinary revolution in Germany. Today it is hard to imagine what Germany was like before this revolution. Consider the town of Siegburg, located between Cologne and Bonn. Let's take a look at the Yellow Pages of 1955, right before the first Italian *Gastarbeiter* started arriving. There are the eateries Aggerblick and Lindenhof, the Heinz Inn, the Fish Bar Peter Leuchter, and Hotel-Restaurant Driescher Hof. In 1985, following three decades of labor migration, we find the Balkangrill, Pizzeria l'Odissea, the Greek Grill Restaurant Zorbas, and the Chinese Restaurant Peking.[57]

New branches of culture emerged, literature, theater plays, and films by migrants. The poet Yüksel Pazarkaya translated classic Turkish-language literature into German for Ararat Publishers and thus made it more palatable for a wider audience, not least to get it out of the position of the eternally catching-up and underdeveloped, and to compete with the Germans in the area of "high culture" on an equal basis. Aras Ören became the "father" of "foreigners' literature" (*Ausländerliteratur*), fiction about life in Germany, usually written in the first languages of migrants and then translated into German. Increasingly German became the language of composition – by authors who had grown up with a different first language and later learned German, or by those who had grown up bilingually or multilingually. Authors like Rafik Schami or Feridun Zaimoğlu, later Wladimir Kaminer, Olga Grjasnowa, Nino

Haratischwili, Alina Bronsky, Lena Gorelik, Katja Petrowskaja, and Yōko Tawada: all of them don't just produce "great" literature that has become part of the canon of Germanophone world literature, but also in their writings discuss questions of Self and Other, migration and German identity.[58]

The 1980s as a "Lost Decade" of Migration Politics?

"Foreigners' literature," the first Commissioner of Foreigners in 1979, linguistic changes, such as the shift from *Gastarbeiter* to "foreign fellow citizens," pizza, gyros, cevapcici, döner kebap, and Italian ice cream parlors – these were but some of the signs that the labor migrants who had stayed and the majority of German society in the late 1970s began getting used to the prospect of living together permanently in the Federal Republic. "Integration" was the buzzword for this coming to terms with reality. The experts – social workers and migration scholars – made propositions for integration measures. The ruling political parties reacted with a "defensive refusal to learn," a term coined by the historian of migration Klaus J. Bade, and reiterated like a mantra that the former labor migrants' stay in Germany must remain limited in time and that Germany was no immigrants' society. The experts spoke and wrote "to a wall" (Bade), the SPD–FDP coalition government proclaimed as late as 1982: "There is a consensus that the Federal Republic of Germany is no immigration country and shall not become one."[59] The Commissioner of Foreigners Kühn resigned in 1980 in protest. "With this cross-party delusion of German migration politics," says Bade, "the 1980s were a historically lost decade for tackling the issues of migration, integration, and minorities."[60]

In 1982 the SPD–FDP coalition government, which had been in power since 1969, collapsed. Helmut Kohl and his conservative CDU came to power. Amidst growing unemployment the new CDU/CSU–FDP parliamentary majority in 1983 passed a "law for the advancement of the readiness to return among foreigners." In its wake, unemployed *Gastarbeiter* who applied between October 1983 and June 1984 got a "bonus for return," in popular parlance a "get-the-hell-out bonus," of 10,500 D-Mark plus 1,500 D-Mark per child.[61] A total of 133,000 persons, including family members, returned to their home countries, most importantly Turkey.[62] Generally speaking, the situation on the labor market remained tense throughout the 1980s, which had to do with short-term and long-term factors. In the short term the new rise in oil prices after the Islamic Revolution in Iran in 1979 had an effect; in the long term there was a transition from an industrial to a postindustrial, knowledge- and computer-based society. Although the economy expanded in many individual years, unskilled labor was in less and less demand. The booming regions of the 1950s to 1970s, first and foremost the Ruhr region, became deprived regions with high unemployment, depopulation, and massive social dislocation – if in 1979 fewer than 1 million were unemployed in Germany, in 1983 this number had climbed to more than 2 million.[63] The north–south asymmetry was reversed: instead of the shipyards and mines in the north now the high-tech multinationals in the formerly poor agrarian regions of Bavaria and Baden-Württemberg boomed – Bosch, Siemens, SAP, BMW, and Mercedes-Benz.

On the whole the climate became tougher for "foreigners," as they were now mostly called. Kohl ushered in the conservative "intellectual–moral turn," which went hand in hand with a new politics of historical memory. CSU leader Franz-Josef Strauß advocated drawing a line under the Nazi past ("it is high time that we step out of the shadow of the Third Reich and the orbit of Hitler and become a normal nation again"), Kohl in 1985 met with US President Ronald Reagan at the military cemetery of Bitburg, where, among others, SS soldiers were buried, and 1986 saw the beginning of a "historians' debate" about the comparability of Nazism and Stalinism, which always revolved around not just memory of the Holocaust, but actually German identity.[64] As the historian of migration Rita Chin has shown, this conservative turn was intertwined with the "foreigner question": "A revived national identity needed historical narratives capable of inspiring pride, but also required a reassertion of borders and clear definitions of cultural belonging."[65] There was a real renaissance of phantasies of national purity. As early as 1981 a group of right-wing professors had published a "Heidelberg manifesto" on migration. It warned about the "corrosion of the German people through the immigration of many millions of foreigners and their families" and the "foreign infiltration [*Überfremdung*] of our language, our culture, and our ethnonational identity [*Volkstum*]."[66] Polls showed a significant change in attitudes: if in 1979 39 percent of those surveyed said that the *Gastarbeiter* should disappear, in 1982 60 percent felt this way. If in 1979 42 percent of those polled were in favor of state investment in integration, in 1982 this number was down to 11 percent.[67] Civil society became active in the protest against "foreigners," for example the Bochum "Citizens' Initiative Stop Foreigners" and the Kiel "List against Foreign Infiltration [*Überfremdung*]" were founded.[68] And there was radical, sometimes murderous violence: thus in 1980 not only was a Turkish store in Hannover attacked and devastated, but also in Leinfelden near Stuttgart fire-bombs were thrown into the hotel room of Ethiopian asylum seekers and in Hamburg two Vietnamese asylum seekers died in an arson attack with Molotov cocktails on their shelter.[69] In the end, two new right-wing extremist parties gained in popularity: the Republikaner and the "German Volk Union" (Deutsche Volksunion, DVU). The Republikaner in their election campaign showed images of families of Turkish descent accompanied by the melody of *Once Upon a Time in the West*, known in German as *Play the Song of Death* – in January 1989 they gained representation in the West Berlin legislature with 7.5 percent of the vote. Thus the SPD's progressive move toward "integration" in the 1970s paradoxically had negative long-term effects: because the former *Gastarbeiter* were no longer perceived as temporary labor migrants, but as potentially permanent residents, they became a screen onto which all political forces, right and left, projected their vision of national identity. During the 1980s in high politics conservatives dominated and propagated the image of a homogeneous German nation. In this image there was little room for the former guest workers.

At the same time – and this complicates the larger picture even more – the 1980s saw the rise of a new party, the Greens, founded in 1980 and first voted into the Bundestag in 1983. The former 68ers were no longer part of the government, as they had been from 1969 until 1982, and so a more radical part of them ended up with the Greens. Like no other party the Greens were linked with extra-parliamentary, civil society, pro-migration politics. This was the heyday of the citizens' initiatives, the *Bürgerinis*. Associations like Pro Asyl were founded (in 1986), people protested xenophobic violence, others hid rejected asylum seekers in their own homes. Kohl's conservative backlash also forced other minorities to step into the limelight and take a public stance. In 1985 German Jews protested against the premiere of a theater play by movie director Rainer Werner Fassbinder, *Der Müll, die Stadt und der Tod* (*Garbage, the City, and Death*), which included an antisemitic depiction of a Jewish real estate agent from Frankfurt. From then onward Jewish Germans grew more comfortable with the idea of staying and taking, if you want, a few things out of the proverbial suitcases on which they had been sitting since the Holocaust. In 1986 the first countrywide meeting of the Initiative Black People in Germany (Initiative Schwarze Menschen in Deutschland e.V.) took place and the foundation of the Organization of Black Women in Germany in 1987 marked another milestone of the Afro-German movement.[70] In 1989 the Frankfurt City Bureau for Multicultural Affairs was founded, headed by 1968 student revolutionary leader Daniel Cohn-Bendit, who worked in an unpaid, honorary capacity and remained in post until 1997.

Just as regional differences in Germany need to be taken into account, the situation in the home countries of the *Gastarbeiter* must also be factored in. After the 1980 military coup, returning to Turkey was no longer an option for many of the Turkish guest workers. In fact, a significant number applied for family reunions for political reasons, and applications for political asylum started coming from Turkey proper – conservatives often spoke of "pseudo-asylum seekers." In 1982 the Turkish dissident Kemal Altun committed suicide when he was about to be deported to Turkey. In the German parliament Joschka Fischer of the Green Party compared this story with that of the Jewish philosopher Walter Benjamin, who in 1940 committed suicide on the Franco-Spanish border, lest he be handed over to the Germans.[71] Also, the number of asylum seekers from Vietnam (boat people, for whom the special status of quota refugees, *Kontingentflüchtlinge*, was created in 1980) and Poland (after the introduction of martial law in 1981) rose, which played a role in the debate at the time. On the other hand, Southern European countries like Spain and Portugal joined the European Union (EU) in 1986 and began booming. That created an economic pull that attracted former *Gastarbeiter* back to their countries of origin.

The Lived Experience of Generation Two in the 1980s

The first generation continued working and began reaching retirement age: if you had come, for instance, at age 31 after the first recruitment agreement from Italy, in 1989 you were 65 years old and could retire. The second generation had greater opportunities: thus Kemal Şahin, born in Turkey in 1955, finished his engineering studies at RWTH Aachen in 1982, had a poster boy career, and opened his first store with presents for Turkish home leave vacationers. This store he expanded into one of Germany's largest textile manufacturers, the Şahinler Group, with more than 12,000 employees. Şahin calls himself an "Anatolian Prussian."[72]

But there was also Ahmet Arslan, born in Berlin-Kreuzberg in 1976 as a child of Turkish *Gastarbeiter*. In the late 1980s he joined one of the first youth gangs – this too was a migrant reality. The 36 Boys of Turkish descent were the most famous of Berlin's street gangs, and Arslan was a member from the age of 12 until 24. He dropped out of school, saw three gang members die in fights with other gangs and with neo-Nazis, and spent a total of 1 year in jail. Today he works with migrant teenagers in preventing violence.[73] How differently might life trajectories like his have developed had the late 1970s integrationist approaches of Commissioner of Foreigners Heinz Kühn and the migration experts been universally applied? How differently had the "major backlash" not taken place under Helmut Schmidt and especially from 1982 onward under Helmut Kohl?[74]

In real life, on the micro level, quite a bit of what Kühn and the experts had recommended in the 1970s was actually put into practice. In many local communities there were in fact preparatory classes for the children who had come in the context of family reunions, because in regular classes they were at risk of falling behind, not least for language reasons.[75] Even in conservative states like Baden-Württemberg differences could be vast, depending on locale, school, or even the teacher. Journalist Semra Pelek's mother (Semra herself was born in 1976 in Böblingen and is a Turkish citizen) arrived in 1971 as a 21-year-old from Istanbul to marry a Mercedes worker. She saw to it that her daughters spoke Turkish at home. Semra's elementary school teacher in first grade forbade her and Hatice, who also had a Turkish background, to speak Turkish. Semra Pelek became withdrawn and began hating school. In the end her report card read: "Semra knows almost all letters, but cannot read. With assistance she can read simple, short words. She has no good command of script. She cannot express herself coherently. But she copies texts recognizably and legibly." Regarding her comportment the report card said: "Semra is shy in interactions with her classmates. She takes part in games vivaciously, but has difficulties because of her poor knowledge of German."[76] Even though Semra would have been transferred to the next grade, her parents insisted that she repeat the year. The new teacher allowed her to speak Turkish and often asked for the Turkish translation of German words. School became fun for Semra. At the end of the year her report card said: "Semra quickly established good contact with her new classmates. [...] Thanks to her mature and independent personality she was able to help others. Her German was good enough for her to easily follow the lessons. [...] She did written assignments on her own and mostly without mistakes."[77] One country (West Germany), one state (Baden-Württemberg), one curriculum, one school, two teachers – two worlds.

Other everyday situations included encounters with bureaucracy or visits to the doctor: as in all immigration societies the children, who had better German, translated for their parents, grandparents, and other relatives. It's easy to imagine what kinds of consequences this had for the power structure in those families where the elderly were accorded respect and obedience by virtue of their age. For the children and teenagers this was often no fun, especially in teenage it is usually embarrassing enough to have to go an administrative office or the doctor with your parents. It is also possible to imagine how different things could have been in a society where this extra linguistic and emotional labor of generation two would have been appreciated – a society like the United States or Canada which didn't lie to itself about not being an immigration society.

At the same time integration "from below" was also taking place, slowly and silently. Friendships for life were forged, teenagers fell in love, the retired teacher helped with homework at the afterschool club and a long-term friendship developed between her and the entire family – all of this was also a fact in the 1980s. European integration also contributed to the fact that the children of guest workers were considered as less and less Other. And the launching of private cable television in 1984 and new media formats like the music channels MTV and VIVA further helped "normalize" migrants. People who watched Afro-German host Mola Adebisi for 2 hours every day were bound to be slightly less shocked when a black person happened to appear next to them at the bus stop or in the doctor's waiting room.

The Early 1990s

The fall of the wall in 1989 and German unification in 1990 changed a lot for the *Gastarbeiter*, their children, and their grandchildren – some say more than a lot, indeed everything. Years of national navel-gazing began. Former GDR citizens were integrated at lightning speed; they had to overcome far fewer bureaucratic obstacles and their belonging to the nation was much more seldom in doubt than with the *Gastarbeiter*, some of whom had been living in West Germany since 1955, had rebuilt that country a decade after the Second World War, had been paying taxes for decades, held citizenship if they could, and made up the social fabric in clubs, trade unions, parties, and religious communities. At the end of the unification process Germany was more sovereign, the American, Soviet, British, and French Allied powers pulled out – and along with them black and, in the case of the Red Army, Central Asian soldiers. Those who looked "different" ethnically now were no longer automatically "foreigners," often enough they were Germans, the domestic Other, if you like. Germany grew territorially and assumed a more important role not just in Europe, but in the international community of states, and on the world market. Many in Europe and the world harbored (old) fears of this (new) Germany, others thought that it should take on a more active and self-confident role. What's important for our subject is that the new, enlarged, sovereign Germany could no longer make a claim for a special role, and that was why it was increasingly measured against the benchmarks of the "classic" immigrant nations, the United States and Canada.

A lot changed in unified Germany. First of all, the economic cake to be shared at first seemed smaller. With the East Germans, "internal migrants" entered the West German labor market who were prepared to work for smaller wages and commute with their used Volkswagen or Opel cars, newly acquired from West Germans, from Thuringia or Saxony to Bavaria or Baden-Württemberg. With the opening of the German–German border an existing and rapidly growing right-wing extremist, racist subculture pushed eastward, merging with the subculture there. And with the East Germans you suddenly had 18 million new citizens of the Federal Republic, who had had a very different experience with "foreigners" and the Other more generally.

In September 1991 in Hoyerswerda in Saxony neo-Nazis and a mob from the town attacked a dormitory of contract workers, the East German labor migrants, and a refugee shelter, injuring many. This was not the first incident of its kind, but it was the start of a series of attacks that rocked from fall 1991 onward not just East Germany, but also the university town of Münster in North Rhine-Westphalia (in September), Bredenbeck in Lower Saxony (in September), and Pforzheim in Baden-Württemberg (in October). Further low points were a pogrom against contract workers and asylum seekers in Rostock-Lichtenhagen in late August of 1992, an arson attack on a residential house in Mölln (Schleswig-Holstein) on November 23, 1992, in which three Turkish citizens were killed, and an arson attack on a residential house in Solingen (North Rhine-Westphalia), murdering five Turkish citizens. This series of incidents of racist violence was the worst in either West or East Germany since the Second World War. Yet it was also the beginning of an unprecedented mobilization of civil society against racism – with demonstrations, some candle-lit, and vigils. Erci Ergün, born in 1973 in Berlin and a member of Cartel, the first band of world renown with Turkish-language rap from Germany, remembers Mölln and Solingen as "a blatant and shocking sign of how little we were welcome here, by a hell of a lot of people. And that in turn created an energy, a power that screamed, wow, it's not that relaxed here after all, we gotta do something."[78]

And the Country of Origin?

To this day "home leave" during the summer belongs to the annual cycle of many former labor migrants.[79] They buy gifts for their relatives, sometimes they pretend that they have been more successful in Germany than they actually have been – some take out loans in order to pay for the vacation and the gifts. Many experience the trip as being thrown back into their culture of origin – and end up feeling out of place in their supposed true *Heimat*. And some come to the conclusion that they feel more at home in Germany and that they are better off there, economically speaking: all of this is true for a lot of families and for all three generations of immigrants.

By now some of the former *Gastarbeiter* have moved into German care homes – which at first were ill-prepared to take them in. But in the meantime homes have opened that cater to the cultures of origin of the first generation. As for life's end, attitudes in the first generation vary greatly: "I have made a living for myself here. I never thought of returning to Turkey. Still, when I die I want to be buried in Turkey next to my mother, my father, and my relatives."[80] Aliye B. agrees: "Dying abroad is like getting lost somehow. After my death I want to be buried in Turkey. We have a family grave in Ankara, but my brother lives in Izmir. That is why I will be buried in Izmir. I have prepared everything for that and taken out funeral insurance."[81] And Erkan A.: "In my thirty years in Germany I had no bad experiences; I never had thoughts like, 'I'll work for three or five years, then buy a house and go back home.' [. . .] I often meet with my German friends, whom I retired with. When one of us needs help, we all get together. My contacts to Germans are exceptionally good. In spite of all that I signed a funeral insurance a couple of years ago. When I die, I will be buried in Turkey. But if there were a cemetery for us here and the costs for a funeral weren't so high, I could be buried here."[82] Aynur A. doesn't care where he will be buried: "My grandchildren, my children are here; we're growing old here. [. . .] Who will visit my grave when I die? The earth is Allah's earth. It doesn't matter if it's in Germany or Turkey."[83]

Conclusion

The Essen coalmine into which Carlos Pérez first descended in the iron cage in summer of 1972 has long closed – the last coalmine in Essen shut down in 1986. Coal, which had been so profitable in the 1970s, is considered an outdated source of energy and is no longer mined in all but a few places in the Ruhr region, where it is highly subsidized in order to protect the few remaining miners just a little bit. Coal is to be had much more cheaply in Eastern Europe, China, or Latin America anyway. The Bonn hospital, where Ana Maria Ferreira Silva started in 1969, today is called Johanniter Krankenhaus Bonn and part of Johanniter GmbH, a social service multinational with about 17,000 employees (2021) that makes annual profits of over €1 billion and operates in thirty countries.

This alone shows just how closely Germany has come to be interwoven with the global economy. Actually it always has been, what's new is the degree of entanglement in our globalized world. In point of fact, the labor migration of the *Gastarbeiter* cannot be properly understood if examined in isolation. The GDR was one important factor. When its regime had a wall built in 1961, migration across the German–German border became much harder. Labor outmigration from the GDR practically stopped, the supply of cheap labor was cut off overnight. Hence the new recruitment agreements with Turkey in 1961, Morocco and South Korea in 1963, Tunisia in 1965, and Yugoslavia in 1968. The emigration of a part of the labor force from West Germany was another factor. Every year thousands of German citizens left the Federal Republic in order to try their luck in countries like Switzerland or the United States: between 1946 and 1961 alone almost a million Germans emigrated forever, or at least a substantial period of time. Recruiters from Canada and Australia were active in West Germany just like the German recruiters in Italy, Greece, and Spain. These émigrés left holes in the labor market. A third important factor was the international context, above all the pan-European context. There is a widespread belief in Germany that the Federal Republic in the imagination of labor migrants was the only possible destination, that it was a paradise on earth. In truth the Federal Republic was only one option out of many, sometimes actually the last option. Especially for Italian, Spanish, and Portuguese labor migrants France was often much more attractive. To illustrate, Christoforos Stefanidis actually wanted to go to Brazil, but the Greek clerk in Thessaloniki claimed that with his height of 1.74 meters he was 1 centimeter too short – a thinly veiled request for a bribe, which Stefanidis didn't react to. Instead he accepted the alternative of Germany and for 36 years ran a taverna in Karlsruhe near the constitutional court, frequented by judges, politicians, and pimps from the red light district, which was also close-by.[84] Or take this Turkish migrant: "I went to the Turkish Federal Employment Agency and registered with them. My first invitation was for Australia. But that is very far away; I didn't know when I would come back, maybe only in 5 years. So I declined firmly. [...] In Germany, however, I had my older brother. After a short while I got an invitation for Germany."[85] Or this migrant, also from Turkey: "Still in Edirne, when I was serving in the military, I heard that you can go to Germany as a worker. I also went to the Turkish Federal Employment Agency and applied. My first choice was actually Switzerland. I had heard that it had even better social security. About Germany I knew almost nothing. It was the mayor in Kasimpasa, to whom I went to do some paperwork, who changed my mind in favor of Germany."[86] So a variety of countries were competing for labor migrants, a country's reputation could change fast (after an economic crisis, a racist attack, and much more), and path dependencies (the older brother already in Germany, half of the village at the Bahlsen cookie factory in Hannover) also played a role.

It cannot be emphasized enough that the Federal Republic itself caused the (birth) defect. The responsibility lay with politicians and a society that voted these politicians into power – and consequently laws that clung, not facing up to reality, to the idea of *guest* work. They even clung to the temporary status of the labor migrants when it was patently impossible to deny that some *Gastarbeiter* would stay. And when experts had been repeating for years that "there was little time to waste," to quote Sevda Ko, a teacher for students with migrant background who herself was born in Ankara in 1955 and has been living in Germany since 1960. She demanded that companies, schools, homes for the elderly, and the entire society should finally reconcile themselves with people staying.[87] Otherwise there would be social problems everyone would pay for dearly.

If only the *Gastarbeiter* had been given the opportunity to get citizenship much earlier, ideally as early as in the 1970s, many problems would have never come up. If only the *Gastarbeiter* had been granted the right to belong to the German nation while at the same time retaining the languages and culture of their Italian, Greek, Turkish, and Yugoslav countries of origin, Germany would not be debating a lot of problems today. If only their belonging to the German nation had not constantly been questioned, if only people with darker skin and "Mediterranean" looks had not constantly been marginalized as "foreigners," and if only the German nation had not always considered itself in some way superior, how much brighter things would look today.

But in spite of everything the history of *Gastarbeit* wasn't all that bad – if seen dialectically. Despite a lot of resentment, the labor migrants, their children, and their grandchildren made it – they resisted physical and verbal violence: to "caraway Turk" they retorted with "potato Germans." They created hybrid cultures in everyday life, in cuisine, literature, music, art, theater, comedy, and television, without which contemporary Germany is simply not imaginable. And every political–social backlash, no matter how great, also has positive, consolidating consequences. The "intellectual–moral turn" under Kohl since 1982 engendered and propelled the citizens' initiatives, the Greens, and much more. These are the beginnings of the widespread support for refugees in the summer of 2015, "the long summer of migration."

4 Labor Migration to East Germany

In 1974 a scholarly essay entitled "On the Continuity of German Imperialism's Alien Worker Politics (*Fremdarbeiterpolitik*)" appeared in the GDR.[1] It was about the West German recruitment of labor migrants. By using the term *Fremdarbeiter* it insinuated that there was a link between the Third Reich and West Germany: *Fremdarbeiter* was the Nazi designation for the millions of people who had to do forced labor in the Third Reich, especially during the Second World War. The 1974 essay may have been unspectacular, but it was typical. In the GDR's propaganda the Federal Republic figured as the Third Reich's successor and both Hitler's Germany and the Federal Republic were imperialist states, that is, they embodied a particularly aggressive stage of development of capitalism: imperialism.

As for its own recruitment of labor migrants, the GDR depicted this recruitment very differently. The 90,000 *Vertragsarbeiter*, or contract workers, from Vietnam, Mozambique, and several other socialist states in the "Third World" who were present in the GDR shortly before the fall of the wall in 1989 were there for purposes of "socialist economic integration." They came from less developed countries, and the GDR, top of the class among the "worker and peasant states," would, as official rhetoric had it, prepare them in the school of life (according to the Marxist interpretation) for "their future work in the construction of socialism." Recruiting labor migrants was "solidarity through training."[2] So much for propaganda.

Reality was a different matter altogether. With its labor migration politics the GDR pursued hard economic interests just like West Germany or other socialist states, which were signing contract agreements with each other (Yugoslav construction workers to Bulgaria in 1973, Vietnamese factory workers to Czechoslovakia in 1979).[3] Especially in the late 1980s, as the GDR was approaching its end, its main interest was to fill unpopular positions in dirty industrial work, where there was an acute shortage of labor.

Public interest in the history of labor migration to the GDR so far has focused on one question: how could Hoyerswerda 1991 and Rostock-Lichtenhagen 1992 happen, what are the causes for East German xenophobia? Portuguese Armando Rodrigues with the motorcycle he was given as the millionth *Gastarbeiter* in 1964 at Cologne Central Railway Station is the photo icon of West German labor migration. Is, then, the iconic photo of GDR *Vertragsarbeit* that of the night in August 1992 when a mob set the "sunflower house" in Rostock-Lichtenhagen, where Vietnamese families were living, on fire? It shows a drunk East German in the jersey of the German national soccer team, wearing wetted jogging pants and standing in front of the burning house with his arm lifted for a Nazi *Sieg Heil* salute.

That would be a misguided juxtaposition. We could easily have ended the history of labor migration to West Germany with the neo-Nazi attack on Munich's Oktoberfest in 1980, the deadliest terror attack in the entire history of the Federal Republic, or with the arson attack on the Arslan home in Mölln in Schleswig-Holstein in November 1992, killing three members of this Turkish *Gastarbeiter* family. Put differently, there are no grounds for West German arrogance, the West Germans themselves produced loads of hate, racism, and violence toward labor migrants and others. I would go even further and make the claim that the post-1989 West German moral arrogance in general and with reference to xenophobia in particular (to the effect that the mother of all racism is in the East, Westerners are the good guys, the *Ossis* are the evil racists) is one – not the only one, but one – of the causes for the racist attacks after the end of the GDR. Why that is the case is what this chapter tries to explain. Most importantly, however, it foregrounds labor migrants, the *Vertragsarbeiter*, and describes how they experienced life in the GDR. They shall become palpable as subjects in this chapter, not just as objects of East German racism. But that racism too will be described and explained, at least insofar as it is possible to do so.

What Was *Vertragsarbeit*?

"Don't you know? In Germany people get up very early. Then they work until late at night. You need to be super fit, otherwise you're done for after 3 days."[4] This is what 1963-born Ibraimo Alberto got to hear in 1981 during his 3-month-long training in a kind of boot camp in Mozambique for contract work in East Germany. He and a few others had protested against the drill, the waking with a whistle at four in the morning and the 40 kilometer runs, and posed the obvious question: what's the use?

Alberto was part of a first cohort of Mozambican labor migrants. In 1979 the GDR signed an agreement with Mozambique to get contract workers. This was preceded by similar agreements with Poland in 1971, Algeria in 1974, and Cuba in 1975. Agreements with Vietnam in 1980, Angola in 1984, and, for much smaller contingents of workers, with China, Mongolia, and North Korea ensued. If West German *Gastarbeiter* numbers peaked in the 1960s, the GDR reached its apex in the late 1980s. In 1986 a total of 7,134 *Vertragsarbeiter* arrived, the highest number so far since the founding of the GDR. In 1987 this figure quadrupled to 28,197 *Vertragsarbeiter* (of whom 20,446 came from Vietnam and 3,203 from Mozambique), 1988 marked the absolute peak with 38,376 new arrivals (of whom 30,552 came from Vietnam and 6,464 from Mozambique), and even in the year when the wall fell another 12,023 *Vertragsarbeiter* came.[5] Thus a total of 150,000 to 200,000 *Vertragsarbeiter* spent time in the GDR during its phase of labor migration, which lasted from 1971 until 1989. Both as an absolute figure and in terms of percentage of the total population that is a small number in comparison with the 14 million *Gastarbeiter* in the Federal Republic.[6] True, to the *Vertragsarbeiter* we must add Soviet soldiers, international students, several thousand political émigrés (mostly from Chile, from where they fled after the coup against the socialist president Salvador Allende in 1973), and diplomats. Still, the proportion of "foreigners" never exceeded 1 percent of the GDR's population. Even if one counts the ethnic German expellees, and their de facto migration experience, the basic truth remains that the GDR's population was more homogeneous, in the GDR you were less likely than in West Germany to encounter a "visible minority" or, for that matter, any person from another culture.

The problem that the GDR tried to solve through contract work agreements with other states from the socialist camp was a shortage of labor. It was largely emigration to West Germany that had caused this labor shortage. The GDR had signed an agreement with Mozambique because this "socialist brother state" had run up a debt with its "big brother," the GDR. After gaining independence for Mozambique in 1975, the FRELIMO (Front for the Liberation of Mozambique) rebels fought a 15-year civil war (with interference from neighboring states such as Rhodesia, but also the United States and GDR military advisors), for which they needed weapons. They bought these in the GDR, but at some point could no longer pay in hard currency and began paying first in raw materials like coal and coffee, later with labor migrants. So sending the first generation of contract workers like Ibraimo Alberto, who were paid below regular GDR wages and whose government kept another 40 percent of their salaries, was then meant to pay off debts from arms purchases for FRELIMO.

At 5:11 pm the wheels of the airplane touched down on German ground. "Welcome to Berlin, capital of the GDR," the pilot announced in German, then in Portuguese. We got off the plane, everything went chop chop! [. . .] They chased us into a large room and we had to line up. Five white gods marched in, all with suit and tie. They had brought a black interpreter along. He stepped closer to us with an arrogant expression on his face: "My name is José, I have been here for a couple of years. Listen and don't get into trouble. These gentlemen represent the People's Enterprises Kombinat Chemische Werke Walter Ulbricht, Kombinat Plaste und Chemie Wolkenstein, the Petrolchemisches Kombinat Schwedt/Oder, Kombinat Industrielle Mast Karl-Marx-Stadt, and Fleischkombinat Berlin. When they call out your names, go to them and behave quietly."[7]

Ibraimo Alberto was assigned to Fleischkombinat Berlin, the meat factory in Ludwigsfelde, southeast of Berlin. A bus brought him and his colleagues to the dormitory, a ten-story house in which the twenty Mozambicans got an apartment with five rooms, four beds in each room. One of the rooms "was grandiosely called the living-room because it had a television set. Most of us had never seen such a device."[8] There was more culture shock in store at the meat factory with its 3,000 employees (Figure 4.1). Alberto was from the Mateúe, a Mozambican ethnic group that did not eat pork – and now he was working with dead pigs on

Figure 4.1 Mozambican *Vertragsarbeiter* at a meat factory in Ludwigsfelde, *c.* 1982. © Ibraimo Alberto.

a daily basis and got fed pork in every shape and form in the cafeteria: "José, who marched around like a grand supervisor, gloated. 'Folks, dig in, this is what they eat here,' he boasted. 'This is blood sausage, this is liverwurst, and this stuff is called *Sauerkraut.*' [. . .] We were familiar with corn farina, tapioca, perhaps a piece of chicken once in a while. I tasted hesitantly, but was grossed out when the clotted blood of the sausage spread across my plate. With my eyes I looked for [my mentor] Mandy, worked up my courage and asked her: 'What's in there?' 'That's pork head blood sausage,' she replied with a friendly smile. 'It has been standardized as cooking sausage according to technical Norm 29213/02.'"

Consider also the cafeteria. For the first time Alberto saw white people work. In Mozambique he had still experienced the Portuguese colonial master António Ferreira, who forced the Mateúe to do slave labor on his farm and whose son had raped and impregnated Alberto's sister. "Clueless, we stood in front of the food counter. White gods were brandishing spoons and distributing food on plates. I was confused: are they working here?"[9]

Alberto ate next to nothing in the first weeks, until he broke down during work, and was taken to hospital. From hospital he wrote a telegram to his half-brother Pedro, who would later become a professional soccer player for Benfica, Lisbon, and asked him to consult their father, the medicine man in the jungle village Charonga – should he return to Mozambique? Pedro lived in Chimoio, the closest city to Charonga. Pedro took off for the jungle. Four days later Alberto received a telegram from his father: "You can't come back. Eat pork."[10]

Alberto was the only one of twelve siblings who had been able to get a school education. His way to school sounds like a cliché about Africa, but here is how he describes it: twice a day 18 kilometers through the jungle past lions and snakes and across a river with crocodiles. Alberto was considered "exceptional" early on, a "liminal child," where it was unclear whether he was the last child of his mother's first husband or the first child of his mother's second husband. He began watching slave owner Ferreira closely and understood that he, as a white *Muari*, which meant in effect a god, decided over life and death by killing, for instance, a slave, who was sick, old, and could no longer work, through a "coup de grâce." The "white god" spoke Portuguese and had a faucet at home and of course guns. And so Alberto learned how to read and write in the language of the "gods." He volunteered for the GDR because he hoped to be able to study there.

In 1975 FRELIMO guerillas attained independence for Mozambique. Ferreira stayed on and kept his slaves for another full year, then he left for Portugal. A Civil War began in which Alberto's youngest, 13-year-old brother, Mussa, was abducted and turned into a child soldier of the

RENAMO militias, who received support from South Africa's apartheid regime.

Now, in an East Berlin hospital in 1981, Alberto gave up his resistance upon receiving the telegram from his father, the medicine man. In 1982 he was elected brigade leader at the meat factory, later he passed his apprenticeship exam as butcher with the highest possible grade of 1. Later yet he became one of the most successful boxers of the GDR with PCK Schwedt, twice winning the Berlin Box Masters in the light middleweight category of up to 71 kilograms, played soccer for Turbine Treptow, and, after marrying Birgit, became father of two children. After German reunification he was Integration Commissioner in Schwedt and got elected to the city council for the Social Democratic Party (SPD) in 2008, and also in 2008 was decorated Ambassador for Democracy and Tolerance for his life's work by interior minister Wolfgang Schäuble and minister of justice Brigitte Zypries. After repeated attacks by neo-Nazis and because of everyday pervasive racism, to which he and his family were subjected, in 2011 he moved to West German Karlsruhe with his wife and children, where he began working as a caretaker for severely disabled people.

No Brothers in the Brotherly State

"Ghetto" is what Ibraimo Alberto called his contract worker dormitory. The isolation of the *Vertragsarbeiter* from the majority of the GDR population was intentional: "The dormitories must be cordoned off so as to safeguard order and security. The factory must secure 24/7 control of entering the dormitory," stated a February 8, 1982, guideline of the GDR State Secretariat on Labor and Wages.[11] Encounters and true exchange with the German population were never part of the plan. According to official propaganda, the labor migrants were supposed to get an education and then help develop the socialist economies in their countries of origin. At bottom everything was about cheap labor, from which the regimes both in the countries that sent contract workers and in the GDR profited. Everything foreign was suspect in the closed societies of the Eastern Bloc. They may have called each other "brothers" and paid lip service to internationalism on holidays and in friendship societies, but in truth the functionaries in the Party and secret services, be they in Hanoi, Maputo, Havana, Warsaw, Ulan Bator, or in fact East Berlin, were deeply suspicious of contract workers and GDR citizens getting too close.

But they got close nonetheless – life is always more complicated than the legalese of the contract recruitment agreements, as we saw with the *Gastarbeiter* in the Federal Republic. Contacts materialized in the workplace, the sports club, the discotheque, the pub. It would be misleading, though, to imagine that the *Vertragsarbeiter* could move as freely as was the case for West German *Gastarbeiter*. Their scope for movement was even more restricted that that of GDR citizens, they were subject to more control and surveillance through the Stasi was even tighter. What is more, there were restrictions "from below" – discrimination that originated with the GDR population, without coercion from the Party or the Stasi, restrictions reminiscent of the situation under the apartheid regime in South Africa or racial segregation in the United States. A restaurant manager from Heinrichs in Thuringia reported in a 1982 interview that could not be published while the GDR still existed how the new Mozambican contract workers of the automobile and hunting weapon factory Suhl were treated in her restaurant: "The table reserved for Mozambicans, we introduced that. Because before that they sat everywhere. And the Heinrichs locals said, we're not going to sit with them! Seriously. At first I reserved a table in the corner for them, but there I didn't have them in sight and under control. When their table is full, they come to me and ask me if they can sit at other tables. Then I go around and ask people at their tables."[12]

Love and sex between contract workers and GDR locals was a particularly charged issue, especially when Mozambicans, Angolans, and Cubans were involved. "White women think we're great. They find us exotic," Aurélio from Mozambique told his surprised friend Ibraimo Alberto.[13] A lot came together here: the black male contract workers were considered as the ultimate Other, as "exotic." Exoticism in the homogeneous GDR was even more exotic than in West Germany and thus, in a way, more attractive than there. At the same time exoticism was associated with the West because all things non-Eastern were somehow seen as Western, even if incarnated in citizens from socialist brotherly states from Africa or the Caribbean. This was due to the fact, among other things, that most GDR citizens were prohibited from traveling abroad to Western Europe, let alone Africa or Latin America. Exoticism was highly sexualized and was associated with corporeality and movement, with very old stereotypes of wildness and sexualized virility, but also with the child's need of protection. All these stereotypes and associations – which of course were also existent in West Germany (and in many parts of the world more generally) – were hidden under the glossy surface of the socialist friendship of peoples, as it was propagated in films and on posters. In the collective phantasmatic imaginary, the smiling black man on the posters of socialist solidarity was always close to attacking, like a predator, the blonde woman from the socialist youth organization FDJ. This sexualized, threatening phantasy also threatened

GDR men *tout court*, their virility, even their status in all layers of society, from the nuclear family up to Honecker and his politburo.

A contract worker who came to Thuringia from Mozambique in 1981 as a 17-year-old talks about his own phantasies and fears with reference to a pub: “A perfectly normal pub close to where I live. Usually few people are in there, and sometimes they buy a round of beers. [. . .] I don’t know how they would react if I ever came in with a German woman.”[14] Only the Vietnamese, the largest group of male contract workers in terms of numbers, did not fit into this phantasmatic matrix of exoticism, virility, potency, and self-perception of inferiority. That was due to stereotypes of “Asians” as less masculine. The Vietnamese women may have been considered “cuddly,” but were also seen as “inscrutable” and distant – not least because of the impression of strong community cohesion of the Vietnamese, of deliberate self-isolation from the GDR populace. One Vietnamese man traced this self-isolation not to cultural specificity, but to political indoctrination through the Socialist Republic of Vietnam: “Question: The Vietnamese often came across as very self-effacing, quiet, and modest. Was that indeed the mentality of the people?” Response by “S.: That was fear above anything. [. . .] Because /uh/ before we got here, they had /uh/ (laughs) brainwashed us anyway, what we’re allowed to do here and what not: never divulge any Vietnamese state secrets, not too much contact with the Germans.”[15]

Whenever love relationships did materialize, the punishment was severe. Mozambicans were often sent home; when asked about what would happen if a secret romantic involvement were uncovered, Massucage D., born in 1968, answers: “Well, then you need to decide, either break up or airplane and off you go to Mozambique.”[16] Many of the children from relationships between Mozambican men and East German women (relationships between Mozambican women and East German men were much rarer) were placed in special orphanages. “It was politically undesirable,” says Ibraimo Alberto, “to create a second generation of foreigners, and on top of that they did not want any mixing of races. On that count there was no difference between the GDR functionaries and Nazi ideology.”[17] Vietnamese women were pushed toward terminating their pregnancies. Those who refused to have an abortion were sent back to Vietnam. A February 9, 1989, official “Resolution on the regulation of enterprise and local state organization tasks with regard to the pregnancy of Vietnamese women who are temporarily working in GDR enterprises on the basis of bilateral governmental agreements” read: “It is not in the GDR’s economic interest that female foreign workers during their productive labor and training in our Republic give birth to children. The SRV [Socialist Republic of Vietnam], which itself pursues a restrictive natal policy, has no interest in this either. Therefore it seems acceptable to us that the young women are given instructions on the avoidance of pregnancies when taking up employment." Furthermore: "Through the deployment of about 20,000 female Vietnamese laborers, especially in light industry, pregnancy has increasingly become a problem in the deployment of foreign laborers. On the basis of the governmental agreement and at the behest of the Vietnamese side it has been agreed that pregnancy generally prompts a return to the SR Vietnam, as pregnancy and motherhood are incompatible with the mission of the delegation."[18]

Racism in the GDR

As early as 1985 Ibraimo Alberto, together with other contract workers, received a warning from Mozambican diplomats: neo-Nazis were hunting black people. At first he paid no attention to the warning, although he "saw more and more young men in bomber jackets and heavy boots on the streets of East Berlin."[19] He knew things were serious when on June 30, 1986, a Mozambican friend, Antonio Manuel Diogo, was killed by neo-Nazis on his way home to Dessau after visiting Alberto in Berlin: "In the afternoon he boarded a train that was supposed to take him back to Dessau in a little under 2 hours. He never arrived. What happened never reached the light of day because the GDR authorities did everything to cover up the affair. Neo-Nazis, who officially should not have existed in the [self-described 'antifascist state' of the GDR], had been on the train. They beat up Manuel and tied his legs together with a rope. They then hung him from a window and slowly let him down until he was torn to pieces between the wheels. The police later found body parts over a distance of 10 kilometers, his head was discovered only days after the murder. Manuel could be identified only on the basis of his papers. Even though the murderers were caught and went to jail, the media hushed up the case. Nor did they inform Manuel's parents about what happened. According to what I was told, the GDR sent a coffin to Mozambique with the strict instruction not to open it. Presumably because it was empty."[20] The transport police recorded in their protocol: "Male corpse found on same latitude as Borne train station. Head and legs severed. Person concerned has dark skin." The Stasi merely recorded in its files that Antonio Manuel Diogo had "left the train while it was in motion and was run over. No indications of a crime."[21] Historians like Harry Waibel and Stefan Wolle after reunification studied Stasi files, police records, and oral history sources and counted "a total of 8,600 radical right-wing and racist attacks," including murders like that of Antonio Manuel Diogo, Ibraimo Alberto's friend.[22]

The GDR media reported in some detail about the existence of a right-wing extremist movement for the first time after October 17, 1987. On that day at Zionskirche in East Berlin's Prenzlauer Berg district two bands gave a concert, *Die Firma* from East Berlin and *Element of Crime* from West Berlin – Zionskirche was a church and one of the GDR's best-known niches of its "niche society," as the underground was known, and housed the environmental library, in which human rights groups from the environmental and peace movements met. Neo-Nazis hated these. Skinheads stormed the concert and started beating up the audience. The police and Stasi were in front of the church, but did not intervene for a long time. They too hated the young people at the concert. But when Western media started reporting about the incident at the concert, the GDR media were under pressure to report as well. To be sure, they did so in their own peculiar way – the newspaper *Junge Welt* compared the human rights activists to the neo-Nazis, who had just used physical violence against the former. Still, for the first time the state had had to publicly acknowledge that there was a right-wing extremist scene in the GDR.

It was telling that neither the police nor the Stasi intervened in Zionskirche during the neo-Nazi attack. Asked about racist attacks, Massucage D. says: "Yes, there were lots of those. And the worst was that we called the police many times – the police came, watched, and drove away. Even though we were totally screwed, like really screwed. Not twice, not four times, such things happened more often."[23] The legal authorities acted in a similar vein. Some of the neo-Nazis who had taken part in the attack on Zionskirche were brought to court, but got away with minor penalties. Only when public protest became evident were higher penalties meted out in appeals courts.[24]

It must be said that the courts, police, and secret police, in short, state power, often shared the racist attitudes that a façade of socialist solidarity barely managed to hide. To some extent this explains the particularly toxic combination after 1989–1990 of right-wing extremism and state institutions that should have stopped or punished the racist attacks, yet failed to do so. As soon as the GDR façade and the control of the surveillance state were gone, right-wing extremists could do as they pleased, unrestrained. In many smaller towns, where the representatives of the state remained unchanged after reunification, right-wing extremists came to dominate life, including everyday culture – neo-Nazi *Landser* or *Störkraft* as favorite bands, combat boots with white shoe laces and later *Thor Steinar* clothes as the dominant fashion styles among young people, enabled and buttressed by the attitudes of older people: authority, order, feelings of loss because of the bygone, homogeneous *Ost*, feelings of inferiority toward the *Wessi* "occupying power."

But even in GDR times everyday racism periodically broke through the façade of solidarity. The boxer Ibraimo Alberto remembers the difference between home fights and away fights: "The crowd from Schwedt cheered me on just as loudly as my team members. When we had away fights, I heard 'Hu hu hu!' and other sounds that the crowd thought were monkey sounds. I wanted to shout to them: 'Folks, you have never heard a monkey, he makes a very different sound.'"[25] The racism Alberto encountered became a lot more subtle when he started a relationship with a Party functionary's daughter. "You know, Ibraimo, my friends don't feel comfortable when you're around," she told him. "It was a weird kind of double standard," he concludes. "On the one hand there was the allure of the exotic black man, on the other no one was to supposed to find out about it."[26]

The dualism of publicly celebrated internationalist anti-racism on the one hand and everyday racism on the other was specific to the GDR, particularly when compared with the Federal Republic. In the GDR there was even an officially prescribed anti-racist terminology for businesses that employed contract workers. A skilled worker, a woman, from Suhl remembers, "when we were apprentices here, in the work and safety training we had to sign a paper that we wouldn't call the Mozambicans negro or black or something like that, they are our Mozambican work colleagues, and we should be nice to them."[27] The reality was bleaker, as the 1982 recording – which did not pass censorship – of a conversation between the director for cadres and education at the automobile and hunting weapon factory Suhl shows. At first, while the tape is recording, perfect Party officialese: "Care for the individual Mozambican friend for us is our class duty, a duty that grows out of proletarian and socialist internationalism." Then the interviewer turns off the tape and jots down from memory that the 60-year-old functionary said, "if his daughter brought home a black guy, he would kick her out."[28]

However, ethnic hatred – both the brutal, in-your-face kind and more subtle variants – targeted certain whites as well. A woman from Poland, who was married to an East German man, recalls: "Even though he was born in Germany, my son had serious problems in school ... his classmates ... Literally, they said: you are a Polack swine just like your mother. He came home and at first said nothing to me, then he lay down and started crying. And that happened in school. I was so enraged that I went there, to his school. But everything was covered up."[29] When the independent trade union Solidarity (Solidarność) was founded in Poland in 1980 and martial law was imposed following that, the Polish contract workers, many of them commuters from the western Polish border region who worked at the computer chip factory in Frankfurt an der Oder, were made to feel that something like that would never have happened in the socialist poster boy

GDR state. Old anti-Polish clichés were mixed together with rumors about the smuggling of goods in short supply across the German–Polish border, about hard currency speculation, and generally about criminal behavior. In addition there was a lot of arrogance, a feeling of national superiority, which resulted in the idea that the GDR was the country of the founding fathers Marx and Engels and hence ahead of all other socialist states.[30]

Vietnamese Contract Workers

In Ibraimo Alberto's autobiography there is a photograph of him in a plaid shirt with dark sunglasses and hat, his thumbs hooked in the pockets of his blue jeans. The caption reads: "As a 19-year-old I pose as Western hero for a photograph at an East Berlin photo studio in 1982."[31] The preceding page shows his friend Manuel – Antonio Manuel Diogo, who will be killed by neo-Nazis four years later. Manuel is also wearing clothes that look "Western." Mozambican men were considered sharp dressers, a group to whom fashionable clothes mattered, or, in the words of a GDR woman: "Take only the clothes that they were wearing, they were not like ours but modern, jeans and shoes with thick heels, and so on."[32] (Figure 4.2)

Regular GDR stores did not carry this kind of clothing, people got it from relatives in West Germany, bought it in one of the few, expensive hard currency stores, or had it sewn by Vietnamese contract workers outside their regular working hours – this is how Alberto and his friends got their "Western clothing."

Like all labor migrants, the Vietnamese had tried to get the coveted contract worker jobs because they saw advantages in them – to earn some extra money for a slightly improved quality of life at home, or to get training, an education in order to get ahead back at home. In this they were no different from the labor migrants in capitalism, except that the Vietnamese state retained 12 percent of their salary. And the contract workers were often deployed in subordinate unskilled laborer jobs. In Rostock, for instance, in September 1989 between 1,300 and 1,500 Vietnamese contract workers were employed at the following state enterprises: Sea Port Rostock (350), textile factory "Shanty" (also 350, almost exclusively women), and the housing construction combine (300). They worked as ship's side cleaner, kitchen help, junior fitter, track construction helper, rail car cleaner. Only very few of the Vietnamese contract workers in Rostock received further training in specific skills and only one of them, after a long tilting at bureaucratic windmills, was allowed to embark on master training (Figure 4.3).[33]

Figure 4.2 Ibraimo Alberto (right), *c.* 1986. © Ibraimo Alberto.

The Vietnamese contract workers soon understood that they could supplement their earnings through the – illegal – production of coveted commodities in short supply like leather clothing or the famous blue jeans. A report of the Halle District Council from "the last three years of the GDR" (no precise date is given) maintains that the contract workers were working less and less because, "in order to attain a certain amount of surplus money, the sewing of certain coveted types of clothing in the dormitories, in the night hours, plays a not insignificant role. All the measures we introduced against that to this day are largely unsuccessful."[34] Needless to say, the report was silent about the fact that illegal production flourished only because regular production failed to generate deficit goods, in short, because there was demand that the GDR economy wasn't able to supply. Because large numbers of people began frequenting the dormitories to order, try on, and pick up their clothes, and because

Figure 4.3 Vietnamese *Vertragsarbeiter* at light bulb factory Narva, Berlin, 1990. Ullstein bild / Getty Images.

a lot of sewing took place at night, there were complaints about the noise from German neighbors. Even the positive stereotype of the industrious, hard-working Vietnamese took a blow.

The Vietnamese contract workers soon developed forms of resistance, and not only to pursue their work as seamstresses and sewers, but also to visit one another in different East German towns. The dormitories were monitored quite strictly, and so one strategy was to leave through the main entrance and officially check out with the security guard, but to go right back in through a window. And even though Vietnam had a particularly strict rotation system and cohorts of contract workers were regularly exchanged, some managed to defect and to stay on illegally in the GDR in friends' dormitories.

But there was also open, direct resistance in the workplace – and solidarity from German colleagues. One Vietnamese contract worker from Rostock reported: "S.: . . . but later, when the bonuses were handed out, I got too little and became very angry. Another guy, a German, who started at the same time as me and had just finished his training, after two years already had salary tier six, whereas I was still on tier four [. . .]. I felt, 'You took me on and consider me an equal human being to you, but if this is supposed to be the recognition for my work, you've lied. I don't need this money.' So I took the money, went up to the master, and tore the money apart. I said, 'That's no way to recognize my work!' Interviewer: And how did the master react? S.: He organized a /uh/ what do they call it again, a team discussion, and they said that the bonus depends on the salary tier after all, but that they wanted to help me. They put down 20 additional overtime hours per month. For that everyone in the team had to give up 2 to 3 hours for me. [. . .] Then they asked my colleagues if they were okay with that, and they did forgo their hours on my behalf. Interviewer: So they got paid less? S.: Yes, because of that, yes, but they still got more than me. That way I moved up on the bonus ladder at some point."[35]

The Vietnamese contract workers' moonlighting in the shadow economy was a fact. But it was also a rumor. Put differently, had it not existed, the phantasy of GDR citizens would have had to invent it. Or, there was active phantasy production among locals about contract workers that expressed itself in rumor-mongering because of purported material advantages, economic criminal activity, and much more. When 200 former GDR citizens were interviewed after reunification, almost two-thirds said the contract workers had received hard Western currency and had generally been much better off than GDR citizens.[36] And when, still during the GDR, a team from East Berlin's Humboldt University examined right-wing crimes between 1987 and 1989 and conducted interviews with right-wing extremist perpetrators, the latter said "that foreign workers take housing away from GDR citizens, through their speculative buying reduce the availability of manufactured goods, imported AIDS into the GDR, treated every woman like an easily buyable prostitute, with their foreign currency play the 'cool guys' without really living up to it, only wanted fights and riots, through their aggressiveness often caused fatalities among GDR citizens, were spoiled in public and in the workplace while GDR citizens, especially young GDR citizens, got nothing."[37] Kerstin Reimann, born in 1972 and from Erkner outside Berlin, sums up: "Opinion was generally two-sided. The foreign contract workers weren't well-liked, but they were much-liked when it came to the sewing of leather clothes, people loved quickly getting fashionable clothes under the counter, and the Vietnamese did a lot of sewing. But generally speaking there was a racism that was often very direct and very, very hostile. Many East Germans thought the foreign contract workers have Western currency and could afford just about anything – but that wasn't true."[38]

The Fall of the Wall and Its Consequences

On November 9, 1989, Ibraimo Alberto was at the Charité, East Berlin's main hospital, because he had injured his eye at a boxing match. "All excited, a nurse ran in. 'Herr Alberto, Herr Alberto,' she exclaimed. 'You've got to look at this!'" Together they went up to the "window and saw countless people run toward the West. Where the wall was. The end of our world. 'Where do they all want to go?,' I asked. The nurse shook her head in disbelief. 'I can't believe it,' she mumbled. 'Günter Schabowski was on TV. He said that from now on any citizen of the GDR can travel abroad. Do you know that that means, Herr Alberto? The wall has fallen!'"[39] The fall of the Berlin Wall also came as a shock to the contract workers. Sometimes even more so than for East German citizens because their own countries continued to be uninterruptedly socialist. (Cuba, for example, remained untouched by Gorbachev's Perestroika and the Eastern European velvet revolutions of 1989.)

Everything changed. Since there was now an overabundance of real Westerners, the GDR "Westerners" seemed less Western. The Algerian contract workers who had been paid their vacation allowance in French francs and who often wore French clothes that they brought with them from Algeria, lost their attractiveness from one day to the next.

What the coming down of the wall meant for the half-million-plus Soviet soldiers and their families, who were in the GDR on November 9, 1989, and whose own empire would implode two years later, we can only guess. We know far too little about them, partly because they were the true masters of the house that was the GDR, with their own secret police and jurisdiction. We do know that a then obscure KGB agent by the name of Vladimir Putin burnt secret files at the Dresden KGB residency until the oven burst. That the Federal Republic after German reunification agreed to build housing for soldiers in Russia worth 15 billion marks. And that an unprecedented selling off of tanks and much more to unsavory buyers, especially the warring parties in former Yugoslavia, began, until the last Red Army soldiers of the Western Group of Forces pulled out of Germany in September 1994.[40]

For the contract workers "return" or *Rückführung*, a euphemism for deportation, became the order of the day. Deportation took place in very different ways: sometimes it was structured, sometimes chaotic. Some whose contract expired were simply not given a new contract. Others received a return bonus of 3,000 marks. The contract workers received redundancy letters from their employers, such as this one:

> People's Enterprise Combined Fiber Works Crimmitschau
> Date: August 1, 1990
> Due notice
>
> Owing to the conversion of our People's Enterprise into a corporate entity and the rationalization measures connected with that we must terminate the existing employment contract with you prematurely.
>
> On the basis of the governmental agreement we terminate the existing employment contract with you duly as of August 1, 1990, so that you leave our enterprise on August 19, 1990. [...]
>
> After termination the Regulation on the Change in Employment Contracts with Foreign Citizens will come into effect for you (Law Gazette Part 1 No. 35 of June 27, 1990), especially paragraph 5.
>
> Saxonian Fiber Works Inc. thanks you sincerely for your efforts and wishes you personally all the best.[41]

Kerstin Reimann, who was 17 when the wall came down and had Mozambican friends, remembers "cloak-and-dagger operations, it was terrible, just terrible."[42]

What was also terrible was the post-unification racist mob violence directed at former contract workers and new asylum seekers who were now being housed in the eastern parts of Germany. Hoyerswerda was the start of a whole series of pogroms. On September 17, 1991, neo-Nazis attacked Vietnamese traders on the marketplace of the small town in Saxony. When these traders escaped into a dormitory for contract workers from Vietnam and Mozambique, the neo-Nazis started throwing Molotov cocktails and stones into the building. Several hundred people stood by, watched, and cheered the neo-Nazis on. Two hours passed before the police intervened and cordoned off the building; on September 20 the contract workers were evacuated from Hoyerswerda in buses, many were deported to Vietnam shortly thereafter. The mob had its way. In the evening of the same day a shelter for asylum seekers was attacked, again with a crowd applauding, and many refugees were injured. The shelter too was evacuated. Neo-Nazis celebrated Hoyerswerda as "free of foreigners" (*ausländerfrei*) – a neologism that derived from the Nazi term "free of Jews" (*judenfrei*) and was voted "unword of the year," *Unwort des Jahres*, for 1991 by a panel of linguists.

A year later something similar happened in Rostock-Lichtenhagen, only on a much larger scale. On August 22, 1992, right-wing extremists attacked with stones and Molotov cocktails the so-called "sunflower house" that housed the state of Mecklenburg-Vorpommern's Central Reception Center for Asylum Seekers and a contract worker dormitory. They screamed slogans like *Sieg Heil!* and "Germany to the Germans, foreigners out!" A crowd of as many as 3,000 cheered them on. When the police arrived, the police officers were attacked and their cars set on fire. On the following days water cannons were put to use and more and more police deployed. On August 24 the mob set the lower floors on fire; the police managed to push back the neo-Nazis only after they had already entered the building with screams like "We'll get you all!" and "Now you'll be roasted!" The Vietnamese contract workers, including women and children, fled onto the roof; they were not rescued until 2 hours after the fire had started.

The violence in East Germany was not new, but what was new was its all-out unleashing, which began after the state had retreated. Also new were the *ausländerfrei* city districts and villages, the "nationally liberated zones," the "no-go-areas." Racism became firmly woven into the fabric of everyday life. A Vietnamese woman reported about Rostock shortly after reunification: "I was in a streetcar and sat down with my child next to an elderly lady. She immediately got up and sat down in another seat. My daughter noticed this."[43] A Mozambican man reported in the middle of the 1990s: "Yes, well, you encounter that every day. You just have to pretend that it's not directed at you. I only once experienced a direct physical threat. That was in July 1992. I wanted to go to church and all of a sudden someone pushed me and threatened me with a gun. But luckily he then walked on."[44] And here is an Afro-Cuban man: "My children are mixed-race because my wife is a German woman. Although they have gotten used to a lot of difficulties, it's not easy for them. When someone, for example, another teenager, calls my daughter, 'you black negro' or 'little negro,' she can't really get over it."[45] When pupils from the state of Brandenburg were interviewed 2 years after the fall of the wall, in November 1991, 29.5 percent agreed with the statement "we need to beat up and drive out the foreigners."[46]

Just to enumerate the former contract workers who were killed out of racist motives in the former GDR: Amadeu Antonio Kiowa from Mozambique (trampled to death on November 25, 1991, in Eberswalde), Jorge Gomondai from Mozambique (pushed out of, or forced at knifepoint to jump out of, a rolling streetcar on April 6, 1991, in Dresden), Nguyen Van Tu from Vietnam (stabbed to death on April 24, 1992, in Berlin-Marzahn), Phan Van Toau from Vietnam (nearly beaten to death on January 31, 1997 in Fredersdorf, died in hospital 3 months later), and Alberto Adriano from Mozambique (nearly beaten to death on June 11, 2000 in Dessau, died in hospital 3 days later). And this enumeration comprises only those cases where the courts came to the unequivocal conclusion that the attacks were motivated by right-wing extremism. As late as the 2010s Ibraimo Alberto reported from

Schwedt: "Our mailbox was constantly stuffed with NPD leaflets, with which the neo-Nazis drove home the point: We're watching you. We know where you live. You and your family will never be safe. [...] When we dared to venture out of the house my kids first checked if right-wingers were around. [...] After the World Cup in South Africa it got particularly bad. 'Waka, Waka, Bimbo, Bimbo, negro into the jungle' – I don't know how often we had to listen to this."[47]

Whence this scale of racism, this degree of violence? One explanation is the scapegoat theory, here in the words of a woman from Magdeburg, born in 1969: "I think that these insecurities became stronger, that they looked for someone to blame and then turned these people into scapegoats."[48] But it wasn't just that contract workers were scapegoated for job losses and economic insecurity. When people's mental cosmos suddenly unraveled, when the patterns with which people interpret the chaos of reality were suddenly gone, some East Germans resuscitated deeper layers of their identity: they were *after all*, they were *at least*, German. This "at least" comes into being only through juxtaposition, it requires an Other, real or imaginary. The former contract workers became a screen upon which this Other was projected, they began to embody it. That was true for the entire Eastern Bloc: in Poland, Hungary, and other countries xenophobia and right-wing radicalism began to thrive. Even in the former Soviet Union a large neo-Nazi skinhead movement formed, although for instance Hitler had written about the "inferior Slavic race" in *Mein Kampf*.[49] An anthropologist has described this Russian, post-Soviet neo-Nazism as part of a patriotism of despair – this can be generalized for the entire ex-Soviet Bloc.[50] This hypothesis is all the more plausible when considering that East Germans, as opposed to those from "socialist brother states," after the fall of the wall did not suffer huge impoverishment: in this regard they were the major exception. To be sure, compared with the West Germans they were a lot poorer, but the social security networks of the Federal Republic did cushion their fall. For them the loss of a secure perspective for the future (the GDR had 100% job security) or more generally of security and plannability of life mattered more. In addition, people in the GDR quite simply were less versed in dealing with difference and ambiguity. That continued to have an effect. Moreover, East Germans saw themselves as heirs to the "good guys" during the Third Reich, the antifascists. That was one of the reasons why Nazism had not been processed or "worked off" (as in "working off the past," *Vergangenheitsaufarbeitung*), for instance in schools, at least not to in the same way and to the same extent that this had played out in the Federal Republic in the course of decades of contestation around the politics of memory. On some level the GDR's relationship with German nationalism was much more continuous, less broken. As the historians Jan Behrends, Dennis Kuck, and Patrice Poutrus put it, it was "paradoxical that the GDR demanded a continual balancing act between nationalism, patriotism [*Heimatliebe*], and international solidarity – in the absence of an open discussion about the content of such terms in the controlled public sphere of the state socialist dictatorship."[51] The three historians furthermore argue that the GDR had a legitimation problem, especially toward the end. Ordinary East Germans perceived the contract workers as part of the regime, that is, as lacking in legitimacy, as forced on them from above. Nor should we forget the homegrown culture of right-wing radicalism while the GDR was still in existence, as we have seen. Finally, after the GDR's collapse the inhibiting factors were simply too weak: policemen and judges often shared the attitudes of the right-wing extremists and let them act unfettered, so that in many parts of towns and in smaller villages a de facto disappearance of the state's monopoly of violence resulted. And the churches, parties, and civil society organizations were too weak to bring their mitigating influence to bear. None of these many factors worked in isolation, they mutually reinforced each other: complex phenomena require complex, multicausal explanations.

What speaks against an exclusively economic explanation, as is sometimes advanced, is the fact that for instance parts of the Ruhr region suffered a lot more from the transformation from an industrial to a postindustrial economy than did former East Germany. And of course the "potty thesis" is nonsense, that is, the idea, popularized in the 1999 "potty controversy," that the GDR's authoritarian upbringing of children and the simultaneous going to the toilet on meticulously arranged rows of potties was responsible for the authoritarian, nationalist attitudes.[52]

Political scientist Franz Walter in 2017 directed an interview- and participant observation-based study about the causes of arson attacks and other attacks on asylum seekers since the 2015 Syrian "refugee crisis." It largely reads like a continuation of the causes of racist violence against contract workers in the 1990s and 2000s. First of all there was "the search for order." Next the "sense of having been humiliated." Many viewed themselves as victims – of city-dwellers (if they lived in the countryside), of West Germans (as East Germans), and of immigrants (whom they considered to be receiving preferential treatment from the state). Added to the sense of humiliation was the impression that they constantly had to justify themselves because of right-wing extremism in East Germany. That caused many East Germans to reject all the more emphatically coming to terms with the – real – problem of right-wing extremism in their own part of the country. The past left a big mark too: the superficial GDR friendship of peoples in conjunction with viewing contract workers as temporary "guests" created particularly skeptical attitudes toward present-day immigrants who chose to stay. And of course the GDR's ethnic homogeneity played an important role, especially in the countryside. Unlike in the West, people often quite simply had no direct, lived experience of interacting with migrants. The "depoliticization of everyday life" constituted another factor. Because civil society and politics continued to be associated with "us" versus "them up there," that is, the ruling Socialist Unity Party (SED), people preferred to stay away from politics. At the same time they expected the state to "care" and solve all problems – in a top-down manner. Finally, "deficient political education" was part of the problem, especially in Saxony. If – here the study gets policy-oriented – the state would only offer more by way of political education, immunity to the extreme right might increase. This is one of the areas where some political will would do considerable good, Walter's study concludes.[53]

As a positive counter-example the study highlights Erfurt, where political forces from a broad spectrum and civil society organizations have come together to fight right-wing extremism and xenophobia, and this seems to work quite well. The power of such alliances became clear immediately after reunification. For Rostock, the social scientist Britta Müller reported after the pogrom in the Lichtenhagen part of town about a broad counter-public that created a "surge in self-confidence," so that even those who had previously not dared to do so began acting in favor of migrants in public.[54] Rostock's Commissioner of Foreigners at the time was a key player in this change. He attained permanent residency rights for the Vietnamese contract workers, which was successful not least because the victims of the pogrom organized collectively and founded a mutual aid society. Shortly after the Lichtenhagen pogrom "visible minorities" reported from Rostock: "F.: Students have become nicer to us . . . for example, now they almost always greet us, which wasn't always the case." Or: "S.: [. . .] I am a member of a club [. . .] and there they /uh/ protect me. They know very well that I'm afraid to go to sports practice alone in the evenings, so they pick me up by car and bring me home and wait in the car until I'm safely inside my house, and it's not just one or two people who do this, it's the entire club."

Others, however, beg to differ. G., for instance, also senses paternalism: "I don't want to be treated differently. I don't like that either. There are people who feel /uh/ obliged to me because I am a foreigner. They pity foreigners. Interviewer: You mean professionally? G.: No . . . there's a layer of society that considers these riots unjust and they want to do something for foreigners, want to support them, because they feel obligated after foreigners were attacked by other Germans, they want to mend things ... I don't want to receive special treatment. [...] Interviewer: Meaning that you want to be perceived the way you are? G.: Exactly. [...] Take my job, I have to do it well, no matter if I'm foreigner or not, black or white or purple ... But there happen to be people who don't know any blacks, don't know if they're good or bad, but they treat them as a priori good persons, just because they see that there are some right-wing radicals who attack them. And they want to help them, no matter whether they need help or not. If you do, for example, something bad or forbidden, the reaction shouldn't be: 'Oh well, he's a foreigner and being discriminated against, we didn't see anything!' I want that you stand by what you do and, if necessary, will be held responsible for it."[55]

Conclusion

In 2013 Ibraimo Alberto travels to Mozambique. He wants back the 40 percent that the FRELIMO functionaries used to subtract every month from his GDR contract worker salary. The Mozambican contract workers were always told that their 40 percent would be returned. Alberto has an appointment at the Ministério do Trabalho, the labor ministry. Without taking his eyes off his computer screen, a clerk tells him: "Well, bad luck. You're too late. I don't understand why you didn't get in touch earlier." After Alberto has proved that he did try to get his compensation on time, the voice behind the screen says: "Write a letter to the minister. You have to lie in it, though, you understand? You have to make up a reason why you only got in touch now. Perhaps a disease, is that an option? What do you think about a disease?"[56]

Alberto leaves and gets in touch with the German embassy – *his* embassy because Birgit and he got married in 1990. After that he got naturalized. His citizenship test in Potsdam lasted two whole days – German history, contemporary politics, singing the national anthem. When he enthusiastically shares the news of his citizenship, friends and fellow athletes are happy for him. Others react differently: "You a German? Ridiculous!"[57] Alberto stops telling people about his naturalization or, for that matter, calling himself German. The German embassy in Maputo advises him against the letter to the minister and the made-up disease. But they can't really help him either, even though he leaves an entire file that documents his case.

The history of the contract workers is one of the most dreadful chapters of German postwar migration history, which has plenty of dreadful chapters. Brought to the GDR to do dirty jobs. Paid with dumping salaries below the general wage level. Cheated out of their hard-earned money by their corrupt countries of origin. Deliberately isolated from GDR locals.

Subjected to racist attacks, ranging from physical annihilation, murder, to hate speech – as late as October 31, 1989, nine days before the fall of the wall, a poster at a demonstration read, "Germany to the Germans, blacks out of the GDR."[58] In 1989–1990 the contract workers were dropped like hot potatoes, deported to their home countries as quickly and cheaply as possible. There they were often forced to live on the margins of society instead of being able to profit from their labor migration. All of that happened with the active participation or silent approval of the reunified Federal Republic, a democracy subject to the rule of law. In this Federal Republic for the longest of times they had no lobby, no press coverage, no organized memory. Those who somehow managed to stay on were marginalized and attacked by neo-Nazis and the mob in East Germany, where the police and judiciary often looked the other way.

Actually, the contract workers deserve a national holiday, a museum, ex post financial compensation, school essay contests, and films. Or at least some respect – a thought about what kinds of obstacles the Vietnamese vegetable grocer on the corner or the Cuban salsa teacher had to overcome until they made it in today's Germany. All the more so since Germany actually has a long colonial past in Africa and Asia, which did not result in migration only because the former German Empire had its colonies taken away after the First World War, no matter how loudly it protested.

During his trip to Mozambique in 2013 Ibraimo Alberto goes to eat at the restaurant *Escorpião*, the "scorpion," in Maputo. It is teeming with Portuguese. Since the beginning of the world economic crisis in 2008 they are migrating to their former colony Mozambique. There they find jobs and send money back home to economically depressed Portugal – marking a progression from colonial overlords, who kept Mozambicans as slaves and decided over their life and death until 1975, to labor migrants. Who knows, perhaps one day the Germans will be in a similar position with respect to the countries that used to send them labor migrants, Vietnam, Mozambique, Poland, Cuba, Algeria, and so on? Or with former colonies like Namibia (German Southwest Africa) or Cameroon? Lo and behold, there is a historical Mozambique connection: in the far north of Mozambique there is the 400-square-kilometer large Kionga Triangle, which was a colony of the German Empire from 1885. In 1916, during the First World War, it was occupied by the Portuguese, and it was allocated to them at the 1919 Versailles Conference. When will the first labor migrants from Germany show up there? When will the first Western Union branch open so that these Germans can keep their families in Ingolstadt and Bad Homburg afloat with remittances?

5 Asylum

Hassan Ali Djan fled from Afghanistan to Germany at age 16 as an "Unaccompanied Minor Refugee," abbreviated UMF. "On the day that will decide whether I can stay in Germany, I wake earlier than usual," he remembers. "And immediately I'm wide awake. Outside it is still dark. Music is blasting from the room next to me, a babble of voices, so loud that I can barely hear the regular breathing of my four roommates." The day is November 3, 2005, and ahead of Hassan is the hearing at the aliens department.[1]

Notwithstanding the countless changes in asylum practices over the decades, one thing has remained the same: the hearing at which a person who is applying for asylum gets up in front of an official representative of the state and is questioned, if necessary with the help of a third person who does the interpreting. Hassan had tried to get information from the other Afghans at his shelter. But "everyone told me a different story about the hearing. Some said the clerk had asked first and foremost why Germany was the destination. Others said he had only been interested in why they had left Afghanistan. Yet others reported being asked mostly about the escape route."[2] "Only much later, long after my hearing," says Hassan, "will I learn that they were almost all partly right. The clerks ask about the escape route to find out whether they can deport the refugee to another European country. They want to know why someone left their home country and came to Germany because only those who were persecuted at home will be granted asylum. Those who came from a war zone or a region in crisis can stay for the time being. Those who fled poverty and hunger stand no chance of getting asylum."[3]

If Hassan's hearing in November 2005 were part of a movie, this would be a four-part mini-series with the first part starting as early as the 1940s. The period from 1948 until the late 1970s was marked by the Cold War. People from the Soviet Bloc fled to the Federal Republic, and the annual number of applications for asylum rarely surpassed 10,000; 1969, the year after the suppression of the Prague Spring, was a highpoint with 11,664 applications. From the late 1970s until 1992 – the second part of the movie – most refugees were from the so-called Third World. The number of applications went up and reached a temporary peak with 438,191 applications in 1992. In 1993, and this is where the third part starts, the German constitution was changed and the basic right to asylum circumscribed. From now on applications had to be filed in the country of entry into the EU and, since Germany has no EU outer borders, the number of applications immediately plummeted.

Yet, as time went by, the international law that had been codified in the 1951 Geneva Refugee Convention became more and more important in the EU and the circle of those who were granted refuge grew larger again. This refuge, however, was not granted in line with the article granting the basic right to asylum in the German constitution, the one that had been restricted in 1993, but on the grounds of the Geneva Convention – hence "Convention refugees." Hassan Ali Djan's 2005 application is part of this phase of historical development, which started around 1997. This fourth phase was marked by the agreement that sealed the European standardization of asylum politics in 1990 in Dublin. Dublin was a consequence of, among other things, the Schengen area. The Schengen Agreements of 1985 and 1990 created in 1995 an area without border controls among the signatory states. Now borderless mobility inside the Schengen area was allowed for EU citizens. At the same time new barriers were erected for refugees because the signatories of Schengen wanted to continue to negotiate their asylum status within the nation-state. Dublin I came into effect in 1997 and stipulated not only that applications be filed in the country of initial entry into the EU, but also that the actual case be processed there. The countries this affected most were Greece (the eastern Mediterranean escape route is from the Turkish mainland to the Greek islands), southern Italy, the endpoint of the middle Mediterranean escape route from North Africa, and southern Spain, which can be reached via the western Mediterranean route from Morocco.

Dublin II came into effect in 2003, replacing Dublin I. Dublin II instituted a central biometric database called EURODAC for collecting the fingerprints of asylum seekers. The intent was to prevent refugees from applying for asylum in another country than the one they first set foot on in the EU, or in several EU countries simultaneously, or under different identities. In addition, the external borders of the EU were fortified ever more securely – with old technology like high barbed wire fences, as in the Spanish exclaves Ceuta and Melilla in Morocco, and with new technology like satellites and drones. In 2004 the European agency FRONTEX was created to further strengthen and monitor "fortress Europe." In 2013 the surveillance system Eurosur was added.

Unmanned drones, for example, now began flying during the night above the Strait of Gibraltar, where a mere 14 kilometers separate the African continent from Europe. They detect refugees with night sight and thermal imaging cameras. At the same time efforts were stepped up to stop refugees from even getting as far as EU coastal border shores. Thus the EU paid money, camouflaged as development aid, to kleptocratic African dictators to keep inside their countries the refugees who were fleeing the violence of these very dictators. That is what "combating the causes of displacement" (*Bekämpfung von Fluchtursachen*) usually means: it is but a euphemism.[4] The more freely EU citizens could move, the more the mobility into the EU of those seeking protection was restricted. And if they made it into the EU after all, their mobility inside the EU was severely restricted.

In 2012 Dublin III went into effect. This regulation officially legalized the internment of refugees in camps. It moreover reaffirmed that the responsibility for an asylum application lies with the EU country to which a refugee first comes. Refugees who try to apply in other countries must be transferred to their country of entrance into the EU. Already during the Dublin III negotiations there was criticism that the EU border countries were overburdened with asylum cases as it was. A rise in cases would hopelessly overburden them. But the countries of the European North, among them Germany, prevailed. That was due, not least, to their enlarged economic power since the world economic crisis of 2008. Greece was on the brink of collapse, there was open talk about Grexit, departure from the Eurozone. The granting of new loans, the austerity measures imposed by the EU, and the negotiations about migration were always conjoined – in this sense too migration is indeed one of the "mega-topics" of the times we inhabit.

When the numbers of refugees from Syria, Afghanistan, and Iraq skyrocketed in 2015, Dublin III had its "stress test." The countries of first entry to the EU increasingly began to circumvent the Dublin III Regulation. Among other things, they stopped registering the refugees so that these could move on and claim in other countries that they had first entered the EU there. What is more, they deliberately neglected the shelters and camps to such a degree that conditions there fell below what judiciary authorities deemed humane. Courts up to the European Court of Justice decided in favor of litigants who filed suits against being transferred, so that they ended up staying in the North. Finally, Germany during the 2015 refugee crisis admitted that the Dublin Regulation wasn't working. The Germans signaled understanding for the plight of countries like Greece and announced that they would temporarily stop returning refugees.

As for legal status, toward the end of the fourth phase there were seven groups of refugees in the Federal Republic. First there were the "classic" refugees according to Article 16a of the German constitution, the Basic Law, whom a state had persecuted on political grounds in their country of origin. This group today comprises very few people, and throughout the fourth phase their share was almost always below 1 percent. The second group are Convention Refugees according to the Geneva Convention. They are nearly on a par with Basic Law Article 16a asylum seekers. The difference is that the Geneva Convention also recognizes non-state actors as instigators of a displacement. This means that if people in their home country are threatened not by the state but by groups like the Taliban in Afghanistan or the "Islamic State" in Syria and Iraq, they too are granted asylum. These persons are protected according to the Geneva principles that informed Paragraph 3 of the German Asylum Law. Throughout the entire phase they constituted the absolute majority. The third group receives subsidiary protection according to Paragraph 4 of the Asylum Law; this group is also large. Subsidiary protection means that in the estimation of the authorities there is no persecution by the state or other groups, but these refugees would be in serious danger if they were to return to their country of origin. For refugees with this status it is much harder to have family members join them and get residency permits. The fourth, also quite large, group consists of rejected asylum seekers whose deportation has been adjourned. This happens when the situation in their countries of origin is deemed critical enough that a temporary stop of deportation comes into force (according to Paragraphs 60 V and VII of the Residence Law). The fifth group comprises those who have filed a suit – often successfully – against their rejection and are waiting for a court decision. Those who have exhausted all legal possibilities and are now awaiting their deportation form a sixth group. Finally, some decide to go underground to avoid deportation. They form the seventh group and live in Germany as the paperless (from the French *Sans Papiers*) or "illegalized" – in contradistinction to "illegals," this term, which some activists and migration specialists use, is meant to signify that no person can ever be illegal, or, as the slogan has it, "no one is illegal": it is unjust laws that brand a person illegal.

To quote some figures, in 2017, out of a total of 222,683 applications, 0.7 percent came under Article 16a, 19.8 percent were according to the Geneva Convention, 16.3 percent received subsidiary protection, and 6.6 percent were granted protection from deportation. In that year nine out of ten of those whose applications had been rejected filed suits against their asylum decisions. In 2005, when Hassan Ali Djan came to Germany, the total annual number had gone down for the fourth year in a row and amounted to 42,908 asylum applications.[5] Of these only 411 or 0.9 percent came under Article 16a, the rest fell within the other categories.[6]

But what do displacement and asylum mean in real life, for example for Hassan Ali Djan? This chapter foregrounds the subjective perspective of asylum seekers – Hassan Ali Djan, who had his hearing at the aliens department in November 2005, is one of them, but others who applied for asylum in the 1980s and 1990s before him will also speak. And we will home in on the associations, citizens' initiatives, church parishes, and individuals who engaged in activism on behalf of asylum seekers. They represent the perspective of civil society. How did they all deal with asylum politics as codified in laws? How did their words and actions impact asylum practices? And what remained the same despite all the changes in politics and practices, what constants can we identify?

Escape in 2005 – Hassan Ali Djan

At eight o'clock sharp the office door opens and Hassan is asked to enter for his hearing at the aliens department. The official and an Afghan interpreter greet him. The official opens Hassan's thick file.

Here we go. "The interpreter explains that an important thing is about to start. '*Die Anhörung.*' He says the word in German as though only that would help me grasp its full meaning." The interpreter reminds Hassan: "You must tell the truth."[7] The official first asks about his reasons for fleeing.

First-person sources of asylum seekers usually treat the time after arrival in Germany cursorily.[8] The emphasis is on life in the country of origin and on the escape story: the unbearable situation in a refugee's home country, escape, dangers, horrors, and surprising turns of the actual escape, finally arrival in Germany. That is usually how the stories end. Is this because life in Germany, especially after arrival, is so monotonous? Preparing an application for asylum, killing time in the shelter, no chance of taking a job, restricted freedom of movement, finally the hearing, and thereafter once again: waiting, waiting, waiting. Perhaps the escape story, after it has been told and retold verbally in hearings and in writing in various bureaucratic documents several times, has become an internalized narrative, whereas asylum seekers' time in Germany hardly figures anywhere in their accounts.

Hassan's story starts in 1989 when he is born in the Afghan village Almitu as the first of seven children of a poor day laborer. His family belongs to the Hazara ethnic group, whom the Taliban persecute. The entire family lives in a single room. They are all illiterate, no one has gone to school. The rhythm of life is all about hard agricultural labor that they do for an independent, wealthier farmer.

When Hassan was 11, his father died. After the mourning ritual, Hassan's oldest uncle told him: "Now it's your job to feed the family."[9] But there were hardly any possibilities of earning money for him, and the family, already scraping by at subsistence level, fell deeper into poverty.

Hassan heard that a couple of men from his village were working on construction sites in Iran and sent home more money than he could ever hope to earn in Almitu. He borrowed money from a cousin for the traffickers who organized the difficult passage via Pakistan to Iran. He had to promise his cousin to return the loan as soon as he started making money as a labor migrant in Iran – in the end it took two years, much longer than planned, to pay back the fee for the traffickers. This is no exceptional case, many go into debt in order to reach their destinations. Often families, clans, even entire villages collect money to send off the member of their society with the best prospects, usually a healthy, young man. If he gets deported without having earned enough to pay back the money, he stands to die a social death. Some try to avoid deportation through suicide, such as a Vietnamese deportation prisoner in Dresden. In December 2007 he tried killing himself twice because he had not yet been able to pay back his debts for the trafficker fees.[10]

For four years, from 2001 until 2005, Hassan worked on construction sites in Tehran: he started at age 12; when he finished he was 16 and had not only kept his family afloat but also saved up several thousand dollars. These were years of world historical cataclysms with Afghanistan at the center: 9/11, the Afghanistan War and the driving out of the Taliban, and from 2003 onward the Iraq War. During these years there was an increased likelihood of being recognized or at least tolerated as an asylum seeker from Afghanistan in the Federal Republic.

In one of his rare telephone conversations with his mother – there was only one satellite phone in all of Almitu – she told him: "You are old enough to get married. I am going to find you a woman."[11] Hassan liked the idea until he met another Afghan of his age from his village. He had worked in Tehran a while back and finally returned to Almitu to get married. But for the wedding and dowry he had go into debt again. As a farmer, he could have never settled these debts and offer his future children a perspective for a better life. So he took off for Iran again.

Meeting this man got Hassan thinking. He imagined life in Almitu with its limited possibilities. But life in Iran was also limited, that he knew. There, Afghans were (and are) "third-class people" and harassed in various ways.[12] And so, together with his friends Naem and Hamit, he decided to go to Europe.

Hassan and his friends paid a trafficker €900 for the first leg of the trip to Istanbul. A public bus first drove them to the Iranian–Turkish border region. Iranian Kurds brought the three, together with more Afghans, Pakistanis, and Bangladeshis, in night marches through the mountains across the border – this week was one of the most dangerous parts of the escape. From Istanbul they were driven to Izmir on the Mediterranean coast, where they paid another trafficker $500 so that he would hide them for a few days and get them a rubber boat to cross to the Greek island of Kos. They were constantly on the watch for the Turkish police, who would have deported them to Tehran.

After a couple of days, they were brought to the coast at night-time. With a boat designed for four people, Hassan, his two friends, and three other men managed, after eight hours of paddling in the rough sea between cargo ships, to reach Kos safely.

There the police picked them up, brought them to a police station, took their fingerprints, and interrogated them. The police officers confused them with the passengers of a Turkish fisherman who was moonlighting as a trafficker. They were looking for witnesses who would corroborate their hypothesis. During the interrogation Hassan and his friends were repeatedly pulled by their hair and kicked in the face with boots. When the policemen understood that they were wrong, they let go of the three and brought them to a camp with 200 more refugees from Afghanistan, Turkey, Iran, and various African countries. They received a 4-week residence permit for Greece; after that they were expected to leave the country.

They crossed by ferry to Athens, where they wanted to go into hiding and work without papers. But it wasn't long before they noticed that in the capital even Greeks were homeless, "normal people, not drug addicts or alcoholics."[13] If even the locals don't have a roof over their heads, they figured their chances would also be bad. They sounded out other Afghans and heard – this was 2005, so before the stock market crash of 2007 and the ensuing world economic crisis – that Sweden and Britain were the most popular. One of the reasons, at least according to hearsay, was that you could bring over your family. By the way, "no one wanted to go to Germany, rumor had it there you would have to wait forever, could not work, and would most likely be sent back."[14]

They took a train from Athens to the port city of Patras. From there they wanted to attempt to travel further, to Northern Europe. They ended up in a pine forest in an improvised tent camp where 150 Afghans were waiting for an opportunity to escape to Northern Europe; some of them had been waiting for years. The best method, everyone said, was to hide in the spare tire under a truck and to cover oneself with a dark plastic bag – at border controls customs officers routinely checked the undersides of trucks with mirrors.

The three friends decided that from now on each of them was on his own. The trucks were in a parking lot with strict security. Through a fence Hassan observed the guards for weeks on end. One day, when the guards were distracted for a moment with another migrant whom they had caught, he tried his luck: he sprinted to the truck he had decided on and quickly crawled into the wheel arch on the underside.

The truck boarded a ferry to Italy and from there drove northward. None of the border controls discovered Hassan. "The exhaust burned in my throat. I was freezing cold and afraid of dropping out of the tire, nonetheless dozed off, stared at the asphalt and just hoped we weren't driving to Germany." Then he decided: "The destination of this truck will also be my destination."[15] For two days he neither drank nor ate, nor did he move at all, and was more dead than alive when the truck one day in the middle of October reached its destination, an industrial zone in Munich.

Hassan's hearing at the aliens department is drawing to a close. "The interpreter is now reading aloud sentences that I have said. Some sound good. Some not. My head is buzzing, he reads and reads, I can barely follow. At some point he asks: 'Do you agree?' I nod my head, like in a daze. Then both get up and shake my hand. Before I leave through the door, the interpreter says: 'You will hear from us at some point.' I don't ask what at some point means. I'm simply happy that the hearing is over."[16]

After his hearing Hassan returns, as if in a trance, to his container shelter on Rosenheimer Straße, where he quickly falls asleep. The next few days he impatiently waits for mail from the aliens department. So as not "to go crazy or get depressed, like a lot of my housemates," he successfully applies for a cleaning job at the shelter. After breakfast he now cleans the kitchen – and doesn't check the mail until the afternoon.

Hassan in 2005 was lucky: yes, he ended up in conservative, CSU-governed Bavaria, but in the social democratic island of Munich within Bavaria. Even though as an asylum seeker he was not entitled to a German language course, his social worker looked hard for a solution because she had rarely seen anyone ask as persistently as Hassan. She got him onto the charity-funded program SchlaU, which offers language classes for child refugees.[17] On this program Hassan had 1 hour of German language lessons a day. For him this was, at age 16, the first visit to school in his life. He did his homework, in addition practiced with tapes – and effectively became literate in German. Schooling in combination with his cleaning job at the shelter made waiting for his asylum decision more bearable.

"'To meet. I meet, you meet, he meets ...' On my way to the blackboard I repeat, as always, one of the irregular verbs that we have just gone through in my German lesson. It's a July day in 2006 and I want to check, once again, whether I've got any mail."[18] Hassan had long ago got used to not seeing his name on the blackboard. But on that July day he finds a note with his name. Hassan picks up the letter, runs to his room and tears open the envelope: a letter with many stamps and written in German legalese. Hassan doesn't understand a word.

The next morning he is first in line at the door of his social worker, Sabine Hodek. Hodek reads the letter. "'That's a deportation letter,' she says, holding the sheet of paper gingerly. Dazed, I take in her words."[19] Actually, she explains, he would now have to leave Germany within 4 weeks, but he could file an appeal, and then a court would have to make a decision on his case. That is precisely what Hassan does next.

Several months later, Hassan gets a call from his Afghan friend Arif, who got a deportation letter shortly before Hassan. Arif had also contested his deportation and later received a document (*Duldungsbescheid*) stating that his presence in Germany will be tolerated until further notice. At this point in time neither he nor Hassan knows that this temporary stay permit could be converted into a residence permit after a while. They only know that those given a temporary stay permit have to continue to live at the shelter; get food parcels; that it is well-nigh impossible to legally get a job, vocational training, or go to school; that they are entitled neither to unemployment benefits nor to social benefits. Only the residence requirement will be relaxed, if ever so slightly: now they are allowed to move within the state of Bavaria, no longer being limited to the confines of their aliens department.

Later in the fall Hassan gets more mail, this time a thick letter. His social worker opens it: "She's leaning over the letter, she's leafing. I concentrate on her face, I'm trying to read its expression. She starts smiling. Her grin gets broader and broader. Sabine brims. [...] Finally she looks up and nods. And I understand: I can stay, I didn't get another temporary stay permit or a deportation letter. [...] I can go to school, get vocational training, look for work. I can build a life for myself in Germany. [...] I jump up, want to run out of the room, but Sabine holds me back, calls for another Afghan guy. He explains to me that I received a temporary residence permit, subsidiary protection, provisional asylum. That I can first stay for another year for the time being. She also says that I will most likely get another residence permit after that."[20]

Now he still had to get an Afghan passport at the General Consulate in Bonn, a precondition for a residence permit. Hassan needs a while until he understands what subsidiary protection means. Afghanistan is ravaged by war, and this war is a serious threat to his life, that is why he gets protection. Yet why he got subsidiary protection and his friend Arif, an Unaccompanied Minor Refugee just like Hassan, only a temporary stay permit, is a mystery to him: "It can't simply have been luck that I'm able to stay? That doesn't fit with what I've seen in Germany so far. There must be a reason. I mull this over. Could the reason be the remote location of Arif's shelter? That he had no access to the help of social workers, that he no longer has any contact with his legal guardian in Munich?"[21]

But often it's just that – small structural inequalities of individual asylum seekers who actually have the same background. Or contingency, pure and simple. Asylum law and asylum practice are so complex that unfairness and absurdity are inevitable. Even asylum lawyers admit openly that they are often at a loss. Given such a confused situation, no wonder Arif got a temporary stay permit, whereas Hassan got a residence permit.

Hassan had to move out of the shelter, he stopped getting food parcels or his €40 pocket money per month. Instead he began receiving a monthly €350 allowance, the Hartz-IV level of welfare benefits. He had to find a room on the rental market. That is nearly impossible in Munich. He found a place only when he met an elderly lady, Frau Zopfy, through a mentoring program for refugees. Frau Zopfy would become very important for him: she gave him additional German lessons, showed him Munich and its vicinity, the countryside, and the world of books and museums. At their first meeting she invited him home, adding: "By the way, in Germany people greatly value punctuality."[22] Looking back, Hassan says Frau Zopfy was decisive in helping him "understand Germany."[23]

Frau Zopfy also helped him with room-hunting, a process that lasted more than a year – the officials of his Upper Bavarian jurisdiction repeatedly demanded that he finally move out of the shelter. In the end it worked, and he found an apartment on the ground floor of a house for €500 a month, which he rented together with another Afghan. Meanwhile the SchlaU program had turned into a full-fledged school that Hassan attended. In the end he received a Certificate of Secondary Education (*Hauptschulabschluss*). "When the principal handed me my diploma, he said: 'Hassan, you impressed us all.' My classmates applaud. A warm feeling inside spreads, I have to smile. I have taken the first step!"[24] Hassan had higher ambitions: he wanted to get a Qualified Certificate of Secondary Education, the Bavarian *Quali*. A *Quali* is needed in order to become an electrician. And that is what he has been aiming for ever since he saw in a handicraft business at an employment agency's open day what electricians do: talk about solar power as a "future technology" left an imprint on him. So he went to *Hauptschule* for another year.

In the meantime he periodically gets calls from Arif. At one point Arif has just spent a week in prison because he had violated the residence requirement. Arif has also tried his luck in Italy, Austria, Britain, and France – to no avail. He cannot find a job anywhere. It is risky for employers in the rest of Europe to take on an asylum seeker with merely a German temporary stay permit and a German residence requirement. In many respects it is easier to employ entirely underground refugees without any rights – the paperless.

Hassan gets his *Quali* with the good grade of 2.2 and immediately finds an apprenticeship position with an electrical engineering firm in Munich. Now he is an apprentice and goes to vocational school. During the second year of his apprenticeship he makes €550 a month, so the social welfare agency halts its payments. He speaks with his family in Almitu as often as possible. After the Taliban have been driven out, school reopens in Almitu in 2006 and three of his sisters attend it. One has almost finished school and wants to go to university in Kabul. To get into university, she needs to attend a preparatory course. She calculates that she would need €300 per month for herself and her two sisters in Kabul – in total, including room, food, and fees for the preparatory course. Hassan is still sending money back home to his mother, as is his brother Ehsan, who, like Hassan once did, works on a building site in Tehran, but this isn't enough to pay for university for the three sisters in Kabul.

Hassan finds himself a side job with a cleaning company and now cleans three evenings a week. On his way home on the commuter train he regularly falls asleep – during one journey he suddenly feels a hand on his shoulder: his old social worker Sabine Hodek. They are happy to meet again. He tells her about his apprenticeship, the vocational school, and the side job. "I don't tell her that I sometimes doze off in vocational school. Nonetheless she is immediately worried. 'Are you managing?,' she asks. 'Yes, of course,' I reply. I don't want to hear from her that I've got too much on my plate. I know that myself."[25] Sabine arranges an article in the pre-Christmas *Adventskalender* column in the local pages of the newspaper *Süddeutsche Zeitung*: "Hassan A. has two jobs – and therefore hardly any time to study."[26] Hassan gets a cheque for almost €1,000 from donations by readers. Then a woman gets in touch with him via the newspaper. She tells him that the article made a deep impression on her and that she and her husband want to support him and his sisters in Afghanistan with €200 per month. "'You know, we're not a rich family, we have two children who are still in university,' she continues, apparently without expecting a reaction from me. She tells me that she is a translator and her husband a surgeon who went to university as a mature student. 'We know how important education is. We just want to help you.' I am still speechless and am searching for the right words. I simply say 'Thank you' in the end."[27]

Hassan quits his job at the cleaning company, although his boss offers him the position of shift supervisor and a pay raise. But Hassan wants to focus on his apprenticeship and vocational school. He successfully finishes the apprenticeship and is taken on in as a journeyman.

Even Arif manages to make it in Bavaria. His temporary stay permit is extended twice, then the aliens department changes his status and he too gets subsidiary protection and a residence permit. He finds a job with a cleaning company in Dachau. "He didn't have the opportunity to go to school or do an apprenticeship. He never really learned German, didn't go to school. In the town of his shelter there was no program like SchlaU, no German language lessons at all. The refugee minors were left to their own devices," says Hassan.[28]

At vocational school Hassan was elected class representative and later became something of a celebrity. It all started with an invitation to a conference of the Federal Expert Association on Unaccompanied Minor Refugees. Later he went on stage at the Munich Kammerspiele theater, then the Bavarian Integration Commissioner invited Hassan to accompany him regularly to events and to tell his story. To be sure, Hassan is a sort of poster boy UMF, but he never forgets that others like Arif had it much harder than he did and that he would not have found a room on the rental market without Frau Zopfy. Because on that market he was at the very bottom of the reputational pecking order. And even now he is still stopped on the street by the police at least once per month and asked to show his papers: this is what one calls ethnic or racial profiling.

Hassan's story is a success story. Despite similar starting conditions, Arif's story is a more mixed one, but at the end of the day it too is a success story. This is not at all the case for everyone, especially if refugees are older or from different countries, or if they end up not in Munich but in poor areas of Germany. In those places there are no jobs, even young locals mostly move away to more affluent cities. And there is a much smaller likelihood that there will be an opportunity like the SchlaU program for learning German, a social worker like Sabine Hodek, a mentor like Frau Zopfy, or a couple that will donate €200 extra support every month (Figure 5.1).

Hassan Ali Djan's escape is one of many similar stories from the last decades. The laws change (in the 1980s the majority of applications were filed under Article 16a of the Basic Law, whereas in 2005 the majority were filed under the Geneva Convention), the number of refugees varies

Figure 5.1 Hassan Ali Djan, 2016. © Anja Schuchardt.

(during one period there are more, then at other times there are fewer of them), the major countries of origin vary (at one point Bosnia, at another Syria), the escape routes vary (at one point the eastern Mediterranean route, at another the middle Mediterranean route), the popularity of destinations changes (at one point Britain, at another Germany is most popular). But much has stayed the same over the years: causes for which it is seldom possible to make a clean distinction between "political persecution" and economic, religious, ethnic, and a few other factors; the refugees, who are rarely the oldest, the weakest, and the sick, but rather are young and dynamic; the reliance of refugees on word of mouth and local networks; the role of the traffickers and others who are inextricably involved in the economy of refugee migration logistics; rescue, relief, gratitude; and countless threats to life and limb, countless traumas and tragedies.

Looking Back

But why did Hassan have a hearing on November 3, 2005, in the first place? Why does a clerk at the aliens department or the German Federal Office for Migration and Refugees in Nuremberg decide on these questions? Does the law not unambiguously fix the criteria according to which asylum is granted so that the executive branch merely implements it?

No. And that was intentional at the time. When the authors of the Federal Republic's Basic Law in winter 1948–1949 formulated Article 16, Paragraph 2, Sentence 2, they were deliberately fundamental and deliberately open: "Persons persecuted on political grounds shall have the right of asylum." Unlike other constitutions, the German Basic Law grants the "politically persecuted" individual the basic right to asylum. In other countries the state has the right to grant asylum, rather than the individual being endowed with the basic right to asylum. It may seem like hairsplitting, but the difference was huge until the general European transition in the 1990s to the Geneva Convention: in Germany the state cannot simply pause asylum law because, say, it does not want to accept any asylum seekers for the next two years; to achieve that end the constitution would have to be changed.

Moreover, the meaning of *political* persecution was deliberately not more precisely defined. People should have the right first of all to cross the German border and get themselves into safety – only thereafter should it be determined whether persecution on political grounds had actually happened. The authors of the Basic Law were still mindful of the years during which German refugees from the Nazis were saved (or not) by being granted asylum in other countries. "Asylum Law is always a question of generosity," said Carlo Schmid of the social democratic SPD, "and if you want to be generous, you have to risk erring once in a while with a person."[29] The constitutional law expert Hermann von Mangoldt (of the CDU), another "father" of the Basic Law, agreed. He never again wanted to have a situation in which the legality of asylum applications would be decided ad hoc at the border, as had been the case on the German–Swiss border during the Nazi era: many refugees had been denied entrance there. With this approach, however, the "fight about four words" (Klaus J. Bade) was transposed into the legislative bodies (such as the Bundestag), the courts, and the offices of the aliens departments with their Formica-topped desks and potted plants.[30]

Sometimes there was no contestation, sometimes the situation was crystal clear. In El Salvador in 1982, for example, Claudia R. fought in the underground against the military junta. Military units filmed her during a hunger strike in a church, before firing into the group. Claudia R. was wounded, other hunger strikers died in the hail of bullets. Claudia R. had a large scar. Using a passport she had obtained through dissident networks, in December 1982 she flew to Germany and applied for asylum. She paid for the ticket with money that her mother had sent her – her mother had fled to Germany with her two younger daughters a year earlier. Claudia R.'s application for asylum was accepted after half a year – this was very fast.[31]

The goal of all asylum cases is to check that there were justified reasons for an escape. To that end the authorities look for contradictions in the escape story. In the case of the escape of the mother of Claudia R. from El Salvador, for example, the testimonies of the two younger sisters were cross-checked with that of the mother. The mother reported that she had supplied fleeing, wounded, underground fighters with medicine. But since the testimonies of the 11- and 15-year-old daughters diverged from the mother's with respect to the quantity of medicines and the number of underground fighters who visited them at home, their application was rejected – in contrast to the application of her daughter Claudia.[32] That is but one of many cases in which the authorities reach very different decisions with family members whose persecution and escape biographies are nearly identical. The father of Safwa Hangalay (who was born in 1971) was murdered in prison in 1981 in Asmara, Eritrea's capital, as a high-ranking member of the Eritrean Liberation Front (ELF). (At that time the ELF and the Tigray People's Liberation Front were engaged in an armed struggle against the Ethiopian central government.) As youths, Safwa and her siblings were active in the ELF as well. When their lives were also under threat, Mona, their father's wife, helped them escape via Sudan, Egypt, and East Berlin to West Berlin, where they started going to school – Safwa wanted to become a dental assistant. "Shortly after our escape Mona and her small son also had to flee," Safwa recounted in 1989. "She now lives in a Bavarian village and was recognized as a political refugee. Yet the administrative court in Berlin refused to recognize my siblings and me as political refugees. A few days ago we received from the aliens department the eviction order, now we are threatened with deportation to Ethiopia. There they will either lock us up in a 'reeducation camp' or execute us as 'deserters of the republic.'"[33]

To gain recognition according to Article 16a the reason for escape must be political persecution at the hands of a state. With Claudia R. from El Salvador that was the case beyond reasonable doubt. The same was true for Samira, a southern Iranian nurse and a member of the Arab minority. In 1985 the hospital she was working at was stormed by the Persian-Shiite Revolutionary Guard. Samira and other hospital staff were accused of supporting opponents of the Mullahs' regime that had come to power in 1979. She managed to escape to Turkey and from there to West Berlin via East Berlin. In Germany her asylum application was recognized without problems.[34] What we have here are two cases in which economic and political grounds are not mixed. But these are the minority. Usually escape has multiple causes that are very difficult to disentangle.

Once they arrive in Germany, it is highly contested whether and how asylum seekers may work, how they are housed, and which social benefits they are entitled to receive while waiting for a decision. Over the years so much has changed, and the general situation in the respective state or municipality – sympathetic or unsympathetic toward asylum seekers? – despite the Europeanization and unification of Asylum Law still has enormous consequences in individual cases.

The core of the problem is that asylum seekers are merely asylum *seekers*. The Federal Republic's entire system was and is geared toward disincentivizing staying. It is also geared toward not encouraging other asylum seekers to come to Germany: the principle is one of deterrence.

In 1993 the restriction of the basic right to asylum was restricted through the "asylum compromise" and the passing of a new law (the *Asylbewerberleistungsgesetz*) that reduced state benefits for asylum seekers to a level below social welfare. (Until then the Federal Social Welfare Law had also applied to asylum seekers.) In 2012 the German constitutional court declared this *Asylbewerberleistungsgesetz* anti-constitutional because it failed to provide a minimal level of subsistence and thus violated the basic right of human dignity. As a consequence of this judgment, benefits specified in this law were raised to approximately Hartz-IV level.

The general tendency was and is that the more politically conservative the place where one is accommodated as an asylum seeker, the more restricted the options. Some places only hand out non-cash benefits (food parcels, clothes, and sanitary products) and it is prohibited to leave the territory of the aliens department, let alone the state (for instance to visit relatives). Other places, by contrast, do indeed grant cash benefits and allow movement between states.

For decades there has been resistance to the conditions in which asylum seekers are forced to live. The agents of this resistance are the asylum seekers themselves and German civil society. In October 2012, with the occupation of Oranienplatz in Berlin-Kreuzberg, which was to last for 17 months, this resistance became a broad social movement that extended far beyond the original activists.

Here's a flashback to the early years of the resistance. Let's go into some detail. Berlin-Kreuzberg, the Lutheran Martha Congregation, January 20–22, 1984. Twenty-six organizations, among them the Refugee Council and the Society for Threatened Peoples, a human rights NGO, had summoned an asylum hearing. By that they meant a sort of international tribunal at which asylum seeker activists and civil society representatives debated the situation in West Berlin in front of a jury. On the subject of food stamps for asylum seekers Ralf Roschinski of the social welfare organization Diakonisches Werk Berlin reported: "A young man enters a supermarket on a busy crossroads in Schöneberg. He walks through the aisles and puts into his basket what he needs for the next day, just like any other customer in the store. He joins the line at the cashier desk and waits, just like any other customer in the store. Now it is his turn. His items add up to 44.43 marks. He hands the cashier 45 marks. So he should get back exactly 57 pfennigs. *Should* – just like any other customer in the store, but the cashier starts arguing. He would not get any change, instead he should buy something else to reach the full 45 marks he has given. Why? [...] Quite simple: he is a foreigner and has applied for asylum. As an asylum seeker he mustn't work. He receives social benefits on a monthly basis, 185 marks in food stamps and 55 marks in cash. And he wanted to pay for his groceries with these stamps. The man is self-confident and well-informed. He points out the so-called 10 percent rule to the cashier, meaning that she is allowed to return up to 10 percent of his coupon in change. [...] But the cashier has not heard of this and categorically refuses to give change in cash. There is an exchange of words at the cashier's desk. [...] Nasty words are said about foreigners who don't work, live off our tax money, and on top of everything act up in the supermarket. Suddenly he is at the center of negative interest, he becomes ashamed and nervous, threatens to call the police. The cashier gives in. Finally he gets his 57 pfennigs change."[35]

Other complaints voiced at the hearing concerned healthcare, the shelters, and the confinement in prisons of those to be deported. A 4-year-old child, for instance, dislocated their shoulder joint and the doctor sent a note and a referral to hospital to the Central Social Welfare Department for Asylum Seekers – whose terse reply was: "Rejected!"[36] There was also a report on the shelter on Friedrich-Olbricht-Damm near Plötzensee prison. The shelter houses 240 asylum seekers, families from Sri Lanka and Lebanon, three-quarters of them children: "There are up to seven people in a room, sometimes the number of beds is smaller than the number of family members. Many children need to share beds. [...] The mattresses are often very old, dirty, tattered, and only made of thin rubber foam. The plumbing is often broken and doesn't get fixed for days. The condition of much of the electrical wiring is 'shocking,' unprotected cables for example. [...] Food rations are far below the social welfare agency's minimum. [...] Once a week onions are distributed as 'vegetable salad'! Food service is on Mondays, Tuesdays, and Fridays. [...] There are only 12 toilets for the 240 tenants. [...] The open junkyard directly next to the shelter contains toxic materials, and is particularly dangerous for the children. [...] Even though the families started a hunger strike in

December 1983 because they could no longer bear the catastrophic conditions, so far their situation hasn't changed at all."[37]

The 1984 hearing also highlighted the plight of the female asylum seekers incarcerated in the women's prison on Lehrterstraße before deportation: "Their situation is even worse than that of the male asylum seekers because Lehrterstraße is a prison for drug addicts or for pre-trial custody. Six to eight female foreigners live cramped in a room, where apart from their beds there is not even enough space for a table and chairs. The women are not allowed out into the prison yard and have no speaking contacts, all the more so since they cannot communicate with one another because they are of different nationalities and have lawyers in only the rarest of cases. [...] These women in custody pending deportation are illegally treated exactly like the above-mentioned offenders ... some women spent several months there, before they were deported."[38]

Lutheran Pastor Ehrhard Mische opened the asylum hearing with the following words: "On New Year 1983/84 six deportation prisoners burned in prison on Augustaplatz, Lichterfelde. Among them were two Tamils who wanted to apply for asylum. [...] On August 31, Turkish Kemal Altun jumped to his death from the window of a court because he could no longer bear the psychological pressure of looming deportation, even though his asylum case was still pending. [...] In 1983, 5,578 people sought protection from political persecution in Berlin (West) and applied for asylum. They came from the Middle East, Sri Lanka, Iran, Turkey, and several African countries. At the end of the year (of 1983) there was a total of about 18,000 asylum seekers in our city. Among them fear, desperation, and bitterness are on the rise. Day in, day out they feel, when shopping or in the streets, during interactions with the authorities and in their apartment buildings, that they are not welcome, that they are explicitly and implicitly branded as 'parasites,' 'freeloaders,' 'criminals.' They are treated in ways we can no longer call humane."[39] The pastor concluded his introduction by quoting from the Bible (3 Moses 19:34): "You shall treat the stranger who sojourns with you as the native among you, and you shall love him as yourself, for you were strangers in the land of Egypt: I am the Lord your God."[40]

In 1983 and 1984 the context was that of the backlash under the new Helmut Kohl government. The other context was that in 1980 there were, for the first time, more than 100,000 applications for West German asylum (after that numbers went down significantly: 1981: 49,391; 1982: 37,423; 1983: 19,737; 1984: 35,278). In the early 1980s there was a real increase of applications in West Berlin because the GDR government let Tamil asylum seekers, who had flown from civil war-torn Sri Lanka to East Berlin, move on with the commuter train to West Berlin. The goal was to destabilize capitalist, enemy West Germany (the GDR herself took in hardly any refugees). Throughout these years the city-state of Berlin's Senator of the Interior, Heinrich Lummer, a CDU hardliner who later moved into the right-wing extremist camp, agitated against asylum seekers. Finally, some media took the same line by writing about "a flood of asylum seekers," "economic refugees," and "fake refugees."[41]

The asylum hearing in Berlin-Kreuzberg in January 1984 is a snapshot and at the same time a high-resolution closeup picture. In the following years the topic subsided, until it returned at the decade's end and began dominating all of political discourse in the early 1990s – in the so-called asylum debate. There were several stages to this. First, the CDU/CSU capitalized on the subject early on and demanded a limiting of the Basic Law to asylum in the Bavarian state election campaign of 1986. Second, right-wing extremist parties successfully pushed the topic of asylum (the Republikaner got 10.9 percent of the vote in the Baden-Württemberg state elections in April 1992). That in turn emboldened conservative parties like the CSU to prioritize this theme in order not to concede electoral ground to the far right. Third, applications for asylum from refugees from Yugoslavia rose, especially after the beginning of the Yugoslav Civil War: 57,379 (1987); 121,315 (1988); 103,076 (1989); 193,063 (1990); 256,112 (1991); 438,191 (1992). Fourth, at the same time real immigration figures of ethnic Germans, especially from the Soviet Union, went up: 78,523 (1987); 202,673 (1988); 377,055 (1989); 397,073 (1990); 221,995 (1991); 230,565 (1992). Fifth, Germany from 1989 onward was preoccupied with German unification and German–German internal migration. Sixth, the racist attacks of Hoyerswerda 1991 and Rostock-Lichtenhagen 1992 were interpreted by many as a sign that the population would not tolerate any further asylum seekers. Seventh, conservative media like the tabloid *Bild* heated up the climate. Thus the *Bild* headline on April 2, 1992 read "The flood is rising – when will the boat sink?," and underneath in capital letters: "Almost every minute a new asylum seeker." And even the left-of-center *Spiegel* had a title page on April 6, 1992, with the headline "Asylum. Politicians Are Failing" and the image of a long line of dark-haired people overrunning the German border.

Throughout 1992 there was a lively debate, in the end the SPD budged and agreed to a change in the Basic Law. This was possible only with a two-thirds majority in the Bundestag, for which the votes of the CDU/CSU and FDP would not have sufficed. On December 6, 1992, the CDU/CSU, FDP and SPD passed the "asylum compromise," and on May 26, 1993, 521 members of parliament voted in favor of the change in the Basic Law, while 132 voted against. That was the necessary two-thirds majority for a change in the Basic Law. In the government quarter in Bonn there was a mass demonstration, and celebrities such as the writer Günter Grass left the SPD.

The asylum compromise was to add to Article 16a a second paragraph that circumscribed Paragraph 1 ("Persons persecuted on political grounds shall have the right of asylum"). Ever since then it is no longer possible to invoke Paragraph 1 if one has arrived through a "safe third state." The law defined as "safe third states" those countries in which the European Human Rights Convention and the Geneva Convention are operative. All EU member states, but also Switzerland and Norway, belong in this category. Equally, it is no longer possible to invoke Paragraph 1 if one is a citizen of a country that Germany classifies as "safe." Among such countries classified as "safe" since 1993 there have always been African countries like Ghana, but also Albania, Kosovo, and Montenegro (from November 1, 2015), and Algeria, Morocco, and Tunisia (from January 1, 2016). This amendment to the Basic Law, especially the clause concerning the safe third state, made legal entry to Germany nearly impossible. The only way of traveling to Germany overland is via third states defined as safe, where one should, then, file one's asylum application. Traveling to Germany by air is exceedingly difficult because of airport controls – states at war or dictatorships obviously don't customarily let their people leave, and even if they do, Germany would not grant an entry visa: "Cynics now say: since the amendment to the Basic Law you have to jump into Germany with a parachute in order to apply for asylum."[42] Realistically, the only remaining option is an illegal one, namely overland with the help of human traffickers.

The asylum compromise also ushered in the so-called airport case trial. The few asylum seekers who actually made it to Germany via air travel and whose applications were deemed hopeless – "clearly unfounded" – were prohibited from entry. They were forced to stay in special shelters on the territory of the airport and after a while directly deported to their countries of origin.[43] For that purpose the airport's transit area had to be declared "extraterritorial" – five airports were retrofitted for that: Frankfurt, Berlin, Düsseldorf, Munich, Hamburg. The Catholic Caritas charity and civil society initiatives decried this practice because often months went by during which families or solo traveling teenagers, sometimes even children, were kept in "asylum prison" until their papers were ready and they could be sent back.

The consequence of the restriction of the asylum law was indeed a sinking number of applications: if in 1993 there had been 322,599 applications, a year later the number was down to 127,210. As the numbers fell, the topic moved out of the focus of attention, but of course it returned in 2015 with a vengeance, shaking the entire political edifice of the Federal Republic. Without familiarity with this long prehistory neither the refugee crisis nor the welcoming culture of 2015 makes any sense. Apart from the basics of some legal preconditions and statistics, both changing over time, one must never lose sight of Germany's historical specificity: ever since the drafting of the Basic Law and thus the beginning of the Federal Republic, asylum has been connected with the plight of Jewish and other Germans who had to escape the Nazis. Some of them were taken in abroad, but too many were turned away and thus handed over to their murderers. This historical experience is palpable in the asylum debate – the most heated of the migration debates together with the debate on labor migration (*Gastarbeiter*) – and palpable in an acute way: as a warning, a yardstick, and a moral argument.

Conclusion

August 17, 1987. School is restarting in the state of Baden-Württemberg after the summer vacation. I have just returned to Tübingen from my exchange year in the United States, now I have two more years of school left. My school is on Uhlandstraße and the closest supermarket is Pfannkuch on Karlstraße, 5 minutes walking distance.

Two days later the 20-year-old Iranian asylum seeker Kiomars Javadi enters Pfannkuch supermarket shortly after 5 pm. He wants to buy something to drink. An 18-year-old apprentice tells him to take his shopping cart back outside; Javadi explains that he's got nothing to do with the shopping cart. The two start arguing. At some point the apprentice Andreas U. grabs Javadi, drags him into the basement and starts beating him with a rubber baton. Javadi bites the apprentice's finger and runs off. In the supermarket's backyard Andreas U., the store manager, and another employee catch him. They throw him on the floor and take him into a choke-hold. Fifteen gawkers stand around, only an older couple tries to intervene. They hold him like that for a total of 18 minutes, then the police arrive and handcuff him. At this point Javadi has been dead for at least 10 minutes, as the forensic doctor Volker Schmidt's autopsy will later conclude. The emergency doctor Dr. Warth reports: "The diagnostic finding when we took him in was that the patient had wide, fixed pupils. There was cardiac and respiratory arrest. He was already clinically dead."[44]

In 1988 two of the three Pfannkuch workers go on trial. They claim to have caught Javadi shoplifting. Allegedly there were stolen groceries in his shopping cart. But no fingerprints of Javadi are found on the groceries.

The two Pfannkuch workers are sentenced to 18 months on probation. The gawkers are not sentenced – no one gets charged for failure to give assistance. The judge Rolf Dippon interrupts Javadi's wife Marjan, who is joint plaintiff, saying "pull yourself together even though you are from the Orient."[45] In tears, she runs out of the courtroom.

Tübingen shows solidarity, there are vigils and demonstrations. A classmate organizes a student demonstration. For many, myself included, the Javadi case is an example of brutal racist violence and the loss of our political innocence: if something like this can happen in broad daylight in a liberal university town, it happens in other places as well, and probably a lot more often. After the murder, many Tübingen locals walk past Thiepval-Kaserne on Schellingstraße, since 1981 one of the largest refugee camps for asylum seekers in Baden-Württemberg, less indifferently; some get involved in civil society initiatives and NGOs like Amnesty International.[46]

Together with the refugees, these people keep alive the memory of the murder – Rahim Shirmahd, like Javadi a refugee from Iran and a resident of Thiepval-Kaserne, in 1991 films a documentary; halfway between Pfannkuch supermarket and Thiepval-Kaserne there is the Epple-Haus, a leftist cultural center, and on it a plaque: "Kiomars Javadi (died August 19, 1987) / Cause of death: racism / . . . and insufficient moral courage!"[47] The refugee movement and its occupation of Oranienplatz in Berlin-Kreuzberg in 2012, the welcoming culture of 2015 – these did not come from nowhere, for all long-term historical developments there are beginnings and events that accelerate the course of history in catalyst-like fashion.

1989

Hamburg, October 2, 1989, Neuengamme Concentration Camp Memorial. Two police squadrons of 100 officers each move in. They break open the doors of the brick factory with chainsaws and haul off 150 Roma, among them many women and children. Fire engines and ambulances are waiting: the Roma activists had threatened self-immolation. They had come from former Yugoslavia and applied for asylum in Germany, which was rejected. The reason given: there were no grounds for political persecution according to Article 16 of the Basic Law. Once before Roma had prevented an impending deportation with a dramatic protest: on February 18, twenty of them had started an open-ended hunger strike that they stopped only when their deportation deadline was extended by 6 months.

There are roughly 6 million Sinti and Roma in Europe today. They speak a multitude of indigenous languages and are exoticized and discriminated against to this day. In the past they were persecuted and annihilated, the nadir of which was the Nazi genocide in which between 200,000 and 500,000 Sinti and Roma were shot or gassed. Yet persecution did not end with the Second World War: in Czechoslovakia from the 1970s onward they were forcibly sterilized, in all polls they end up at the very bottom in popularity ratings of minorities, and hatred of Sinti and Roma, Antiziganism, is rampant.[1]

At the end of the 1980s, 6,000 Roma migrated from the Balkans and Eastern Europe to Germany and applied for asylum. Hysterical anti-immigration rhetoric in the media accompanied the immigration numbers, which had indeed risen; in 1988 for the first time in 8 years the number of asylum applications had gone above the 100,000 mark, at the same time 202,673 *Spätaussiedler* (late resettlers, see Chapter 6) had arrived.[2] All the major parties, even the Social Democrats, tried to make a mark by playing tough, especially toward whom they called *Zigeuner*, a term with even more pejorative connotations than "gypsies" in English.

When their deportation became imminent, the Hamburg Roma activists on August 29 occupied the Neuengamme Concentration Camp Memorial. They chose this date deliberately. On August 29, 1942, the Nazi Chief of Civil Administration in Serbia had written to the Wehrmacht Commander

Southeast: "Serbia only country in which Jewish and Gypsy question solved."[3] The location was symbolic as well: "a concentration camp is apparently the only place where Gypsies are welcome today," said Rudko Kawczynski, the Head of the Rom & Cinti Union, and banners read: "Gassed in Auschwitz – persecuted to this day."[4] The symbolism was lost on no one, and the BBC, CBS, and other international media reported; parliaments, from the US Congress to the Israeli Knesset, declared solidarity.

One month after the evacuation of Neuengamme, Rudko Kawczynski is back. It's November 9, 1989, and an event commemorating the anti-Jewish pogroms of 1938 is taking place at the concentration camp memorial. Rudko Kawczynski gives a dramatic speech. He recalls the persecution of the Roma and the fact that several hundred Roma were imprisoned in Neuengamme during the Nazi era. And he warns that deportation to civil war-torn Yugoslavia comes close to committing another genocide.[5]

Meanwhile another drama is playing out in Berlin.

***

International Press Center of the GDR, Mohrenstraße 36–37. A press conference is edging, or rather, moving at a snail's pace, toward the end. The day before had seen the sensational announcement of the resignation of the politburo, but today's conference is deadly dull – until an Italian journalist at 6:52 pm asks Central Committee member Günter Schabowski about the new GDR travel law. Schabowski reads out a draft version of the law. Asked when the law would go into effect, he answers: "immediately, without delay."[6] Everyone is electrified, the journalists in the room just as much as viewers at home in front of their TV sets. At first there is confusion, but shortly thereafter the first East Berliners leave their houses for the border checkpoints.

At checkpoint Bornholmer Straße a reporter chances upon a man whose pyjamas show under his coat. "I was already in bed," he explains in Berlin dialect, "my missus goes out to walk the dog, returns right away, and says: 'Listen, they're all going to the West!' I threw on some clothes and came here."[7] Around 8:30 pm at first hundreds, later thousands of locals residents have congregated at the border crossing. About an hour later the border guards open the barrier. Another hour later they stop checking: "We're flooding now! We're opening everything!"[8]

After midnight Westerners start crossing over into the East. Journalist Jürgen Petschull climbs over the fence on Pariser Platz and reaches the Brandenburg Gate: "For 28 years the Brandenburg Gate was shut off by the wall and men with submachine guns. Even if you're not an emotional type, this is an unforgettable moment. Total strangers are hugging. Many are crying. We walk through the spaces between the columns, back and forth. Again and again."[9]

West Berlin's Kurfürstendamm becomes a party zone, GDR citizens drive their Trabant cars up and down, honking without end, West Berliners offer them Western food classics like chocolate-covered cream cakes (*Schokoküsse*) through the open windows of their cars. "It was really incredible, we simply walked across without anyone checking. It was fantastic," an East Berlin man says into the camera. "Just once across the border, feet touching the ground, just to see if it's true," explains an overjoyed woman from East Berlin. "And, what did it feel like?", asks the journalist. "Amazing, my entire body shook."[10]

On November 10, 1989 alone 600,000 East Germans visited West Berlin. In the remaining 7 weeks of 1989, 343,854 East Germans moved to West Germany.[11] In the following years there would be many, many more – entire villages in Brandenburg or Mecklenburg-Vorpommern were depopulated. Add interior migration to that: on Monday morning by car from Thuringia to a construction site in Bavaria, back home on Friday evening.

As early as by summer 1989, tens of thousands of East Germans had emigrated to West Germany via Hungary and Czechoslovakia. That had become possible because East Germans could move quite freely inside the Soviet Bloc, and Hungary had opened the border to Austria, from where East Germans went on to West Germany. Others sought refuge in the embassies of the Federal Republic in Budapest, Prague, and Warsaw. Between the establishment of the GDR in 1949 and the construction of the wall in 1961 a total of 3.8 million East Germans had emigrated to West Germany. Between the construction and destruction of the wall another 787,000 East Germans emigrated, most of them officially by applying to the authorities, no matter how difficult and how long the wait – today that has been forgotten; we remember only the spectacular escapes through tunnels or in balloons.[12]

***

Russian Disco: Tales of Everyday Lunacy on the Streets of Berlin, the debut novel of Wladimir Kaminer, a writer born in Moscow in 1967, starts like this: "In the summer of 1990, a rumor was doing the rounds in Moscow: Honecker was taking Jews from the Soviet Union . . . [. . .] Word got around quickly. Everyone knew, except maybe Honecker."[13]

Literary scholars regard Kaminer as part of a growing number of translingual writers who write in a different language from their first. In terms of genre, his books are picaresque, he himself a modern *picaro* (rogue) who says such outrageous things that you never know whether he seriously believes them with a deadpan face and strong Russian accent:[14]

> Many people of various nationalities suddenly wanted to be Jews and emigrate to America, Canada or Austria. East Germany joined the list a little later on, and was something of an insider tip. I got the tip from the uncle of a friend who sold photocopiers he imported from West Berlin. On one occasion we visited him in his apartment, which was already completely empty because the entire family was shortly departing for Los Angeles. All that remained was a large, expensive TV set with integrated video recorder, which sat squarely on the floor in the middle of the room. The uncle was reclining on a mattress, watching porn movies. "Honecker is taking Jews in East Berlin. It's too late for me to change course, I've already moved my millions to America," he told us. "But you're still young, you don't have anything, Germany's just the job for you, it's crawling with layabouts. They've got a stable welfare system. They won't even notice a couple more lads."[15]

Kaminer became quite a phenomenon – a precursor of the 230,000 Jewish quota refugees (*Kontingentflüchtlinge*), bestselling writer, cult figure, and "professional Russian" (*Russe vom Dienst*), who will speak about Putin and Russian foreign policy after the eight o'clock news on public television and later DJ in Berlin's Kaffee Burger with Yuriy Gurzhy.

***

Olga, a 19-year-old ethnic German from Kazakhstan, emigrated to Germany in 1988. "We had to wait 8 years for our exit permit," she recounts in March 1990. "The authorities had kept saying 'no, no.'"[16] She explains the push for the great emigration of the Russian Germans at the end of the 1980s in economic terms: "They showed demonstrations [on TV], only the bad things. Capitalism and unemployment and films about fascism. Even though life in Russia is much harder than here. [. . .] When shopping you always have to stand in lines there, they don't sell any sausage or meat. I think that is why many ethnic Germans want to come here. Of course not those who are directors or ministers. But among the regular population nobody believes Gorbachev when he speaks about Perestroika. He talks so much, but people want to to have something to eat and enough clothes."[17]

About her own family she says: "My father was director in a gas plant in Russia. Here he works in a factory. He is very happy because he makes a good living."[18] The fact that her family is faring better than most is not just due to her father's high position in the Soviet Union, but also to the fact that they already had relatives in Germany: "When we got here we didn't have to live in a shelter for a long time. My uncle had emigrated years ago. He had a big house where we lived, and in the meantime my parents bought their own apartment."[19]

In the end she does provide an explanation for ethnic German emigration that goes beyond purely economic aspects and is connected with identity and minority status: "Yes, in Kazakhstan the official language is Russian, even though many more Kazakhs than Russians live there. In the streets they speak Kazakh, but with the authorities Russian is prescribed. We Germans didn't have contact with anyone at all: in Kazakhstan we had no contact with our neighbors. The Russians hated us and said that we are fascists, the Kazakhs wanted to get rid of all foreigners, the Russians just as much as us Germans. Here in Germany it's good, here we're among Germans and can speak with our neighbors."[20]

***

"Germany," opined the American Holocaust historian Raul Hilberg about the nationalist temptation after 1989, "is like a recovering alcoholic. Woe betide us if he gets near a bottle."[21]

***

"Turkish Gastarbeiter are scared to get pushed out by – Saxonian dialect-speaking – competition," wrote Germany's weekly magazine *Der Spiegel* in late 1989.[22] For many migrants who were already in Germany, the fall of the wall and unification engendered fears for a variety of reasons. They were afraid that Germany from now on might be preoccupied with national navel-gazing and that they would drop off the radar; that the cake would get smaller and East Germans would receive preference ahead of other migrants; that excessive forms of patriotism would increase and that neo-Nazis and racism would make life unbearable; that the opening of East Germany was only the first domino to fall and that masses of migrants from Eastern Europe would now invade, further stoking competition among migrants.

***

YouTube has plenty of Russian clips about the withdrawal of Soviet soldiers in 1994 from their GDR headquarters in Wünsdorf south of Berlin. Some clips are television documentaries, others DIY mixes by soldiers who were stationed in the GDR. Many begin with images of hoisting the Soviet flag on the Reichstag on May 2, 1945. All of the clips, even the most subdued, those that try to remain objective, have something in common: nostalgia. How is it that the proud Red Army, which had vanquished fascist Germany in the bloodiest of all wars, the "Great Patriotic War," 49 years later had to pull out of Germany shamefully, as though it had lost this war? How could one fall so low?

Between 1945 and 1994 a total of 6.1 million people served in the Soviet armed forces on the territory of the GDR; including family members we get the even higher number of 8.5 million.[23] When the wall fell in 1989, 400,000 were left, in absolute numbers by far the largest group of foreigners in the GDR. The Soviet soldiers represented the actual landlords in the house that was the GDR. They were isolated, their communication with the East German population was restricted to a few rituals of German–Soviet friendship a year, but everyone knew that Moscow had everyone in their grip and that its representatives sat in Wünsdorf.

In 1985 Gorbachev came to power and started reforms. His reforms developed a momentum of their own, they were fast-paced, one taboo after another was broken – and the GDR didn't keep pace. Before long it was more conservative than the "big brother" in the east, before long Honecker et al. looked like dinosaurs in comparison with "Gorbi."

First the Honecker regime was swept away in November 1989, two years later the Soviet Union also imploded. The next two years until the final withdrawal of the troops was a kind of extra rotation of history: the record had already reached its end, but it continued to rotate nonetheless and the sapphire stylus of the pick-up scratched: the soldiers took with them or sold whatever they could unscrew, they went on a rampage buying video recorders and Nintendos, stereos and cars – all the consumer goods that were so hard to come by in the impoverished former Soviet Union. The higher the rank, the more could be carried off: some generals became millionaires by selling tanks and weapons to the Balkans where a civil war was raging. Later millions of marks that the German government had earmarked in the Treaty on the Final Settlement with Respect to Germany, or the Two Plus Four Agreement (the two Germanies and Britain, France, the United States, and the USSR), for the construction of apartments for officers in Russia went into the top brass's mansions and dachas in Moscow's affluent suburbs. All corruption lawsuits were kicked into the long grass.

There remained in Wünsdorf hastily abandoned homes for officers, swimming pools, cafeterias, barracks, concert halls in which the Soviet pop singers had loved to perform, and even a small television studio belonging to the station "Telestudiya Wyunsdorf," as well as tons of waste oil, asbestos, and scrap metal. Astonishingly few soldiers defected. What prevented them from going into hiding and trying out a new life as migrants in the West?

Memories too stayed behind. The more time went by, the more bitterness became admixed with them: "You come here, look at everything again, it almost breaks your heart and tears flow, well, they say guys don't cry, but . . .," says Sergei Pavlov from St. Petersburg, who was stationed in Wünsdorf from 1984 until 1986 and in 2014 returned to the ghost town on a memory tour.[24]

In 2005 Putin called the dissolution of the Soviet Union "the twentieth century's greatest geopolitical catastrophe." Wünsdorf was a western outpost of the Soviet empire. And in its own way a beacon and a place of longing. Any diagnosis of contemporary Russia's postimperial phantom limb pains must take that into account. Without knowledge of these phantom limb pains we cannot understand why a portion of the over 3 million Germans of ex-Soviet descent can be mobilized by Putin's Russia, as happened in the "Lisa case" in January 2016 (see Chapter 6).

***

A street in Berlin, a house is being converted. A Persian grill is going to replace the Vietnamese restaurant in the front building. All of the builders speak Polish. They do not live in Berlin: in front of the house are a van and a station wagon with Polish number plates. More precisely, with number plates from a voivodeship (province) in western Poland.

A hotel in Berlin-Mitte. You pull your magnetic key through the lock and let the door of the hotel room slam shut behind you. The chambermaids are already in the hallway, with their carts, fresh towels, toilet paper rolls and pungently smelling cleaning detergent. Two of them are conversing in Polish. If you followed them after their shift, you would end up at Ostbahnhof, hop on the Berlin–Warszawa-Express and get off exactly 2 hours and 36 minutes later in Poznań.

Thousands, perhaps tens of thousands, of Poles commute to Berlin on a daily basis. This commuter labor migration became possible because of Poland's accession to the EU in 2004. In May 2011 all limitations on the free movement of labor for Poles in Germany were lifted. Many are in irregular types of employment – with subcontractors in the building industry, which do not make social security payments, as private cleaning ladies, or as full-time carers for nursing cases.

The "ant flows" (*Kriechströme*, to coin Karl Schlögel's term) of cross-border commuting always go from a low-wage country to a high-wage country – from Poland to Germany, or conversely, from the region of Lörrach in Germany's southwest to Switzerland. Increasingly, this kind of migration is not just to the neighboring country, but by airplane to more distant countries – low-cost airlines make this possible. In this way new networks are developing across Europe. Thus, before Brexit, there used to be van companies at the Berlin airports that drove Polish labor migrant commuters from the border region to the airport – residence in western Poland, transfer to Berlin airport in Germany, toolbox as hold luggage and then by plane to Manchester, laying tiles for two weeks on a construction site, then back home again.

In 2016 the case of a London student by the name of Jonathon Davey made international headlines. He had calculated that it was cheaper for him to live in a hostel in Polish Gdańsk (formerly Danzig) and fly to his lectures at Goldsmiths College in London with low-cost airlines than to rent a room in London.[25]

What happened to the Polish floor tilers in Manchester and the London students in Gdańsk after Brexit? What will happen to the German cross-border commuters from Lörrach, if Swiss voters go down a nationalist route?

***

Beginning in summer 1990 the Treuhand (privatization agency) sells 8,500 East German state-owned enterprises. Italian mafiosi sense the opportunity for a huge money laundering operation. Investing profits from drug trafficking and prostitution pro forma in the defunct East German firms allows the dirty money to enter regular circulation.

After 1989 not only did European and global interconnectedness grow, not only did more people move across borders, but also organized crime became Europeanized and globalized. As a result mafia groups like the Calabrian N'drangheta and the Neapolitan Camorra entrenched themselves in Germany.

***

A hospital in Bad Bevensen in Lower Saxony, 1997. Charlotte Meškauskienė, née Milowski, steps up to the bed of her 93-year-old father who is slowly recovering from a stroke. "Here's your Lotti!," says his wife through her tears, "Did you understand?" "Yes, I understood everything. And now I can die."[26]

Charlotte and her father Fritz had lost track of each other during the Second World War – she didn't know whether he had been captured as a POW or disappeared. Her mother and grandmother starved to death in summer 1945 in their home village of Schakuhnen in the district of Elchniederung, East Prussia, today's Levoberezhnoe in the Russian exclave of Kaliningrad Oblast.[27] Her grandfather brought 11-year-old Charlotte across the nearby border to Lithuania, where a farmer's family took her in as a nanny. The grandfather himself survived for a while as a cobbler, but then he too died of malnutrition. When Charlotte's Lithuanian family was deported to Siberia by the Soviet secret police, because the family had allegedly collaborated with the Lithuanian resistance fighters, the "Forest Brothers," Charlotte became a "wolf child." The wolf children were approximately 5,000 children of German descent who became orphans in the chaos of war, ended up homeless, and lived in the wild in Lithuania's forests.

Their fate had largely been forgotten until documentaries and feature films like *Wolfskinder* (*Wolf Children*, 2013) brought them back into public memory. More generally, Charlotte is one of hundreds of thousands of Germans from East Prussia, West Prussia, Pomerania, and Silesia, whom special battalions of the Soviet secret police, the NKVD, deported to the Soviet Union at the end of the war or in the immediate postwar period. They ended up in the Gulag, had to do forced labor, were adopted, were given new names, and became Soviet citizens. Until the end of the Cold War very little was known about these German deportees: they had to remain silent.[28]

After a few weeks in the woods, Charlotte found new employment as a nanny and her time as a wolf child was over. Later she ended up in the Soviet exclave of Kaliningrad, formerly Königsberg. In the early 1950s she found her father through the Red Cross and they began exchanging letters. Her father tried everything to get Charlotte out of the Soviet Union to join him in West Germany – to no avail. It was not until 1997 that Charlotte was granted a tourist visa and could travel to see her father. Six weeks later the visa expired and she went back. The very hour that her train entered Kaliningrad, Fritz Milowski died in Bad Bevensen.

There were quite a few reunions like that of Charlotte and Fritz Milowski after 1989. The Second World War, the postwar chaos, and the epoch of the greatest migration movements in modern Europe in some ways only really ended after the fall of the wall, the opening of the Iron Curtain, and the end of the Cold War.

***

In the week of the dual drama in Neuengamme and in Berlin – one, the protest of the Roma, forgotten, the other, the fall of the wall, a world historical turning point, the protesting Roma received an offer from Dresden – Dresden *of all places*, one is tempted to say after Pegida and an infamous neo-Nazi speech by AfD politician Björn Höcke. The human rights activists from Dresden's Neues Forum suggested, "that Dresden, Hamburg's twin city, offers to take in as many Roma as Hamburg has promised, so 150."[29] Later the "Roma question" was negotiated on a pan-European level. The EU classified them as an official minority in 1993, since 1997 this applies also for unified Germany, where they are recognized as a minority along with the Friesians, Danes, and Sorbs.[30] Throughout his entire life Günter Grass defended the Sinti und Roma and in a speech once said: "As natural Europeans, from centuries of experience they are in a position to teach us how to cross borders, more than that, to lift the borders in and around us and to [. . .] create a borderless Europe."[31]

The events of 1989 accelerated the pace with which, and changed the directions in which, people move in Europe. In 1989 Europe opened toward the east. European unification accelerated: migration within an expanding EU became ever easier. The 1989 events turned East Germans and West Germans into new migrants, even though after German unification on October 3, 1990 these forms of migration were only entered as changes of residence in the registry offices or recorded in tax declarations. The year 1989 marked the second caesura of German migration since the end of the Second World War.

6 Germans There, Russians Here

"I have always felt German and spoken up for the Germans in the Soviet Union all of my life, and now I get to Germany, and I am not longer a real German," says a 50-year-old man in the early 2000s. "There are a lot of ethnic Germans from Russia who are torn between having left Russia with the label 'German' and having the label 'Russian' attached to them in Germany," seconds another man in his fifties.[1] We could expand the chorus of voices, we would always hear the same song: Germans there, or worse yet, fascists; Russians here. After emigrating with the expectation of returning home and being among people like them, they are now excluded as aliens and fall between all stools: that is the tragedy of the Volga Germans. The same goes for the other ethnic Germans who had stayed on as minorities in Eastern Europe after the end of the expulsions in 1950 and later emigrated to Germany: Upper Silesians from Poland, Banat Swabians and Transylvanian Saxons from Romania, Danube Swabians from Yugoslavia, and many more.

Let us fast-forward. January 2016. A crowd has gathered in front of Angela Merkel's Chancellery in Berlin. They are holding placards with slogans like "Children cry same language," "Today my child – tomorrow your child," "Respect for German culture," and "Lisa – we are with you." From the handwritten script of the placards one can tell that they have been produced by people who learned how to write in Cyrillic. And indeed, most of the 700 demonstrators are Volga Germans.

What happened? On January 11, 2016, Lisa F., a 13-year-old Volga German from Berlin-Marzahn, does not come home after school. When she continues to be missing in the evening, her parents file a missing person report. The next day she surfaces and claims to have been confined and raped in an apartment by "Southern-looking types," *Südländer*. A police analysis of the geodata on her smartphone shows that she was at a friend's house. She admits having been scared to go home because her parents would punish her for the poor grades on her report card. In the meantime Russian state television has taken up the case and portrays it as a rape of "our" Lisa by Muslim refugees. The news spreads in the

Russian-speaking diaspora across the globe via satellite television and social media. This leads to demonstrations by Volga Germans all over Germany, including the one on January 23 in front of Merkel's Chancellery. The case grows bigger by the minute; the Russian foreign minister Sergei Lavrov gets involved and on January 26 accuses the German authorities of a cover-up.

There is a connection between the Volga Germans' falling between the stools and the ease with which they let Putin's propaganda machine instrumentalize them as a "diaspora" in 2016 so that Volga German Lisa mutated into *nasha Liza*, *our* Russian Lisa. This connection is linked with one of the central themes of this book: how to reconceptualize the German nation so that the Volga Germans – and all other migrants – feel at home in Germany. Once that happens, they will no longer respond to the siren calls of an increasingly muscular Russian state that increasingly defines itself in ethnonational terms. And they will not have to search for their identity in Germany at the expense of others, in this case Syrian refugees, to whom the phantasma of *Südländer* was attached.

Looking Back in History

Once the Lisa scandal had passed its zenith and reflection set in, it became clear that this was not only an early case of fake news. With the Volga Germans there came to the fore a migrant group who, considering their number – about 2.3 million have immigrated to Germany since 1987 – have received comparatively little media attention.[2] Who are these people, where do they come from? Where are the other ethnic Germans from, those who get lumped together under the terms *Aussiedler* (resettlers) or *Spätaussiedler* (late resettlers)? Why were they "invisible" for so long?

Aussiedler is a legal term. It designates persons of German descent who from 1950 onward emigrated to West Germany from the "really existing socialist states" of the Soviet Bloc. For the early phase of the 1950s the distinction between expellees and *Aussiedler* is an arbitrary one. A political decision was taken that the expulsions ended on December 31, 1949, and that all ethnic Germans who immigrated from January 1, 1950 will be called *Aussiedler*. In 1953 this was codified in the Federal Expellee Law (*Bundesvertriebenengesetz*), where *Aussiedler* come up in Article 1, Paragraph 2, No. 3 as a subgroup of the expellees discussed in Article 1. But how would "Germanness," literally "belonging to the German people" (*deutsche Volkszugehörigkeit*), be defined? On that count the law stated: "Those belonging to the German people are those who have committed themselves in their homelands to Germanness (*Deutschtum*), insofar as this commitment is confirmed by certain facts such as descent, language, upbringing, or culture."[3]

In late 1992 a new law (the *Kriegsfolgenbereinigungsgesetz*) largely replaced the Federal Expellee Law. January 1, 1993, became an important cutoff date. On the one hand, *Aussiedler* who immigrated to Germany after January 1, 1993, were now called "late *Aussiedler*," *Spätaussiedler*. On the other hand, people born after this date were stripped of their status as *Spätaussiedler*. In other words, an ethnic German born in Kazakhstan after 1993 cannot emigrate to Germany as a *Spätaussiedler*. The immigration of *Aussiedler* thereby acquired a temporal limitation because at some point in the future in Kazakhstan, Russia, and Eastern Europe there will be no living ethnic Germans who were born before 1993. This has an additional, more far-reaching consequence: a termination of ethnonational immigration to Germany has now been put in place, and, compared with it, other forms of migration, such as labor migration, have gained in standing. Put another way, the definition of the German nation has become slightly less ethnic and slightly more civic. Put yet another way, the legal, official German concept of the nation has become more French.

In terms of numbers, the most important countries of origin for *Aussiedler* are the USSR and its successor states, alongside Poland and Romania. From the former Soviet Union since 1950 a total of about 2.5 million *Aussiedler* immigrated, from Poland 1.5 million, and from Romania another 450,000. An additional 300,000 came from such countries as Yugoslavia and Czechoslovakia.[4]

Jannis Panagiotidis, a historian of migration, divides the immigration of *Aussiedler* into four phases. During the first phase, from 1950 until the late 1960s, the majority of *Aussiedler* came from Poland and had personally experienced the mass expulsions at the end of the war – we could dub this generation of *Aussiedler* "late expellees." The GDR in this phase also took in *Aussiedler*, more than 100,000; in official East German parlance they were called *Übersiedler* (literally "trans-settlers"). The second phase lasted from 1970 until 1987. In this phase (and those after it) the *Aussiedler* had mostly been born after the expulsions. The 1970s were dominated by détente when the regimes in the Eastern Bloc relaxed their barriers to emigration. The majority of *Aussiedler* continued to be from Poland, but West Germany also bought out – for Western hard currency – ethnic Germans from Romania. Phase three, 1987–1992, was short and dramatic: in the wake of Gorbachev's Perestroika, the 1989 Velvet Revolutions in Eastern Europe and the dissolution of the Soviet Union at the end of 1991, the Eastern Bloc's restrictions on emigration fell away, and since Germany had yet to erect new barriers, the astounding figure of

1.5 million *Aussiedler* immigrated in only 5 years. The fourth phase started with the erection of such barriers, first in the shape of a law, the *Kriegsfolgenbereinigungsgesetz* in late 1992. This phase continues to this day. The *Spätaussiedler*, as they have been called ever since, came (and this is true to this very day) almost exclusively from the former Soviet Union.[5]

The ancestors of these almost 5 million immigrants to West and East Germany had come to Eastern Europe as migrants from the various German regions and states that existed before 1945. In Chapter 1 we touched on the German labor migrants in Muscovy and the Russia of Peter the Great (1682–1725), the artisans, merchants, and doctors, but we could go further back. In the twelfth century German-speaking peasants from the Rhineland took up the invitation to emigrate to the Kingdom of Hungary and started tilling virgin land there. In return they received tax and other privileges that guaranteed that they could keep their own language and culture. Hungarians called them Transylvanian Saxons, even though they had nothing in common with Saxons in our contemporary understanding. Whether in today's Slovakia around Bratislava or in the Banat region in today's Romania, Serbia and Hungary, the principle was always the same for several centuries: Eastern European rulers invited peasants from the German states so that they would colonize virgin, often recently conquered land, buttressing the power of the ruler and contributing to feeding the population. In return they received economic and cultural privileges: they paid lower taxes, were exempt from military service, and were allowed to live in linguistic–cultural "parallel societies."

This was precisely what happened in the Russian case, as we saw in Chapter 1. Invited in 1763 by Catherine the Great, German-speaking peasants came in several waves and colonized newly conquered or under-governed areas of the expanding Tsarist Empire, first on the Volga, later in what today is Ukraine. This pattern held for a century until nationalism spread in Russia. The less the Romanov monarchy saw itself as a multinational empire and the more it defined itself as a nation-state, the less hospitable it became for the settlers of German origin. Many of them left Russia and migrated further. Thus pacifist Mennonites of German origin and colonists of other denominations emigrated to North and South America after the introduction of universal conscription in 1874.[6] Discrimination peaked with the liquidation laws and pogroms against ethnic Germans during the First World War.

The liquidation laws of February and December 1915 involved the expropriation and deportation of ethnic Germans from the western parts of Russia to Siberia.[7] At first these laws applied only to those ethnic

Germans who lived near the front line and in border areas, later they applied to all ethnic Germans of the Tsarist Empire. About 110,000 were expropriated and deported before the laws were suspended in the wake of the February Revolution of 1917. Also during the democratic spring of 1917 a first Congress of Volga Germans was held. The Soviet Union was founded in 1922, and on January 6, 1924, the Autonomous Socialist Soviet Republic (ASSR) of the Volga Germans was created: it was located in the original area of settlement on the Volga and inside the largest of the fifteen Soviet Republics, the Russian Soviet Federative Socialist Republic (RSFSR). If after 1917 there had been a small window to remigrate to the German Empire or later the Weimar Republic (120,000 used this opportunity, 60,000 migrated further to North and South America during the economic crisis), the Volga Germans were now, like all Soviet citizens, confined to the USSR without any chance of leaving it.

From then on their history developed more or less like that of other Soviet ethnic minorities. The difference was their region of origin, which consisted of many different states in the times of Catherine the Great, becoming a nation-state in the shape of the German Empire in 1871, a democratic republic after 1918, and, on January 30, 1933, a dictatorship. And not just any dictatorship, but an exceptionally aggressive dictatorship whose agenda included the "expansion of living-space into the east," the fight against "Jewish Bolshevism," and the extermination of the Jews. In addition, this dictatorship sought to resettle those ethnic Germans who did not live within the borders of the Reich, and it partially achieved this – they were brought "back into the Reich" (*heim ins Reich*). Some of them were integrated in the Wehrmacht.

So how, generally speaking, did the Russian Germans fare in the Soviet Union? The deportation of purportedly wealthy farmers, dubbed kulaks, during Stalin's forced collectivization of agriculture between 1928 and 1932 affected all farmers equally, and with it the high mortality that resulted from hunger, the cold, and the many arbitrary executions. The famine of 1932–1933, primarily in Ukraine, affected the Volga Germans too (about 250,000 Black Sea and Volga Germans starved to death in this catastrophe).[8] Just a few population groups, however, were covered in the special lists drawn up by the NKVD in 1934 – this concerned all of the Volga Germans as well as Communist refugees from Germany and Austria. This kind of registration was connected with the potential diaspora homeland, Germany, since 1933 National Socialist and a potential aggressor against the Soviet Union. Exceptional too were the deportations of Volga Germans from the western Ukrainian border regions to Central Asia, all carried out on the basis of these lists. Exceptional, moreover, was the proportionally extraordinarily high number of arrests (and often executions) of Germans and ethnic Germans during the Great Terror of 1936–1938. Volga Germans comprised only 0.8 percent of the Soviet population, yet amounted to 5.3 percent (75,331 between October 1, 1936, and July 1, 1938) of all those arrested. In terms of percentage only ethnic Poles were hit harder in the same period (0.4 percent of the population, 7.4 percent of all arrests).[9] Exceptional, finally, was the forced resettlement of 800,000 Volga Germans from the European part of the USSR to the Urals, western Siberia, and Central Asia, especially Kazakhstan, in August 1941 after the German attack on the Soviet Union on 22 June; the liquidation of the Volga German ASSR, including the expropriation of property; the prohibition of German as an official language, a media language, and a language of instruction; and the demotion of Volga Germans to second-class citizens. From 1941 onward, at first men, then a year later also women and teenagers, were sentenced to forced labor in the so-called *Trudarmiia* or *Trudarmee* ("Labor Army") to build up the military industry and imprisoned in camps. This affected in total 350,000 people, of whom 150,000 died as a consequence of these deportations and the violence that accompanied forced labor, malnutrition, and numerous diseases. To be sure, some of these tribulations also affected members of other nationalities who lived as diasporas in the Soviet Union: Koreans, Poles, Finns. But since there were many more Volga Germans and since their diasporic home was by far the most aggressive warring party (after all, the Germans had started a war that in the end would claim 27 million Soviet lives), the Volga Germans were most affected. Whether they identified with Germany, or approved of its war aims, was irrelevant.

What happened to the Volga Germans after the war had most in common with what happened to the Jewish minority. Both had external homelands, the Jews from 1948 in Israel, the Germans from 1949 in the Federal Republic, both of which became magnets for the respective "diasporas" across the world, especially in the Soviet Union, all the more so since the "laws of return" in both countries made immigration easy. Later both the German and the Jewish diaspora formed the seed of dissident human rights movements in the Soviet Union. Those who applied for emigration ran into great trouble. Since the Soviet authorities (almost) always rejected their applications, they had to stay put, which often meant decades-long discrimination: loss of their jobs, unemployment, surveillance by the KGB, but also incarceration in the camps and forced labor. Some resisted actively: they became dissidents (Figure 6.1).

The rehabilitation of the Volga Germans after Stalin's death in 1953 was half-hearted and piecemeal. In December 1955 the status of "special settlers" was lifted and their reporting to the local NKVD office ended;

Figure 6.1 Volga Germans demonstrate in Bonn, West Germany, for the right of Soviet Volga German dissidents to emigrate, *c.* 1984–1985. © Museum für russlanddeutsche Kulturgeschichte, 2017/92.

that granted the Volga Germans a bit more freedom of movement inside the Soviet Union. The key demand for a restoration of the Volga German ASSR, however, was never met, either in Soviet or in post-Soviet times. To avoid losing the votes of nationally minded ethnic Russians, in 1992 President Yeltsin, too, disappointed the hopes of the Volga Germans in this regard. In addition to this push factor there were others: the economic downturn of the late Soviet Union and its successor states; and the nationalism of Central Asian former Soviet Republics after their independence in 1992, with increasing attacks on all non-Central Asians and civil wars, especially in Tajikistan. Since this was combined with the West German "law of return," a strong pull factor, the situation led to the emigration of 2.3 million people after 1987.

"Of all nationalities and minorities of the former USSR," writes Viktor Krieger, a well-known specialist on the history of the Volga Germans, "it was the Volga Germans who suffered by far the most under the Soviet regime."[10] Is that true? There was at least some rationality behind the decision in 1941 to forcibly resettle the Volga Germans far out of reach of the attacking Wehrmacht, so that they could not go over to the enemy.

After all, the Nazis had symbolically incorporated the Volga Germans, and the German and Romanian occupying forces went further still by incorporating the 340,000 ethnic Germans (especially Black Sea Germans) in Ukraine as *Volksdeutsche*. What is more, Volga German men fought in the ranks of the Wehrmacht and Waffen-SS, and later, in 1943 and 1944, when the Soviet Union pushed westward, these *Volksdeutsche* fled the Red Army to Germany. The context of an external aggressor, of the same nationality as this diaspora, who unleashed unprecedented violence against the Soviet Union, makes the history of the Volga German minority different, for example, from that of the Chechens or Circassians (or Crimean Tatars), who were "innocently," without an external "homeland," deported to Central Asia in 1944, in the course of which as many as a third of them died. Put differently, in light of Nazi policies Stalinist paranoia vis-à-vis the Volga Germans seems somewhat less paranoid.

The history of those who started coming to West Germany from Poland as *Aussiedler* in 1950 is more complicated still.[11] After not having been a sovereign state since 1795, the aftermath of the First World War saw the foundation of the Republic of Poland, also known as the Second Polish Republic or interwar Poland. There was a large German-speaking minority in this independent Polish state. It lived predominantly in Upper Silesia in the south of contemporary Poland. This territory at the time of the Polish partitions after 1795 belonged successively to Prussia and, after 1871, the German Empire. After the First World War it was divided between the Republic of Poland and the newly founded German Republic. A part of Upper Silesia henceforth belonged to Germany – until the end of the Second World War. The ethnic Germans who emigrated from this and other regions to Germany from 1950 onward comprise the first large subgroup of *Aussiedler*. The second group consisted of people from the part of Upper Silesia (and other parts of Poland) that had been Polish before the Second World War. Some of them had been naturalized through the *Deutsche Volksliste* during the Nazi occupation following the German attack on Poland on September 1, 1939. The *Deutsche Volksliste* of March 1941 had four categories: category I were Germans "who were actively engaged for Germanness before September 1, 1939, in the *Volkstum* struggle"; category II comprised Germans "who during the Polish period may not have been actively engaged for Germanness, but who nonetheless demonstrably conserved their Germanness"; category III were "ethnic German persons, who over the years formed attachments to Polishness," as well as "members of the *völkisch* hard to classify, blood-based (*blutmäßig*) and culturally inclined to Germanness (*kulturell zum Deutschtum hinneigend*) population groups with Slavic home languages" (Kashubians, Masurians, and Poles in

Danzig, who are "inclined to Germanness"); category IV consisted of "ethnic German persons [. . .], who dissolved politically in Polishness."[12]

The *Deutsche Volkliste* was not only an expression of Nazi racial fanaticism, but also an instrument of domination.[13] Depending on the list, citizens' rights were granted or curtailed, food rations were allocated or not, and individuals were conscripted into the Wehrmacht or not. That said, not only were the four categories inherently arbitrary and the boundaries between them porous – how, for instance, can one determine whether someone is "culturally inclined toward Germanness"? – but also putting them into practice differed from one *Gauleiter* (regional administrator) to the next: in one place people who thought of themselves as Poles were forcibly registered in the *Volksliste*, in other places as many as possible were denied registration. By January 1944 almost 2.8 million persons had been entered in the list, the vast majority (1.7 million) in category III.

After the Second World War the *Deutsche Volksliste* had a toxic effect on living together in the People's Republic of Poland. Anyone whose name was in the list was suspected of collaboration; most had to seek rehabilitation in court or in front of a commission. They often managed to do so, especially if they had been classified as category III or IV.

Ethnic Germans in Upper Silesia and Poles who had been naturalized into the Nazi *Reich* through the *Deutsche Volksliste* comprised the two main groups of *Aussiedler* who came to West Germany from Poland, although no proper statistics were ever generated that might have shown who acquired their *Aussiedler* status by which means. The immigration of the *Aussiedler* took place in several waves. During a phase of liberalization after Stalin's death – during the Polish Thaw of 1955–1959 – 250,000 people emigrated. During a second phase, in the 1960s, another 150,000 persons emigrated. The *Aussiedler* of these first two waves had personally experienced German occupation. The third wave of the 1970s, during which 220,000 persons emigrated, was more "Polish" – most of these *Aussiedler* were Polish-speaking and Polonized, not least because of the long assimilation drive and the stigma attached to the so-called *folksdojcz* (Polish transliteration of *Volksdeutsch*) in Poland. Also new in this third wave was that *Aussiedler* became political bargaining chips: the politics of détente always involved political and financial concessions, as was the case in 1970 during the negotiation of the Warsaw Agreement as part of the Moscow and Warsaw Agreements or in 1975 in the question of special loans. The largest wave was that of the 1980s – between 1988 and 1990 alone, 520,000 *Aussiedler* from Poland came to Germany.

Numerically, Romania was the third-most-important region of origin for *Aussiedler*.[14] The collective term Romanian Germans in fact bundled together very diverse ethnic German groups. The largest among them were the Transylvanian Saxons and Banat Swabians. Bukovina, Bessarabia, and Dobrujan Germans had been resettled as ethnic Germans (*Volksdeutsche*) after 1939 as part of the Nazi "back into the Reich" policy, especially to the Warthegau around contemporary Polish Poznań (from where many Poles and Jews had been deported for the sake of "Germanization"; later they were also confined to ghettos and murdered). Insofar as these ethnic Germans returned to Romania after 1945, many of them were deported to the Soviet Union together with Transylvanian Saxons and Banat Swabians – 10 to 15 percent of them were killed during in these deportations or died as a result of forced labor. In 1949 the Romanian Germans got back their rights as citizens and some cultural autonomy. But time and again they were subjected to repressive measures, especially the intellectuals among them, as in the 1959 "German writers' trial" after the Hungarian Revolution of 1956. From the 1970s onward West Germany bought out Romanian Germans for several thousand marks per person, which Romania, economically ailing and short of hard currency under the dictator Nicolae Ceaușescu, badly needed. Thus every year about 10,000 Romanian Germans entered the Federal Republic as *Aussiedler*, among them in 1987 the writer and later Nobel Prize winner Herta Müller. After the 1989 Velvet Revolution and the opening of borders, this immigration peaked in 1990 with 111,000 *Aussiedler*.

Friedland

Irrespective of whether you entered West Germany at the height of the Cold War with a Lufthansa plane from Moscow or in the transition period between 1989 and 1992 with your own car via Ukraine or Poland, during these decades what followed was a stay at the Friedland transit camp, sometimes for a few days, sometimes for weeks. This camp was built by the British in 1945 near Göttingen in the border triangle between the British, American, and Soviet occupation zones, and a great variety of people passed through Friedland. It was an initial reception center (*Erstaufnahmestelle*) for Displaced Persons, expellees, and released POWs, for refugees from the Hungarian Revolution in 1956 and from Chile (after the military coup of 1973), Vietnam (after 1978), and the former Soviet Union, and for asylum seekers from Lebanon, Iraq, India, Eritrea, and Turkey. What it continually did across all these years was function as an initial reception center for *Aussiedler*, the first of whom arrived in 1950. Since 2000 it is Germany's only initial reception center for *Spätaussiedler*.[15]

The first thing that happened in Friedland was registration: personal data were recorded, there was a test to establish whether people were eligible for *Aussiedler* status and whether all of the accompanying family members could be accorded the same status as well. During the Cold War many *Aussiedler* were interrogated by the secret services of Britain, the United States, France, and West Germany, purportedly to prevent the infiltration of spies, but of course also to gather intelligence about the Soviet Bloc. Many *Aussiedler* to this day remember the interrogations by the Western services as being uncannily similar to those by the KGB before emigration. Even between 2000 and 2005, 4,639 *Aussiedler* were interrogated by the *Bundesnachrichtendienst* (the German secret service) in Friedland.[16] During all these years Friedland furthermore tested the immigrants' "belonging to the German people," and as part of that their "commitment to German *Volkstum*." A Friedland clerk described this ritual as a farce: "It's the same sad game every day: unending streams of applicants from Poland sit in front of us and pretend to be Germans. And we have to pretend that we believe them."[17]

After Friedland, *Aussiedler* are distributed across Germany according to an allocation method known as *Königsteiner Schlüssel*, which, among other things, strives to reunite families. The *Spätaussiedler* Erich Kludt, for instance, who immigrated in 1995 from Kazakhstan, had relatives in Baden-Württemberg and Hamburg. A social worker in Friedland recommended that he go to Hamburg, where the job market was better.[18] Once they had arrived at their destinations, the *Aussiedler* were first housed in *Aussiedler* shelters. At the height of the *Aussiedler* immigration, in the late 1980s to early 1990s, many were sheltered together with asylum seekers, for example in container ships in Hamburg harbor, or with other *Aussiedler* exclusively, for example in a repurposed gym or homeless shelter in Osnabrück and Berlin-Neukölln, respectively.[19] After that, they moved to their first apartment, mostly a social welfare apartment, which was often organized by relatives who had emigrated earlier. The first years were eased through integration assistance benefits, which in this form exist only for this group of immigrants: "transition benefit" (*Überbrückungshilfe*), health insurance, unemployment benefits, and a language course. In addition, years of labor in their country of origin count toward their German retirement benefits (Figure 6.2).

The journalist Emilia Smechowski, who arrived in 1988 as a 5-year-old from Poland, went back in 2015 at the pinnacle of the refugee crisis to the homeless shelter in Berlin-Neukölln where her family had been placed after emigrating. In one of the kitchens she started chatting with refugees

Figure 6.2 Volga German men wait in front of an office at a reception camp in Unna, 1992. Ullstein bild / Getty Images.

from Syria. "They are telling me in English about boats, human traffickers, panic, and screaming. [. . .] At some point, during a break, I say: 'I too lived here once.'" She immediately regretted saying this because, despite some commonalities, there were more differences, and the reason for that was German "bureaucracy which mixes the cards anew and deals them out. Our cards, those of *Aussiedler* in 1988, were excellent. We were treated in hospital when we got sick. We had German lessons until we found work. What do these people get? A trifling minority gets the right to asylum. Most will obtain a temporary stay permit. For years." Smechowski concludes: "We were premium refugees, aristocracy. The Syrians today are, if they are lucky, solid middle class. Serbs and Macedonians? They are so far down that they won't even be recognized as refugees. Our chances in Germany were always better than those of other refugees. Even though it is they who seek refuge from bombs, hunger, and disease. How fair is that?"[20]

We will return to the question of fairness; here we note that the status of being "premium refugees" applied to *Aussiedler* who came, like Smechowski, in 1988 or earlier. After 1992 the privileges of *Aussiedler* were continually scaled back. And yet the differences between *Aussiedler* and other migrants were huge. Why does an activist of the trade union Solidarność who fled after Polish military leaders imposed martial law in 1981 have disproportionately worse cards as an asylum seeker than a politically conformist Polish family who emigrated in that same year of 1981, but could prove that a great grandfather had appeared in the *Deutsche Volksliste*? Often the dividing line runs right through a single family. The Volga German electrical engineer Viktor Petri, born in 1950, immigrated in 1996 as an *Aussiedler*. "Already in the container village I could start a language course that the employment agency paid for," he remembers. "I had received the status conferred by Article 7 of the Federal Expellee Law and was thus entitled to integration assistance benefits. First I did a 6-month-long language course, then after a short break a 3-month specialized language course. After that I enrolled in the job integration program, the BIP course. There too language was at the center during the first months. Finally there was a 7-month internship."[21] In the end he landed a permanent job as an electrical engineer with a forklift truck company. The experience of his wife Natasha, an ethnic Russian, and their son was very different: "She, as a Russian, and our son, who as a minor had yet to receive his own passport with the entry 'German,' received a different – worse – legal status. As a result they got fewer integration assistance benefits. For my wife this was, and still is, dramatic."[22] Petri concludes: "We came as a family, as equals. Now we are in Germany, but inside the family we are very unequal Germans. There are many like Natasha because intermarriage is very common."[23] Indeed, the later people emigrated to Germany, the more commonly one of the spouses is not Volga German.

The Past and Divided Memory

Viktor Petri had actually never planned to emigrate. His family had migrated once before, from Siberian Krasnoyarsk to Moscow in 1969. In Moscow there were few Volga Germans, and as for discrimination, he can't remember any either in Krasnoyarsk or in Moscow. But there were prying questions; for instance, when someone inquired about his wife's unusual surname, she sometimes shook that person off by replying, "It's an Italian name."[24]

Petri worked in a prestigious job at a famous institute. Only when the Soviet Union collapsed did he seriously begin to consider emigration. His boss rented out institute space to private companies and kept the profits for himself. The institute paid salaries less and less frequently, mafia structures began spreading, and more and more colleagues went into private business or emigrated to the West. In addition there was hyperinflation and the attendant devaluation of all savings and general economic uncertainty. And there was the prospect that his son would have to serve in the Russian army – at that point, at the very latest, he would be reminded of his minority status, as Volga Germans, just like Jews, Armenians, and other ethnic minorities, to this very day are subjected to brutal hazing and harassment.

What tipped the scales for Petri, however, was the debate about the restoration of the Volga German ASSR. Yeltsin destroyed all hopes and actually added insult to injury by saying that the Volga Germans deserved at most a – contaminated – rocket testing ground in Kapustin Yar in the southern Russian steppe on the border with Kazakhstan. True, his ethnically Russian colleagues were embarrassed, but the insult irks Petri to this day: "I was interested in moral equality for the Germans. With Yeltsin our hopes faded. He was shameless enough to whip up ethnic hatred against us when it seemed opportune at rallies. I thought that was a very dangerous development. More acutely than in Soviet times did I feel unwanted, as a German, by political state power."[25]

Unlike Petri, most Volga Germans actually lived in the Soviet countryside. Often entire villages emigrated collectively, social pressure being another push factor. In Germany the former village-dwellers then again settled close to each other. Emma Neumann, born in 1936, grew up in Friedental near the city of Orenburg. "Nearly all of my fellow villagers," she says, "today live in the city of Kamen near Dortmund. In the early nineties twenty-five families left Friedental in one swoop. A neighbor, Alexander Rommel, had taken things into his hands and organized the emigration, because there were many older villagers who were illiterate. He filled in more than 100 applications so that everyone could emigrate."[26]

Typically, after a village emptied, Chechen, Armenian, and Kazakh migrants moved in from other parts of Russia (Chechnya) or former Soviet Republics like Armenia and Kazakhstan, all fleeing civil war or in search of better economic conditions – entirely new migration movements within the post-Soviet realm. As for Kazakhstan, the Volga Germans there in the early 1990s often sought refuge from the racial hatred of the Kazakhs, who had, after splitting from the Soviet Union, become aggressively nationalistic. Faced with this new Kazakh nationalism, not only the Volga Germans, but also Jews, Tatars, and ethnic Russians fled – after decades of peaceful cohabitation. The Kazakh case goes to show once more how fast things can change: in Soviet times they were one titular nation among several other nationalities in the Soviet Republic of Kazakhstan; after the end of the Soviet Union they became chauvinist oppressors of the members of these other nationalities, among them ethnic Russians; and today many Kazakhs live as labor migrants in Russia while Kazakhstan presents itself as a multiethnic "Soviet Union in miniature."

In the 1970s the motivation for emigration among the *Aussiedler* was very different. At that time one had to have strong reasons to want to emigrate. After applying for emigration "on the German ticket" and usually being turned down, fierce exclusion and discrimination followed – from job loss, refusal of study at university for one's children, and social ostracism by colleagues and neighbors to prison and labor camp. The most powerful motivation that might make one able to face this kind of sanctioning was the memory of the experience of violence during Stalin's rule, for which the state under Khrushchev later at best half-heartedly attempted to make amends. In addition to that, there was the inability to speak publicly about this collective historical experience – because of the taboo and silencing surrounding it.

One of the most traumatic experiences for the Volga Germans during Stalin's rule was the chaotic cloak-and-dagger deportation after the invasion by the Wehrmacht. Here is the account of an *Aussiedler* born in 1916, which was recorded on tape in West Germany in the 1970s: "When the Germans drew closer, we were deported together with almost all other families in the village. That happened within just a few hours. We were allowed to take nothing other than what we were wearing. Trucks brought us to the nearest railway station 45 kilometers away, and from there we were taken by train to the sea. On the shore they had rounded up large crowds of people, then they penned us up in the boats that were waiting there. Those were boats otherwise used to transport cattle and pigs, but they were not made for people. It's hard to imagine what they looked like inside and how they stank!"[27] The boats floated on the Caspian Sea for 2 months, the passengers went hungry, diseases spread, "and ever more people died, especially children. One after another they starved to death, and the corpses were simply thrown into the sea. They sank my 4-year-old boy in the water, too. The other, the 7-year-old, had to watch this, and so he clung to my skirt and said: 'Dear mother, don't let them throw me into the water as well.'" But this boy too starved to death. When the Volga German men tried to mutiny, the Russian overseers sank four boats – the Volga Germans had to watch how "people drowned helplessly, after that nobody dared speak out against them."[28]

Once the deportees had finally arrived in the designated western Siberian or Kazakh places of exile, a hostile local population often waited for them. One *Aussiedler*, born in 1915, remembers: "Now they're dropping us off at a school in the Shulyi collective farm. A lot of people are standing around, with whom we're supposed to find accommodation, mostly female peasant farmers who look at us as though we'd come straight from hell. They have heard it many times: the Germans are devils. They check to see whether we really have horns and wonder that we look like them, that we behave like people and speak to them politely."[29]

Sophie Wagner, who was born in 1953 and in Kazakhstan became a German teacher in the village of Rosovka, recalls the leaden silence that surrounded the second key collective event, the deportation of men for forced labor: "February 6, 1942, was a very sad day. The majority of men from our village were forced into the Trud Army [labor army] – 106 men in a single day. My father too had to go to the camp. The Trud Army was certainly the worst thing he ever experienced. Like most of his generation, he never talked about it. Even decades later, when we wanted to record this history for the museum, the older people at first remained silent. They were still scared – scared that we, their children, might get into trouble if we reported the truth."[30]

Volga German activists insisted on speaking out about this experience of deportation and forced labor. They often did so in a religious framework, which became more important again after decades of imposed atheism. The first Christian underground groups formed in the 1950s. They held secret meetings, had a samizdat press, and were of course infiltrated and surveilled by the KGB. During Khrushchev's antireligious campaign (1958–1964) German groups of Baptists, Mennonites, Jehova's Witnesses, and Catholics were uncovered, and their members were arrested and sent to prison, punitive psychiatric institutions, or labor camps.

In the 1970s the Volga German nonconformists started learning and copying from forms of resistance pioneered by other dissidents, especially Jewish Zionists. In April 1972, thirty activists started a sit-in strike at Moscow's Main Telegraph Office and demanded the right to emigrate. A year later a delegation handed the Supreme Soviet an appeal that was also addressed to the General Secretary of the United Nations: 7,000 families, that is 35,000 persons, had signed the appeal. In September 1973 nearly 1,000 police officers and soldiers had to break up a gathering of Volga Germans in Kazakh Karaganda who were demanding the right to emigrate. And in March 1980 Volga German dissidents unrolled banners with demands like "Free emigration for Germans to the Federal Republic of Germany!" on Red Square in Moscow – before they were dragged off by KGB agents minutes later. Human rights activists like Andrei Sakharov also adopted the "Volga German cause" and demanded that those Volga Germans who wished to do so should be allowed to emigrate, and that linguistic and cultural autonomy and their Volga German ASSR should be restored to those who wished to stay.[31]

Memory of Stalinist violence was one thing. There were also memories of German occupation, though these were positive only in exceptional cases. Sophie Wagner's mother was one such case. She had grown up in the village of Hoffental in Ukraine – here is her daughter's account: "On August 22, 1941, the Wehrmacht conquered the village. For my mother the Germans were liberators. The peasants were allowed to take their livestock back home and to run their own farms. [...] The village really came alive again. My mother never tired of talking about the Hitler Youth, about the League of German Girls (BDM), about the summer camps, celebrations, and parties. In spring 1942 they selected in each village the best boys and girls to be deployed as future BDM and Hitler Youth leaders in the occupied territories. My aunt Sophie was one of them. She and her entire family were very proud of this distinction, and for Sophie dreams became reality. As one of 'the elect' she and her group went first to Kyiv, later to Königsberg and Berlin. She felt honored, esteemed, and accepted like never before in her life. The BDM even made possible the first vacation of her life. She was allowed to go to Austria for recreation."[32] So there were also concrete and real advantages for Nazi collaborators. "Later she and my mother dreamed a lot about this 'good time.'"[33]

In fall 1943 the ethnic Germans from Hoffental were moved to the Warthegau as *Volksdeutsche*; the mother became a train conductor with the Deutsche Reichsbahn and in January 1945 escaped the Red Army from Posen (now Polish Poznań) to Leipzig, where Soviet soldiers caught up with her after all. "My mother had been warned about the Russians. 'Escape as fast as you can, go into hiding,' she was told. She didn't hide. She wanted to reunite with her family, with her mother, who, she knew, was working for a farmer in Sigrotsbruch near Neustadt-Dosse in Brandenburg. Had she known what the future held in store, she surely would have done anything within her power to flee to the West. It never occurred to her that she might be deported from Germany as a German. That was a mistake. Because when the Russians moved in, harassment started all over again for her. She was deported to Siberia and had to work in a paper factory there. In 1947 she risked escape and with a lot of luck made it to Lugansk [Ukrainian Luhansk] via Pavlodar."[34] Wagner continues: "When I was about 9 years old we watched a film in school about the atrocities of the Germans in Ukraine. I was spellbound and couldn't believe what I was watching. My mother had never mentioned any atrocities. 'My mother doesn't lie,' I thought. But I couldn't make out at the time what was true and what wasn't."[35]

One social science study calls this kind of family memory "divided." The study points to the fact that membership in Nazi organizations, including the SS, paradoxically was valorized positively when applying for *Aussiedler* status – and quotes in this context Karl-Markus Gauß, who wrote "in a slightly exaggerated manner, but factually correctly"[36]: "A father who had learned and practiced the craft of murder in the SS or in one of the 'self-protection [*Selbstschutz*] units' set up by the SS was always a trump card that could be played with the authorities of the democratic Federal Republic in order to credibly prove one's German heritage."[37]

The Nazi past was an equally ambivalent topic among the *Aussiedler* in Poland. On the one hand, an ancestor with an entry in the *Deutsche Volksliste* was a ticket to the Golden West. On the other hand, that entry in the *Deutsche Volksliste* was associated with shame. Decades of school lessons and war movies had produced indelible images: "Every Polish child could imitate him, the prototype of an SS man, who was shown on state television on a daily basis. Firrrrrrre!"[38] There was even something like a secret code with which one could communicate whether one had any part in this Nazi past: if you had a suspicion that somebody else also . . ., you warily asked: "Do you too have a German shepherd dog in your cellar?"[39]

Other pasts refused to go away, too. Among Romanian German intellectual *Aussiedler* in West Germany a fight broke out about the question who had collaborated with the infamous Romanian secret service, the Securitate. The writer Herta Müller, a Banat Swabian born in 1953 – her father had been in the Waffen-SS, her mother was deported to Ukraine for forced labor after the Second World War – in 1979 refused to inform for the Securitate and as a consequence lost her job. Yet the Securitate spread a rumor among colleagues that she had signed. When Müller emigrated to Germany in 1987, the Securitate used the same tactic – successfully, for both the West German secret service (the BND) and the domestic *Verfassungsschutz* (the Federal Office for the Protection of the Constitution) followed these hints and interrogated her for days. She continued to receive threats from the Securitate in Germany.[40] Her former husband, the Romanian German writer Richard Wagner, in 2009, when Müller received the Nobel Prize and was at the center of attention, started a public debate about the involvement with the Securitate of other writer colleagues, especially Oskar Pastior, and about the infiltration of the Territorial Association of Banat Swabians by the Securitate.

Invisible in the Federal Republic?

Romanian German intellectuals had a certain visibility, but Polish *Aussiedler* have aptly been dubbed "the invisible ones," and the same could be said of the Volga Germans. In relation to their large absolute number and their high percentage among migrants from the late 1980s onward, the *Aussiedler* have indeed remained invisible. How many would know, for instance, that Russian and Polish are, depending on which statistics one believes, respectively the second and fourth most commonly spoken languages in Germany?[41] To be sure, in almost every city there is a "little Moscow," a "Russian ghetto," where *Aussiedler* live – Lahr in the Black Forest for a while was notorious in the media. To be sure, there is an infrastructure of stores, clubs, and home care services for senior citizens, and large supermarkets nowadays often have an "ethnic" corner, a few meters of shelf space with Russian cranberry juice, Polish *bigos* and *ptasie mleczko* alongside boxes of Turkish rice pilaf. To be sure, there is an infrastructure of social work that lives off the *Aussiedler* – and periodically the media have carried sensationalist reports about the drug biographies of Volga German teenagers ("from vodka straight to heroin") or about Volga German networks in German prisons.[42] To be sure, some celebrities are known to have *Aussiedler* background: pop star Helene Fischer from Russia, soccer players Lukas Podolski and Miroslav Klose from Upper Silesia.

And yet they do remain invisible. Among members of the German chattering classes the *Aussiedler* are considered uncool. German intellectuals are largely postnational and view as archaic the politics of letting them immigrate so easily and giving them citizenship before others. Plus, they are seen as being a bit like embarrassing redneck relatives, of whom one is slightly ashamed. If anything, the German chattering classes aspire to be Jewish – we turn to the Jewish *Kontingentflüchtlinge* and philosemitism in the next chapter.

Only since 2016 and the Lisa scandal have the Volga Germans been at the focus of media attention. The situation is similar to that with Russia more generally. There is hardly any positive attention paid to them, rather it's almost always negative. Volga Germans are now seen as tending toward right-wing extremism and authoritarian-leaning. News about the "GDR-ization" (*Ossifizierung*, to coin Michael Wolffsohn's term) of the German army, the Bundeswehr, reinforces this impression.[43] People then quickly resort to making facile connections between authoritarian conditions in the Soviet Union and archaic, patriarchal family structures.

But all of that is oversimplified stereotyping – and unfair. Many Volga Germans lived a lot more multiculturally in Central Asia or Russia than is known among the German public. Erich Kludt, born in 1918, reminisces: "I used to work with Russians, Jews, Tatars, Kazakhs, and other nationalities and felt that we were equal."[44] Consider also Emma Neumann, born 1936: "Jews and Chechens lived there, there were Kazakhs,

Russians, and we Germans. But at the time I paid hardly any attention to a person's nationality. To me, everyone was equal."[45] Maria Kessler, born in 1976 and until emigration at the age of 14 a student at a Soviet–Bulgarian, Comecon-supported school near Vorkuta, recounts: "95 percent of the students were Bulgarian. [...] It was super nice with the Bulgarians. [...] There was a creative and friendly atmosphere in our little multicultural world."[46] It would not be an exaggeration to say that most Volga Germans had more interaction with Asians and Jews than most West Germans. Why not remember this positive experience of the Soviet multinational empire? Why not generalize and take as a warning above all for the Federal Republic the later renationalization, the move toward homogeneity, the former Soviet Republics' difficulty in dealing with difference?

And why not celebrate the nonconformism of the Volga German dissidents and the connection to other dissident movements like the universalist human rights activists or Jewish Zionists – in the media, in schools, at events, etc.? Israel honors as heroic the defiance of the human rights activist and refusenik Natan Sharansky, who was imprisoned under high-security conditions from 1977 onward for nine years and was released only in 1986 under Gorbachev in a spy exchange on the Glienicke Bridge. And Germany also honors the resistance against Hitler. The symbolic effect that the Volga German dissidents created cannot be underestimated. One *Spätaussiedler*, born in 1916, after years of humiliating bureaucratic struggling finally got her permission to emigrate – "but only after a woman, I think her name was Oldenburger, had tied herself to a chain in Moscow and in that way won her right to emigrate. Like many other Germans who had been waiting a long time for their passports, we also profited from that."[47]

Conclusion

When Russian foreign minister Lavrov in January 2016 at the height of the Lisa scandal spoke of "our Lisa," some were appalled by this linguistic appropriation of a German citizen by a foreign power. Here is what hardly anyone knows: in addition to German citizenship, Lisa also had Russian citizenship, and to that extent Lavrov was correct.[48] We have here one of the greatest contradictions of the *Ausländer* discourse in Germany: those people who are defined "most German" via culture, language, and "blood" and fast-tracked for citizenship in the most comfortable way, the *Aussiedler*, can retain citizenship of their country of origin. And Germany quietly accepts this. (In some cases, as in that of Kazakhstan since October 2004, the country of origin itself prohibits dual citizenship and forces ethnic Germans to decide between the two passports.)

It is a serious paradox indeed. Since 2000 it has been possible for the descendants of labor migrants from Turkey who have been living in Germany for three generations to be naturalized, but they must decide between Turkish and German citizenship before they reach the age of 23. At the same time there is an extremely charged, politically speaking, debate about Turkish-German citizenship that revolves around issues like loyalty, Islam, belonging, and patriotism, in which, to conservatives and right-wingers, dual passports seem to embody pure evil – consider the Mesut Özil debate of 2018, when Özil posed for a photograph with Turkish President Recep Erdoğan, prompting questions about his loyalty to Germany and eventually leading to Özil resigning from the German national soccer team. On the other hand, there are hundreds of thousands of Germans of Polish-Upper Silesian, Russian, or other descent who have dual citizenship.[49] They do so according to agreements that go back to the times of the Iron Curtain, which for this group of people wasn't so iron after all: it was an open secret for the German authorities that *Aussiedler*, when going on vacation to Gdańsk or Poznań, showed their old passport of the People's Republic when entering Poland and their German passport when returning to West Germany. Increasing numbers of Volga Germans are using the same privilege and alternate working temporarily or for longer in Germany with working in Russia. If during the Cold War every *Aussiedler* migration meant emigrating forever, *Aussiedler* today are increasingly "transnational."[50]

In some way that defuses the explosiveness of the question of belonging – just consider the book title *Zuhause fremd – Russlanddeutsche zwischen Russland und Deutschland* (*Foreign at Home: Volga Germans between Russia and Germany*). The *Aussiedler* are no longer *between* two stools, but sitting on two stools at the same time.[51]

However, that is true for only a part of the *Aussiedler*. They may legally be Germans and have privileges, but on an emotional-symbolic level the majority of Germans do not accept them as their own. What remains is a feeling of rejection: for many it is a stinging pain that never subsides. This lack of acceptance creates a vacuum insofar as national belonging is concerned.

For a while now the Russian state has been filling this vacuum, a state whose self-definition is increasingly ethnonational, a reversal from Soviet times and the first post-Soviet decade under Yeltsin. Part of this is the concept of a "Russian World." Putin launched it in 2006. He made an appearance at a preparatory meeting for the "Year of the Russian Language" (2007) and said: "the Russian World can and should unite all those for whom the Russian language and culture are dear, whether they live in Russia or beyond its borders. Use this term, 'Russian World,' more often."[52] The concept presupposes a community of people with felt attachments to Russia: they speak Russian, feel close to Russian culture, and tend to be Orthodox by denomination. The strength of this version of diaspora nationalism lies in its vagueness. It is primarily a cultural–linguistic–religious definition.

The Russian World is underpinned by a TV channel, a radio station, and *Russkiy Mir*, that is, "Russian World," institutes across the globe. Via social media and satellite TV the concept also reaches Volga Germans in Germany – and is all the more successful because Germany does not compete with it in any way whatsoever. Germany offers no possibilities for emotional-symbolic attachment, on the contrary. The majority population excludes Volga Germans; they continue to be seen as "Russians," not as Germans. No wonder, then, that Putinite Russia's overtures fall on receptive ears.

By the way, the same applies to the nationalist propaganda of Erdoğan and the Justice and Development Party (AKP): it too falls on receptive ears, among Germans of Turkish descent. And in both cases, that of Russia and of Turkey, the proposed ethnonational definitions of nation are new constructs: the Soviet Union itself was defined supra-ethnically, and under Yeltsin too Russia with its supra-ethnic *rossiiskii* (rather than ethnic *russkii*) banked on a supra-ethnic, civic identity. The secular concept of Turkishness that prevailed before Erdoğan was also not defined ethnically. It must be said that German arrogance would be completely out of place here: essentially, Russia has arrived at precisely the kind of German ethnonational concept of nation that hollowed out the Soviet Union from the inside, whereby Volga Germans and Jews followed the siren calls of the two most important ethnic/religious/national "homelands," emigrating to Germany and Israel.

There is only one path through which Volga Germans can some day feel like Germans and identify with the country: the German population must stop ostracizing them as "Russians" and the Federal Republic as a state must offer emotional-symbolic opportunities for attachment. A part of this should be attractive media formats in Russian: so attractive that they will win out against Putin's propaganda.

It's also true that not all *Aussiedler* are hostile toward refugees as the events surrounding the scandal of "vanished" Lisa might suggest – here too we should be wary of oversimplifying. Smechowski, for instance, writes: "We didn't cross the Mediterranean in a rubber dinghy. We were not at the mercy of human traffickers, we were not at risk of drowning or dying of thirst, of being tortured or raped. In 1988, from

Wejherowo to West Berlin, we traveled on Polish cross-country roads. True, with a car we had at some point inherited from my grandparents and with which we were relieved to make it to the border at all. But by car. And yet, the 65 million people worldwide who are currently refugees, from Syria, Afghanistan, Sudan and South Sudan, Iraq, the Democratic Republic of the Congo: they affect me. I know how inappropriate and outright ridiculous this is, yet I cannot but read their stories against the backdrop of our own escape."[53]

7 Jewish *Germaniya*

In 2018 the German TV channel RTL launches a new series, *Sankt Maik* (*Saint Maik*). Maik Schäfer is a small-time criminal who puts on a deceased priest's robe to escape the police in one of his con games. Good-looking Maik ends up as the new priest in a Catholic parish – where he gets involved with the choir leader, who actually happens to be a police officer and from all of which more complications and mix-ups happen.

Maik is played by Daniel Donskoy. Donskoy is 1.90 meters tall, red-haired, has freckles, and a broad smile from ear to ear. The viewing figures are fantastic, fans post video clips with Sankt Maik with a naked torso on YouTube, Donskoy's Instagram followers increase by the day, Google suggests "Daniel Donskoy girlfriend" when you start entering his name.

Donskoy was born in Moscow in 1990. In that year his parents emigrated as Jewish quota refugees to Berlin, where Donskoy grew up in Marzahn. His parents separated. In 2002 Donskoy moved to Tel Aviv with his mother and stepfather, where he was discovered at age 16 and started modeling. In 2008 he finished high school, returned to Berlin – as a German citizen he was exempt from Israeli military service – and entered university, which he soon quit in favor of the stage: "I can't help it, I'm a stage tiger," he says about himself.[1] Already in 2008 he had made it to the preliminary round of *Kokhav Nolad*, the Israeli version of the *American Idol* franchise. He then studied acting and singing in New York and London, from where he commuted to the shooting of *Saint Maik*.

Berlin-Marzahn is a hotspot for Volga Germans who remain below the radar of the media, the exception being the Lisa scandal in January 2016. Unlike the Volga Germans, the second group of immigrants from the former Soviet Union, the Jewish quota refugees, is very visible in culture and the media. It is enough to recall some names who have made a splash in recent years, for example the writers Alina Bronsky, Lena Gorelik, Olga Grjasnowa, Kat Kaufmann, Lana Lux, and Sasha Marianna Salzmann. Or in theater and television: Marina Frenk, Alisa Levin, Palina Rojinski, and Donskoy. Or in classical music: Igor Levit, Olga Scheps, Anatol Ugorski, and Jascha Nemtsov. This visibility in culture and the media stems from the fact that they are disproportionately from educated, urban intelligentsia families. They were well set up to make it as a writer, pianist, or violinist, or also as a computer programmer and dentist. But of course German history also plays a role: in 1989 no one in their right mind would have dared to imagine that after the Holocaust Germany might again become a destination for Jewish immigration, let alone the country with the world's fastest-growing Jewish community. That this has nonetheless happened is what generated media interest – internationally.[2]

Since 1989, 230,000 Jewish quota refugees have immigrated. Most of them are secular and have no interest in religion, but some are registered in the Jewish communities with their roughly 100,000 members.[3] These communities and Jewish life in Germany more generally have, however, changed massively.

Quota Refugees

The beginnings of this Jewish immigration go back to Gorbachev's Perestroika. In the late 1980s the Soviet Union loosened its travel restrictions, which increased mobility inside the Soviet Bloc. It became quite easy to obtain tourist visas and travel, for instance, by car from Leningrad – renamed St. Petersburg in 1991 – via the Baltic states, Belarus, and Poland to the GDR.

When the GDR dissidents began meeting at round tables after the opening of the wall, there was one such table specifically devoted to the subject of the Jews and Israel. The GDR had never established diplomatic relations with Israel, which was typical of the pro-Palestinian states of the Soviet Bloc. The dissidents took this as a point of departure for moral and political discussions about, for example, the GDR's self-description as an antifascist country that supposedly had nothing to do with Nazism. Meanwhile the Jewish Cultural Association, an organization of, among others, secular Jews that had been founded in January 1990, heard rumors of impending pogroms against Soviet Jews. (Note that in 1989 in the entire GDR a mere 500 Jews were registered in synagogue congregations.) There had also been the first cases of Soviet Jews who were in the GDR on tourist visas and had not returned to the USSR for fear of antisemitism. At the Jewish Cultural Association's behest a motion was filed at the round table: "We request that the GDR government make it possible, irrespective of current regulations, for those who feel discriminated against and persecuted in the Soviet Union as Jews to stay here."[4]

The GDR's first free elections took place on March 18, 1990. The Volkskammer, the legislature, convened on April 12 and passed a resolution proposed by various parliamentary fractions that originated from discussions at the round table: "The first freely elected parliament of the GDR on behalf of the people of this country admits its joint responsibility for the humiliation, expulsion, and murder of Jewish women, men, and children. We feel sad and ashamed, and acknowledge this burden of German history. We ask the Jews of the whole world for forgiveness. We ask the people of Israel to forgive us for the hypocrisy and hostility of East German policies toward Israel and also for the persecution and degrading treatment of Jewish citizens in our country after 1945."[5] The last sentence was a reference to the antisemitic purge in the communist party (SED) of 1952–1953, a time when Eastern European communist parties excluded, imprisoned, and sometimes executed Jewish members. Finally: "We support granting persecuted Jews asylum in the GDR."[6]

After the passing of this resolution, 650 Soviet Jews came on tourist visas. In the meantime representatives of West Germany, the Central Council of Jews in Germany, the State of Israel, and the Soviet Union became involved in the discussion. On July 11, 1990, the GDR Council of Ministers resolved: "The government of the German Democratic Republic grants, initially for limited numbers, foreign Jewish citizens who are threatened with persecution or discrimination the right to stay on humanitarian grounds."[7] This declaration was a diplomatic walk on eggshells. It tried to neither embarrass the still fairly powerful big brother Soviet Union nor infringe upon the self-definition of the State of Israel, with which the GDR wanted to establish diplomatic relations (there can be no "asylum" for Jews, since for all the Jews in the world there is only one homeland: Israel). Three months later the GDR collapsed, diplomatic relations with Israel were never established, and a year and a half later the Soviet Union dissolved.

Between the resolution of July 11 and the end of the GDR on October 3 another 2,000 Soviet Jews immigrated. Now the ball was in the court of unified Germany. The behind-the-scenes negotiations between the Federal Republic, the president of the Central Council of Jews in Germany, Heinz Galinski, the State of Israel, and probably also the Soviet Union have yet to be fully reconstructed. It is also contested whether it was Chancellor Kohl or Galinski who insisted on going beyond the halakhic definition of Jewishness and accepting people who had only one Jewish grandparent.[8] On the other hand, we do know that Israel wanted to limit Jewish emigration to Germany – for Zionist reasons and because of the Holocaust. In 1990 Germany still seemed a very unlikely place to live happily and safely as a Jew. At the same time there was a consensus in the German media, from leftist newspapers to the conservative Axel Springer outlets, that if Jews – after what had happened –

knocked on Germany's door, this was an unbelievable gift, and it would be a shame not to accept it. Even though many details of the negotiations remain unclear, their result is known. The conference of interior ministers decided to grant Jews who were seeking asylum the legal status of quota refugees.

This legal status had been created in 1980 for the Vietnamese Boat People, refugees from communist Vietnam, whom international rescue ships like the *Cap Anamur* of German human rights activist Rupert Neudeck picked up from their boats in the South China Sea.[9] This status derives from to the Geneva Convention, not the basic right to asylum in Article 16 of the German Constitution. Compared with an asylum seeker, the status of quota refugee has the advantage that persecution in the country of origin is presupposed rather than subject to examination. So there is no asylum case as such, no hearing, and additionally all quota refugees are enrolled on a language course paid for by the state and receive a work permit. However, quota refugees too, like other refugees and *Aussiedler*, are distributed among the federal states according to the *Königsteiner Schlüssel* allocation method. So their mobility is restricted and they cannot, for instance, move to Berlin if they have been sent to Saxony-Anhalt. Since 1980 the federal government can implement quotas in the context of humanitarian actions following refugee movements. Germany most recently made use of this option in 2013 and 2014 for 20,000 refugees from Syria, who thus ended up getting a more comfortable legal status than other refugees from the civil war-ravaged country.

After the USSR dissolved in late 1991, it became even easier to emigrate because the new, democratic Russia guaranteed full freedom of movement. Germany became increasingly attractive as a destination. In 2002 for the first time more Jews from the ex-USSR emigrated to Germany than to Israel or the United States: 19,262 went to the Federal Republic, 18,878 to Israel, fewer than 10,000 to the United States.[10] The immigration wave of Jewish quota refugees came to a halt only in 2005, when a new immigration law came into force that raised the bar: ever since then, those interested in immigrating must furnish proof that a Jewish community is prepared to take them in and that they "can permanently provide for themselves in the Federal Republic of Germany." Quota refugees also have to pass a language test at a certain level.[11] Since then Jewish immigration has become a trickle.

The ageing West German Jewish communities, with their mere 30,000 members in 1990, were in danger of disappearing sooner or later. Naturally, they placed great hopes in the Soviet Jews. But when they celebrated the first Passover Seders and other High Holidays, they were disappointed: some of the new arrivals took out Ukrainian *salo*, cured pork fat, wrapped in greasy parchment paper – needless to say, this was not compatible with Jewish dietary laws. Instead of Jewish songs, or at least the Hebrew folk song *Hava Nagila*, they sang, accompanied by accordion or guitar, Russian romances or the songs of the underground bards of the 1960s. In short, they didn't have the faintest idea about Jewish traditions and rituals. The 74 years of Soviet atheism had thoroughly expunged religion from them.

West German Jews had themselves originally come from the east. When Hitler came to power in 1933, there were only half a million Jews in Germany. Many of them fled Germany, some were exiled – in 1939 roughly 250,000 Jews were left in the German Reich. The vast majority of these, about 200,000, were murdered between 1941 and 1945. After the war only very few of the Jewish refugees returned to Germany. Instead, East European Jewish DPs, mostly from Poland, remained stuck, as it were, in the Federal Republic. Take Marek Lieberberg, who was born in 1946 as the son of Polish Holocaust survivors stranded in the Zeilsheim DP camp. In 1970 he founded the agency Mama Concerts and that same year brought The Who to the city of Münster. His later company, Marek Lieberberg Konzertagentur (MLK), organized Rock am Ring and brought Sting, Guns N' Roses, and many other performing musicians to concerts in Germany and later also in Israel. As a reaction to Mölln, Hoyerswerda, and Rostock-Lichtenhagen, in December 1992 he organized "Heute die! Morgen du!" ("Today They! Tomorrow You!"), a concert against right-wing extremist violence with an audience of 150,000 at the Frankfurt Messehalle.

What is more, and this is not widely known, two decades earlier Soviet Jews had once before immigrated to Germany, more precisely to Berlin. In the 1970s Galinski, then chairman of West Berlin's Jewish community, had arranged through a special agreement with Israel that a small portion of the Jews emigrating via Vienna to Israel (or the United States) would be offered the option of going to Berlin. (Because of the non-existence of diplomatic relations between the USSR and Israel, there were no direct flights, therefore Soviet Jews emigrated via Vienna or Rome.) In this way 3,000 Soviet Jews ended up in West Berlin during the East–West détente between 1973 and 1980.[12]

A snapshot of Jewish life in the Federal Republic before 1989 would have looked roughly as follows: people were sitting on slightly less packed suitcases than 10 years earlier, yet every elementary school, home for the elderly, and synagogue had to be protected by the police. Any Jewish person in the public limelight got anonymous hate mail from old Nazis and neo-Nazis. Most of the Jews in communities were orthodox in terms of religious ritual, men and women sat separately during services. The orthodox ritual applied to everyone, there were unified communities. Yet Reform Judaism with its combined service for both sexes and organ music had emerged in Germany in the 1920s; today it constitutes one of the three branches of American Judaism (Reform, Conservative, Orthodox). Broadly speaking, in 1989 there were few Jews in Germany, the communities were very small, and the Jewish marriage agency Simantov was essential for German Jewry's survival. Most of them spent the summer in Israel, but there as elsewhere in the world they had to justify why they were living in Germany. In public discourse there were a few important, brave voices who fought antisemitism as much as philosemitism with the power of the word: the real-estate agent Ignatz Bubis, Central Council president from 1992 until 1999, the literary critic Marcel Reich-Ranicki, the journalists Henryk M. Broder and Michel Friedman, the historian Michael Wolffsohn, and the writer Maxim Biller. They all constantly had to balance when they wanted to speak just for themselves and when they wanted to speak for "the Jews" *tout court*.

Who and What Is Jewish?

Vladimir Kaminer, who came to East Berlin in 1990, was clearly Jewish since both of his parents were Jewish. Jewish religious laws, the Halakha, define as Jews those whose mothers are Jewish and those who have converted to Judaism. Conversion is an elaborate process because Judaism, unlike Christianity or Islam, does not proselytize. When the interior ministers of the federal states discussed in fall 1990 who should qualify as a quota refugee, the "who is a Jew?" question came up – it is also highly contested in Israel ever since its foundation: should persons who have only a male Jewish parent be recognized? The Central Council of Jews in Germany rallied for a generous definition. The German state agreed and brought Nazism into the equation, arguing that, since the Germans adopted a capacious definition of who was Jewish (in the 1935 Nazi Nuremberg Laws), they should not now, when helping Jews who were being persecuted yet again was at stake, create the impression that they wanted to keep the group of potential immigrants small. This is how the political will to have a generous rule came about, the concrete result being that one Jewish grandparent was sufficient for immigration to Germany. The next question then became: how could a person from Astrakhan or Vladivostok prove to the German Consulates or the German Embassy in Russia and other USSR successor states that at least one of their grandparents is Jewish?

Just like "German" in the case of the Volga Germans, "Georgian" with Georgians, or "Russian" with ethnic Russians, "Jewish" was recorded as a "nationality" (*natsional'nost'*) in Soviet domestic passports and other documents. Equally, as for the Volga Germans (the Volga German ASSR until 1941), Georgians (the Georgian Socialist Soviet Republic), or ethnic Russians (the Russian Socialist Federative Soviet Republic), there was also for the Jewish nationality an ethnoterritory – the Autonomous Jewish Republic of Birobidzhan in the Far East on the Mongolian border. True, that was largely pro forma, very few Jews actually lived there. Jewish Soviet citizens mostly lived in the cities of the fifteen Soviet Republics.

After the October Revolution of 1917 they migrated there. The tsarist empire had been a "prison of the peoples," and it had limited the mobility of Jews to the Pale of Settlement, an area that consisted of parts of contemporary Ukraine, Russia, Belarus, Poland, Moldova, Lithuania, and Latvia. As soon as it became possible, many Jews migrated from the sthetls, the poor villages, to the cities: to them the Soviet Union meant modernity, Bolshevism meant emancipation. They were spectacularly successful at modernity, many converted wholesale to Marxism and tried shedding anything Jewish, especially religion, once and for all. Many early Bolsheviks – Leon Trotsky, Yakov Sverdlov, and Lazar Kaganovich – and many Soviet celebrities in the arts and sciences were Jewish: the poet Osip Mandelstam, the violinist David Oistrakh, the gymnast Maria Gorokhovskaya, who won seven medals at the 1952 Olympic Games in Helsinki, more than any other woman before or after her in a single Olympics, the World Chess Champion Mikhail Botvinnik, and the poet Joseph Brodsky, who won the Nobel Prize in literature in 1987.

Yet time and again the Soviet Union descended into antisemitism, especially after the foundation of the State of Israel in 1948. Stalin's fight against "rootless cosmopolitanism" in 1948 or against the alleged "Doctors' Plot" in 1952 cost a lot of Jews their jobs and their freedom – hundreds were imprisoned. Later there was less violence, but systemic, institutionalized antisemitism continued: there were strict, unofficial acceptance quotas at universities (no more than a certain percentage of those admitted could be Jewish, even though, judging by their levels of qualification, many more students in a given year should have been Jewish), and many Jews were not allowed to join the Communist Party. And there was always plenty of antisemitism in everyday life. By the late 1960s it would have been unthinkable for a Jew to join the Politburo, as Kaganovich had in the 1930s. In this situation an underground movement of those who wanted to emigrate to Israel formed, consisting of Zionists, who were called refuseniks because their applications for emigration to Israel had been refused. They were not allowed to work and were subjected to numerous other forms of harassment while waiting for their emigration permits for years – much like the Volga German activists.

When Gorbachev came to power in 1985 and introduced elements of a market economy, Jewishness became an opportunity, but also a renewed liability. It was an opportunity because it became possible to emigrate to the "golden West" – the joke regarding marriages of convenience between Jews and non-Jews was that Jews had become the fastest means of transportation from Moscow to New York, but it applied for emigration to Haifa or Berlin as well. Many oligarchs were and are Jewish: Roman Abramovich, Piotr Aven, Boris Berezovsky, German Khan, Mikhail Fridman, Yuri Milner, Viktor Vekselberg. They no longer had to hide their Jewishness; the oligarch Vladimir Gusinsky, for example, was President of the Russian Jewish Congress from 1996 until 2001. On the other hand, a new liability was that antisemites could now act unchecked and openly threaten Jews. The facade of fraternity of peoples (*druzhba narodov*) had collapsed, and after the bankruptcy of Communist ideology many shifted to Russian nationalism, with Jews and people from the Caucasus becoming "the Other" incarnate. With this, nationalists took up old antisemitic traditions of the tsarist empire. Rumors about pogroms started circulating in 1988, "in the first months of 1990 such rumors reached a peak."[13]

Born in the USSR, Life in *Germaniya*

For the family of 8-year-old Dmitrij Kapitelman, emigrating to Germany, not Israel, was a last-minute decision. The visas for Israel were ready and the suitcases had been packed – when an immigration permit for Germany also arrived. "You would have always been a second-class Jew here," answers his father, 20 years later during their first trip to Israel, when his son asks him why they chose Germany. Kapitelman's father is Jewish, but his mother is not, therefore, according to the Halakha, their son Dmitrij is not Jewish.[14]

Also the 20-year-old Dmitrij Belkin, a history student, ultimately decided in favor of Germany. In early 1992 he had tried the embassies of the United States, Canada, and Australia in Moscow, but everywhere the hurdles would have been too high for him. In the United States one needed close relatives there to immigrate as a Jew. And Israel wasn't ideal because he, like Kapitelman, was paternally Jewish (his father at the time had no intention of emigrating). In the German Embassy in Moscow it was explained to him, as he recounted, that "Hitler also persecuted paternal Jews (and I am one), therefore the country would accept this group of people."[15]

"Jewish citizens over here!," Belkin hears in Russian with a German accent several months later, though in Kyiv rather than in Moscow. A clerk called this out to the people lined up in front of the German Embassy.[16] Moscow, where Belkin had first traveled, was the wrong capital, because on January 1, 1992, he had become a citizen of a new country, Ukraine. The clerk at the embassy, Kurt Schatz, was also from a country that had ceased to exist, the GDR. He was one of the few diplomats the West German diplomatic service had taken on. In Kyiv he decided on 40,000 applications. He not only checked for the criterion "Jew" in Soviet documents, but also interviewed applicants to determine whether at least one grandparent was Jewish and whether they had experienced antisemitism.

Belkin told Schatz about "how in 1984 the striker of the opposing team, after his team had lost, came into our locker room and brought a jar of jam. Out of respect for the performance of our team." "But don't let the Jew have any of it," he added.[17] But more than anything else Belkin feels embarrassment about having to "sell" his own experience of antisemitism in order to be able to emigrate to Germany. This doesn't fit with his self-image of a proud, self-respecting young man who wants to be anything but a victim. Later in Germany he was surprised how poorly people were able to identify Jews "phenotypically," that is by looks, as though Nazi caricatures like those in *Der Stürmer* had never existed. "Dmitrij, are you actually Greek, Iranian, or Italian?," he is often asked; if anything, people perceive his looks as *südländisch*, "Southern."[18]

In the Soviet Union there was a widespread belief that minorities like Jews could be identified by looks through a trained, purportedly laser-sharp gaze with the help of external markers like nose, facial features, and hair. Even those Jews who had "Russian" as nationality in their documents because one of their parents was ethnically Russian and the family had decided, for obvious reasons (better life chances for the child), in favor of the hegemonic nationality of ethnic Russian. Antisemitism was a common experience not only for halakhic Jews or those who were Jewish according to their documents, but also for those whom non-Jews identified as Jewish, no matter if this was true or not.

By the way, Jews and Volga Germans were not the only ones who emigrated from the (former) Soviet Union on the ethnobiological or ethnoreligious ticket. A lot more countries than is commonly known have Laws of Return; the idea that only Germany (ethnobiological) and Israel (ethnoreligious) have such a law is a myth. Finland has "repatriated" at least 30,000 persons of Finnish descent from the former Soviet

Union since 1991, especially from Estonia and Russian St. Petersburg.[19] Greece has taken in at least a quarter of a million persons of Greek ancestry since 1991, and Armenia, Estonia, Lithuania, Poland, Hungary, and other countries all have laws of return as well.[20] As always with such emigration, there is some fraud with forged papers – Greece in particular for a long time was a well-known gate for EU citizenship. It used to be easy to buy forged documents in Russia and Ukraine that showed Greek heritage. The trick was to enter Greece with these papers and then use the right of intra-EU mobility to settle in another European country, such as Britain or the Netherlands. In this way wealthy Russians who wished to emigrate but had no Jewish, German, or Finnish background got a coveted EU passport.

In December 1993 Belkin and his classmate "Edik," Eduard Fleyer, who is also Jewish and will later switch from History to Law and become a successful lawyer in Frankfurt, start their bus trip from Ukraine via Poland to Germany. The trip takes four days. After the bus has passed the German–Polish border, Belkin sees the first half-timbered houses in his life – and thinks that the advent lights in the windows are Hanukkiahs: "The thought that so many Jews lived here was both overwhelming and comforting."[21]

Through the *Königsteiner Schlüssel* allocation system Edik ended up in the state of Hesse, whereas "Dima" found himself in Baden-Württemberg, where he spent the first 9 months in a shelter for asylum seekers in Reutlingen. In 1994 he started studying History in Tübingen, later got a Ph.D. there, and ultimately ended up working as a curator for exhibitions, publicist, and consultant at the Ernst Ludwig Ehrlich Scholarship Fund (ELES) for Jewish students in Germany, one of thirteen federally funded foundations that provide scholarships for gifted students (Figure 7.1).

In Tübingen Belkin often ended up being irritated by the relationship of educated Germans, *Bildungsbürger*, toward Jews. There was the drop in temperature, the seriousness that begins to pervade a conversation when it turns to Jews, the palpable tensing when merely pronouncing the word *Jude*. But there was also the philosemitic celebration of anything Judeo-Christian in a protestant parish. Belkin noticed that the Jews were always seen in terms of an abstract Judaism, or as the Jews murdered in the Holocaust, or as those Jews who represent the "German–Jewish symbiosis," the Kafkas and Einsteins. Yet the Germans looked straight past the concrete, living Jews, the Jewish new arrivals from Russia, who were making ends meet as cleaning ladies, security guards, or pool attendants. Belkin also noticed the emphatically irreverent approach to the subject among some 68ers. These former student revolutionaries seemed critical

Figure 7.1 Dmitrij Belkin, 2022. Photographed by Jonatan Schwenk, © Dmitrij Belkin.

both of antisemitism and of philosemitism, and were so concerned with normalization that they wanted to include Jews too among the butts of their all-pervasive sarcasm. Consequently they sometimes made deliberately politically incorrect remarks that sounded, if taken literally, antisemitic – a complicated, intellectual form of antisemitism once removed, an antisemitism of actually well-intentioned anti-antisemites.

The attitude in Kapitelman's Leipzig housing projects was much more in-your-face. Neo-Nazis terrorized the eight housing complexes with their 80,000 inhabitants: "In Grünau I fled from neo-Nazis with knives, neo-Nazis with dogs, and neo-Nazis with baseball bats. Once I made it into our house, I took the elevator up to our apartment on the eighth floor. A sticker on the neighbors' apartment door announced: 'Rudolf Heß – people's hero [*Volksheld*]. Friday party here.' After several years in Grünau, around the time when we first had the Holocaust in history lessons at school, my dad gave me the following advice: 'If you want to avoid problems, never get mixed up in others' business. Unless something directly concerns you, stay out.' Stay out of everything. Become invisible. 'Dad, but wasn't the Holocaust possible only because non-Jews stayed out and nobody protested?' 'Yes, but – ' Before my father could finish his sentence, a neo-Nazi asked us for a light. 'I not have fire,' replied my dad in an accent that could hardly have sounded more East European. The Nazi exploded: 'I don't want no fucking fire from you, Abraham.' Silence. Dad tried appearing physically threatening. The two heads taller Nazi actually did appear physically threatening. Then he suddenly turned around and left. With a facial expression as though he had postponed a necessary, but arduous job. He will mow the Jew lawn later."[22] In 2002 Shahak Shapira came to Germany as a 14-year-old with his younger brother, albeit not as a quota refugee, but as the son of an Israeli woman who had fallen in love with an East German and moved in with him in his hometown Laucha in Saxony-Anhalt. In the NPD stronghold Laucha and later in Berlin, Shapira had similar experiences to Kapitelman: from the 16-year-old fellow student who, with a smirk on his face, gets up in front of him, gives the Hitler salute, and calls out "Sieg Heil!," to the neo-Nazi, who abuses his brother in 2010 as *Judenschwein*, "Jew pig," and beats him up, to New Year's night 2014 when he films with his smartphone on the Berlin subway seven men of Arab ancestry shouting slogans like "Fuck Israel" and "Fuck Jews," and then gets beaten up by them, which had a global media fallout.[23]

With all of these Jewish voices it is tangible how difficult it is to find an adequate language for the antisemitism they have experienced: they don't want to engage in tear-jerking, that wouldn't mesh with their ideas of masculinity either. Yet they have experienced it and simply want others to be spared it. Kapitelman is resentful toward his parents for a long time because it is their Soviet-inflected ideas about the superiority of new apartments, in their case an apartment in a GDR *Plattenbau* made of prefab concrete slabs, that turns his way home from school into running the gauntlet: "To this day they don't understand how much I suffered from Grünau. [...] As for me, it took me years to detect the Grünau poison in myself. But when I finally found it, playing guitar in Berlin-Schöneberg, I lay down on the floor, cowered, and started crying."[24]

In recent years antisemitism in its new forms has become louder and more aggressive – on al-Quds Day in Berlin 2014 the demonstrators shouted "Hamas, Hamas, Jews to the gas," in schoolyards *Jude* has become a common swearword, and criticism of the Israeli government's political actions often spills over into antisemitism, for example when "the Jews" in general, that is the world's approximately 14 million living Jews, get consistently equated with Israel and are held responsible for its politics, or when Israel's right to exist is questioned.[25]

But apart from this negative identity brought to them from outside: what does being Jewish mean for Jewish Germans of Soviet extraction? What is Jewishness to them?

For one thing, there is the memory of the negative ascription in the Soviet Union. The semi-official antisemitism, the quotas in university and in the workplace, the terrible hazing in the army that led many to commit suicide, and especially everyday antisemitism – little taunts, microaggressions, epithets, physical violence: these experiences in some cases led to an overidentification with Russianness and a rejection of anything Jewish, that is, a wish to escape being Jewish by any means. Most often, however, they led to the contrary, to a defiant counter-reaction: bonding with similarly excluded Jews, pride in Jewish celebrity soccer players, singers, writers, actresses, scientists, and chess players. In addition there was the certainty that one would have to try harder as a Jew – Sasha Marianna Salzmann in her debut novel has the Jewish mother figure impress on her son: "You must be the best in school, much better than the Russians. If you are three times as good, you will perhaps be considered half as good as them and make it as a good Russian doctor. If you don't make it, you will always remain a poor Jewish loser." Salzmann's punch line: "Later she replaced the Russians by the Germans."[26]

Only in the rarest of cases did Jewishness signify religiosity. True, there were Jewish communities in the Soviet Union, but very few Jews had anything to do with them. There were some who practiced underground religion below the radar of state control (like Russian Orthodox or Lutheran churches, synagogues were also infiltrated by KGB informers). Yet religiously inclined Jews emigrated to Israel rather than Germany, even before the collapse of the Soviet Union (or they were prevented from emigrating: the refuseniks). Some Jewish customs survived nonetheless, for instance where food was concerned: most families had the odd Jewish dish in their diets. Many avoided pork, simply out of family tradition, even while loudly denouncing Jewish dietary laws as "medieval." Some Yiddish expressions also lingered in their speech. The choice of spouse also often happened in the traditional way. The later quota refugees Semen and Tatiana Gostrer, both atheists, were introduced to one another in 1979 in Voronezh, a city of a million inhabitants, by a Shadkhan, a Jewish matchmaker who in this way earned some extra money on the side.[27]

The Gostrer family remained secular in Germany. The same is true for the Kapitelman family and most others. A little fewer than half of the immigrants turned to religion over time. The efforts of the Jewish communities and institutions (such as the Central Welfare Board of Jews in Germany) focused on the children: Jewish kindergartens and elementary schools, summer camps (machanot) in Europe and Israel, soccer, ping-pong or chess in Makkabi sports clubs, trips (if qualified) to the Maccabi Games, the Jewish Olympic Games that take place every 4 years in Israel, and of course the coming of age ritual in the Jewish community at age 12 for girls (bat mitzvah) and 13 for boys (bar mitzvah). But, much like Catholics or Lutherans after confirmation, after bar/bat mitzvah many no longer pray regularly in synagogue or celebrate the High Holidays. Anastassia Pletoukhina is very much aware of that: "I am a member of a group of people with experience of migration, a religious minority, but also a minority of people who practice religion. It's the principle of the matryoshka doll: a minority in the minority in the minority."[28]

Dmitrij Belkin was not allowed to participate in the religious life of a Jewish community – to Jewish communities he was a non-Jew because of his non-Jewish mother. Belkin went on a long journey of soul-searching that at one point brought him to Russian Orthodox Christianity. In the end he and his wife (who has no Jewish parent) decided to convert to Judaism. The bar for giyur, or conversion, is high. The family started following the commandments of the Torah. Belkin and his 6-year-old son got circumcised. In 2006 at the Oranienburger Straße Synagogue in Berlin they stepped before a beth din, a rabbinical court. This was a special beth din because it consisted of liberal and reform rabbis. Until 2005 the only rabbinical conference was orthodox, and it would have barred a family like the Belkins from giyur. The immigration from the USSR has also diversified German Jewry, from very progressive to ultra-orthodox. Thus in major German cities you can now sometimes see black-clad Jews with peyot and black hats. Generally speaking, in large German cities you now have representation of all denominations of Judaism, as they also exist in the United States, France, England, or Israel. Nowadays the Abraham Geiger Kolleg, a rabbinical seminary in Potsdam, is training non-orthodox rabbis: one graduate, Alina Treiger, originally from Ukraine, was ordained in 2010 as the first female rabbi in Germany after 1945.

At the Belkin family's giyur the son was last in line to get up in front of the beth din. "'And you?,' the rabbis asked Mark, who went to a Jewish school in Frankfurt. Mark didn't need any rational arguments, it was right before Hanukkah and he simply sang a Hanukkah song, so our appointment at the rabbinical court ended with collective singing by the rabbis and the giyur-happy family from the Soviet ruins together with their 6-year-old, Tübingen-born son."[29]

As for memory of the Holocaust and the Second World War, the Soviet immigrants differ from German Jews. For the older German Jews November 9, the pogrom night of 1938 (previously euphemistically known as *Kristallnacht*, the "Night of Broken Glass") and increasingly January 27, the day of liberation of Auschwitz in 1945, are important days of commemoration. For Jews from the Soviet Union, May 9 (1945) is the central day of commemoration. The former USSR continues to celebrate it as "Victory Day." The West marks it on May 8 as the day of capitulation – the ceasefire at 11:01 pm Central Europe Time was past midnight in Moscow, a different time zone, hence May 9. The name "Victory Day" encapsulates the key difference: Soviet Jews feel like victors, since many of their relatives fought even harder than ethnic Russians in the

Red Army against the Wehrmacht; they were even greater antifascists because they knew what was in store for them if Nazism prevailed. November 9 and January 27 by contrast stand for the commemoration of a catastrophe and a collectivity of victims. What is more, for many Jews from the former Soviet Union the Germans of the Second World War are primarily fascists who attacked the Soviet Union, not Nazis intent on annihilating the Jews. It was difficult to separately remember the Shoah, since in the innumerable Soviet war movies it was subordinated to the suffering of ethnic Russians and the victory of the USSR as a whole. Some learned about the Holocaust as a separate phenomenon, not an aspect of the war, only when they came to Germany – in history lessons at school or through Western movies like *Schindler's List*.

The Russian Jews have, however, also brought to Germany a Shoah experience that serves as a corrective to the dominant memory narrative. In Germany the Holocaust was long remembered solely as industrial mass killing, encapsulated by systematic murder through gas in death factories like Auschwitz and other extermination camps. In reality at least a third of the 6 million Jews who were murdered were shot in Ukraine, Belarus, or elsewhere in Russia and Eastern Europe. In Auschwitz primarily Central and Eastern European Jews as well as Western European Jews were killed. The depiction of the Holocaust in the German media to this day doesn't adequately reflect this. Nor does its depiction in German museums (such as the Information Center at the Memorial to the Murdered Jews of Europe in Berlin next to the Brandenburg Gate), the United States Holocaust Museum in Washington, D.C., the French Mémorial de la Shoah, or even Israel's Yad Vashem. The museums and media mostly tell the story of the killing in the extermination camps. A disproportionate number of German Jews is shown, as though they constituted the largest group of victims. This skewed imaginary then spills over into quotidian life: many Germans view Russian Jews as "Russians" and not as survivors of the genocide that they committed, whereas they are more likely to see Israelis or American Jews as victims of the Shoah.

Most Russian Jews – because of a Shoah memory that was differently configured or suppressed by the Soviet state – have a relaxed attitude toward Germany. They definitely do not want to be reduced to the role of victims in the Shoah, they often don't even want to talk about it. Mascha Kogan, the quota refugee protagonist in Olga Grjasnowa's bestselling novel, mocks a German philosemite, who treats her as "his personal pet Jew": "My only flaw was that I didn't come straight from a German concentration camp"[30] (Figure 7.2).

Russian Jews decided in favor of emigration to Germany for reasons that bear little relationship to the past: they want to live in "old" Europe,

Figure 7.2 Olga Grjasnowa, 2012. Photographed by Stephan Röhl, CC BY-SA 2.0.

not in the United States or dangerous, conflict-ridden Israel, where their children, both sons and daughters, would have to serve in the army. Israel is also too hot; in terms of climate Hamburg is much more like St. Petersburg, Munich much more like Kyiv.

Something else was really key to the Jewish immigrants: the recognition of academic degrees and quick integration into the German labor market. The fact that highly qualified doctors with international publications had to wait for years for the approval of their MD degree or their license to practice medicine, that accomplished pianists or engineers had to work as beauticians or in a *Spiela* (*Spielhalle*, that is, a casino), all of this meant an enormous loss of status for them – this left deep wounds and to this day is the quota refugees' number one grievance. All the more so when they hear from friends who emigrated to America how quickly these people entered the job market and how much in demand their skills acquired in the USSR are over there. To put it differently and emphasize the point, while Sergey Brin could focus on coding the Google algorithm, immigrants in Germany had to wrestle in German government agencies with forms written in impenetrable German and the hostile clerk Frau Müller –

a demoralizing struggle with red tape that set them back for years. These immigrants wanted recognition of their know-how as mathematicians, doctors, or engineers, not for the fact that they happen to be Jewish. After all, they chose Germany as one of several options because they thought they could there continue their careers and would have correspondingly good prospects of promotion.

These problems apply mostly to the middle age cohort, those who emigrated between the ages of 30 and 50. The younger and older age cohorts in many ways have it easier. The children do exceptionally well in school, but have to overcome the typical obstacles for children of "second-class" immigrants (not those from France or Britain, but "the Turks" or "the Russians"): they are initially sent to vocational school instead of university-bound *Gymnasium*, or they are held back: "On my third day in Germany I went to school and was promptly demoted two grades. Instead of practicing algebra, I was supposed to color mandalas with crayons," as Grjasnowa has her heroine Mascha Kogan say.[31] The older generation, those aged over 50, also has fewer problems. The German social welfare state protects them, they care for their grandchildren, and they are themselves definitely much better taken care of in the Jewish homes for the elderly than in their ex-Soviet countries of origin. There a move into a nursing home continues to be perceived as a death warrant. Yet also among the older generation there are justified grievances: they are not on an equal footing with Volga Germans and their working years in the USSR do not count toward their German pension.[32]

The visibility of the younger generation in culture, politics, and the media is already remarkable and likely to grow in the future. Marina Weisband (born 1987) was leader of the Pirate Party from 2011 until 2012, and generally the public face of her party. Sergey Lagodinsky, born in 1975 and since 2019 a Member of the European Parliament for the Greens, in 2007 founded the Jewish Caucus in the SPD. Then he resigned from the SPD in 2011 because the party failed to expel Thilo Sarrazin (see Chapter 8). Both Weisband and Lagodinsky are religious and never made a secret of their background as Jewish quota refugees. Male quota refugees, such as Belkin, Kapitelman, and the rapper Sun Diego aka SpongeBOZZ (Dimitri Chpakov), write autobiographies. Female quota refugees publish novels: writers like Grjasnowa and Salzmann have already figured in this book.[33] Some of the most stimulating inputs in the migration debate are from resident author Salzmann and her Studio Я at Berlin's Gorki Theater, for example the "disintegration congress" that brought to the fore the public debate about the exclusionist character of the German concept of *Integration*. Jewish quota refugees in some ways are the vanguard, the pace-setters of the debate on migration.[34] It is only a question of time until they break through the glass ceiling of the old, West German Jewish establishment and become as widely represented in the Jewish institutions, the Central Council, and the leading bodies of the Jewish communities as they ought to be, given their numbers in contemporary German Jewry.

One thing is certain: a Russophone infrastructure has come into being in Germany. There are grocery stores that sell Soviet *tvorog* (a kind of cottage cheese) or *vobla* (dried salted fish). And the leading Russian theater stars and pop singers regularly come to Germany during their international tours performing for the Russophone diaspora.

What about lumping together all immigrants of Soviet background as a "Russophone diaspora"? Sometimes they do so themselves and deliberately so, as in the Federal Association of Russophone Parents, where Russian-Jewish and Volga German parents have come together as a lobby group.[35] Yet often they go their separate ways, both spatially (Volga Germans in the Berlin districts of Marzahn, Hellersdorf, and Spandau; Jews in Charlottenburg, Wilmersdorf, Schöneberg, and Prenzlauer Berg) and personally (there are few friendships and marriages between the two groups). A social scientist studied the Potsdam district of Bornstedt in the middle of the 1990s: "Close contacts only exist in rare cases, which is why so far there has been no stable cross-group entanglement. Indeed, spatial yet segregated proximity amplifies the perception of social differences, because after all the two immigrant groups are treated differently in legal and social terms. Small or large successes of members of one group are commented on with eagerness to criticize by the other group. Under the pressure of a highly competitive climate in contemporary Germany the often diverging lifestyles are perceived not less starkly, but in fact more acutely. On the Jewish side, the get the same stereotypes are attached to *Spätaussiedler* as to Russians: they 'drink,' they 'are physically violent,' they are 'antisemitic.' The *Aussiedler*, by contrast, readily contest in principle the very right of Jews of Soviet extraction to live in Germany."[36]

Whence the chasm between the two groups? Is it because Soviet Jews were Mercurians, Volga Germans Apollonians? The historian Yuri Slezkine calls modern service nomads Mercurians, sedentary farmers Apollonians. Mercurians are "urban, mobile, literate, articulate, intellectually intricate, physically fastidious, and occupationally flexible." Modernity is the age of the Jews, modernization "is about learning how to cultivate people and symbols, not fields or herds." Modernity signifies education and meritocracy instead of inherited privileges and estate society. Slezkine's conclusion: "Modernization, in other words, means that everyone will become Jewish. [. . .] but no one is better at being Jewish than the Jews themselves. In the age of capital, they are the most creative entrepreneurs; in the age of alienation, they are the most veteran exiles; and in the age of expertise, they are the most competent specialists."[37]

There is some truth to this. Many Volga Germans did indeed come from agricultural jobs and rural areas on the Volga, in Kazakhstan, or in Siberia. Many Jews are from the urban intelligentsia. But in the Soviet Union there were also unions, alliances, and coalitions that have been forgotten. Thus Gerhard Dick (1896–1998), descendant of a Russian German Mennonite dynasty of beer brewers, and Sophia Dick, who was Jewish, were happily married for 60 years. They were from similar urban milieus, both had been imprisoned in the Gulag, and they were united in the certainty that Soviet power considered them a minority – persecution as a minority in the Soviet Union was a common denominator of Volga Germans and Jews.[38] In other cases the common denominator was that after the collapse of the USSR and renationalization processes the dominant people, for example the Kazakhs in Kazakhstan, discriminated in equal measure against Jews and Germans.

At any rate, for both groups the term "mobility" often describes their forms of movement better than does "emigration." They fly back and forth between Munich and Moscow, Hannover and Almaty, Berlin, St. Petersburg, and Tel Aviv, and at the border they present the passport of the country they are entering. For Russia and Ukraine allow multiple citizenships. And the Germans silently tolerate this. Marina Weisband, for example, has dual German and Ukrainian citizenship.

Over the past few years another group of Jews in Germany has grown, especially in Berlin: Israelis. Perhaps 10,000 to 20,000 live in the German capital, but counting them isn't easy because many of them have a German or other European passport. A person whose ancestors the Nazis stripped of citizenship is eligible for German citizenship without having to renounce their other citizenship(s) according to Article 116, Paragraph 2 of the Basic Law. Israelis in Berlin are seeking to break out of the relatively parochial small State of Israel, they seek out the sexual diversity of the queer community, and they appreciate the cheaper cost of living and also the possibility of interacting with Palestinians and other Arabs beyond the limits that life in Israel imposes: "Ever since I've been here and living in Neukölln," says Meytal Rozental, "and my neighbors are Turks, Palestinians, Lebanese, people with whom I had no contact before – because I wasn't allowed to have contact – my feeling that life in Israel is very, very confined and very much circumscribed by political factors has become stronger. With whom you are allowed to talk, what you know about others."[39] Since Brexit and Trump, some British and American intellectuals have applied for German passports with media fanfare – it would have been hard to imagine just 10 years ago that Germany after the Shoah might some day become a beacon of political-democratic opposition among Jews worldwide.[40] This proves once more that the place from where you migrate can become the place you escape to overnight, that the migrants of yesterday are the autochthonous of today, who are the migrants of tomorrow, who are the ...

A conspicuously high number of the younger Jewish immigrants became active on behalf of refugees in 2015, even though it would appear that all Jews might resent immigration from Arab Muslim countries because it can bring with it antisemitism and terrorism, and not very well-off older Jews of Soviet descent might worry because such incomers would be new competitors for social benefits.[41] In 2016 Dmitrij Kapitelman was asked in an interview: "It's impossible to compare your immigration as an 8-year-old with the arrival of an 8-year-old refugee from Syria. Can you nonetheless imagine how these children must feel?" His response: "I saw the video of the bus that arrived in Heidenau a year ago and had stones hurled at it and was attacked by a mob. There's a small boy there who is about to get off the bus and can't understand what's going on outside. He cries bitterly. Given my experiences, which came at a later age and weren't as brutal, I know that he will never forget this feeling of rejection. [...] And after what my family has been through I can but feel empathy and solidarity."[42]

Thus there are refugee charity aid projects sponsored by the Jewish and Muslim student scholarship foundations ELES and Avicenna. Akiva Weingarten, an ELES scholarship student alumnus and now a rabbi, comments: "As human beings we must of course have a sense of responsibility for other people who are suffering. As Jews we have experienced this again and again, and when it took longer until other countries recognized that we are in trouble, it cost us millions of victims." Weingarten can "understand that some people say, 'Yes, but how can we know who is a terrorist and who isn't?' Of course, when we accept millions of people from these countries with open arms, there will be a few terrorists among them. [...] But that doesn't mean that we have no responsibility, just because there might be terrorists in this group."[43] Josef Schuster, president of the Central Council, warns of a new, imported antisemitism, but at the same time says about the AfD: "It is a party that stokes fears of minorities. At the moment primarily against Muslims. I am, however, convinced that, when the subject of Muslims is no longer interesting and it would furthermore be politically and socially opportune, then it could easily concern other minorities. Among these I also count Jews."[44] There is an echo here of Marek Lieberberg's concert after Rostock-Lichtenhagen in 1992: "Today They! Tomorrow You!"

Conclusion

"My mother tongue is Russian, but I would *no way* call myself Russian. [...] I don't go to synagogue, don't observe Jewish laws and rituals, know neither Hebrew or Yiddish, yet still feel an attachment to the Jewish people. How, what explains this? I don't know. But I also feel attachments to Ukraine and to Germany, the country where my family and I have been living for 13 years, whose language I know quite well and find fascinating and whose citizenship I have, after all. Who am I then? A monster thrown together from very different parts? Or a human being of the future who belongs to several cultures at the same time?"[45] This could be read in an internet forum in 2008. For the writer Lana Lux, who immigrated from Ukraine as a 10-year-old quota refugee in 1996, the "Who am I then?" question also came up. She had become a mother, and suddenly Jewishness was an issue. She and her husband celebrate Shabbat and High Holidays in order to pass on to their daughter elements of Judaism before she gets externally identified as a Jew – before she learns about the Holocaust at school or is confronted with Israeli politics in everyday life.[46]

Jewish quota refugees from the former Soviet Union juggle their own set of attachments. It bears emphasizing – *contra* a common misconception – that these quota refugees are not German Jews who had been expelled in 1933. The vast majority of Soviet Jews are descendants of the Jews who were cramped together in the Tsarist Empire's Polish–Ukrainian–Belorusian Pale of Settlement, who after the Russian Revolution moved to the cities of the USSR and became Russian-Soviet in terms of language and culture. But they also have little in common with the more than 200,000 Russian Jews who in the 1920s populated Berlin-"Charlottengrad," published newspapers and books, and ran theaters and student associations: these were directly from the Pale and predominantly spoke Yiddish.[47] They also have little in common culturally and linguistically with the locals of the German postwar Jewish communities, for these were descendants of the Polish Jews in the DP camps after the Second World War. If they resemble anyone, the quota refugees most resemble the several thousand Soviet Jews who came in the 1970s – the Berlin writer Friedrich Gorenstein, for example, or the Jewish Russians around Radio Liberty/Free Europe in Munich.

Judaism and Jewishness are notoriously difficult to pin down. If religion isn't practiced in some form, if no one marries within the Jewish community and there are no converts to Judaism, it will disappear some day. Secular Jews too complain about this: Judaism will have been annihilated through assimilation, in retrospect Hitler will have won after all.[48] That is why it was important for Belkin to convert to religious Judaism even though in his family only his father is Jewish. Circumcision to him was particularly important in this: "Circumcision to me meant the repairing of something that had been violently interrupted. Not just by the Nazis, not just by the Soviets, not just by the twentieth century. It was the course of life itself, and now it had been repaired. It had begun with my father's love for my mother and was reconstituted through my marriage with Lyuda, our emigration, Mark's birth, and now this covenant. We'll see about the rest."[49]

One aspect of the Jewish immigration from the Soviet Union is that the Jewish religion is again practiced more openly and less dominated by anxiety in Germany. The same kind of openness can be observed with Islam. Both are positive developments. It is to be hoped that some day it will no longer be necessary to have policemen in front of synagogues. And that mosques continue moving into the city centers from where they are now, hidden away in the most distant corners of the industrial estates. Perhaps the time has come to consider introducing general, non-Christian religious holidays? How about at least one holiday for the other two Abrahamic religions, Judaism and Islam? Christianity is historically so prominent in the Federal Republic's festive culture that for instance Lana Lux considers Christmas "irritating": "There are a lot of people who don't celebrate Christmas and they are also part of society. [...] I've got the feeling [...] that we somehow get run over."[50] A Jewish (and Muslim) religious holiday per year on which everyone in Germany takes a day off could mitigate this feeling.

Apart from that, it is very specific, job market-related, economic and social policy questions that are at the top of the list of many Jewish quota refugees. It is important to them that academic degrees be recognized more easily and faster. That the glass ceiling in Germany's Jewish institutions starts crumbling so they can move up into leading positions. That the glass ceiling in non-Jewish institutions starts crumbling and the general public becomes accustomed to museum directors, professors, and politicians who speak with an accent. That they get put on equal footing with the Volga Germans insofar as the recognition of work done in the Soviet Union for German pensions is concerned, for poverty in old age is widespread among them.[51]

But there is room for symbolic improvement. Symbolic empowerment is also the express goal of the website www.rentajew.org, through which one can invite a Jewish person as speaker: "For contemporary Jewry," says Lea Simon, "it is essential to get across to non-Jews that there are still living Jews around today. And very diverse ones indeed. This can be done through an action like 'Rent a Jew.' You can rent a Jew/Jewess. The title is pretty provocative, just the idea that one can rent another human being. But the concept behind it is what counts. We need visibility for the fact that there are very different people with very different biographical trajectories. Not all Jews are dead or Israelis. And suddenly they are again like you and me. Plus Jewish."[52]

8 Welcoming Culture

In November 2015, at the height of the "refugee crisis," 10.9 percent of Germans or roughly 9 million people were engaged in volunteer work for refugees. In May 2016, despite the harassment of women by predominantly North African men in Cologne on New Year's Eve and the supposed end of the welcoming culture (*Willkommenskultur*), this number had gone up rather than down: 11.9 percent or roughly 10 million people.[1] In November 2017 an Allensbach Institute poll even counted 19 percent or almost 16 million who were active in helping refugees – despite exhaustion, despite the first-ever election of a party to the right of the conservative CSU, the AfD, to the German parliament in the 2017 general election, and despite the constant relentless criticism of the German government's refugee policy by the ninety-two AfD parliamentarians.[2]

One can cast doubt on the numbers, one can adjust them downward, but even the most conservative estimates confirm that civil society volunteering for refugees since 2015 has been at its largest in the entire postwar history of West and East Germany. When classifying this volunteering – donations in kind, accompanying refugees to bureaucratic institutions, taking on guardianships for Unaccompanied Minor Refugees, after-school private lessons for children – as a social movement, as a lot of social scientists do, then we are talking about Germany's largest social movement since 1945.[3] Larger than West Germany's peace movement in the early 1980s or the protest movement against the GDR regime in fall 1989. On October 22, 1983, a total of 1.3 million people gathered in Bonn, Hamburg, and other West German cities for demonstrations against the stationing of Pershing II missiles. On October 23, 1989, the GDR saw the largest Monday demonstration, with 300,000 participants in Leipzig and several tens of thousands in other East German cities.

What is truly astonishing about the "long summer of migration" of 2015, a play on "A Summer's Tale," the term used for the 2006 Soccer World Cup that Germany hosted, is not that the mood changed in 2016.[4] That was to be expected, considering the economy of feelings: it is hard to keep up so much passion in the long run. Nor were the specific circumstances – the large number of refugees, their privations and suffering in summer 2015 – astonishing. Catastrophes and war were just as horrific in the 1980s or 1990s. The most astonishing thing about the long summer of migration is: the long summer of migration. Especially in the historical longue durée, it begs the question how and why so much voluntary activism was possible. This was an extraordinary event in the history of the Federal Republic – the broad solidarity, the broad activism of so many people for migrants, and their positive talk about them. How did it come about?

A New Start around the Millennium

Germany started the new millennium with a firework display of migration politics. The new citizenship law went into effect on January 1, 2000. Now also children born in Germany to non-German citizens became eligible for German citizenship as long as, when they were born, at least one parent had legally resided in Germany for 8 years.[5] This birthright citizenship (*ius soli*) was added to the right of blood (*ius sanguinis*), which continued to be valid. According to the right of blood, German citizenship is available to those who have at least one parent with German citizenship. The new citizenship law replaced the Nationality Law of 1913 (*Reichs- und Staatsangehörigkeitsrecht*) and was perceived by many as a long overdue modernization. At long last birthplace instead of blood, at long last arrival in the West – that is how many saw the change.

But not everyone. Long fighting preceded the reform. In September 1998 Helmut Kohl's coalition of the CDU/CSU and the FDP, which had governed since 1982, was voted out of power. For the first time ever a coalition of Social Democrats and Greens started governing at the federal level. The new government under Chancellor Gerhard Schröder made the change of the citizenship law a cornerstone. It initiated a law that not only brought in the birthright principle, but also allowed the possibility of dual citizenship. (In practice the authorities already tacitly tolerated this with some groups, as we saw in the case of the *Aussiedler* and Jewish quota refugees.) The CDU/CSU organized a campaign "Yes to integration, no to dual citizenship," it won the state elections in Hesse in spring 1999, the majority in the Bundesrat, the chamber of parliament representing the sixteen federal states, changed, and Schröder's government had to settle on a compromise regarding dual citizenship. Children with two passports now had a "duty to choose" (*Optionspflicht*): between the ages of 18 and 23 they had to opt for one or other of the two citizenships.

Compromise or not, during the early years of the Red–Green government it seemed as though a long gridlock on reforms had ended and as though things were finally moving forward in terms of migration politics. The new citizenship law of January 1, 2000, lowered the duration of residency required for naturalization from 15 to 8 years. In August 2000 the German Greencard was launched. And in September 2000 the cross-party Independent Commission "Immigration," chaired by the CDU politician Rita Süssmuth, started working. Its aim was to prepare the ground for a unified, streamlined immigration law so that finally the legal chaos would disappear and more clarity might reign.

In July 2001 the Commission presented its closing report. The very first sentence broke with the "Germany is no immigration country" mantra of the entire postwar epoch: "Germany needs immigrants."[6] The 1973 ban on *Gastarbeiter* recruitment had halted labor immigration, but now it was expressly invited – the Green Party's Commissioner for Foreigners, Marieluise Beck, welcomed the report as "springtime in migration politics."[7] The basic right to asylum should remain intact. In addition, the report opened a window for grounds for asylum other than political persecution: "The Commission affirms that women who are persecuted on account of their gender are in need of protection."[8] The Commission also advocated the introduction of a Canadian-style points system through which applicants could "earn" their citizenship. This "model of labor market-oriented immigration" recommended the recruitment of six groups of immigrants: entrepreneurs (with ideas for new businesses); qualified permanent immigrants (in professions for which long-term employees were sought); students (who had been educated in Germany at considerable cost anyway); apprentices in an "18-plus-program"; workers in fields in which there was a shortage of labor; top achievers in business and science ("top" being measured by a high salary or a scientific quality label). This was a complex model meant to merge at least three contradictory aims: the "competition for the best minds"; a renunciation of the old West German *guest* worker myth and recognition of the fact that Germany was a country of immigrants; but also acknowledgment that in 2001 "almost 4 million people were unemployed."[9]

The recommendations of the Commission were in almost all respects more progressive than the CDU's position after 2015 – and the CDU was Commission president Süssmuth's party. Two examples: first, the vast majority of refugees from Syria were admitted on the basis of the Geneva Convention of 1951 because a civil war like the Syrian one is not considered grounds for admission on the basis of political persecution according to Article 16 of the Basic Law. However, the Commission would have made them equivalent to asylum seekers according to

Article 16 and thereby given them automatically the right to family reunification.[10] Second: "Civil war refugees too have access to the points system." In other words, a person with sought-after IT skills, for example, would have earned points, and this would speed up their asylum application process. This would have meant a blurring of lines between refugees and labor migrants, lines conservatives insist on when clamoring for a distinction between "true asylum seekers" and "economic refugees."[11]

The widely and publicly debated report of the Süssmuth Commission became the basis for a law drafted by the Interior Ministry in August 2001. But a month later something unexpected happened that fundamentally shifted the coordinates of the entire debate about migration: on September, 11, 2001, Islamist terrorists flew two airliners into the twin towers of New York's World Trade Center, and almost 3,000 people died. After that the United States started wars in Afghanistan and Iraq. The Iraq War, not just the Arab Spring of 2011, stirred up the Middle East and was the medium-term main cause of the Syrian Civil War. As such it was also the medium-term main cause of one of the largest refugee movements in the history of humanity, in which in 2015, according to an estimate of the UNHCR, for the first time since its records began in 1951, more than 60 million people were on the move as refugees, including more than 4 million from Syria. And Islamism, indeed Islam itself, since 9/11 embodies terrorism in the imagination of a part of the world and is seen as intimidating.

Yet even before 9/11 not everything spelled progress. In October 2000 the head of the CDU/CSU parliamentary group, Friedrich Merz, started the *Leitkultur* debate. According to him, the success of immigration depended on "a capacity to integrate on both sides: the receiving country must be tolerant and open; immigrants, whether they want to live among us temporarily or forever, must for their part be willing to respect the rules of living together in Germany." Merz proposed calling these rules "free German *Leitkultur*." We should not discuss the necessity of such rules, "but rather argue about their content."[12]

For Merz the most important ingredient of these *Leitkultur* rules was the constitution, the Basic Law. Central to him was also the European idea, democracy and a social market economy, the equality of women, and the German language. This was a paradoxical argument. He demanded a discussion about *Leitkultur*, the rules of living together, the contents of what he called the "minimal consensus." But what he proposed as the minimal consensus was not only not open-ended and future-oriented but rather the status quo, that is conservative. Put differently, the contents of Merz's *Leitkultur* were very durable, almost transhistorical – you can't argue with the Basic Law or democracy as a "value." For who would propose, content-wise, to exclude the Basic Law or democracy from *Leitkultur*? The Basic Law and democracy are the framework within which content can be debated; what is more, they are the precondition for debate in the first place. This was the first fudge factor in Merz's *Leitkultur*.

Moreover, Merz launched the *Leitkultur* concept against the negative backdrop of "foreigners" (*Ausländer*): "Cultural interaction and mutual enrichment through cultural experiences from different countries hit their limits where the minimal consensus on freedom, human dignity and equal rights is no longer adhered to. This has consequences for living together with foreigners. In a free country people of diverse backgrounds can shape their future together only on the basis of commonly accepted values." This, then, is the second implication of the *Leitkultur* debate as prompted by Friedrich Merz: he defines the values about which there should allegedly be debate in juxtaposition to "foreigners," for which one can read migrants, and their "parallel societies," claiming they would not share these values. What is the basis for this claim? The fact that some Muslim women wear a hijab? Is that per se oppressive and in violation of personal liberties? Many Christian denominations prohibit premarital sex. Is that in conformity with values of liberty and equal rights?

Also, many of the elements that allegedly belong to a "free German *Leitkultur*" are not shared by all politicians and members of the CDU (Merz's own party) and CSU – this contradiction is inherent in the conservative position: gender equality, the decriminalization of homosexuality, and other minority rights in the Federal Republic too were achieved only in a decades-long struggle, and to this day many conservatives prefer a traditional family model, for example. Yet they pretend that these liberties won with such great effort have always been part of Western values. As late as 1984, for instance, only 16 years before Merz's *Leitkultur* debate, the CDU politician Elisabeth Motschmann said in a talkshow about gays: "a homosexual on average has 600 different partners in his life. [. . .] I find very disturbing any idealization of homosexuality, any attempt to view it as equal with heterosexuality." In 2015 CDU politician Julia Klöckner suggested that refugees should sign a contract with the German state in which they pledged, among other things, to accept homosexuality.[13] Incidentally, what would a poll among the members of Klöckner's own party say if they had to tick a box: "I pledge to accept homosexuality, yes or no"?

In point of fact the true instigator of the debate wasn't Merz: the term *Leitkultur* has a longer history (and an epilogue – more about that in the conclusion of this book). But Merz reframed the debate so that large parts of the German population, especially PlusGermans (whom Merz equated with literal foreigners, that is persons without German citizenship), perceived *Leitkultur* not as an invitation for democratic participation but as a "this is the dictate to which you must submit" top-down discourse.

Still, a picture in broad brushstrokes of the migration situation in Germany during the first decade of the new millennium would look as follows. First, laws were finally adapted to reality. Despite the many compromises that had to be made, after 16 years of conservative stagnation under Chancellor Helmut Kohl the new Red–Green government brought fresh air into the migration debate and got extensive reforms off the ground. For these there was and exists to this day a majority that goes beyond the voters of the SPD and the Green Party: it includes economic laissez-faire liberals, classic FDP voters who in a globalizing age consider national borders increasingly archaic, with regard to not just the flow of goods and money, but also the mobility of people. In addition there are those among the CDU/CSU voters who take seriously the "C" in their party names and adhere to the asylum seeker-friendly position of the Christian churches, which in turn impacts their general attitude toward migration. Second, and this is genuinely new, demography now has a constant presence in the public debate, for the Germans are getting ever older and ever fewer: how, if not through immigration, can a balance be struck between a low birthrate and a long life expectancy? Who, if not working immigrants, will pay for the pensions benefits of the older generation? And yes, third, the world has become more interconnected and smaller, people in all regions of the world seem more alike in the age of the Internet, global 24/7 supply chains, and global warming.

Fourth, German society itself has become more diverse. This is noticeable not just in cuisine – Döner has become a German national dish, in fall 2000 the first "German Döner" eatery opened in Beijing, and "German Doner Kebap" is now sold everywhere in the United Kingdom.[14] It is palpable in the elementary schools of large cities, in sports clubs, in pop music, in television, in consumer behavior (cue ethnomarketing), and in the political class, where politicians such as Cem Özdemir, Aydan Özoğuz, Tarek al-Wazir, Omid Nouripour, Dilek Kolat, and Raed Saleh have attained key positions. Fifth and finally, in the early 2000s a movement of refugees began, which in 2012 culminated in the protest camp on Berlin-Kreuzberg's Oranienplatz.

The 2000s

In March 2002 the German parliament passed the immigration law. In many ways it was more restrictive than the Süssmuth Commission's final report, which had served as the basis for this law: the points system was only hinted at; gender discrimination no longer counted as a reason for asylum.[15] The recommendations of the Süssmuth Commission were watered down because of the terrorist attacks of September 11 that occurred 8 weeks after the final report was presented and concessions to the CDU/CSU opposition parties, not least because of the fact that federal parliamentary elections were coming up in September 2002 and the CDU/CSU had kept open the possibility, in the wake of 9/11, of running an election campaign in which they would take a hard line on migration.

Now the law still had to pass the Bundesrat, the second chamber of the German parliament, in which the sixteen federal states are represented. There was a lot of anxiety around the outcome of this vote, since the Red–Green coalition no longer had a majority in the Bundesrat because it had lost several federal state elections to the Christian Democrats. Through a trick in the voting procedure, it passed on March 22, 2002. The CDU/CSU governments of six federal states immediately filed a lawsuit at the Federal Constitutional Court, Germany's supreme court. On December 18, 2002, the Federal Constitutional Court declared the law anti-constitutional. Everything that had already been put into practice became null and void. The government initiated a new compromise that was passed in 2004 and went into effect in 2005 (more on this shortly).

A lot of zigzagging notwithstanding, the years 1998–2005 of the Social Democratic–Green coalition were key years in which the ground was prepared for a greater acceptance of immigration and a wider solidarity with refugees, as manifested in the summer of 2015. After migration had been at the center of parliamentary and public debates, no party, no civil society organization, no individual could avoid taking a stance. And once Islamist terrorism had been conjoined with the migration topic, here too one needed to position oneself – should one distinguish between Islam and Islamism? Try hard not to regard all Muslims as deserving to be treated with suspicion?

On the first day of 2005 the immigration law went into effect. The law was meant to simplify older regulations and adapt them to newer EU laws, to restructure institutions of migration policy along more rational lines, and to tackle changes in the areas of asylum and integration. Just two residence titles were supposed to replace the confusing multitude of titles: a temporary one (*Aufenthaltserlaubnis*) and a permanent one (*Niederlassungserlaubnis*). EU citizens no longer had to apply for anything; they were granted full mobility and merely had to register, like German citizens, with the local German registration-of-address office.

The Federal Office for Migration and Refugees in Nuremberg became the new super-agency for migration issues. It took over a lot of the functions of the local employment agencies and social welfare offices. The "Advisory Council on Immigration and Integration," which had started working in 2003 under Rita Süssmuth and had been meant to become as important as the "German Council of Economic Experts," or the "Five Sages" in common parlance, was eliminated. Really novel was the fact that integration measures now became compulsory. New immigrants could be coerced to take language and integration courses; if they didn't comply, their residence status could worsen. Immigrants who had come to Germany longer ago could also be coerced; the social benefits of those who were receiving them could be decreased if they failed to comply. Proof of language ability was introduced for *Spätaussiedler* and Jewish quota refugees. As a result, immigration from the former Soviet Union was reduced to a trickle. Foreigners who planned to move to Germany following their spouse now had to furnish proof of language ability before entering the country. And almost nothing survived of the points system and the "competition for the best minds," only the rule that foreign students were allowed to stay if they found work within 18 months of finishing university.

In March 2002 Interior Minister Otto Schily (SPD) had announced with fanfare "Europe's most modern immigration law." What transpired 3 years later was not a great success, but merely the smallest common denominator. Instead of simplifying things, a lot actually got more complicated – one migration expert reported a decade later that "according to Gerda Kinateder, who in Stuttgart directs one of Germany's largest aliens departments, there are now, believe it or not, seventy-seven temporary and fifteen permanent kinds of residence status. [. . .] The administrative regulations that accompany the residence law alone comprise 390 pages."[16]

All of this took place against the backdrop of economic decline. After the dotcom bubble burst in March 2000, in the middle of the 2000s unemployment figures reached their highest point since reunification.[17] In November 2004 *The Economist* called Germany "the sick man of Europe."[18] The ruling Social Democrats, against great resistance among the party rank-and-file, in 2003 decided on a package of labor market reforms, "Agenda 2010."

The architects of Agenda 2010 could not reap its fruits. In a September 2005 snap election the Red–Green coalition was ousted, and Chancellor Angela Merkel's grand coalition of Christian and Social Democrats came to power. The effects of Agenda 2010 became tangible only under Merkel's chancellorship – or at least that is how various economists see it. Many had the feeling that already in summer 2006 (the summer of the World Cup in Germany) an unusually long economic boom began, which only experienced a dent in 2009 because of the world financial crisis of

2008. Precisely the mixed economy with its emphasis both on services *and* on industry, combined with the social market economy with strong trade unions, proved the more sustainable model in comparison with financial industries-driven economies like Britain's.

The World Cup wasn't just important for the economy. With players like Gerald Asamoah, Miroslav Klose, David Odonkor, and Lukas Podolski, the national soccer team mirrored Germany's diversity. For the first time new forms of playful *Party-Patriotismus* became commonplace – public viewing and dancing with fans from all over the world, and Hawaiian flower garlands in black, red, and gold, the colors of the German flag. There were also hybrid versions like German–Turkish flags with the Turkish white star on the red stripe of the German tricolor. The hospitality of the German population was widely noted – foreign journalists produced headlines like "Germany and the World Cup: The Liberating Normality," while others commented on the "international love-in."[19] For the first time it seemed possible even for anti-national, skeptical Germans to practice symbolic patriotism – if you want, postmodern symbolic patriotism.

Merkel's government kept the Red–Green migration reforms, it did not usher in a conservative U-turn. In July 2006 it started its first "integration summit." Ever since, every summer representatives of migrant organizations, politicians, and others congregate to discuss migration issues. In September 2006 the German Islam Conference was inaugurated, where representatives of Muslim denominations and organizations confer with politicians about the relationship between the state and religion. In July 2010 the CDU politician Christian Wulff began his term as President of the Federal Republic, a largely representative but nonetheless key function next to that of the Chancellor. Three months later, on the occasion of the Day of German Unity, October 3, 2010, he gave a now famous speech in Bremen. In it he said something about Islam that made history. This was because all of Germany at the time was debating migration. That in turn was because of a book that had just appeared.

Sarrazin, or, the Battle for Discursive Hegemony on Migration

On August 30, 2010, a book came out that sold more than 1.5 million copies and became postwar Germany's bestselling work of non-fiction ever – and turned the migration debate to the right: *Deutschland schafft sich ab: Wie wir unser Land aufs Spiel setzen* (*Germany Abolishes Itself: How We're Putting Our Country in Jeopardy*). Its author was the SPD politician Thilo Sarrazin, Berlin's Senator of Finance from 2002 until 2009 and at

Figure 8.1 Thilo Sarrazin at the book launch of *Germany Abolishes Itself* on its release date, August 30, 2010. Toni Passig / Getty Images.

the time of the book's publication an Executive Board member of Germany's central bank (Figure 8.1).

The book is a mixture of first, dry social analysis with statistics about demography, PISA tests, and unemployment; second, a genetic argument; and third, a fictious horror scenario for the future. The social analysis is spot on in many respects and seems motivated by genuine concern about the future of the social welfare state; the genetic argument is scientifically unsound and awash with nasty mistakes; the horror scenario is muddled and just nasty.

Not just I, everyone has an opinion about this book. How many read the 464 or 512, depending on the edition, pages is hard to tell. In any case, it has been asserted that it is the most successful non-fiction book since Adolf Hitler's *Mein Kampf* – and, like Hitler's, a book that few buyers actually read.[20] I have read it. Several times.

So what does it say? Germany will abolish itself, claims Sarrazin, if it fails to change its politics with respect to migration, labor, education, and the social welfare state. The Germans live ever longer, but have ever fewer children. More precisely, not all Germans, and the wrong people continue to have enough children. Those who have a lot of children are, according to Sarrazin, uneducated Muslims who live off social benefits instead of paying into the social welfare systems and thus securing the well-being of the older generation. Because of these many economically unproductive Muslim children, society as a whole is becoming dumber: "Our society is shrinking, it is getting older, more heterogeneous, and, in terms of educational indicators, less productive. Since disproportionately many children in Germany are growing up in so-called uneducated strata with often below average intelligence, we are on average becoming dumber for purely demographic reasons. The proportion of people who can only with difficulty be integrated into the modern labor market because of their inadequate education and intellectual deficiencies is structurally increasing."[21]

Sarrazin's genetic argument about the intelligence of groups is the most controversial part of the book – and this needs to be prefaced by the fact that even research on individual intelligence is a minefield, but when it comes to groups, such as "the Muslims" or "the Germans" or "the Jews," it is all the more so. For historical reasons group-genetic arguments trigger associations to do with social Darwinism, racism, and eugenics – because of South African apartheid, US racial segregation, and Nazism. So it's no wonder that Sarrazin's point of departure elicited protest: "Among serious scientists there is no longer any doubt that human intelligence is 50 to 80 percent hereditary."[22] In the footnote to this – much-quoted – sentence, Sarrazin refers to the psychologist Elsbeth Stern.[23] Three days after the publication of *Germany Abolishes Itself*, Stern begged to differ in the weekly paper *Die Zeit*: "With his much-repeated sentence 'intelligence is 50 to 80 percent hereditary' Thilo Sarrazin proves that he doesn't understand fundamental things about heritability and intelligence. That is why we must question many of his conclusions."[24] A cardinal mistake of Sarrazin's was that he assumed the same starting chances for everyone, as though school children in first grade started the rat race of life under the same conditions: "But because we are very far from such educational equality, the following applies: if the son of college-educated German parents achieves 'only' an average IQ, we can be quite certain that his genes simply do not allow for more. If, however, the daughter of working-class parents of Turkish descent attains the same IQ, we can assume that she has not been able to realize her full genetic intelligence potential. In better circumstances she would have likely achieved a higher IQ. Among children with a migration background there is thus more hidden potential in terms of intelligence to be found than there is among children of German descent."[25]

Sarrazin makes further scandalous errors concerning facts and logic. He writes, for example: "From today's perspective, the immigration of *Gastarbeiter* during the 1960s and 1970s was a gigantic mistake: for the most part, the *Gastarbeiter* worked in dying industries. This slowed down the unavoidable structural transformation to a postindustrial economy and obstructed our view of the worrying nature of Germany's demographic decline."[26] But hasn't economic history shown that the *Gastarbeiter* markedly contributed to the economic miracle?[27] And how can one seriously blame the *Gastarbeiter* for slowing down the transition to a postindustrial economy – should they have had a premonition (and why they of all people?) that this transition was around the corner?

Sarrazin writes, moreover: "People call Neukölln Germany's largest Turkish city. There are a lot of Neuköllns in Germany. The city of Ahlen in Wesphalia, for example, has about 56,000 inhabitants, but south of the railway tracks there is a compact Muslim city of 15,000 inhabitants. Today there are hundreds of residential areas and entire urban districts in which Turkish or Arab migrants constitute a majority or a strong minority. In all of these settlements similar problems occur. They are growing much faster than the cities in which they are located (those are actually often shrinking), and they are growing faster than the German population anyway. Someone who passes through one of these areas as a German feels like a stranger in his own country."[28] Yet the parents and grandparents of Neukölln's or Ahlen's inhabitants of Turkish descent never volunteered to move into these quarters and to settle there compactly. We saw in Chapter 3 that in the 1960s and 1970s they had no choice but to move into these dilapidated quarters where no one else wanted to live. Even today the so-called free housing market is anything but free, as many social science studies go to show; there are more or less subtle mechanisms of exclusion if you want to move into certain parts of town but have Öztürk as a surname and place your first phone call to the property management or real-estate agent.[29] And by the way, the people who live in Neukölln or Ahlen are often just as much German citizens as Sarrazin. He cannot feel like "a stranger in his own country." Neukölln is inhabited by people who are in their own country. This country belongs to them just as much as it belongs to Sarrazin.

Whenever Sarrazin looks beyond the German borders, especially to the UK and the United States, he gets things particularly wrong. Thus he writes: "Parallel societies usually go hand in hand with regional concentration, but this isn't necessarily the case. They easily become ghetto-like where the population is largely unemployed and mostly lives off social welfare benefits. That holds for northern Neukölln with its Turkish and Arab population as it used to hold for Black Harlem in New York. Parallel societies form all the more readily and exist all the longer, the greater the migrants' lack of interest in dominant society and the more they prefer to stick to themselves."[30] "Prefer"? It is testimony to considerable history-falsifying energy to presuppose voluntarism with reference to Harlem's "parallel society." This "parallel society" came into being because of de facto apartheid: until the Civil Rights movement of the 1960s African Americans in New York too were practically *coerced* to live among themselves, they had no choice.

Apart from these factual mistakes, half-truths, logical fallacies, and internal contradictions, Sarrazin's greatest mistake is essentialism: this is the book's most fundamental problem. Sarrazin thinks about culture and the nation as essences, as unchangeable phenomena. Thus he writes: "I would like my great-grandchildren to be able to live in *Germany* 100 years from now, if they so wish. I don't want the country of my grandchildren and great-grandchildren to be predominantly Muslim, that women wear a headscarf, and the daily rhythm is governed by the call of the Muezzins. If I want to experience that, I can book a vacation trip to the Orient."[31] Leaving aside for a moment the special, provocative Sarrazin sound, the Germany that he dreams of here will not exist in 100 years. No one can know what Germany will look like then, whether Germany will still exist, which languages are spoken, whether there will still be religions or which religions will dominate and how people will practice them. Even the quickest of glimpses into history brings home that it is absurd to want to conserve the present for 100 years: the Germany, spoken German, and its religions of 1871 (before that "Germany" as a nation-state did not exist) have very little in common with the Germany of 1971. Moreover, immigrants never simply blend into the existing culture. Through their "integration" they invariably change what already exists, much like the German immigrants in the United States or Russia never simply "integrated," but in reality changed the United States and Russia.

"Those who grew up in Germany," Sarrazin writes about the *Almancı*, "notice at the latest in Turkey that they are now 'Germanites' and no longer real Turks. The horrible thing is that many of these 'Germanites' in the end are neither real Turks nor real Germans."[32] Only someone who imagines "Turks" and "Germans" as homogeneous, essential entities can find surprising what Sarrazin finds "horrible." If culture is understood, as is common today, to be hybridic, the state of the *Almancı* appears normal: it is the same normality that allows Bavarians or Swabians to live in the Federal Republic without identity conflicts.[33] "But we don't want any national minorities," Sarrazin goes on. "Whoever wants to remain a Turk or an Arab and wants the same thing for their children, should be removed to their country of origin."[34] Apart from the fact that Germany has exactly four recognized national minorities (the Danes in Schleswig-Holstein, the Friesians in northern Germany, the German Sinti and Roma, and the Sorbs in the Lausitz region), the question is why does being German and being Turkish or Arab need to be defined in mutually exclusive terms? We need a concept of the nation according to which the collective identity of being German is unreservedly compatible with a simultaneous maintenance of Turkish or Arab identities (and many more). These particularist identities should be cherished and actively promoted. Multilingualism and being comfortable in more than one culture are crucial in our globalizing world.

Is Sarrazin's concept of culture already racial (*völkisch*) or even neo-Nazi, as some commentators opined?[35] No, I believe, or at least not at first glance, because immigrants, in theory, have the option of totally assimilating in the culture imagined by Sarrazin in essentialist terms, namely through "integration," which for him actually means complete assimilation, that is, acculturation. If Muslims shed their faith, male Muslims regard women as equal, female Muslims do not wear a headscarf, and all contribute to the GDP through hard and honest labor, learn German to perfection, and can recite Goethe's *Wandrers Nachtlied* (*Wanderer's Nightsong*) by heart, they would contribute to a Germany that Sarrazin today dreams of for his great-grandchildren in 100 years' time. On looking more closely, however, Sarrazin does indeed slip into racial thinking. For his future forecast is based on the idea of two Germanies, a white, Christian Germany and a Muslim, Arab–Turkish one. When Sarrazin conceives a horrific scenario for the future in which the latter will be in the majority, what becomes visible is a concept of religion as nature that cannot be changed, much like one's body height or skin pigmentation. That is racial.

Germany Abolishes Itself is a polemic with a presupposed opinion. It is pseudo-scholarly because the sole function of scholarship here is to buttress ready-made opinions; the aim is not, as should be the case in scholarship, to arrive at the truth even if it is uncomfortable for one's opinion. As long as they fit his argument, Sarrazin has no compunction about citing infamous, repeat-offending charlatans whom serious scholars would not touch with a bargepole.[36] In addition, he cites as token voices a few atypical PlusGermans like Necla Kelek, Seyran Ateş, or Güner Balcı.[37] Finally, the book is worded in a hurtful tone that makes the reader wince at every page.

Take this example: "Society is its own object and through the parameters it sets for itself can change its form. If this were not the case, all human societies would, much like the different chimpanzee tribes in the jungle, still be at the same level of development, namely that of the African bush."[38] Sarrazin perhaps thinks this is straight talking, not mincing words. Or funny. Or both straight talking and funny. PlusGermans, however, perceive Sarrazin's rhetoric, which aims at provocation, as hostile and degrading. More precisely, hostile and degrading in a way that is all too familiar to them. Sarrazin's language is never hard-hitting argumentation among equals. He reopens wounds among PlusGermans that others, from fellow students in the school courtyard to their bosses at work, have caused them again and again. Hate speech, hostile, hurtful talk against women, gays, Muslims, Jews, and blacks is, as all microaggressions are, a form of violence.

Germany Abolishes Itself poisoned the atmosphere – in school, at the workplace, in the neighborhood, at the sports club.[39] PlusGermans saw the book as confirmation that they are, at the end of the day, not welcome. No matter how hard they try to "integrate," they will never belong. If more than 1.5 million people buy such a book, there must exist a huge groundswell of rejection. The 1988-born feminist, hijab-wearing blogger Kübra Gümuşay felt that in Germany "there was always a basic framework of decency that I could rely on – that is gone now. For me it started with Thilo Sarrazin's book in 2010."[40]

For others the book lent corroboration to their own prejudices, all the more so since its author is a Social Democrat and thus not suspected of being a right-winger, and on top of that a statistician who works with numbers as "hard facts." They felt as though they had finally been lent a voice that the mainstream media had ostensibly suppressed. Sarrazin himself had planted the seeds for such an interpretation when writing, "It is almost considered politically incorrect to worry about Germany as the land of the Germans. That explains the many taboos and the completely messed-up German discussion of such topics as demography, family policy, and immigration."[41] Four years later he expanded on this and published his book *Der neue Tugendterror: Über die Grenzen der Meinungsfreiheit in Deutschland* (*The New Terror of Virtue: On the Limits of Freedom of Speech in Germany*). To be sure, Sarrazin did not invent the our-opinion-is-suppressed narrative, that was the New Right. But he made it palatable for wider parts of the public. Sarrazin's book is an important way station on the path to slogans like those of *Lügenpresse*, "lying press." For quite a while now these charges are no longer being made in the most remote corners of the World Wide Web, but in Germany's most influential media – we will get to Jens Spahn, Peter Sloterdijk, and Rüdiger Safranski.

Ever since Sarrazin, the Right has been controlling the narrative and setting the agenda. That is the situation in which Germany finds itself in since 2010: a majority of the population has positive attitudes about migration, indeed 19 percent are engaged in refugee charity work, Germany's largest social movement since the Second World War, but public discourse about refugees, migration, and the nation is dominated by the right-wing minority: it is hegemonic.

The 2010s

Bremen, October 3, 2010, the central ceremony for the twentieth anniversary of German reunification. The new Federal President, Christian Wulff, who has been in office for 3 months, steps up to the rostrum. He starts with German reunification, the European idea, then moves on to "visionary statesmen" like Willy Brandt, Helmut Schmidt, and, of course, Helmut Kohl from the ranks of his own party, the CDU.

He continues with the contemporary Germany of 2010: "Our country has become more open, more cosmopolitan, more varied – and more diverse. [. . .] global competition, global trade routes, new technologies, borderless communication, immigration, demographic change . . .." On to the transition to the Sarrazin debate, if only, to be sure, in innuendos: "Some differences trigger fears. [. . .] When German Muslims write to me: 'You are our President' – then I respond from the bottom of my heart: Yes, of course I am your President!" Wulff now takes apart "three grand delusions": *Gastarbeiter* are only temporary "guests"; Germany is not an immigrants' country; multiculturalism, defined as simply letting things run their course without making demands on immigrants, works. Germans must part with all three delusions. Then the broad hint at Sarrazin: "We have come a long way, further than the current debate might suggest." And finally the famous sentence that would be quoted over and over: "But by now, Islam also belongs to Germany."[42]

One day before that, October 2, 2010. Berlin. The Dutch right-wing populist Geert Wilders gives a lecture at a hotel, praises Sarrazin, and speaks about the specter of Islam that is haunting Europe. His audience consists mainly of white, male Germans who have paid an entrance fee of €35. The event was fully booked in no time.[43]

Clearly, by the 2010s migration had become one of the key issues of political debate, and with the 2015 refugee crisis it moved to the top of the agenda. Not having an opinion became ever more difficult. Three longer-term developments characterize the 2010s: the polarization of politics; the self-organization and radicalization of an increasingly united refugee movement; and welcoming culture, that is, charity work on behalf of refugees, which turned into postwar Germany's largest social movement. These three developments are entangled and can only be narrated jointly.

Today the 2010s are often remembered for right-wing populism's ascent. In truth, politics on the whole polarized during that decade, the left and right extremes gained in strength. In the immediate aftermath of really existing socialism's collapse in 1989–1991 left-wing alternatives at first seemed to have been discredited for good. Social democratic parties in Europe and the United States renounced social reform programs and tended toward centrism; no word had a greater taboo attached to it than the r-word (redistribution); the market was considered the solution to just about anything; what increasingly came to be called "neoliberalism" triumphed. Social democracy's new centrism was spectacularly successful: Tony Blair's New Labour in the UK (1997–2010), Schröder's SPD in Germany (1998–2005), but also Clinton in the United States (1992–2000).

It wasn't until the great crash of 2008 that the image of neoliberalism as the sole remaining, functioning economic system showed serious cracks. New emotion-based social movements against neoliberalism, austerity politics, and gentrification ensued: in Germany "citizens in rage" (*Wutbürger*) against the rebuilding of Stuttgart's central railway station, an expensive infrastructure project known as Stuttgart 21, from 2010 onward; "the outraged" (*Indignados*) in Spain from 2011 onward, inspired by the 93-year-old French Second World War resistance fighter Stéphane Hessel's 2010 manifesto *Time for Outrage*, and the new left-wing party Podemos that emerged from the Spanish anti-austerity protests; the Occupy movement on New York's Wallstreet and in London's and Frankfurt's banking districts (2011); the success of the new left-wing party Syriza in the Greek parliamentary elections of 2012 and its subsequent victory in 2015: for the first time in years a European country came to be governed by an anticapitalist left-wing party. And all of this against the backdrop of the Arab Spring from 2011 onward – we will return to this. Later social democracy in England and America also moved further to the left, as manifested in the surprise success of the Momentum movement and Jeremy Corbyn's ascent in the British Labour Party and Bernie Sanders' near-presidential candidacy for the Democrats in 2016. Germany was the outlier. There the move away from the center to the left began only in 2019 and so far no credible "angry, old white man" like Corbyn or Sanders, who stubbornly held on to an alternative to capitalism during the decades of neoliberalism between 1989 and 2008, has emerged.

Why do we collectively remember the post-2008 years mostly for the return of the Right? Whence this distorted image? Possibly because the Right represented the new for the first time since the 1920s. In terms of ideas and protest forms, symbols and rituals, the Left, at least in Germany, had a monopoly on innovation for a long, long time, at least since 1968. The Red–Green government of 1998–2005 marked the institutionalization of 1968, the arrival in the establishment after the "long march through the institutions." In the 2010s left-wing sit-ins, demonstrations, and slogans seemed somewhat tired. Occupy, Stuttgart 21, and so on were iterations of familiar forms, slightly tweaked, but actually the return of the same.

So much for what I have to offer by way of explanation for the Right's discursive dominance. Embodying novelty and freshness was also the express goal of the Right itself – consider Björn Höcke at the booth of Götz Kubitschek's New Right Antaios publishing house at the 2017 Frankfurt Book Fair: "We are living in a key transition period. Just as the 1968ers once pushed through their cultural hegemony [. . .] the turn will now be to the conservative, right-wing position."[44] Höcke represents the far-right wing of the AfD, a right-wing populist party that managed to get into the Bundestag in 2017 and in this surpassed its predecessors, the NPD, which in 1969 with 4.3 percent of the votes fell slightly short of the 5-percent threshold, but also the Republikaner, who were successful in the 1980s, or the Partei Rechtsstaatlicher Offensive (Party for a Rule of Law Offensive), whose Ronald Schill from 2001 to 2003 was Senator of the Interior of Hamburg, one of Germany's sixteen federal states.

A loose right-wing International formed, whose unifying "idea" is the rejection of migration and Islam; that employs social media ever more frequently and adeptly and spreads fake news and conspiracy theories ever faster, accelerating cycles of emotional heating-up; that found a new reservoir of financial and ideational support in Putin's Russia, especially after the annexation of Crimea in 2014. There, the poles sometimes touch each other: thus left-wing *Putin-Versteher* (Putin sympathizers) of the German party Die Linke, the AfD, the French Rassemblement National, the Austrian FPÖ, Russian Neo-Eurasians, and the American Alt-Right have come together in Russia for conferences.

Just how clueless Germans had been about the activity of those even further to the right – right-wing extremists – became painfully obvious when in 2011 a series of right-wing terrorist attacks was uncovered. Uwe Mundlos, Uwe Böhnhardt, and Beate Zschäpe had undergone radicalization in Jena in the early 1990s. Their main sources of inspiration were the US White Supremacy movement and the international neo-Nazi scene. They went underground in 1998, in 1999 they founded their terror group National Socialist Underground (NSU), and between 2000 and 2009 they killed nine people with a migration background and one policewoman, and organized bomb attacks and armed robberies. After the two men had committed suicide on November 4, 2011, Beate Zschäpe was arrested, and one of Germany's largest-ever criminal trials began, ending on July 11,

2018. Zschäpe was sentenced to life in jail. The verdicts of the helpers of the terrorists, against whom the more than fifty joint plaintiffs, among them many surviving family members of the murder victims, had filed cases, were widely seen as too mild. For the terrorists were able to rely on a large network of up to 200 supporters whose tentacles reached into the police authorities. The practice of infiltrating the right-wing scene with paid police informers was tarnished, perhaps discredited definitively. The fact that for nearly 10 years people of Turkish and other backgrounds could be murdered, that these murders were not solved and even attributed to people of Turkish background themselves ("migrant milieu," "Döner murders"), led to a crisis of the entire German domestic secret service (its head had to resign in the end) and destroyed trust in the German legal system among PlusGermans in the long run.[45]

Let us move on to the second development that *taz* journalist Christian Jakob tracked in his 2016 book *Those Who Stay: How Refugees Have Been Changing Germany for the Past 20 Years.*[46] Thuringia, 1996. Osaren Igbinoba, a Nigerian whose application for asylum has just been rejected, opens an office in the attic of a left-wing center. His organization is called The VOICE Refugee Forum Germany. The center is located right behind the theater in Jena, the town where at the same time the NSU trio is radicalizing. A year later, in September 1997, someone deposits a bomb in a suitcase in front of the theater; a swastika is drawn on the suitcase. During the investigation Böhnhardt, Mundlos, and Zschäpe are among those interrogated. The VOICE grows into the leading German refugee movement, managing to bridge national, ethnic, political, and gender differences.

It is no coincidence that the movement emerged in the same (eastern) German federal state as the right-wing terror of the NSU. In the ex-GDR asylum seekers were housed in the former barracks of the East German army (NVA) and the Western Forces of the Soviet Army. Here conditions are worse than anywhere else in Germany because the barracks are in remote areas, completely isolated, and asylum seekers, who must not even move outside the confines of their aliens department, are cramped together for years on end, without being allowed to work. Racist attacks from the local population are more frequent and more brutal than in the west, and even those Germans who would be willing to come into contact with the asylum seekers can hardly do so because of the isolation. The camps themselves are in a deplorable condition. Take Katzhütte in the Thuringian Forest, once a vacation resort of the GDR federation of trade unions – cracked prefab walls, damp and cold, mold, no soap, no toilet paper, the kitchen locked from 4 pm, the shower from 5 pm onward.[47]

Igbinoba and The VOICE visit one asylum shelter after another, first in Thuringia, later also in other states. Their message is simple: we all have the same problems, let's organize! Self-organization of refugees had taken place earlier, but it had been restricted to recognized refugees (not asylum seekers) and organized according to country of origin or ethnic-political identity, as in the case of Communist Kurds from Turkey. The four main demands of The VOICE will remain the same over the course of 20 years: lifting of the prohibition on working; freedom of movement instead of the residence requirement; monetary support instead of benefits in kind, especially not the hated, monotonous food packages; housing in apartments in the midst of society rather than isolated in shelters. The residence requirement is unique in Europe. Until 1996 asylum seekers in several states still had to get permission from the aliens department if they wanted to travel to the territory of another aliens department, even if it was for only a few hours. Other places had residence requirements limited to within the entire federal state. Since 2013 these residence restrictions have been lifted almost everywhere, only Bavaria and Saxony continue to cling to them.

Before the parliamentary general election of 1998 The VOICE joins with other groups and travels across Germany as a caravan, clamoring for the rights of refugees and migrants: "we have no vote but a voice" is their main slogan. The refugee movement gains traction: in 1999 soon-to-be-deported refugees occupy the office of the Green Party in Cologne, they start a hunger strike; in 2000 the first large refugee convention takes place in Jena, with 600 participants, many of whom have to violate the residence requirement in order to travel there. Others come from France from the Sans Papiers movement, which in any case is the great model because it proves how self-organization even of those with the least rights, those who went underground or were illegalized, can have spectacular successes. In France politicians were repeatedly forced to implement amnesty programs for the Sans Papiers.[48] And thus the Jena Convention of 2000 above all also marks self-empowerment.

And so it goes on for more than a decade in which ties are forged – with the anti-globalization movement; from the late 1990s with the border camps on the Oder–Neiße border, for example in Görlitz in 1998 and in Zittau in 1999; from the middle of the 2000s with the No-Lager (No-Camp) network; later with groups in Mali, Morocco, Greece, Ukraine, France, and other countries. What supports and flanks the refugee movement is the grandchildren generation of the *Gastarbeiter*, some of whom are now calling themselves postmigrants, others New Germans. Their motivation was a feeling of "rage. About living in a society in whose self-image we don't exist."[49]

The asylum topic truly enters the national conversation in 2012. From then on it gains momentum; society has shifted, it is no longer willing to accept the 1993 change of the constitution that restricted the basic right to asylum. From 2011 the self-organized refugee movement widens and becomes more radical. This radicalization is mostly due to refugees from Iran, many of whom were tortured in its prisons. The spark is Mohammed Rahsepar's suicide in a Würzburg shelter on January 29, 2012; according to the organization Anti-Racist Initiative from Berlin he is number 167 of a total of 179 refugees who by late 2014 had committed suicide out of fear of being deported. Thousands wound themselves in suicide attempts, such as the 33-year-old deportee Kokou D. from Togo, who in his Hamburg prison cell "rams a ball pen refill into his trachea."[50] On March 19, 2012, Rahsepar's Iranian housemates build a protest camp in the center of Würzburg and begin a hunger strike. Well into the second week of the hunger strike, the media start reporting about them. The CSU Minister of Social Affairs, Christine Haderthauer, warns against speaking with the protesters, lest the state appear "susceptible to blackmail."[51] At the same time the asylum applications of four of the by now ten hunger strikers are expedited and accepted – after nothing had happened for years with their applications.

The activists interrupt their hunger strike. Their main demands continue to be the abolition of residence limitations and compulsory housing in camps and also the end of deportations. When these demands are not met, the Iranians recommence their hunger strike and escalate it in early June: Arash Dosthossein and Mohammed Kalali sew their mouths shut, now they can only take in liquids through a straw (Figure 8.2). In the following days five

Figure 8.2 Iranian refugees Arash Dosthossein (left) and Mohamed Kalali (right) in Würzburg with sewn-up mouths, June 4, 2012. Daniel Peter / epd.

other Iranians follow suit. At first the city of Würzburg tries to impose an information blackout: no images must get out – "shock news" and "self-mutilation" are invoked as justification for the ban. The courts immediately declare the ban null and void, arguing that it violates free speech. Images of the emaciated protesters with their sewn-up mouths in Germany's richest federal state go around the world. More and more refugees and German activists come to Würzburg and build a protest camp, first there, then in other towns – they call this "tent actions."

On September 8, 2012, the Iranians in Würzburg embark on a protest march to Berlin. Along the whole route there isn't a single intervention by the police, even though many of the marchers are violating their residence requirements. While on the road, supporters house them, and television crews soon arrive. Neo-Nazis attack them in Erfurt. When they arrive in Berlin on October 5 after 600 kilometers marching on foot, Germany's number one television daily news broadcast, the *Tagesschau*, reports about the refugee movement for the first time. "They broke through into the consciousness of the general public," writes Christian Jakob.[52] (Figure 8.3)

The movement builds a camp on Oranienplatz in Berlin's Kreuzberg district. Until its clearing in April 2014, Oranienplatz is the nerve center of an expanding political movement. Berlin refugees, left-wing groups, civil society initiatives, and church groups all show solidarity. Increasing

Figure 8.3 Refugee hunger strike in Berlin, October 31, 2012. Adam Berry / Stringer / Getty Images.

numbers of people come to express support and donate blankets, mattresses, and money. Several times the protesters go on hunger strike, they occupy the Nigerian Embassy, and even ultra-conservative CDU politicians like Wolfgang Bosbach feel obliged to receive a delegation from the camp.

In June 2013 refugees set up another protest camp on Munich's Rindermarkt Square and start a hunger strike. In a letter to Angela Merkel they demand recognition as victims of political persecution according to Article 16 of the German constitution rather than merely subsidiary protection or exceptional leave to remain. And not just for themselves, but for all asylum seekers. Wado Watol from Ethiopia says: "We have lost our families, our country, and now we live here in the same kind of prison as before." "In our country we are killed with a bullet, here we die a slow death," seconds Lukas Johannes, also from Ethiopia.[53]

The refugees begin to resort to more radical methods, they stop drinking. The Bavarian CSU government sets up an emergency taskforce, Munich's Mayor Christian Ude (SPD) says the refugees "are knowingly facing their death."[54] In the camp there are children, babies, and pregnant women. The situation is becoming more dramatic by the hour. On a Sunday at the crack of dawn the police brutally clear the camp, and those on hunger or thirst strike are brought to hospital. They are tacitly given permanent residence permits. Alexander Thal of the Bavarian Refugee Countil, a civil society organization, concludes: "The more confrontational you are, the more likely it is you'll be allowed to stay."[55]

Meanwhile on Berlin's Oranienplatz the situation is deteriorating. People's nerves are on edge after the first winter, there is a lot of argument. Then something happens that triggers mass empathy in the German population: on October 3, 2013, near the Mediterranean island of Lampedusa a boat with 360 refugees catches fire and sinks. "It is like in a horror movie, down there, there is a mass of trapped bodies, one over another in the freight hold," says an Italian diver.[56] The images become an icon of the refugee crisis, much like the September 2, 2015 photograph of dead Kurdish-Syrian boy Alan Kurdi. Europe is shocked, although so far an estimated total of 25,000 refugees have drowned, attempting to cross the Mediterranean in boats. High-ranking EU politicians take a stance, as does Pope Francis. On November 3, 2013, 15,000 people in Hamburg participate in a demonstration against the EU's refugee policy, more than ever before.

The protests are widening across Europe, but in Spring 2014 media interest declines and the refugee movement visibly splinters – along lines of country of origin or political allegiance. In early 2015 the protest cycle that began in January 2012 in Würzburg with the radical Iranians has run its course. Some demands have been met, twelve of the worst east German shelters, against which Igbinoba organized the first protest in Jena, have been closed. But many problems persist. Still, through the vigils, pickets, protest camps, foot marches, demonstrations, and hunger strikes countless contacts have been forged, networks have been built, and wider society has been sensitized; the topic is now firmly anchored in the collective consciousness.

Let us now home in on volunteering for refugees, the third of the three intertwined processes. When looking for a beginning, 1979 is one possibility. Back then Rupert Neudeck, a former Jesuit, started a rescue operation for Vietnamese Boat People who had fled the Communist regime in Vietnam in boats on the South China Sea. Neudeck raised funds and chartered the cargo ship *Cap Anamur*, with which he rescued over the course of many years in the open sea a total of 11,300 Boat People, got them medical treatment, and brought them to Germany. There they received asylum as quota refugees.[57]

A second possible beginning is 1983 and also in the Christian-alternative milieu. In October 1983 three Palestinian families asked the Lutheran clergyman Jürgen Quandt and his Holy Cross Parish in Berlin-Kreuzberg for protection from impending deportation.[58] Recall from Chapter 5 how the refugee Kemal Altun jumped to his death from the sixth floor of Berlin's Landgericht court on August 30 during his legal hearing because he understood that his application for asylum stood no chance and that he would be deported to Turkey, where the military leaders, who had come to power in a coup in 1980, had accused him of attempting to assassinate a minister. When six refugees in deportation prison burned to death on New Year's Eve 1983–1984, religious people became increasingly skeptical "about the argument that what is happening on legal grounds should be accepted merely because it is legal."[59] Working groups were formed in both of the major Christian Churches, and more and more parishes started hiding refugees threatened with deportation in their buildings.

At the same time civil society initiatives were founded, especially in locales with refugee shelters. In 1986 PRO ASYL, the national umbrella movement of the local citizens' groups, came into being.[60] In the early 1990s, as a reaction to Hoyerswerda, Rostock-Lichtenhagen, Mölln, and Solingen, the civil society activism of the citizen groups and leftist activists expanded. Antifa activists risked their lives, it bears remembering, in the reconquest of so-called "nationally liberated zones" in their struggle with neo-Nazis, who abused the leftists as "ticks" (*Zecken*) and brutally attacked many of them: at least six have been murdered since 1990.[61]

New forms of commemoration and protest emerged, especially candle-lit demonstrations: 400,000 people came together in December 1992 in Munich for such a candle-lit demonstration, among them many celebrities – this was one of the milestones on the path to the welcoming culture of 2015. In 1997 the network Kein Mensch ist illegal (No One Is Illegal) brought together anti-racist groups from the Antifa spectrum with citizen groups and Church organizations. The forms of activism were diverse and ranged from fictitious marriages and the hiding of rejected asylum seekers to protests against the EURODAC biometric database, founded in 2003, which centrally stores fingerprints and enabled the Dublin System in the first place, to the blocking of deportation charter flights.

Clearly, then, historical actors have *agency*, within corridors of possibility they decide their own fate. Through networking and later the collective fight for their interests, through novel forms of resistance, through radical tactics, such as sewing up their mouths or the refusal to take in liquids, which had previously not existed in Germany, refugees successfully gained attention and moved their concerns to the center of Germany's political–ethical agenda. Refugees are anything but compliant objects of the state or the well-intentioned helper scene, they are thinking, feeling, acting, and oftentimes contradictory subjects. The same is true for the volunteers, from religious milieus, to local citizen groups, to Antifa groups. Both the refugees and the helpers had to position themselves in the political field in which they were moving. This field was always demarcated by right and left extremes. In the years preceding 2015 these extremes became stronger: both the Left and the Right became stronger; the conventional wisdom that just the Right was in the ascendant is in need of correction. None of the three developments, the self-organization of refugees, volunteering on behalf of refugees, and political polarization, can be understood on its own; they are inextricably intertwined.

Welcoming Culture 2015

Late 2010 saw the start of a series of revolutions that swept away dictators and their regimes in Arab countries such as Tunisia, Egypt, and Libya. The mass protests of the Arab Spring reached Syria, where deserting soldiers formed their own army and soon fought in a civil war against the troops of President Bashar al-Assad. This civil war became increasingly brutal – poison gas was used, and, by the time of writing in 2022, up to 610,000 people have died. And it became increasingly intricate and confused – different religious and ethnic parties fought each other, Russia and the United States got involved, and for a while the terror group *Daesh* (the so-called Islamic State) controlled large parts of Syria and Iraq.

The Syrian civil war triggered one of the worst refugee crises in recent decades. Four years after the beginning of the war, in 2015, more than 11 million Syrians had been displaced, of whom 6 million remained inside Syria, while 5 million managed to escape the country. Of these 5 million, the overwhelming majority ended up in the adjacent countries Lebanon (1 million in March 2015), Jordan (625,000 in March 2015), and Turkey (1.7 million in March 2015). In Lebanon (population 4 million) and in Jordan (population 9 million) this signified a vastly higher percentage of refugees in relation to the domestic population than in Germany.

The direct cause of the subsequent migration from these countries neighboring Syria across the Mediterranean to Greece and from there via the Balkan route to Northern Europe was the cut in financial contributions to the UNHCR by donor countries, including Germany. The United Nations ran large refugee camps in countries neighboring Syria. The cuts led to painful curtailments of food rations and medical services. António Guterres, at the time Director of the UNHCR, in November 2015 did not mince his words: "The trigger was the sudden scaling-back of humanitarian aid. Over the past year the UN World Food Program in one fell swoop had to reduce its support for refugees in countries neighboring Syria by 30 percent."[62] The prospect of a longer stay in the camps or even of returning to Syria became ever more implausible. Those who could, collected money and left for Europe – via a similar route to that of Hassan Ali Djan in Chapter 5: to Turkey, from there with human traffickers to one of the Greek Islands, and further north to Germany or Sweden on the open Balkan route through Macdedonia, Serbia, and Austria (this was different from the route used in 2005 by Hassan, who came to Germany underneath a truck with the ferry from Patras to Italy and later reached Germany via the Brenner Pass).

Increasing numbers of refugees began arriving in Austria and Germany. In June 2015, for instance, 35,449 applications for asylum were filed in Germany, up from 14,019 applications a year earlier.[63] The topic began garnering more attention in the German media, and for the first time since the asylum compromise of 1993 the mood was almost invariably positive, even among many conservatives. At some point Chancellor Merkel was going to have to react; up until now she had been avoiding the subject, so much so that in April the *Süddeutsche Zeitung* ran the headline "What Merkel Is Avoiding."[64] In a July 15 television show Reem Sahwil, a 14-year-old girl with impaired mobility who had come to Germany with her parents as a Palestinian from Lebanon, spontaneously asked Merkel in front of running cameras for an improvement in their residence status so that they would not be deported. Merkel insisted on the letter of the law, Reem started crying. The Chancellor's reaction was widely perceived as overly harsh and cold. Later in July an Emnid poll found that 81 percent thought Merkel should "visit an asylum-seeker shelter in the near future."[65] This shift in public opinion in favor of asylum and Merkel's perceived coldness were important factors in this extraordinary time that Germany is still coming to terms with.

Another factor was the extreme political polarization between Right and Left that dramatically came to a head over the refugee question. On August 18 a mob, supported by right-wing extremists, had attacked a bus carrying refugees in the Saxonian town of Heidenau. On August 26 Merkel visited Heidenau – as we now know, mostly to avoid getting outempathized by her Social Democratic political rival Sigmar Gabriel, who had already visited and scolded the Heidenau demonstrators as "scum." Merkel was attacked in ways she had never experienced in her 10 years as Chancellor: "You whore!," "You c**t!," "Traitor to the people!" She was visibly repulsed and let herself be provoked into making a statement that also excluded the demonstrators from society, much like Gabriel's labeling them "scum," albeit more politely: "There can be no tolerance toward those who question the human dignity of other people."[66] From then on there was a dichotomy of light versus dark Germany, the Germany of the refugee helpers versus the Nazis. The welcoming culture after the non-closure of the border on September 4 in many ways was a reaction to Heidenau: let's *not* be like this, let's be different.

A third factor was the dissemination of new and shocking images of dead refugees: a refrigerated truck used by human traffickers with seventy-one corpses, discovered on a highway near Vienna on August 26, 2015 because a noxiously smelling liquid was dripping from the cargo compartment; and the drowned three-year-old Kurdish-Syrian boy Alan Kurdi on the beech of Bodrum on September 2, 2015.

Whether the key political actors, above all Merkel herself, in the drama that played out over the next few weeks were "Driven Ones" (*Getriebene*), as journalist Robin Alexander claimed in his eponymous book, or whether they were rational beings guided by ethical, Christian, *Realpolitik*, and other motives, will be a bone of contention for historians in decades to come. One thing is certain: it was a drama.

In late August more and more refugees are stuck at Keleti Train Station in Hungary's capital Budapest. Merkel had been pushing for an EU solution from late July onward, but the other EU countries were opposed to distributing the refugees among themselves. Hungary's President Viktor Orbán negotiated a de facto acceptance of a part of these refugees; in reality he went much further and had them bussed to the Austrian border, which they passed, only to then move on to the German border. More and more were passing into Germany across the barely supervised border. On September 4 Germany stopped registering these refugees – this news traveled fast via social media. From then on the Austrians waved the refugees through instead of taking in some themselves – with Germany's tacit agreement, in turn amplifying the pull factor. According to Alexander, this was not an opening of the border (the border was open), nor a premediated non-closing of the border, and certainly not a humanitarian act on the part of Chancellor Merkel. She simply refused to take responsibility for the fortification or closing of the border: "Thus on this weekend the German border stays open for everyone. The 'exception' of the border opening becomes a months-long state of exception because no political force can muster the courage to end the exception, as had been planned. The border does not stay open because Angela Merkel, for instance, or someone else in the federal government deliberately decided to keep it open. In the decisive hour there is simply no one who wants to take responsibility for closing it."[67]

Six days later Merkel visits a branch of the Federal Office for Migration and Refugees in Berlin-Spandau and lets professional photographers capture how refugees are taking selfies with her. These images immediately go around the world; the digital revolution has accelerated everything, including in matters concerning migration. This was an additional pull factor. Today the key politicians from back then are in agreement that instead some kind of deterrent signal should have been sent after the fateful day of September 4 (Figure 8.4).

On September 13 this would be rectified, and the German cabinet decides to close the border. But what kind of closure: to everyone? To everyone except asylum seekers? To everyone except Syrian asylum seekers? This is the subject of an ongoing argument that lasts to this day. It is doubtful whether closing the border – any kind of closing – would have been legally possible at all. The term closing of borders is, furthermore, misleading because neither barbed-wire nor a wall had been planned; what was discussed was rather the reintroduction of border controls. At any rate, everything was ready for such controls (21 groups of 100 police, water cannons).[68] The President of the German federal police, Dieter Romann, had put border controls in place during the G7 summit in Elmau in June and had, without informing the powers that be, left the equipment in the border region. Even a thirty-page mission order was ready: Romann had drawn it up in advance.

In the meantime, the welcoming culture took on unbelievable proportions. In Munich people from all walks of life greeted the new arrivals in "trains of hope" at the Central Station with water and food, distributing

Figure 8.4 Angela Merkel's selfie with Syrian refugee Anas Modamani at a branch of the Federal Office for Migration and Refugees in Berlin-Spandau, September 10, 2015. Sean Gallup / Getty Images.

cuddly toys to the children. In all of Bavaria people got into their cars to bring refugees from Hungary to Germany via Austria; in the weekly newspaper *Die Zeit* a law professor explained how German tourists could bring refugees with them to Germany while driving back from their vacations in Italy, without violating the law. When 1,000 refugees arrived in Hamburg, 400 potential helpers spontaneously showed up at the shelter, within an hour they founded 16 working groups, ranging from "German lessons" to "sports & fun." "Refugees Welcome" t-shirts became an Amazon bestseller. Artists co-opted the language of the leftist, anti-racist milieu, who had long been using the term "escape helpers" (*Fluchthelfer*) in lieu of the pejorative "human traffickers": a Munich theater hosted a "Congress of Traffickers" for "image improvement" and "new appraisal of the trafficking service industry." Even the Union of German Criminal Investigators called for "an end to the continued criminalization of refugees," for there is "no legal possibility at all for refugees to enter Germany and make use of their right to asylum."[69] Activists in the asylum citizen groups, NGOs, and refugee organizations, who had been saying pretty much the same thing since the 1980s, only to no avail, could not stop rubbing their eyes (Figures 8.5 and 8.6).

Figure 8.5 Welcoming culture: Syrian refugees arrive from Hungary via Austria at Munich's Central Station, September 6, 2015. Christof Stache / AFP / Getty Images.

Figure 8.6 "Refugees Welcome," Frankfurt am Main Central Station, September 5, 2015. Shen Zhengning / Xinhua / Alamy Live News.

Now the September 13 order for the border closing would only have had to be carried out. Yet the Chancellor would have to give a signal to that effect. Why didn't she? Merkel herself has offered different explanations at different moments. On October 7 she cited technical, pragmatic reasons in Anne Will's television talk show: "You can't close the borders. We have 3,000 kilometers of land border. Then you have to build a fence. There is no such thing as a freeze on entrance (*Aufnahmestopp*)."[70] At the CDU Party Convention on December 14 in Karlsruhe, which ex post facto legitimated her non-closing of the border – again, the border *was* open, there was no border opening – she cited moral reasons: "Thousands of refugees were stranded in Budapest, they were making their way on foot via the highway to Austria. This was a situation in which our European values were put to the test. This was no more and no less than a humanitarian imperative."[71] Journalist Robin Alexander posits that Merkel prevented the reintroduction of border controls because of a combination of polls-obsessed mathematical calculus and irrational self-intoxication. On the one hand, she closely followed the polls with regard to the refugee euphoria and then tried "surfing the wave instead of dampening expectations."[72] On the other hand, she was carried away by the quick change in her image: from "ice queen" after the Reem Sahwil incident in July to Chancellor of the refugees in September, to holy "Mother Angela," first in leading German media, including among left-wing intellectuals, later globally.[73]

At the same time, the key political actors in this phase constantly seem to have been aware that the mood of the population might turn.[74] Therefore, behind the scenes they were feverishly working on a European solution. This solution was meant to suspend the Dublin regulations, according to which asylum cases should be decided where refugees first cross a border of the EU – Greece, Italy, or Spain, and instead distribute asylum seekers among all EU states according to specified ratios. When this solution faltered because of the resistance of East European states such as Hungary and the Czech Republic, the German government, with a heavy heart, entered into negotiations with Turkey and its quasi-dictator Erdoğan. These negotiations pivoted on control of the Turkish–Greek sea border, the taking back in of refugees with bad prospects for European asylum status, and the acceptance (via airplane) of all refugees with plausible reasons for asylum in the EU. In return Turkey was meant to get money, easier access to visas for entry into the EU, and the reopening of serious EU accession talks. This EU–Turkish agreement, signed on March 18, 2016, went down in history as the "EU–Turkey deal." Subsequently refugee numbers did indeed drastically decrease, not, however, because of the EU–Turkey deal, but because Macedonia closed its border with Greece on March 9 with a fence. The EU–Turkey deal was only partly put into practice – true, the Turkish–Greek waters are now indeed more strictly patrolled, but next to no refugees were ever flown out of Turkey to the EU, just a fraction of the earmarked EU monies was remitted, and the easing of the visa system and so forth never materialized.

Welcoming culture notwithstanding, there was resistance right from the start, and by this I do not have in mind just the record number of arson attacks on refugee shelters from the beginning of 2015 on. On September 4 the border had not been closed, and immediately there was criticism and skepticism from many quarters, including the ranks of the governing CDU – on September 13, for example, Jens Spahn told the *Süddeutsche Zeitung*: "The opening of the borders last weekend for refugees from Hungary was right in this extraordinary situation, but the consequences are enormous. This must remain an exception. Refuge migration too has gone digital. Messages and images circulate via WhatsApp within seconds and set tens of thousands of people into motion in the direction of Germany. Some still underestimate this."[75] The chattering classes followed suit – Jörg Baberowski on September 14 in the *Frankfurter Allgemeine Zeitung*, Peter Sloterdijk on September 18 in the *Handelsblatt*, Rüdiger Safranski on September 28 in *Die Welt*. "The political class has taken the decision to flood Germany," said an outraged Safranski. "If the Chancellor says Germany will change, I would like to be asked, please."[76] Many others sang the same tune. And with similar metaphors: "wave," "stream," "inundation," "avalanche," "flood," "overflow." This was taking place in leading mass media, often on the first page of the culture section, a key institution in German intellectual life, and shared many times via social media. Even further on the Right, the AfD, Pegida, and the like started relentlessly pounding, usually far afield from the traditional mass media: countless apocalyptic book titles and subtitles testify to this, such as *The Secret Migration Agenda* or *The Unsparing Truth about the German Asylum Madness!*[77] One of the most astonishing myths about the "refugee crisis" is that an oppositional public sphere ceased to exist. This is simply not true. Jens Spahn fed this myth as early as September 13, and since then all those who are skeptical about the welcoming culture have nourished it further.[78] To be sure, this mythical leitmotif originated with the New Right and was normalized by Sarrazin in 2010 (the "terror of virtue"). Among its later iterations are the "mainstream media" and the "lying press."

Yet what really remains in need of explanation about the welcoming culture is the welcoming culture itself, welcoming culture from below, if you want. For it was created by the population. Even a conservative journalist like Robin Alexander concedes that "Angela Merkel did not create the welcoming culture, not even through her spectacular opening of the border. It was the other way around: the population's enthusiasm about its own morality swept up the government, too."[79]

What might have been expected: isolation instead of opening, national egotism instead of international humanitarianism, marking refugees as "Other" instead of stressing commonalities ("people like you and me"), overproduction of phantasmas (metaphors of disease and sexuality, images of refugees as sources of epidemics and as rapists).

As with all extraordinary, complex events, scholars are going to be searching for explanations decades from now – and will find ever new ones. Here is an attempt, my attempt. Three kinds of factors interacted: long-term, medium-term, and short-term. I believe the medium-term factors were the most important, that is, the three intertwined processes described above, namely the self-organization of the refugees, the volunteers, and political polarization. Among the more short-term causes were the economic boom years since 2006, symbolized by Germany's victory in the 2014 World Cup, in other words, the luxury of being able to afford to be generous, and finally the digital revolution which accelerated the spreading of shocking images such as that of Alan Kurdi. Among the long-term causes was the wish to compensate for Nazi crimes, the felt need to atone for the refugee catastrophes produced by Germany in the wake of 1933, but also the memory of the 12.5 million expellees, a memory that was recalled in a climate of increasing displacements through the images of the refugee treks with strollers and babies on the Balkan route in Macedonia, Austria, and Bavaria.

I believe that no moral superiority or suchlike accrues to Germany from the welcoming culture of 2015. It was not that Germans showed solidarity, but humans showed solidarity with other humans. Since this still happens much too rarely, all humans, without exception, can feel good about and take pride in this. U2 singer Bono is right in saying: "As a European I feel proud thinking back to when Germans welcomed frightened Syrian refugees."[80]

Conclusion

Refugee migration raises serious moral questions. Is freedom of movement a national basic right or a universal human right? How much responsibility arises from past wrong-doing by the West – must the history of colonialism be counted among today's causes for migration? How just is it if the poorest citizens of rich countries like Germany have to accept cuts in benefits and other parts of the social welfare state because refugees are taken in?

There is an entire scholarly field of migration ethics, and its answers to these questions are often surprising.[81] For instance, some leftist philosophers reject the demand for open borders.[82] They maintain that open borders would lead to the emigration of the healthiest and most dynamic citizens of poor countries and make the Global South even poorer. For the sake of equity they are *in favor* of borders and controls on migration. Economic justice comes before all forms of freedom, including freedom of movement. Some leftist philosophers even argue that colleagues, also of the political Left, who are in favor of open borders are using "neoliberal arguments": the unfettered movement of capital, goods, and people is at the core of neoliberal thought, with its erroneous assumption that markets best organize everything automatically.[83]

To me, the open border position is more convincing for certain historical and present-day reasons which trump all other reasons. Among the historical reasons is first and foremost colonialism and its consequences in the Global South, such as civil wars because of artificially imposed borders, and economic backwardness because of the exploitation of natural resources, and also because of the high losses of people due to chattel slavery, especially to the United States and Latin America. The colonial economy also contributed to the accumulation of German wealth during the German colonial era dating from 1884 until 1919. This has largely been forgotten. The photo artist Philip Kojo Metz has made this forgotten, repressed colonial legacy tangible through objects in private households by photographing Germans in their apartments in such a way that next to the Biedermeier desk the African Herero mask, inherited from their great grandparents, colonial officers in German Southwest Africa (now Namibia), also becomes visible.[84] And there were numerous colonial crimes, above all the genocide of the Herero and Nama in German Southwest Africa between 1904 and 1908, which according to some historians functioned as a kind of laboratory for the later Nazi genocides.[85] The fact that there has been no financial recompense for these crimes, especially the genocide, is evidenced by the class action suits of the Herero and Nama, the result of which is still to come.[86]

Among the causes in the here and now are land-grabbing, that is the purchase of the Third World's most productive agricultural lands by First World banks and investment funds, which then speculate with these lands or let them lie fallow because fertile grounds are a key resource for the future (food for the growing world population, biofuels); closing the markets of the Global North to competitive agricultural products from developing countries (partly through import barriers or tariffs, partly indirectly through agricultural subventions, for example in Europe) and the simultaneous flooding of the markets of developing countries with products from rich countries; climate change, overwhelmingly produced by the rich North (industry, cars, airplanes) and its disproportionately negative, indeed increasingly catastrophic, impact in poor countries around the equator; the Western military sector and its eminent interest in civil wars because of weapons sales.

A politics of open borders would need to be achieved democratically: we would have to forge majorities – through fact-based arguments, through persuasion within the framework of our deliberative democracy. Refugees too, who have become German citizens and might be in favor of open borders due to their own experience, could use their democratic options and fight for their demands. They could do so either within existing political parties and parliaments or through the foundation of a new single-issue party, much as ecology was the single issue of the Greens in their founding phase in the late 1970s and early 1980s. Or they could organize in extra-parliamentary fashion, which would facilitate participation by those who do not have citizenship.

The big question with global topics is who is sovereign and hence democratically in charge, the citizens of a nation-state or the citizens of the world? How should one conceive of democracy when local actions have extreme consequences across the globe? What if, for example, the lifestyle of German citizens indirectly causes the flooding of the Ganges delta through climate change – why should the citizens affected there not vote for migration to Europe; on what ethical grounds can Germans have the right to destroy the livelihoods of Bangladeshis without then endowing these Bangladeshis with the right to create the conditions for a new livelihood in Germany? I cannot think of any ethical grounds for this. If democracy is conceptualized in a truly global way, new majorities emerge: there are 80 million Germans, but twice as many Bangladeshis. If only a part of these 160 million Bangladeshis avail themselves of their global human right of freedom of movement, if they "vote with their feet" and indeed set themselves in motion, nothing will hinder them from crossing the border between the Republic of Austria and the federal German state of Bavaria.

Conclusion

Oscar Handlin's *The Uprooted*, a 1951 classic in American migration history, begins as follows: "Once I thought to write a history of the immigrants in America. Then I discovered that the immigrants *were* American history."[1] Ibraimo Alberto, Dmitrij Belkin, Leonie Biallas, Hassan Ali Djan, Osaren Igbinoba, Emma Neumann, Ioannis Petridis, Ana Maria Ferreira Silva, Emilia Smechowski, Alev Yildirim – all of them and many more, who figure in this book, *are* German history. Taken together, their stories and the stories of those who arrived earlier are the history of the Germans: "the New We," the original German title of this book. The New We is also the idea for a national collective identity.

But what for? Is the German constitution not sufficient as glue beyond citizenship? After all, the constitution is more than just a collection of rules regulating social life. The constitution is above all an expression of values, and people should also identify emotionally with these values. "Constitutional patriotism" is what this concept of national pride is called; the idea originates from the philosophers Dolf Sternberger and Jürgen Habermas.[2]

The literary scholar Marina Münkler and political scientist Herfried Münkler expanded on this concept in 2016. To them, Germanness has five characteristics, two "socioeconomic" and two "sociocultural," plus constitutional patriotism. First, Germans are industrious and try to get ahead through their own, hard labor, falling back on social benefits only in emergency situations. Second, a German person thus defined can assume that "they will attain personal respect and some level of social mobility by means of their own efforts."[3] Third, Germans separate religion and the state; they do not demand, for instance, that jurisdiction must follow religious laws. Fourth, they do not interfere in the choice of life partners of their children, who can decide freely whom they love and with whom they live. Fifth, they subscribe to the constitution, the German Basic Law.[4]

It's good that the Münklers don't define Germanness ethnically. What fails to convince me, though, are the first two, economic characteristics. What about low-pay or gig economy employees who work extremely hard, yet never make it? What if things get genuinely tight economically and growth contracts permanently? What if digitization and automatization – work 4.0 – destroy a lot of jobs? Or if an Unconditional Basic Income is introduced after all? We need a definition, I believe, that safeguards some degree of social cohesion through more than just the economy.

To cut a longer discussion short, I consider the existing concepts of belonging inadequate. I believe Germany needs a collective identity that serves as a more effective emotional glue than love for the constitution or a dishwasher-to-millionaire mentality.[5]

Others hold a similar position. Some simply call this collective identity plus emotional glue patriotism (without adjectives like "constitutional patriotism"), others *Heimat*, and yet others leading culture, *Leitkultur*. I share some things with the proponents of these three concepts, but ultimately submit that we will do better with a fresh term. For whether speaking of patriotism, *Heimat*, or *Leitkultur*, these terms are all occupied, especially from the Far Right. Perhaps they could be reconquered, but it's unclear whether that would succeed.

Let's start with the concept of patriotism. Robert Habeck of the Green Party was the first left-of-center politician who said something on the topic – following the more relaxed attitudes in thinking about the nation that came with the 2006 soccer World Cup. However, his 2010 book *Patriotism: A Left Plea* lets you fathom how big the taboo he broke must have been. Because, according to Habeck, patriotism is not for the nation, but for some murky "commonwealth," by which he sometimes has in mind a neighborhood, sometimes a state institution like school, sometimes the EU.[6] The liberal-conservative Thea Dorn ventured into the same field 8 years later – and the resulting book read very differently. Intended as an alternative to the AfD, Dorn's "enlightened patriotism" stressed Germany as a nation of culture (*Kulturnation*).[7] Yet Dorn's canon of Goethe, Schiller, and the like comes across as awfully essentialized. And it bears little relation to real life, in which the German population is much more likely to experience German culture via Herbert Grönemeyer, Bushido, or Kraftklub than Schiller. Therefore I doubt that such an approach could truly emotionally engage all citizens. What is more, it is to be feared that the term patriotism has been lost irretrievably to the extreme Right – in times of "Patriotic Europeans Against the Islamicization of the Occident" (Pegida).

The term *Heimat*, the second concept for a collective, emotionally enriched identity, on the one hand was on everyone's lips after the 2018 renaming of the Federal Ministry of the Interior as the Federal Ministry of the Interior, Construction, and *Heimat*. In everyday usage, however, *Heimat* is restricted to smaller units at the sub-national level, such as a town, a place, or a region.[8] And the extreme Right has been employing the term for a long time in an exclusionary, nostalgic sense: *Heimat* must remain *theirs*, *Heimat* is the allegedly homogeneous, pre-migrant golden past that must be protected at any cost.

The concept of *Leitkultur* too is by now occupied. Bassam Tibi, a political scientist, introduced the original term in 1996, albeit in a different sense. To Tibi *Leitkultur* was a commonality of values, such as the separation of religion and state, human rights, and democracy. Tibi spoke of a European *Leitkultur* precisely because German identity was conceived even more ethnically back then in the middle of the 1990s. He thought "German *Leitkultur*" was impossible.

As I have detailed, around 2000 conservatives took over the term *Leitkultur*, first and foremost the CDU politician Friedrich Merz. *Leitkultur* to him was not a community of values as it had been for Tibi, to be attained by democratic means, but rather an unchangeable, historically fixed set of rules and institutions: the Basic Law, the European idea, democracy, the social market economy, equality between men and women, the German language.[9]

From then on, despite shifts in meaning, *Leitkultur* invariably meant something fixed, unmalleable. This was true in 2017 with Thomas de Maizière, at the time Interior Minister, who defined *Leitkultur* in the tabloid *Bild* in ten points – consider only the first point: "We value a couple of social customs, not because they are the content, but rather because they are the expression of a certain stance: we say our name. We shake hands when we meet. At demonstrations we have a ban on wearing face-coverings. 'Showing one's face' – that is a sign of our democratic cooperation. In everyday life we attach significance to whether we are looking at a friendly or sad face in interactions with our interlocutors. We are an open society. We show our face. We are not burka."[10]

Since the refugee crisis of 2015 leftists like the journalist Jakob Augstein and the Berlin SPD politician Raed Saleh have intervened and attempted to co-opt *Leitkultur* for the Left.[11] Their view hinges on the conviction that mere *multikulti*, multiculturalism, defined as the coexistence on an equal level of diverse PlusGerman cultures, is insufficient. But neither is it sufficient to constantly demand that immigrants have to integrate. What they should integrate into needs to be defined. For too long the Left has avoided such a definition. Because of Nazism, anything national was suspect, which, however, ultimately allowed the Right to occupy this field unchallenged.

Generally speaking, I share the view that *multikulti* is insufficient and that it was a mistake of the Left not to enter into competition with right-wingers over defining the nation. However, unlike Saleh, for example, I do not want to define the "felt German *Leitkultur*" (*gefühlte deutsche Leitkultur*) as a stable, fixed set of values and practices.[12]

Instead the national collective identity, the New We, should be defined and periodically redefined through democratic process and in accordance with changing historical circumstances. The collective identity of the German nation cannot be fixed once and forever since German society, like any society, is constantly changing. The contents of the We should be determined – to be sure, within the framework of the Basic Law, as no one's basic rights must be violated – via democratic decision-making processes, such as legal initiatives, parliamentary debates, committees, and competitions with juries.

To illustrate, in practice such a democratic *search* for a collective German identity might look as follows. A political party in parliament proposes legislation for a national migration museum in Berlin and a broad media debate ensues. At first it centers on the fact that the Federal Republic of Germany's status as a country of immigrants is not reflected in its museums. Various voices wonder in public that Bremerhaven has a Deutsches *Aus*wandererhaus, a German *e*migration museum, yet nowhere in Germany is there a *Zu*wanderermuseum, an *im*migration museum. For a while the debate continues to home in on Bremerhaven, and many articulate their bewilderment that the Auswandererhaus got an extension on immigration in 2012, but is still called the *Aus*wandererhaus and still located in Bremerhaven, the former port for transatlantic emigration, instead of moving to the symbolic center of the nation, Berlin. At some point everyone ashamedly looks to Cologne, where the Documentation Center and Museum of Migration in Germany, DOMiD, has been demanding such a museum since 1990 and indeed, thanks to the enormous, mostly unpaid work of PlusGerman volunteers, has morphed into the central archive on migration matters in Germany. In parliament the debate takes a turn – two parliamentary groups say that a separate migration museum would only continue "ghettoization" and demand a complete overhaul of the two sites of the German Historical Museum, the German Historical Museum in Berlin and the House of History in Bonn: the museums must be closed for several years and migration in all of its many, many dimensions inscribed into the permanent exhibitions, and every child must go on at least one school trip to one of these permanent exhibitions. In the end there is a vote – construction of a new national migration museum in Berlin or the substantive recalibration of the museums in Berlin and Bonn? In fact, and I am writing this in 2022 for the English edition, in November 2019, 9 months after my book appeared in German, the federal government earmarked €22 million for a national German migration museum in Cologne-Kalk; other government agencies and donors followed suit, and construction of what one day will be the largest migration museum in Europe has started.

Let us take a glimpse at one more example of what a democratic search for a New We might look like in practice. The federal government proposes a new national holiday, the Day of the Citizen. A parliamentary committee then starts figuring out the exact aesthetic execution of 15 naturalization ceremonies for 50,000 new citizens in soccer stadiums – what kind of music will be played, what will be sung, which symbols will be used? How can we balance diversity and unity? How should we represent PlusGerman cultures, which musical traditions do we use in order to show that the Germans have become "one out of many" (*e pluribus unum*)? Public debate about the issue soon picks up and for a while focuses on the odd fact that there are now more and more official naturalization ceremonies in Germany, but that these are done at local level, in Berlin, for example, at the level of the city-state Berlin and the Berlin district in which you are registered. When you get citizenship, the city-state of Berlin invites you to celebrate in the ballroom of its state parliament, the council of the district Steglitz-Zehlendorf, one of twelve districts, to the rococo room at the former Steglitz manor house.[13] But why? People start pointing out that you don't become a citizen of the state of Berlin or a citizen of the district of Steglitz-Zehlendorf. We're talking about the nation here, they say. Symbolically, Germany continues to be a blind spot, a nonentity, they say. The debate then shifts to what everyone begins calling by the buzzword "national ersatz symbols," such as the soccer national team or the EU, for important debates about what it means to be German take place in discussions about European values.[14] In the end broad support for the introduction of a Day of the Citizen emerges. The naturalization ceremonies in stadiums take root. Their symbols and rituals turn out to be flexible enough to adapt over the course of decades to the German population, the composition of which keeps changing as a consequence of emigration and immigration.

What could become a central element of the We – and here I am actually sketching a proposed content – is tolerance, if tolerance is defined as respect for the Other, whom I do not try to change even if they seem different from me or I do not like them. Of course, some degree of that kind of tolerance is guaranteed through existing laws. But when tolerance becomes a kind of brand, when the Germans start taking pride in respecting difference, that would be a wider, more active understanding of tolerance. This understanding would be along the following lines: tolerance as a stance is typical for us, we identify emotionally with it and are proud of the fact that visually marked Others, visible minorities, can be certain that they are safe and well in

Germany. Thus respect for PlusGerman difference would become a cornerstone of collective national identity.

Memory of the Holocaust could prop up historically, as it were, this cornerstone. It could do so in the sense that the causes of genocides need to be avoided by all means. Among the key causes are phantasies of purity and homogeneity. And lack of respect for the Other, for diversity, for plus-identities – in short: lack of tolerance. This would be a new kind of Holocaust memory, no longer a Holocaust memory predicated on belonging to the nation that has carried out a horrific genocide and now needs to be forever wary of having this genocidal gene break out again phenotypically. This kind of, if you will, ethnobiologized Holocaust memory no longer works for a number of reasons, not least because many contemporary Germans would have themselves become victims of Nazi extermination policies. A different kind of commemorating that presupposes the genocidal as a universal human possibility would be preferable. Yet it is and remains a part of our history that the Germans carried out this systematic, horrible genocide. Any civic, emotionally enriched belonging to the German nation therefore has to involve coming to terms with this fact.

***

But is such a collective national identity, a national New We, really necessary and desirable? Aren't we postnational? Isn't it at most supranational entities like the EU or the UN that deserve emotional identification? A lot of people think along these lines, and, by the way, beyond the political Right–Left camps. Postnational leftists and economic liberals, who would like the global market to be as free, meaning as unrestricted by borders, as possible, meet here. I too thought like this most of my life, identifying as an internationalist of the Left.

But I have come to be persuaded that we do need this kind of collective national identity. For one thing, there is an obvious, tangible demand for it. For many the nation continues to be an important source of identity, much more important than supranational sources. Many can't afford to be postnational, since they lack the money to travel outside Germany to reap the benefits of the mobility that a German passport affords (with a Ukrainian or Iranian passport these possibilities are much more circumscribed). Not to mention the many, many people in the world who are, as I type these lines, risking their lives to get to safe Germany from places of war, hunger, and other catastrophes, many of them caused by the German (Western) way of living, and who dream of one day acquiring a German passport. In short, postnational talk is an elite posture.

On the other hand, there is demand for a national, German identity on the part of the immigrants themselves. Many new citizens are from cultural contexts where the nation is not a blind spot or nonentity, but instead an important source of identity. If you've got nothing to offer to fill this empty place, you leave the filling to others. People will then identify with the impressive, emotionally charged offerings of their countries of origin, such as those proffered by Turkey's AKP and by Putin in Russia. Finally, arguing that the essence of Germanness is not being German, saying that being a German citizen is about not having a national identity, can, though coming from a well-meaning position derived from lessons of the horrors of Nazism, end up being undemocratic and outright paternalistic. What right do these well-meaning German citizens have to deny other German citizens the option of having a national identity? Why should they have the last word if others, who do want a definition for German national identity, are in the majority?

***

In conclusion let me summarize what I am arguing for.

- Our point of departure is the infinite number of identities that we all live, that change every time we live them, and between which we switch without difficulty or conflict: a concept of plural and performative identity.
- Among these identities are heritage cultures and heritage languages of Germans plus or PlusGermans: these should be valued and promoted by the state. Multilingualism and multicultural skills should be celebrated and fostered through language teaching in schools.
- However, we need to move beyond demands for radical plurality of heritage cultures *only*, that would be *multikulti*, multiculturalism without glue, without a We. There has to be access to a collective German identity. That would mean, for example, that a person of Syrian heritage experiences appreciation for, and active promotion in German schools of, Arabic, their first language, at the same time as they experience appreciation and respect as a German and can consequently comfortably identify as German.
- The two aspects go together; individual and collective identity don't cancel each other out, they are not mutually exclusive. German politicians once before managed to bring the two together: around 1950 the expellees from Silesia, the Sudetenland, and so on had their heritage cultures sponsored (*Brauchtumspflege*) and were simultaneously defined as belonging to the German nation. Ultimately this recipe is that of the American salad bowl model which in the 1960s superseded the melting-pot: like the ingredients of a salad, the many identities come together in a large bowl where they coexist but are kept together by the bowl itself.

- There should be collective belonging for citizens and it should consist of more than simply holding a passport: there must be some kind of emotional, symbolic celebration as glue, if only because there is a clear and proven demand for such a glue among citizens.
- Symbolic-emotional celebration can also be called collective identity or the New We.
- The contents of this collective German national identity, the New We, should be determined via democratic means, though always within the framework of the German constitution so that nobody's basic rights are infringed.

***

To be sure, the personal stories in this book are also meant to contribute to an emotional-symbolic celebration. Every nation tells itself stories about itself and thus makes meaning, creates some kind of coherence. The stories in this book are parts that in sum add up to a success story, even if so much remains to be done so that Germans manage to balance their diversity and unity. The history of migration to Germany is a success story, first, because of the immigrants themselves. They, the Germans plus, have overcome incredible obstacles and achieved so much. But it is also, second, a success story because of the so-called do-gooders, or *Gutmenschen*, a term that is only waiting to be reconquered and used again without irony or malice, indeed instead with pride. This is the part of German civil society that has been volunteering on behalf of PlusGermans for decades – in working groups, *Aktionsausschüsse* and *Flüchtlingskoordinationen*, in Sri Lanka and Lebanon groups, at PRO ASYL, Terre des Femmes, or Amnesty International, in antifascist and left autonomous anti-racism initiatives, in the churches, political parties, trade unions, and charities, in sports clubs, with candle-lit demonstrations (*Lichterketten*), or in their neighborhood.

There are grounds for optimism when PlusGerman politicians get elected to city and state parliaments or the Bundestag; that PlusGerman writers, artists, actresses and actors, anchormen and anchorwomen, are popular and respected; that so many people volunteer on behalf of those who have been less fortunate, such as recent refugees. To be sure, too many racist microaggressions and attacks, even right-wing terrorist murders, have happened and continue to happen, today there still is far too much racism, hatred, and racist violence, but at the end of the day the stories in this book add up to a success story, a history of progress.

If the narrative of this book – a *different* history of the Germans that cannot be imagined without migration, the New We that includes the Germans plus – wins, the question "Where are you from?" will one day be okay, because coming from another place and being German will no longer be mutually exclusive. Then there will be Turkish Germans (*Türkendeutsche*), Turkey Germans (*Türkeideutsche*), or Turkogermans (*Turkodeutsche*) instead of German Turks (*Deutschtürken*). No one will call the national soccer team the "International Eleven." My daughter Olga and her friends will no longer call themselves "foreigners" (*Ausländer*). And "integration" will no longer actually mean assimilation, will no longer mean: you are different, throw overboard everything that you bring along in terms of plus and become like us, while we're not going to tell you what "like us" means, or rather, while we're going to change this meaning whenever you think you've just made it, much like a carrot that we keep dangling in front of you, only to pull it away whenever you get close to catching it.

Now, it would be naïve to assume that a civic (rather than an ethnobiological or ethnoreligious) definition of the nation that is celebrated symbolically-emotionally (the New We) excludes no one. Such a definition also generates an Other. Through this recalibration of identity all non-citizens are more marked than is the case today with the current definition.[15]

The production of the Other will not even cease when the national level at long last recedes behind the supranational EU level. Then the difference between EU citizens and non-EU citizens will be felt more acutely. It will not even stop being operative when humanity finally organizes as such, as humanity, for instance in a world federation. In this world federation economic difference, socioeconomic inequality, will be more palpable.

Still, it is critical to dream of collectives beyond the nation and to work toward the realization of these dreams – this book shall not end in the telos of the nation, it shall end in further goals: a functioning, truly democratic EU, a genuine world federation. It is generally essential for survival to think from a vantage point outside the here and now, an imagined future of what things should rather look like, a non-place humanity has yet to get to: a utopia.

One day national borders will seem like a remnant from a bygone epoch, much like slavery or the exclusion of women from general elections do today in the Western world. There will be a truly universal right, a human right, of freedom of movement. The German welcoming culture of 2015 was like a foreshadowing of this future of human solidarity beyond national borders, borders that artificially divide us into citizens of different countries even though these borders are so arbitrary and young. Someday 2015 will be the norm, it will be the rule rather than the exception. The future is, in every respect, borderless.

Coda

Let us remember here how fortuitous citizenship actually is. The newborn child has no influence on the country and times they are born into. We do not earn this fortuity. Migration specialist Ayelet Shachar speaks of "the birthright lottery": just as you are born into a poor or rich family, you are born into a citizenship that either opens opportunities or closes them off.[16] To remind ourselves just how fortuitous citizenship is, let's take a last glance at history. As late as the eighteenth century many more people from German states were still trying to emigrate than the other way around. Seen from a longue durée perspective it is very likely that Germany in the future will again become a country for outmigration. It is no exaggeration to state that migration is the human default position that is merely interrupted by periods of sedentary life. For this reason alone, a bit more humility would behoove us. For most, German citizenship is not something that they have earned through their own merits; German citizenship is a historical accident that is a privilege today but could turn into a liability tomorrow.

It is worth remembering this in everyday life once in a while. When eating in a restaurant, you can be quite sure that your plate was washed by someone in the kitchen whom historical contingency has put at a disadvantage: a paperless person. When buying Italian olive oil at the supermarket, you can be quite sure that the olives were harvested by a paperless person. The paperless do the hardest, most unpleasant, most precarious jobs. They are invisible. And they are particularly vulnerable. No employment protection, no trade union, no insurance shields them. When they fall ill, they can only hope to fall back on a network of – brave – doctors who treat them semi-legally. They live in constant fear of our state, that tries to find and deport them – our police.

Politically, we could translate our humility in the face of the historical accident of citizenship into amnesties: every few years we could turn the paperless into Germans, much like countries such as Spain already do with their paperless. The minimal translation work our humility can do is to call attention to them one last time right here: that is why, at the very end of this book, I want to erect a memorial of letters for those who are also named at the very beginning of this book, in the dedication: the paperless.

Appendix: Dates and Facts

May 8–9, 1945:	Nazi Germany capitulates first to the Western Allied powers, then to the USSR.
1944–1949:	12.5 million ethnic German expellees immigrate from Eastern Europe, including 4.5 million to the Soviet Occupation Zone/German Democratic Republic (GDR).
1946–1961:	1 million Germans emigrate, especially to the United States and Switzerland.
1949:	Federal Republic of Germany (FRG, or West Germany) and GDR (East Germany) founded. West German constitution ("Basic Law") promulgated, including Article 16, Paragraph 2, Sentence 2, "Persons persecuted on political grounds shall have the right of asylum," and Article 116, Sentence 1: "Unless otherwise provided by a law, a German within the meaning of this Basic Law is a person who possesses German citizenship or who has been admitted to the territory of the German Reich within the boundaries of 31 December 1937 as a refugee or expellee of German ethnic origin or as the spouse or descendant of such person."
1949:	The Allies lift the ban on political parties and coalitions; expellees form the League of Expellees and Deprived of Rights (BHE): it gets 23.4 percent of the vote in the 1950 state elections in Schleswig-Holstein. In 1957 lobby organizations of expellees unite under the umbrella organization Federation of Expellees (BdV).
1949–1990:	From the creation of the GDR until the building of the Wall in 1961, 4 million emigrate from East

to West Germany and 400,000 the other way around. Between 1961 and the dissolution of the GDR in 1990 another 1.2 million emigrate from East to West.

1950: German expellees from Eastern Europe arriving in the Federal Republic from now on are called *Aussiedler*, from 1993 *Spätaussiedler*. 4.5 million immigrate, including 2.5 million from the USSR and its successor states, 1.5 million from Poland, 450,000 from Romania, and 300,000 from Yugoslavia, Czechoslovakia, etc.

1951/1967: The 1951 Geneva Refugee Convention (GRC) guarantees protection for those seeking refuge "owing to well-founded fear of being persecuted for reasons of race, religion, nationality, membership of a particular social group or political opinion" (Article 1A). Signatories (almost 150 states in 2022) guarantee to neither expel nor return such refugees (the "principle of non-refoulement"). There was a perceived need for a legally binding convention at the end of the 1940s because of Cold War refugees from the Soviet Bloc, but also because of memory of the 1938 Evian Conference bilateral agreements for contingents of Jewish refugees that had never been put into practice. The 1967 Protocol expanded the GRC's remit by lifting temporal and geographical restrictions.

1953: The Federal Law on Refugees and Exiles (BVFG) effectively codifies the salad bowl model by allowing for the coexistence of a German Federal Republican national identity and particularist identities (Silesian, etc., state-sponsored expellee cultural sponsorship [*Brauchtumspflege*]).

1955: First labor migration ("guest work," *Gastarbeit*) recruitment agreement of West Germany with Italy, followed by agreements in 1960 with Spain, in 1961 with Turkey, in 1963 with Morocco and South Korea, in 1965 with Tunisia, and in 1968 with Yugoslavia. A total of 14 million guest workers recruited, of whom 11 million return to their countries of origin; 3 million stay and bring over their families or start a family in Germany.

1961: The GDR builds the Berlin Wall to prevent mass migration to West Germany.

1965: New Aliens Law. Temporary permits for labor migrants could now lead to permanent residency after 8 years of living in West Germany.

1966–1967: Recession, labor migration declines. The halt to recruitment of 1973 concludes this process. At the same time family reunions begin in the 1970s.

1971–1989: The GDR signs labor migration ("contract work," *Vertragsarbeit*) agreements with Poland in 1971, Algeria in 1974, Cuba in 1975, Mozambique in 1979, Vietnam in 1980, and Angola in 1984. A total of 150,000 to 200,000 labor migrants are recruited, numbers peak in the late 1980s. However, Soviet soldiers are numerically the largest group of foreigners in the GDR: a total of 6.1 million between 1945 and 1994, or 8.5 million, including family members.

1973: A halt to recruitment stops labor migration to West Germany.

1979: Heinz Kühn appointed as West Germany's first Commissioner of Foreigners.

1979: 40,000 Vietnamese Boat People arrive as refugees in West Germany (in 1980 they receive the legal status of quota refugees).

1980: Neo-Nazi attack on Munich's Oktoberfest, the deadliest terror attack in the entire history of the Federal Republic: 13 dead, 211 injured (to compare, the Islamist attack on the Berlin Christmas market in 2016 caused 12 fatalities and injured 55).

1980: Military coup in Turkey, applications for asylum in West Germany surpass 100,000 for the first time.

1981: Polish martial law, Poles seek asylum in West Germany.

1982: New conservative CDU/CSU–FDP government under Chancellor Helmut Kohl, increasingly restrictive immigration policy. Rise of the Green Party.

1986:	PRO ASYL is founded.
1987:	Poland and the Soviet Union ease the emigration of *Aussiedler*, start of the numerically largest *Aussiedler* immigration first to West Germany, later to unified Germany: 2.3 million until 2022, of whom 1.5 million arrived before the restrictive changes to the Federal Law on Refugees and Exiles in late 1992.
1989:	Velvet Revolutions in Poland, Hungary, and the Czech Republic.
January 29, 1989:	7.5 percent of the vote in elections to the West Berlin parliament goes to the right-wing Republikaner.
1989:	From summer onward emigration of GDR citizens via Hungary and the West German embassy in Prague.
November 9, 1989:	Fall of the Berlin Wall.
1990:	Jewish quota refugees from the Soviet Union start immigrating (about 230,000 to date).
October 3, 1990:	German unification.
1991:	Aliens Law of 1965 liberalized. People who have legally resided in the Federal Republic for 8 years are now entitled to a permanent residence permit.
January 1, 1992:	The USSR ceases to exist.
1993:	The Single European Market and mobility of citizens within the EU.
1991–92:	Racist attacks and pogroms in Hoyerswerda (September 17–23, 1991), Rostock-Lichtenhagen (August 22–26, 1992), Mölln (November 23, 1992: three dead), and Solingen (May 29, 1993: five dead). Solidarity movement with the victims (candle-lit demonstrations, etc.).
1992:	A new law (the *Kriegsfolgenbereinigungsgesetz*) replaces the Federal Expellee Law. *Aussiedler* who immigrate from 1 January, 1993 are now called *Spätaussiedler*.
1992:	Asylum applications peak at 438,191 because of the Yugoslav Wars.
1993:	"Asylum compromise." A two-thirds majority in parliament restricts the Basic Law's Article 16a ("Persons persecuted on political grounds shall

have the right of asylum") to exclude people arriving via a "safe third state," which includes all EU countries plus Switzerland and Norway. Legal entry into Germany is now practically impossible. Moreover, a new law (the *Asylbewerberleistungsgesetz*) that reduces state benefits for asylum seekers to a level below social welfare is passed (hitherto the Federal Social Welfare Law had applied also to asylum seekers).

1996: The VOICE Refugee Forum Germany, the first united movement of asylum seekers that manages to bridge political and other differences, forms in Jena. Four main demands: lifting of the prohibition on work; freedom of movement instead of the residence requirement; monetary support instead of benefits in kind; housing in apartments in the midst of society rather than isolated in shelters.

1997: Dublin I Regulation adopted, according to which asylum cases should be decided where refugees first cross a border (usually Greece, Italy, or Spain).

2000: New Citizenship Law goes into effect. Birthright citizenship (*ius soli*) added to the right of blood (*ius sanguinis*), which continues to be valid. Naturalization becomes easier, dual citizenship is permitted until the age of 23, after that there is an obligation to choose one or other of the two citizenships.

2000–2009: The right-wing terrorist group National Socialist Underground (NSU) kills nine persons with a migrant background and one police officer. Uncovered in 2011, trial in Munich 2013–2018.

2002: For the first time more Jews from the ex-USSR emigrate to Germany than to Israel or the United States: 19,262 to Germany, 18,878 to Israel, fewer than 10,000 to the United States.

2003: Dublin II Regulation: fingerprints centrally stored in the EURODAC biometric database.

2004: The EU expands to Eastern Europe (Bulgaria and Romania in 2007). Germany restricts labor mobility for Eastern Europeans until 2011.

2005: New Immigration Law goes into effect: more restrictive for, among others, Jewish quota refugees.

2005: First micro census with question about "migration background" (*Migrationshintergrund*), defined as someone who themselves did not have German citizenship at birth from 1949 or at least one of whose parents did not. The 2015 micro census shifts that date to birth after 1955, much like a moving wall, meaning that migration background is not biologized.

2006: FRONTEX agency for tighter control of the EU's borders established in Warsaw.

2011: Germany extends EU labor mobility to Eastern Europeans. New migration movements, but the feared "surge" from the east never materializes.

2012: Dublin III Regulation legalizes internment of refugees. The EU country where a refugee first arrives continues to be responsible for processing their asylum application. This does not work in practice because countries with external EU borders (Italy, Greece, Spain) either do not record details (fingerprints) for refugees or the refugees, with the help of human traffickers, immediately move on to Sweden, Germany, etc. and get registered there.

2012: Federal Constitutional Court rules the *Asylbewerberleistungsgesetz* unconstitutional, benefits raised to the level of social welfare (Hartz IV).

2012: Radicalization of the refugee movement, occupation of Oranienplatz in Berlin-Kreuzberg for 17 months.

2014: New version of the *Asylbewerberleistungsgesetz* in accordance with the 2012 Federal Constitutional Court ruling. Better regular benefits, but health benefits remain restricted to treatment of "acute illness and pain."

2015: "Asylum Package I": Albania, Kosovo, and Montenegro defined as safe countries of origin, faster deportation of asylum seekers from those countries.

2015: 1 million refugees from Syria, Afghanistan, etc., from August "welcoming culture," but also a surge in racist attacks on refugees. Legally, 95 percent of the 2015 Syrian refugees are GRC refugees. The rest receive subsidiary protection in line with the 2004 European Human Rights Convention (in contrast to the GRC, it prohibits family reunions) or are asylum seekers (in 2013 and 2014, 25,000 Syrians also are admitted as quota refugees). Refugees are recognized, tolerated (i.e. rejected but their deportation is postponed), rejected, awaiting deportation, or deported.

2016: In January Volga Germans protest against the immigration policy of Angela Merkel's government because of an alleged, in reality feigned, sexual assault by refugees against the Volga German teenager Lisa F.

2016: "Asylum Package II": Algeria, Tunisia, and Morocco defined as safe countries of origin, faster deportation of asylum seekers from these countries.

Notes

Introduction

1. Names changed.
2. www.spiegel.de/politik/deutschland/kinder-statt-inder-ruettgers-verteidigt-verbalen-ausrutscher-a-68369.html.
3. Friedrich Merz, "Einwanderung und Identität," *Die Welt* (October 25, 2000).
4. The term is from migration studies, including the field of migration education studies. See Ursula Boos-Nünning, "Kinder mit Migrationshintergrund: Plädoyer für eine sozialraumbezogene Politik," *Frühe Kindheit* no. 1 (2000), 4–19.
5. www.destatis.de/DE/PresseService/Presse/Pressemitteilungen/2018/08/PD18_282_12511.html.
6. For a pan-European history, see Peter Gatrell, *The Unsettling of Europe: How Migration Reshaped a Continent* (New York, 2019).
7. This is based on performativity as conceptualized by, among others, Judith Butler, *Gender Trouble: Feminism and the Subversion of Identity* (New York, 1990); and *Excitable Speech: Contemporary Scenes of Politics* (New York, 1996). Also see Monique Scheer, "Alltägliche Praktiken des Sowohl-als-auch. Mehrfachzugehörigkeit und Bindestrich-Identitäten," in Monique Scheer, ed., *Bindestrich-Deutsche? Mehrfachzugehörigkeit und Beheimatungspraktiken im Alltag* (Tübingen, 2014), 13–15.
8. See Steven Vertovec, "Super-Diversity and Its Implications," *Ethnic and Racial Studies* 29, no. 6 (2007), 1024–1054; Mark Terkessidis, *Interkultur* (Berlin, 2010).
9. Mukherjee quoted in Tina Bauer, "Ihre Herkunft macht sie begehrt. Profs mit Migrationshintergrund," *duz* (October 25, 2013). Keltek introduced the term at an event commemorating the twentieth anniversary of the lethal right-wing extremist arson attack of Solingen in 1993. See Johannes Spätling, "Brandanschlag von Solingen: 'Migranten sind Plus-Deutsche,'" *Kölnische Rundschau* (June 27, 2013), who erroneously credits the journalist Aslı Sevindim with coining the term (email from Sevindim, October 3, 2018). See also the organization Deutsch Plus: www.deutsch-plus.de.
10. https://neuedeutsche.org/de/ueber-uns/wer-wir-sind. See also their excellent glossary, "Formulierungshilfen für die Berichterstattung im Einwanderungsland": https://glossar.neuemedienmacher.de.

11. Rapper Harris : "Wir sind nicht mehr die Türken, die Araber, die Afrikaner, die unsere Eltern vielleicht waren. Wir sind die neuen Deutschen," *Stern* (October 8, 2010); Naika Foroutan, "Neue Deutsche, Postmigranten und Bindungs-Identitäten. Wer gehört zum neuen Deutschland?," *APuZ* (November 15, 2010), 9–15; Özlem Topçu, Alice Bota, and Khuê Pham, *Wir neuen Deutschen: Wer wir sind, was wir wollen* (Reinbek, 2012); https://neuedeutsche.org/de/ueber-uns/wer-wir-sind.
12. Herfried Münkler and Marina Münkler, *Die neuen Deutschen: Ein Land vor seiner Zukunft* (Reinbek, 2016).
13. www.destatis.de/DE/Publikationen/Thematisch/Bevoelkerung.
14. True, the micro census itself expressly avoided biologizing migration background. Its initial 2005 version defined a person with migration background as someone who themselves, or at least one of whose parents, did not have German citizenship at birth from 1949, whereas the 2011 micro census shifted that date to birth after 1955, much like a moving wall.
15. For a study that is similar in approach and at the same time, because of its transnational, pan-European angle, nicely complements *We Are All Migrants*, see Philipp Ther, *The Outsiders: Refugees in Europe since 1492*, trans. Jeremiah Riemer (Princeton, 2019).
16. See Heinrich-August Winkler, *Der lange Weg nach Westen*, vol. 2, *Deutsche Geschichte vom "Dritten Reich" bis zur Wiedervereinigung* (Munich, 2000), 331; Eckart Conze, *Die Suche nach Sicherheit: Eine Geschichte der Bundesrepublik Deutschland von 1949 bis in die Gegenwart* (Munich, 2009), 229–231, 548, 670–672, 784–786.
17. There is nothing comparable to Ronald Takaki, *A Different Mirror: A History of Multicultural America* (Boston, 1993) or Robert Winder, *Bloody Foreigners: The Story of Immigration to Britain* (London, 2004). Two German historians who teach in the United States criticized this as early as 2003: "The failure to incorporate experiences of migration into the national story has created a misleading historical consciousness that treats 'German' as a fixed ethnic category, although it is rather fluid." Konrad Jarausch and Michael Geyer, *Shattered Past: Reconstructing German Histories* (Princeton, 2003), 198.
18. See Paul Lüttinger, "Der Mythos der schnellen Integration. Eine empirische Untersuchung zur Integration der Vertriebenen und Flüchtlinge in der Bundesrepublik Deutschland bis 1971," *Zeitschrift für Soziologie* 15, no. 1 (2016), 20–36.

1 We Are All Migrants, Almost Everywhere, Almost Always – Especially the Germans

1. See Everett S. Lee, "Eine Theorie der Wanderung," in György Széll, ed., *Regionale Mobilität* (Munich, 1972), 117–129.
2. Karl Schlögel, *Planet der Nomaden* (Zurich, 2000); Klaus J. Bade, *Homo migrans: Wanderungen aus und nach Deutschland. Erfahrungen und Fragen* (Essen, 1994). See also e.g. Giovanni Tortora, *Homo migrans* (Geneva, 1971).

3. See Frank Bass, “Deutsche sind wichtigste ethnische Gruppe in USA – Zahl wächst,” *Die Welt* (March 7, 2012). In comparison, 35.8 million self-reported being of Irish ancestry, 31.8 million Mexican, 27.4 million English, and 17.6 million Italian.
4. For introductions see Andreas Fahrmeir, *Die Deutschen und ihre Nation: Geschichte einer Idee* (Stuttgart, 2017); Christian Jansen and Henning Borggräfe, *Nation – Nationalität – Nationalismus* (Frankfurt am Main, 2007); Dieter Langewiesche, *Nation, Nationalismus, Nationalstaat in Deutschland und Europa* (Munich, 2000).
5. See Dieter Gosewinkel, *Schutz und Freiheit? Staatsbürgerschaft in Europa im 20. und 21. Jahrhundert* (Berlin, 2016); Patrick Weil, *How to Be French: Nationality in the Making since* 1789 (Durham, NC, 2008); Rogers Brubaker, “Myths and Misconceptions in the Study of Nationalism,” in John Hall, ed., *The State of the Nation* (Cambridge, 1998), 298–301.
6. See Helmuth Plessner, *Die verspätete Nation: Über die politische Verführbarkeit bürgerlichen Geistes* (Stuttgart, 1959).
7. See John Higham, *Strangers in the Land: Patterns of American Nativism, 1860–1925* (New Brunswick, 1955), 9–11.
8. Douglas Klusmeyer and Demetrios Papademetriou, *Immigration Policy in the Federal Republic of Germany: Negotiating Membership and Remaking the Nation* (New York, 2009), 274.
9. http://founders.archives.gov/documents/Franklin/01-04-02-0037.
10. https://founders.archives.gov/documents/Franklin/01-04-02-0080.
11. https://founders.archives.gov/documents/Franklin/01-03-02-0091.
12. See Bernd Brunner, *Nach Amerika: Die Geschichte der deutschen Auswanderung* (Munich, 2009), 116.
13. Frederick Law Olmsted, *Journey through Texas, or, A Saddle-Trip on the Southwestern Frontier: With a Statistical Appendix* (New York, 1857), 431.
14. Benjamin Franklin, “Observations Concerning the Increase of Mankind, Peopling of Countries, etc.” (orig. 1751), in Leonard W. Larabee, ed., *The Papers of Benjamin Franklin*, vol. 4 (New Haven, 1959), 234.
15. See Brunner, *Nach Amerika*, 33.
16. Ibid., 35–36.
17. Gottlieb Mittelberger, *Gottlieb Mittelberger's journey to Pennsylvania in the year 1750 and return to Germany in the year 1754: containing not only a description of the country according to its present condition, but also a detailed account of the sad and unfortunate circumstances of most of the Germans that have emigrated, or are emigrating to that country*, trans. Carl Theodor Eben (Philadelphia, 1898; orig. 1756), 38.
18. Pastor Mühlenberg quoted in Brunner, *Nach Amerika*, 62.
19. See Simone Blaschka-Eick, *In die Neue Welt! Deutsche Auswanderer in drei Jahrhunderten* (Reinbek, 2010), 38–40.
20. Ibid., 46.
21. http://triptych.brynmawr.edu/cdm/compoundobject/collection/HC_QuakSl av/id/11.

22. See Jefferey Strickland, "How the Germans Became White Southerners: German Immigrants and Their Social, Economic, and Political Relations with African-Americans in Charleston, South Carolina, 1860–1880," *Journal of American Ethnic History* 28, no. 1 (2008), 57.
23. See Brunner, *Nach Amerika*, 111.
24. Table in Blaschka-Eick, *In die Neue Welt!*, 10–11.
25. Gottfried Duden, *Report on a Journey to the Western States of North America and a Stay of Several Years along the Missouri (during the Years 1824, '25, '26, and 1827)* (Columbia, MO, 1980), 176.
26. Quoted in Brunner, *Nach Amerika*, 83.
27. Ibid., 84 (the historian is Wolfgang Helbich, a specialist in émigré letters).
28. www.spiegel.de/panorama/gesellschaft/doener-erfinder-kadir-nurman-ist-tot-a-930140.html; Hans-Jörg Conzelmann, "Der deutsche Döner kommt aus Reutlingen," *Reutlinger General-Anzeiger* (May 6, 2012); Maren Möhring, *Fremdes Essen: Die Geschichte der ausländischen Gastronomie in der Bundesrepublik Deutschland* (Munich, 2012), 421.
29. See Blaschka-Eick, *In die Neue Welt!*, 93.
30. See Brunner, *Nach Amerika*, 87.
31. "Roosevelt Bars the Hyphenated," *New York Times* (October 13, 1915).
32. See Christoph Gutknecht, *Lauter böhmische Dörfer: Wie die Wörter zu ihrer Bedeutung kamen* (Munich, 2004), 69.
33. Quoted in Christopher James Wright, "The Impact of Anti-German Hysteria in New Ulm, Minnesota and Kitchener, Ontario: A Comparative Study," M.A. Thesis, Iowa State University (2011), https://dr.lib.iastate.edu/entities/publication/236d56e5-857c-4fd5-b295-7d389b2a97ea, 12.
34. See Eric Lohr, *Nationalizing the Russian Empire: The Campaign against Enemy Aliens during World War I* (Cambridge, MA, 2003), 33.
35. www.volgagermans.org/history/manifesto.
36. See Blaschka-Eick, *In die Neue Welt!*, 172.
37. Ibid., 176.
38. Aleksandr Gertsen (Alexander Herzen), "Russkie nemtsy i nemetskie russkie," in *Sobranie sochinenii v tridtsati tomakh*, vol. 14 (Moscow, 1958), 155.
39. Quoted in Rudolf Pörtner, *Heimat in der Fremde: Deutsche aus Rußland erinnern sich* (Düsseldorf, 1992), 78.
40. See Viktor Krieger, *Kolonisten, Sowjetdeutsche, Aussiedler: Eine Geschichte der Russlanddeutschen* (Bonn, 2015), 8.
41. See Blaschka-Eick, *In die Neue Welt!*, 182–183.
42. Ibid., 192; www.volgagermans.org/who-are-volga-germans/history/immigration/argentina/entre-rios/general-alvear-colonies/valle-maria.
43. See Blaschka-Eick, *In die Neue Welt!*, 193. For a critical assessment of this thesis, see Jeffrey Lesser, *Immigration, Ethnicity, and National Identity in Brazil, 1808 to the Present: New Approaches to the Americas* (Cambridge, 2013).
44. Quoted in Brunner, *Nach Amerika*, 100.
45. See Dirk Hoerder, *Geschichte der deutschen Migration: Vom Mittelalter bis heute* (Munich, 2010), 56.

1945

1. See Ernst Volland, *Das Banner des Sieges* (Berlin, 2008); Ernst Volland and Heinz Krimmer, eds., *Jewgeni Chaldej – der bedeutende Augenblick: Eine Retrospektive* (Leipzig, 2008); David Shneer, *Through Soviet Jewish Eyes: Photography, War, and the Holocaust* (New Brunswick, 2010), 136–137, 205–207; Jeremy Hicks, *Victory Banner over the Reichstag: Film, Document, and Ritual in Russia's Contested Memory of World War II* (Pittsburgh, 2020).
2. William Gardner Smith, *Last of the Conquerors* (New York, 1948), 67–68, quoted in Heide Fehrenbach, *Race after Hitler: Black Occupation Children in Postwar Germany and America* (Princeton, 2005), 17.
3. See Clarence Lusane, *Hitler's Black Victims: The Historical Experiences of Afro-Germans, European Blacks, Africans, and African Americans in the Nazi Era* (New York, 2003); Raffael Scheck, *Hitler's African Victims: The German Army Massacres of Black French Soldiers in 1940* (Cambridge, 2006), 145–149.
4. Quoted in Sven Reichardt and Malte Zierenberg, *Damals nach dem Krieg: Eine Geschichte Deutschlands 1945 bis 1949* (Munich, 2008), 53.
5. Sam Dann, ed., *Dachau 29 April 1945: The Rainbow Liberation Memoirs* (Lubbock, 1998), 143.
6. Ibid., 143–144.
7. Quoted in Atina Grossmann, *Jews, Germans, and Allies: Close Encounters in Occupied Germany* (Princeton, 2007), 139.
8. Alos Harasko, "Die Vertreibung der Sudetendeutschen. Sechs Erlebnisberichte," in Wolfgang Benz, ed., *Die Vertreibung der Deutschen aus dem Osten: Ursachen, Ergebnisse, Folgen* (Frankfurt am Main, 1995), 109.
9. More than any other book, Miriam Gebhardt's *Crimes Unspoken: The Rape of German Women at the End of the Second World War*, trans. Nick Somers (Cambridge, 2017) helped raise consciousness about the role of Western Allied soldiers in the rapes.
10. Leonie Biallas, *Komm, Frau, raboti: Flucht und Vertreibung 1945–1946* (Hürth, 2004), 22–23.
11. Quoted in Andreas Kossert, *Kalte Heimat: Die Geschichte der deutschen Vertriebenen nach 1945* (Munich, 2008), 48.
12. Quoted in ibid., 49.
13. Quoted in ibid., 73.
14. Quoted in ibid., 75.
15. Quoted in ibid., 68.
16. Quoted in ibid., 50–53.
17. Quoted in ibid., 135.
18. Quoted in Rainer Schulze, "Zuwanderung und Modernisierung – Flüchtlinge und Vertriebene im ländlichen Raum," in Klaus J. Bade, ed., *Neue Heimat im Westen: Vertriebene, Flüchtlinge, Aussiedler* (Münster, 1990), 85.
19. Reichardt and Zierenberg, *Damals nach dem Krieg*, 174.
20. Quoted in ibid., 168.
21. Quoted in ibid., 168.

22. Vladislav Kamyshov, "'V Germanii ostalas' nasha molodost' . . .' (vospominaniia ostarbaiterov)," https://urokiistorii.ru/school_competition/works/v-germanii-ostalas-nasha-molodost.
23. Ibid.
24. See Bade, *Homo migrans*, 35–36.
25. Kamyshov, "'V Germanii ostalas' nasha molodost' . . .' (vospominaniia ostarbaiterov)."
26. Quoted in Reichardt and Zierenberg, *Damals nach dem Krieg*, 40.
27. Quoted in ibid., 41.
28. Quoted in ibid., 42.

2 Twelve-and-a-Half Million in Six Years

1. R. M. Douglas, *Orderly and Humane: The Expulsion of the Germans after the Second World War* (New Haven, 2012), 1.
2. Mathias Beer, *Flucht und Vertreibung der Deutschen: Voraussetzungen, Verlauf, Folgen* (Munich, 2011), 134.
3. See Kossert, *Kalte Heimat*.
4. Quoted in Beer, *Flucht und Vertreibung der Deutschen*, 109.
5. Quoted in ibid., 114.
6. Ibid., 110.
7. See Philipp Ther, *Die dunkle Seite der Nationalstaaten: "Ethnische Säuberungen" im modernen Europa* (Göttingen, 2011), 38–108; Ther, *The Outsiders*, 54–69.
8. Hitler's Reichstag Speech of October 6, 1936, quoted in Joseph B. Schechtmann, "The Option Clause in the Reich's Treaties on the Transfer of Population," *The American Journal of International Law* 38, no. 3 (1944), 356.
9. Quoted in Beer, *Flucht und Vertreibung der Deutschen*, 42, 46.
10. Jean Ancel, ed., *Documents Concerning the Fate of Romanian Jewry during the Holocaust*, vol. 6, no. 15 (New York, 1986), 199–201.
11. Winston S. Churchill, *His Complete Speeches 1897–1963*, ed. Robert Rhodes James (New York, 1974), vol. 7, 7069.
12. Reproduced in Guido Knopp, *Die große Flucht: Das Schicksal der Vertriebenen* (Munich, 2001), 204.
13. On the Valka camp, see Bernd Windsheimer, *Nürnberg-Langwasser: Geschichte eines Stadtteils* (Nuremberg, 1995), 101 (with a photograph of the grocery store owned by Elisabeth Plamper). Also see Steven M. Zahlaus, "Von Kaaden im Egerland nach Nürnberg. Die neue Existenz der Familie Plamper in Langwasser," *Norica* no. 4 (2008), 88–93; (www.nuernberg.de/imperia/md/stadtarchiv/dokumente/norica_4_komplett_low.pdf); www.nordbayern.de/2.5886/nurnberg-wurde-zur-zweiten-heimat-1.847774.
14. See Knopp, *Die große Flucht*, 272, 276.
15. See Beer, *Flucht und Vertreibung der Deutschen*, 100.
16. Lucius D. Clay, *Decision in Germany* (Garden City, 1950), 100.
17. Beer, *Flucht und Vertreibung der Deutschen*, 113.
18. Quoted in ibid., 108.

19. Quoted in ibid., 109.
20. Quoted in ibid., 110.
21. Quoted in ibid., 115 (unattributed quotation).
22. Quoted in ibid., 107 (May 26, 1946).
23. Quoted in ibid., 122.
24. Bernhard Parisius, "Neubürger," *Online-Lexikon zur Kultur und Geschichte der Deutschen im östlichen Europa* (2015) (http://ome-lexikon.uni-oldenburg.de/begriffe/neubuerger) (accessed November 1, 2022).
25. Theodor Oberländer, "Zum Geleit," in Eugen Lemberg and Friedrich Edding, eds., *Die Vertriebenen in Westdeutschland: Ihre Eingliederung und ihr Einfluß auf Gesellschaft, Wirtschaft, Politik und Geistesleben*, vol. 1 (Kiel, 1959), vi.
26. Quoted in Beer, *Flucht und Vertreibung der Deutschen*, 26 (unattributed quotation).
27. Helga Hirsch, *Schweres Gepäck: Flucht und Vertreibung als Lebensthema* (Hamburg, 2004), 16.
28. Parts of the following passages are nearly identical with Jan Plamper, "Die Deutschen als Opfer," *Neue Zürcher Zeitung* (June 8, 2015), 15. Also see, with a less critical perspective, Burkhard Bilger, "Where Germans Make Peace with Their Dead," *New Yorker* (September 12, 2016) (www.newyorker.com/magazine/2016/09/12/familienaufstellung-germanys-group-therapy).
29. Norbert Frei, "'Drittes Reich.' Gefühlte Geschichte," *Die Zeit* (October 21, 2004).
30. Jörg Friedrich, *The Fire: The Bombing of Germany, 1940-1945*, trans. Allison Brown (New York, 2006).
31. Reiner Burger, "NPD sorgt für Eklat: 'Bomben-Holocaust,'" *Frankfurter Allgemeine Zeitung* (January 21, 2005).
32. See Günter Grass, *Crabwalk*, trans. Krishna Winston (Orlando, 2002); Anonymous, *A Woman in Berlin: Eight Weeks in the Conquered City. A Diary*, trans. Philip Boehm (New York, 2006); *Die Flucht*, dir. Kai Wessel, ARD TV film in two parts (2007).
33. For fairness' sake it bears noting that Radebold asked whether these traumas should figure at all as a topic in their own right considering the crimes the traumatized Germans might have committed against Jews, Poles, and others. See Hartmut Radebold, *Die dunklen Schatten unserer Vergangenheit: Hilfen für Kriegskinder im Alter* (Stuttgart, 2005), 28–31.
34. Here an increasing number of books served as orientation, for example Luise Reddemann, *Kriegskinder und Kriegsenkel in der Psychotherapie: Folgen der NS-Zeit und des Zweiten Weltkriegs erkennen und bearbeiten – Eine Annäherung* (Stuttgart, 2018); Meinolf Peters, *Das Trauma von Flucht und Vertreibung: Psychotherapie älterer Menschen und der nachfolgenden Generationen* (Stuttgart, 2018).
35. Sabine Bode, *Kriegsenkel: Die Erben der vergessenen Generation* (Stuttgart, 2009); Anne-Ev Ustorf, *Wir Kinder der Kriegskinder: Die Generation im Schatten des Zweiten Weltkriegs* (Freiburg im Breisgau, 2008).
36. Sabine Bode, *Die vergessene Generation: Die Kriegskinder brechen ihr Schweigen* (Stuttgart, 2004), 300.

37. Gabriele Baring, *Die geheimen Ängste der Deutschen* (Munich, 2011), 33.
38. Ibid., 13.
39. Gabriele Baring, *Die Deutschen und ihre verletzte Identität* (Berlin, 2017), 71.
40. Baring, *Die geheimen Ängste der Deutschen*, 186.
41. Bode, *Kriegsenkel*, 28.
42. Baring, *Die geheimen Ängste der Deutschen*, 49.
43. See Raymond Unger, *Die Wiedergutmacher: Das Nachkriegstrauma und die Flüchtlingsdebatte* (Berlin, 2018).
44. See Hinrich Rosenbrock, *Die antifeministische Männerrechtsbewegung – Denkweisen, Netzwerke und Onlinemobilisierung* (Berlin, 2012) (www.gwi-boell.de/sites/default/files/antifeministische_maennerrechtsbewegung.pdf). Also see Christa Hämmerle, "Genderforschung aus neuer Perspektive? Erste und noch fragende Anmerkungen zum Neuen Maskuli(ni)smus," *L'Homme* 23, no. 2 (2012), 111–120; Andreas Kemper, ed., *Die Maskulisten: Organisierter Antifeminismus im deutschsprachigen Raum* (Münster, 2012); Juliane Lang, "Familie und Vaterland in der Krise. Der extrem rechte Diskurs um Gender," in Sabine Hark and Paula-Irene Villa, eds., *Anti-Genderismus: Sexualität und Geschlecht als Schauplätze aktueller politischer Auseinandersetzungen* (Bielefeld, 2015), 167–181.
45. See Astrid von Friesen, *Der lange Abschied: Psychische Spätfolgen für die 2. Generation deutscher Vertriebener* (Gießen, 2000); Astrid von Friesen, *Schuld sind immer die anderen! Die Nachwehen des Feminismus. Frustrierte Frauen und schweigende Männer* (Hamburg, 2006).
46. See Ruth Leys, *Trauma: A Genealogy* (Chicago, 2000).
47. See Kevin Moss, "Russia as the Saviour of European Civilization: Gender and the Geopolitics of Traditional Values," in Roman Kuhar and David Paternotte, eds., *Anti-Gender Campaigns in Europe: Mobilizing against Equality* (Lanham, 2017), 202–206; Chrissy Stroop, https://politicalresearch.org/2016/02/16/russian-social-conservatism-the-u-s-based-wcf-the-global-culture-wars-in-historical-context.
48. See Moss, "Russia as the Saviour of European Civilization," 207; Thomas Korn and Andreas Umland, "Jürgen Elsässer, Kremlpropagandist," *Die Zeit* (July 19, 2014).
49. Exact figures in Beer, *Flucht und Vertreibung der Deutschen*, 101.
50. Quoted in ibid., 123.
51. Quoted in Reichardt and Zierenberg, *Damals nach dem Krieg*, 73 ("mulatto race") and 47–48 ("potato beetles").

3 Labor Migration to West Germany

1. DOMiD, Interview Obj. Nr. 125 (May 7, 2004).
2. DOMiD, Interview Obj. Nr. 163 (June 25, 2004).
3. DOMiD, Interview Obj. Nr. 174, real name (July 27, 2004).
4. DOMiD, Interview Obj. Nr. 173 (June 25, 2004).
5. See DOMiD, Interview Obj. Nr. 232 (July 8, 2004); Obj. Nr. 179 (July 28, 2004).
6. DOMiD, Interview Obj. Nr. 181 (July 5, 2004).

7. Muzaffer Y. in Hasan Çil, *Anfänge einer Epoche: Ehemalige türkische Gastarbeiter erzählen* (Berlin, 2003), 15.
8. DOMiD, Interview Obj. Nr. 186, real name (May 21, 1996).
9. See DOMiD, Interview Obj. Nr. 72 (January 25, 1996).
10. DOMiD, Interview Obj. Nr. 196 (May 25, 2004).
11. See DOMiD, Interview Obj. Nr. 66 (May 8, 1996).
12. See Karin Hunn, *"Nächstes Jahr kehren wir zurück ...": Die Geschichte der türkischen "Gastarbeiter" in der Bundesrepublik* (Göttingen, 2005), 93.
13. Muzaffer Y. in Çil, *Anfänge einer Epoche*, 15.
14. Bekir Y. in ibid., 69.
15. Muzaffer Y. in ibid., 15.
16. DOMiD, Interview Obj. Nr. 66 (May 8, 1996).
17. See Hunn, *"Nächstes Jahr kehren wir zurück ...,"* 95.
18. Muzaffer Y. in Çil, *Anfänge einer Epoche*, 15–16.
19. See Ulrich Herbert, *Geschichte der Ausländerbeschäftigung in Deutschland 1880–1980: Saisonarbeiter, Zwangsarbeiter, Gastarbeiter* (Berlin, 1986), 184.
20. Muzaffer Y. in Çil, *Anfänge einer Epoche*, 17.
21. "Metin und Martin. Aufsatz eines türkischen Schülers (aufgezeichnet von Alev Tekinay)," in Norbert Ney, ed., *Sie haben mich zu einem Ausländer gemacht ... ich bin einer geworden* (Reinbek, 1984), 50.
22. Aynur A. in Çil, *Anfänge einer Epoche*, 43.
23. For Spain, see especially DOMiD, Interview Obj. Nr. 233 (June 8, 2004), for Greece, see DOMiD, Interview Obj. Nr. 249 (July 8, 2004). See also Carlos Sans Díaz, "Umstrittene Wege. Die irreguläre Migration spanischer Arbeitnehmer in die Bundesrepublik Deutschland," in Jochen Oltmer, Axel Kreienbrink, and Carlos Sanz Díaz, eds., *Das "Gastarbeiter"-System: Arbeitsmigration und ihre Folgen in der Bundesrepublik Deutschland und Westeuropa* (Munich, 2012), 130–131.
24. See DOMiD, Interview Obj. Nr. 237 (= 252), Bert H. (April 21, 2005). On the Ford strike also see Part IV in Jan Motte and Rainer Ohliger, eds., *Geschichte und Gedächtnis in der Einwanderungsgesellschaft: Migration zwischen historischer Rekonstruktion und Erinnerungspolitik* (Essen, 2004).
25. "More than 706,000" between 1960 and 1973 is the figure given in Monika Mattes, *"Gastarbeiterinnen" in der Bundesrepublik: Anwerbepolitik, Migration und Geschlecht in den 50er bis 70er Jahren* (Frankfurt am Main, 2005), 10.
26. See Heike Berner and Sun-ju Choi, "Vorwort," in Heike Berner and Sun-ju Choi, *Koreanische Frauengruppe in Deutschland, Zuhause: Erzählungen von deutschen Koreanerinnen* (Berlin, 2006), 11; Corinna Broeckmann, "Gegen den Pflegenotstand. Migration philippinischer Krankenpflegerinnen nach Deutschland," in Mary Lou U. Hardillo-Werning, *TransEuroExpress: Filipinas in Europe* (Frechen-Königsdorf, 2000), 22–24.
27. Arlie Russell Hochschild, "Introduction. An Emotions Lens on the World," in Debra Hopkins, Jochen Kleres, Helena Flam, and Helmut Kuzmics, eds., *Theorizing Emotions: Sociological Explorations and Applications* (Frankfurt am Main, 2009), 32.

28. See Gülcin Wilhelm, *Generation Koffer: Die zurückgelassenen Kinder* (Berlin, 2011).
29. Ivan Ikić, *"Mein Leben in der Migration,"* in Amt für multikulturelle Angelegenheiten, ed., *"Mit Koffern voller Träume . . .": Ältere Migrantinnen und Migranten erzählen* (Frankfurt am Main, 2001), 44.
30. Hayrire E. in Çil, *Anfänge einer Epoche*, 83.
31. See Wilhelm, *Generation Koffer*, 23. In 1975 Germany cut child benefits for children who resided in Turkey. This created another incentive to reunite families in Germany, which in turn was reflected in the statistics of children brought to Germany to reunite with their parents.
32. See Cord Pagenstecher, "Die ungewollte Einwanderung. Rotationsprinzip und Rückkehrerwartung in der deutschen Ausländerpolitik," *Geschichte in Wissenschaft und Unterricht* 46, no. 12 (1995), 718–737, cited in Wilhelm, *Generation Koffer*, 22, 24.
33. Abedelhamid Afellah, "Gespräch mit meinem Vater," in Amt für multikulturelle Angelegenheiten, ed., *"Mit Koffern voller Träume . . .,"* 73.
34. Hayrire E. in Çil, *Anfänge einer Epoche*, 87.
35. See Rita Chin, *The Guest Worker Question in Postwar Germany* (Cambridge, 2007), 37.
36. See for example Marcel Berlinghoff, *Das Ende der "Gastarbeit": Europäische Anwerbestopps 1970–1974* (Paderborn, 2013).
37. See Chin, *The Guest Worker Question in Postwar Germany*, 90.
38. Jochen Oltmer, "Einführung: Migrationsverhältnisse und Migrationsregime nach dem Zweiten Weltkrieg," in Oltmer et al., eds., *Das "Gastarbeiter"-System*, 12.
39. Bundesvereinigung der Deutschen Arbeitgeberverbände, "Entwicklungspolitisches Gastarbeiterprogramm," *Informationen zur Ausländerbeschäftigung* no. 1 (1974), 23. Quoted in Chin, *The Guest Worker Question in Postwar Germany*, 92.
40. Chin, *The Guest Worker Question in Postwar Germany*, 58.
41. Hayriye E. in Çil, *Anfänge einer Epoche*, 91.
42. Metin K. in ibid., 35, 37.
43. Bekir Y. in ibid., 77.
44. Wilhelm, *Generation Koffer*, 101.
45. Ibid., 89.
46. Ibid., 35.
47. Ibid., 92.
48. Nedret P. in Çil, *Anfänge einer Epoche*, 107.
49. Hayriye E. in ibid., 87.
50. A fall 1963 poll among 500 labor migrants from Turkey found that 41 percent were from Istanbul, 18.2 percent from villages with fewer than 2,000 inhabitants, 12.8 percent from towns with more than 50,000 inhabitants, 5.7 percent from Ankara, and 4.3 percent from Izmir. Hunn, *"Nächstes Jahr kehren wir zurück . . .,"* 71.
51. Aliye B. in Çil, *Anfänge einer Epoche*, 27.
52. Hunn, *"Nächstes Jahr kehren wir zurück . . .,"* 72.

53. Quoted in ibid., 102–103. A 1964 Foreign Ministry report sent to other West German ministries states: "For Turkish workers German businesses note excellent discipline and allegiance [*Einordnungsfähigkeit*], physical prowess and productivity paired with great unpretentiousness. In this regard the attitude of Turkish workers is markedly, and positively, different from *Gastarbeiter* of other countries from within and outside the European Economic Community." Quoted in ibid., 104.
54. See Chin, *The Guest Worker Question in Postwar Germany*, 43.
55. Dursun Akçam, *Alaman Ocağı: Türkler Almanları anlatıyor/Deutsches Heim Glück allein: Wie Türken Deutsche sehen* (Göttingen, 1993), 193, 200.
56. Nedret P. in Çil, *Anfänge einer Epoche*, 111.
57. See www.deutsche-digitale-bibliothek.de/item/4OHBSCCPCBRXZQUK54SXFETY4R6TSERS?lang=de – 6 (Aggerblick), 54 (Lindenhof), 27 (Heinz), 53 (Leuchter), 39 (Driescher); *"Gelbe Seiten" für Bonn und den Rhein-Sieg-Kreis 1985/86* (Cologne, 1985), 142–143.
58. See Chin, *The Guest Worker Question in Postwar Germany*, 105–140.
59. Cabinet meeting of November 11, 1981, www.bundesarchiv.de/cocoon/barch/0000/k/k1981k/kap1_1/kap2_48/para3_4.html.
60. Bade, *Homo migrans*, 40.
61. DOMiD, Interview Obj. Nr. 237 (April 21, 2005).
62. See Wilhelm, *Generation Koffer*, 26.
63. See Chin, *The Guest Worker Question in Postwar Germany*, 144.
64. Franz Josef Strauß, "Mehr aufrechten Gang," *Frankfurter Rundschau* (January 14, 1987).
65. Chin, *The Guest Worker Question in Postwar Germany*, 157.
66. "Originalfassung Heidelberger Manifest," *Deutsche Wochenzeitung* (November 6, 1981); *Nation und Europa* no. 12 (1981); *Deutschland in Geschichte und Gegenwart* no. 4 (1981), 34.
67. See Chin, *The Guest Worker Question in Postwar Germany*, 153.
68. Charlotte Wiedemann, "Sauber und deutsch," *Die Zeit* (April 2, 1982); Dietrich Strothmann, "Witterung der Braunen," *Die Zeit* (April 23, 1982), 5.
69. See Chin, *The Guest Worker Question in Postwar Germany*, 147; www.spiegel.de/spiegel/print/d-14329214.html; Hans Schueler, "Die Angst vor den Fremden," *Die Zeit* (January 1, 1982).
70. See Deutsches Historisches Museum, ed., *Deutscher Kolonialismus: Fragmente seiner Geschichte und Gegenwart* (Berlin, 2016), 254.
71. Joschka Fischer, *Von grüner Kraft und Herrlichkeit* (Reinbek, 1984), 150–159.
72. See David Deißner, Thomas Ellerbeck, and Benno Stieber, eds., *Wir: 19 Leben in einem neuen Deutschland* (Munich, 2011), 30–36.
73. DOMiD, Interview Obj. Nr. 246 (May 3, 2005).
74. Chin, *The Guest Worker Question in Postwar Germany*, 141.
75. See Abdelkader Rafoud, *50 Jahre marokkanische Migration: Dokumentation mit Fotos* (Mainz, 2010), 64–65.
76. Semra Pelek, "Leerstelle Heimat. Eine Kindheit zwischen Deutschland und der Türkei," in Jeannette Goddar, Dorte Huneke, eds., *Auf Zeit. Für immer: Zuwanderer aus der Türkei erinnern sich* (Bonn, 2011), 197.
77. Ibid., 198.

78. DOMiD, Interview Obj. Nr. 259 (July 27, 2004).
79. See for example Rafoud, *50 Jahre marokkanische Migration*, 106.
80. Muzaffer Y. in Çil, *Anfänge einer Epoche*, 21.
81. Aliye B. in ibid., 29.
82. Erkan A. in ibid., 99.
83. Aynur A. in ibid., 45.
84. See Alexandros Stefanidis, *Beim Griechen: Wie mein Vater in unserer Taverne Geschichte schrieb* (Frankfurt am Main, 2010), 7–10.
85. Hayriye E. in Çil, *Anfänge einer Epoche*, 83.
86. Bekir Y. in ibid., 67.
87. DOMiD, Interview Obj. Nr. 170 (September 3, 2004).

4 Labor Migration to East Germany

1. See Lothar Elsner, "Zum Wesen und zur Kontinuität der Fremdarbeiterpolitik des deutschen Imperialismus," in Universität Rostock, ed., *Fremdarbeiterpolitik des Imperialismus* (Rostock, 1974), 2–76.
2. Quoted in Dennis Kuck, "'Für den sozialistischen Aufbau ihrer Heimat'? Ausländische Vertragsarbeitskräfte in der DDR," in Jan C. Behrends, Thomas Lindenberger, and Patrice G. Poutrus, eds., *Fremde und Fremd-Sein in der DDR: Zu historischen Ursachen der Fremdenfeindlichkeit in Ostdeutschland* (Berlin, 2003), 272.
3. See Amalendu Guha, "Intra-COMECON Manpower Migration," in *International Migration – Migrations Internationales – Migraciones Internacionales* XVI, no. 2 (1978), 55; http://dissertationreviews.org/archives/13447.
4. Ibraimo Alberto with the assistance of Daniel Bachmann, *Ich wollte leben wie die Götter: Was in Deutschland aus meinen afrikanischen Träumen wurde* (Cologne, 2014), 80. A more positive, Eastgermanophile impression emerges from the authors, among them former Mozambican *Vertragsarbeiter* and former East German Mozambique functionaries, assembled in Ulrich van der Heyden, Wolfgang Semmler, and Ralf Straßburg, eds., *Mosambikanische Vertragsarbeiter in der DDR-Wirtschaft: Hintergründe – Verlauf – Folgen* (Berlin, 2014).
5. See Almut Zwengel, "Kontrolle, Marginalität und Misstrauen? Zur DDR-Spezifik des Umgangs mit Arbeitsmigranten," in Almut Zwengel, ed., *Die "Gastarbeiter" der DDR: Politischer Kontext und Lebenswelt* (Berlin, 2011), 4.
6. Calculated from the total number of about 127,948 from all states (Zwengel, "Kontrolle, Marginalität und Misstrauen?," 4) plus Polish and Hungarian contract workers. For numbers also see Karl-Heinz Meier-Braun, *Einwanderung und Asyl: Die 101 wichtigsten Fragen* (Munich, 2015), 30–32; Klaus J. Bade and Jochen Oltmer, *Normalfall Migration* (Bonn, 2004), 90–96.
7. Alberto, *Ich wollte leben wie die Götter*, 102–103.
8. Ibid., 105.
9. Ibid., 106.
10. Ibid., 110.
11. Quoted in Kuck, "'Für den sozialistischen Aufbau ihrer Heimat'?," 275.

12. Transcript of interview with R. M., quoted in Landolf Scherzer and Anna-Lena Schmitt, “Mosambikanische Vertragsarbeiter. Ausgrenzung und Rassismus als alltägliche Erfahrung,” in Zwengel, ed., *Die “Gastarbeiter” der DDR*, 104. Quoting from this interview was prohibited in the original GDR publication: Landolf Scherzer, *Bom dia, weißer Bruder: Erlebnisse am Sambesi* (Rudolfstadt, 1984).
13. Alberto, *Ich wollte leben wie die Götter*, 115.
14. “Herr Duave aus Mosambik: Er hat keine Arbeit mehr, ich habe keine Arbeit mehr – wie kann ich ihm dann die Arbeit weggenommen haben?,” in Der Landesbeauftragte für Ausländerfragen des Freistaates Thüringen, ed., *Lebenswege: Ausländer in Thüringen* (Erfurt, 1995), 73.
15. Britta Müller, *Ausländer im Osten Deutschlands: Eine Rostocker Studie* (Cologne, 1996), 63. This study is based on twenty-seven interviews conducted in Rostock between September and December 1993. See ibid., 11.
16. DOMiD, Interview Obj. Nr. 218 (April 6, 2005).
17. Alberto, *Ich wollte leben wie die Götter*, 142.
18. BArch Dokument DC/20/I/3/2774 quoted in Michael Feige, “Vietnamesische Vertragsarbeiter. Staatliche Ziele – lebensweltliche Realität,” in Zwengel, ed., *Die “Gastarbeiter” der DDR*, 50, footnote 29. See also www.argus.bstu.bundesarchiv.de/DC20-I-3-20614/index.htm?search=DC%2F20%2FI%2F3%2F2774&KontextFb=Signatur&searchType=any&searchVolumes=all&highlight=true&vid=DC20-I-3-20614&kid=0ecf176d-ada6-409c-be81-15e7ddaec7f6&uid=aa3c5f8c-4773-4dee-b736-8efafdf392b8&searchPos=1.
19. Alberto, *Ich wollte leben wie die Götter*, 142.
20. Ibid., 156.
21. Michael Hübner, “Gastarbeiter in der DDR. Mosambikaner getötet: Auf zehn Kilometern Körperteile gefunden,” *Mitteldeutsche Zeitung* (July 12, 2018).
22. Stefan Wolle, “Geschlossene Gesellschaft,” *Die Zeit* (December 18, 2015).
23. DOMiD, Interview Obj. Nr. 218 (April 6, 2005).
24. See www.demokratie-statt-diktatur.de/DE/Presse/Themen/Hintergrund/20121016_punkkonzert_1987.html?nn=1755758; www.bstu.de/mfs-lexikon/detail/jugend; Robert Mießner, “Der Zionskirchüberfall vom 17. Oktober 1987 und die Zäsur, die er markiert,” *taz* (October 12, 2017).
25. Alberto, *Ich wollte leben wie die Götter*, 164.
26. Ibid., 167–168.
27. Transcript of interview with C. D., quoted in Scherzer and Schmitt, “Mosambikanische Vertragsarbeiter,” 107.
28. Transcript of interview with E. S., quoted in ibid., 102–103.
29. “Frau M. aus Polen: Dann wäre ich nur auf dem Papier Deutsche, eine richtige Deutsche wäre ich nie,” in Der Landesbeauftragte für Ausländerfragen des Freistaates Thüringen, ed., *Lebenswege*, 43.
30. See Bernd Wagner, “Migrationspolitisch relevante Akteure in der DDR,” in Zwengel, ed., *Die “Gastarbeiter” der DDR*, 23. Also see Rita Röhr, *Hoffnung – Hilfe – Heuchelei: Geschichte des Einsatzes polnischer Arbeitskräfte in Betrieben des DDR-Grenzbezirks Frankfurt/Oder 1966–1991* (Berlin, 2001), 174.

31. Alberto, *Ich wollte leben wie die Götter*, pictorial insert between pages 128 and 129.
32. Quoted in Zwengel, "Kontrolle, Marginalität und Misstrauen?," 13–14.
33. See Müller, *Ausländer im Osten Deutschlands*, 28–29.
34. Quoted in Feige, "Vietnamesische Vertragsarbeiter," 47.
35. Müller, *Ausländer im Osten Deutschlands*, 46-47. Friendships with East Germans were exceedingly rare, yet they existed. See e.g. M. about *Mutti*, or mom, in her GDR ersatz family: "I just need the warmth of the family. My *Mutti* sometimes chokes up when she hears that. Then she says: 'You are like my daughter!'" Ibid., 54.
36. See Zwengel, "Kontrolle, Marginalität und Misstrauen?," 17–18.
37. Quoted in ibid., 11–12.
38. DOMiD, Interview Obj. Nr. 197, real name (November 1, 2004).
39. Alberto, *Ich wollte leben wie die Götter*, 172–173.
40. See www.auslaender-in-der-ddr.com/europa/westgruppe-der-sowjetischen-streitkräfte; Oliver von Wrochem, "Die sowjetischen 'Besatzer.' Konstruktionen des Fremden in der lebensgeschichtlichen Erinnerung," in Behrends et al., eds., *Fremde und Fremd-Sein in der DDR*, 57–74; Jan C. Behrends, "Sowjetische 'Freunde' und fremde 'Russen.' Deutsch–Sowjetische Freundschaft zwischen Ideologie und Alltag (1949–1990)," in ibid., 75–98.
41. Quoted in Feige, "Vietnamesische Vertragsarbeiter," 52.
42. DOMiD, Interview Obj. Nr. 197, real name (November 1, 2004).
43. Müller, *Ausländer im Osten Deutschlands*, 102.
44. "Herr Duave aus Mosambik: Er hat keine Arbeit mehr, ich habe keine Arbeit mehr – wie kann ich ihm dann die Arbeit weggenommen haben?," in Der Landesbeauftragte für Ausländerfragen des Freistaates Thüringen, ed., *Lebenswege*, 74.
45. "Herr A. aus Kuba: Ich habe hier gelacht, ich habe hier geweint," in ibid., 56.
46. Quoted in Zwengel, "Kontrolle, Marginalität und Misstrauen?," 15–16.
47. Alberto, *Ich wollte leben wie die Götter*, 226, 228.
48. DOMiD, Interview Obj. Nr. 244 (April 7, 2005).
49. Christian Hartmann, Ottmar Plöckinger, Roman Töppel, and Thomas Vordermayer, eds., *Hitler: Mein Kampf. Eine kritische Edition*, vol. 2 (Munich, 2016), 1657.
50. See Serguei Alex. Oushakine, *The Patriotism of Despair: Nation, War, and Loss in Russia* (Ithaca, 2009).
51. Jan Behrends, Dennis Kuck, and Patrice Poutrus, "Thesenpapier. Historische Ursachen der Fremdenfeindlichkeit in den Neuen Bundesländern," in Behrends et al., eds., *Fremde und Fremd-Sein in der DDR*, 330.
52. See ibid., 327–328.
53. Peter Maxwill, "Das Peripherie-Problem," *Spiegel Online* (May 18, 2017) (www.spiegel.de/panorama/gesellschaft/rechtsextremismus-in-ostdeutschland-studie-untersucht-freital-und-heidenau-a-1147970.html).
54. See Müller, *Ausländer im Osten Deutschlands*, 11.
55. Ibid., 96.

56. Alberto, *Ich wollte leben wie die Götter*, 88–89.
57. Ibid., 187.
58. Behrends et al., "Fremde und Fremd-Sein in der DDR," 15.

5 Asylum

1. Hassan Ali Djan, *Afghanistan. München. Ich: Meine Flucht in ein besseres Leben* (Freiburg im Breisgau, 2015), 93. Also see www.youtube.com/watch?v=nplNLsM2-NM; www.youtube.com/watch?v=FLqaR8qWyG8.
2. Djan, *Afghanistan*, 93.
3. Ibid., 93–94.
4. See Christian Jakob, Simone Schlindwein, *Diktatoren als Türsteher Europas: Wie die EU ihre Grenzen nach Afrika verlagert* (Berlin, 2017).
5. See https://de.statista.com/statistik/daten/studie/76095/umfrage/asylantraege-insgesamt-in-deutschland-seit-1995.
6. See BAMF, *Asylbroschüre 2007*, 40 (here the higher total of 48,102 is given as the total number of asylum applications in 2005).
7. Djan, *Afghanistan*, 97.
8. See for example Zekarias Kebraeb, *Hoffnung im Herzen, Freiheit im Sinn: Vier Jahre auf der Flucht nach Deutschland* (Cologne, 2011); Mojtaba, Masoud, and Milad Sadinam, *Unerwünscht: Drei Brüder aus dem Iran erzählen ihre deutsche Geschichte* (Berlin, 2014).
9. Djan, *Afghanistan*, 38.
10. Dokumentationsstelle der Antirassistischen Initiative Berlin, ed., *Bundesdeutsche Flüchtlingspolitik und ihre tödlichen Folgen: Dokumentation 1993 bis 2016*, Hefte I–III, 24. Auflage, 458; for the twenty-third edition see www.ari-berlin.org/doku/titel.htm.
11. Djan, *Afghanistan*, 65.
12. Ibid., 56.
13. Ibid., 84.
14. Ibid., 86.
15. Ibid., 91.
16. Ibid., 98.
17. Founded by the Trägerkreis zur Förderung von Bildung und Integration von Flüchtlingskindern und -jugendlichen e.V. See www.schlau-schule.de.
18. Djan, *Afghanistan*, 116.
19. Ibid., 120.
20. Ibid., 127.
21. Ibid., 132.
22. Ibid., 136.
23. Ibid., 138.
24. Ibid., 154.
25. Ibid., 168.
26. "Adventskalender," *Süddeutsche Zeitung* (December 27, 2011).
27. Djan, *Afghanistan*, 169.
28. Ibid., 159.

29. Quoted in Klaus J. Bade, "'Politisch Verfolgte genießen . . . .' Asyl bei den Deutschen – Idee und Wirklichkeit," in Klaus J. Bade, ed., *Deutsche im Ausland – Fremde in Deutschland: Migration in Geschichte und Gegenwart* (Munich, 1992), 411.
30. Ibid.
31. Christine Klissenbauer, "Interview mit Ana V. und Claudia R. über die Situation der Flüchtlinge aus El Salvador," in Gisela Klemt-Kozinowski, H. Koch, L. Scherf, and H. Wunderlich, eds., *Platz zum Leben gesucht: Lesebuch Asyl* (Baden-Baden, 1987), 44–45.
32. Ibid., 45.
33. Safwa Hangalay, "Geschichte einer Flucht," in Anja Tuckermann, ed., *In die Flucht geschlagen: Geschichten aus dem bundesdeutschen Asyl* (Frankfurt am Main, 1989), 52.
34. Karin Hoffmann-Walbeck and Susanne Prior, eds., *Mein Leben ist wie ein fremder Fluß: Der Weg ins Asyl – Frauen erzählen* (Reinbek, 1988), 120–121.
35. Ralf Roschinski, "Wertgutscheine für Asylsuchende," in Tessa Hofmann, ed., *Abgelehnt, Ausgewiesen, Ausgeliefert: Dokumentation zum Hearing über die soziale und rechtliche Lage der Asylbewerber in West-Berlin (20.–22.1.1984)* (Göttingen, 1984), 141.
36. See talk by P. Bischof in ibid., 138.
37. See Heidi Belay and Pari Raffi, "Unterbringung von Asylbewerbern in Heimen," in ibid., 158–159.
38. See Christina Balachandiran and Tessa Hofmann, "Abschiebehaft und Abschiebungen in der Praxis," in ibid., 30.
39. E. Mische, "Begrüßung und Einführung," in ibid., 18.
40. Ibid., 20.
41. On Tamils see Joachim Nawrocki, "Peinliche Kumpanei an der Spree," *Die Zeit* (August 23, 1985); Jochen Staadt, "Nach drüben," *Frankfurter Allgemeine Zeitung* (November 30, 2015), 9; on asylum in the GDR see Patrice G. Poutrus, "Zuflucht im Ausreiseland. Zur Geschichte des politischen Asyls in der DDR," *Jahrbuch für Historische Kommunismusforschung* (2004), 355–378; Patrice G. Poutrus, "Asyl im Kalten Krieg. Eine Parallelgeschichte aus dem geteilten Nachkriegsdeutschland," *Totalitarismus und Demokratie* 2, no. 3 (2005), 273–288; Patrice G. Poutrus, "Zuflucht im Nachkriegsdeutschland. Politik und Praxis der Flüchtlingsaufnahme in Bundesrepublik und DDR von den späten 1940er bis zu den 1970er Jahren," *Geschichte und Gesellschaft* 35, no. 1 (2009), 135–175.
42. Meier-Braun, *Einwanderung und Asyl*, 84.
43. Ibid., 88; www.gesetze-im-internet.de/asylvfg_1992/BJNR111260992.html; www.bamf.de/DE/Themen/AsylFluechtlingsschutz/Sonderverfahren/Flughafenverfahren/flughafenverfahren-node.html.
44. www.epplehaus.de/unvergessen-der-tod-von-kiomars-javadi.
45. I have reconstructed the Javadi case on the basis of Christian Gampert, "'Der schnauft ja noch,'" *Die Zeit* (July 8, 1988); http://unvergessen.blogsport.de/javadi-kiomars; http://www.spiegel.de/spiegel/print/d-13526485.html.

46. In other parts of West Germany pro-refugee activism has similar roots. See for example, for Aachen, Anka Erdweg, "Den ersten Besuch werde ich nie vergessen," in Ulrike Behnen, ed., *In einem Fremdenland: Flüchtlinge und Deutsche erzählen* (Münster, 1995), 163–166.
47. *18 Minuten Zivilcourage*, dir. Rahim Shirmahd (1991).

1989

1. See Gwendolyn Albert and Marek Szilvasi, "Intersectional Discrimination of Romani Women Forcibly Sterilized in the Former Czechoslovakia and Czech Republic," *Health and Human Rights* 19, no. 2 (2017), 23–34; Till Mayer, "'Sie haben mir ein Stück meines Frauseins genommen,'" *Spiegel Online* (March 31, 2009) (www.spiegel.de/politik/ausland/roma-sterilisation-in-tschechien-sie-haben-mir-ein-stueck-meines-frauseins-genommen-a-613610.html); Meier-Braun, *Einwanderung und Asyl*, 72.
2. Ulrich Herbert, *Geschichte der Ausländerpolitik in Deutschland: Saisonarbeiter, Zwangsarbeiter, Gastarbeiter, Flüchtlinge* (Munich, 2001), 276.
3. Quoted in Alexander Korb, *Im Schatten des Weltkriegs: Massengewalt der Ustaša gegen Serben, Juden und Roma in Kroatien 1941–1945* (Hamburg, 2013), 29.
4. Quoted in Jean-Philipp Baeck and Kathrin Herold, "Ein langer Weg," *taz* (July 18, 2015).
5. See Gaston Kirsche, "Anstalt XII," *Jungle World* (November 14, 2001).
6. Quoted in Hans-Hermann Hertle, *Chronik des Mauerfalls: Die dramatischen Ereignisse um den 9. November 1989*, 11th expanded edition (Berlin, 2009), 144.
7. Quoted in ibid., 153–154.
8. Quoted in ibid., 166.
9. Quoted in ibid., 182–183.
10. Quoted in TV clip, "Jubel – Mauerdurchbruch – Stimmung: Jubel auf dem Kurfürstendamm, der Mauerdurchbruch am Grenzübergang Bornholmer Straße – Stimmung am Grenzübergang Invalidenstraße, 9./10. November 1989" (RIAS-TV/Deutsche Welle) (www.chronik-der-mauer.de/chronik/#anchoryear1989).
11. See Christian Wemicke, "Angekommen – auch angenommen?," *Die Zeit* (January 12, 1990).
12. Frank Wolff, *Die Mauergesellschaft: Kalter Krieg, Menschenrechte und die deutsch–deutsche Migration 1961–1989* (Berlin, 2019), 18.
13. Wladimir Kaminer, *Russian Disco: Tales of Everyday Lunacy on the Streets of Berlin*, trans. Michael Hulse (London, 2002), 13.
14. See Adrian Wanner, "Wladimir Kaminer: A Russian Picaro Conquers Germany," *Russian Review* 64, no. 4 (2005), 590–604.
15. Kaminer, *Russian Disco*, 14–15. For a reproduction of Kaminer's East Berlin identity document see Dmitrij Belkin and Raphael Gross, eds., *Ausgerechnet Deutschland! Jüdisch-russische Einwanderung in die Bundesrepublik* (Berlin, 2010), 51.

16. "Seit sechs Monaten lerne ich Deutsch," in Heidi Knott, Horst Hamm, and Wolfgang Jung, eds., *Heimat Deutschland? Lebensberichte von Aus- und Übersiedlern* (Pfaffenweiler, 1991), 55.
17. Ibid., 56.
18. Ibid., 55.
19. Ibid., 56.
20. Ibid., 57.
21. Quoted in Ulrich Schiller, "An Auschwitz war kein Interesse," *Die Zeit* (October 1, 1993).
22. www.spiegel.de/spiegel/print/d-13497885.html.
23. Hans-Albert Hoffmann and Siegfried Stoof, *Sowjetische Truppen in Deutschland und ihr Hauptquartier in Wünsdorf 1945–1994: Geschichte, Fakten, Hintergründe* (Berlin, 2013), 6.
24. www.youtube.com/watch?v=YRVMyDeASHw (9:39–9:48). See also www.youtube.com/watch?v=F63NrKejkJk.
25. See Matthias Fiedler, "Der Extrem-Pendler," *Spiegel Online* (April 9, 2016) (www.spiegel.de/lebenundlernen/job/extrem-pendeln-mit-dem-flugzeug-zur-uni-a-1088700.html).
26. Knopp, *Die große Flucht*, 286.
27. See *Das Ostpreußenblatt* (November 21, 1992), 14 (http://archiv.preussische-allgemeine.de/1992/1992_11_21_47.pdf#search=milowski).
28. See Knopp, *Die große Flucht*, 258.
29. www.spiegel.de/spiegel/print/d-13497181.html.
30. See Sonja Wolf, "Zur sozialen und politischen Lage der anerkannten nationalen Minderheiten in Deutschland," *APuZ* (March 10, 2017), 16–22.
31. Günter Grass, *Ohne Stimme: Reden zugunsten des Volkes der Roma und Sinti* (Göttingen, 2000), 93.

6 Germans There, Russians Here

1. Katrin Vogel, *Psychosoziale Schwierigkeiten im Integrationsprozess von russlanddeutschen Spätaussiedlern: Qualitative Fallanalysen* (Stuttgart, 2008), 327; "Viktor Petri, geb. 1950," in Dorothee Wierling, ed., *Heimat finden: Lebenswege von Deutschen, die aus Russland kommen* (Hamburg, 2004), 102. The loaded question of the Volga Germans' German identity has become an object of scholarly inquiry in its own right, as, for example, in this social science study: Svetlana Kiel, *Wie deutsch sind Russlanddeutsche? Eine empirische Studie zur ethnisch-kulturellen Identität in russlanddeutschen Aussiedlerfamilien* (Münster, 2009).
2. See Jannis Panagiotidis, "Postsowjetische Migranten in Deutschland. Perspektiven auf eine heterogene Diaspora," *APuZ* (March 13, 2017), 24.
3. See Merih Anil, "The New German Citizenship Law and Its Impact on German Demographics: Research Notes," *Population Research and Policy Review* 25, no. 5/6 (2006), 448–449.
4. See Susanne Worbs, Eva Bund, Martin Kohls, and Christian Babka von Gostomski, *(Spät-)Aussiedler in Deutschland: Eine Analyse aktueller Daten und Forschungsergebnisse* (Nuremberg, 2013), 28; also see www.bamf.de/Shared

Docs/Anlagen/DE/Forschung/Forschungsberichte/fb20-spaetaussiedler .pdf?__blob=publicationFile&v=14.

5. Jannis Panagiotidis, "Aussiedler/Spätaussiedler," in *Online-Lexikon zur Kultur und Geschichte der Deutschen im östlichen Europa* (2015) (https://ome-lexikon.uni-oldenburg.de/begriffe/aussiedlerspaetaussiedler) (accessed February 1, 2018).
6. See Deutsches Kulturforum östliches Europa, ed., *Nach Übersee: Deutschsprachige Auswanderer aus dem östlichen Europa um 1900* (Potsdam, 2015).
7. This sketch of the history of the Volga Germans since the First World War is based on Viktor Krieger, *Kolonisten, Sowjetdeutsche, Aussiedler: Eine Geschichte der Russlanddeutschen* (Bonn, 2015); György Dalos, *Geschichte der Russlanddeutschen: Von Katharina der Großen bis zur Gegenwart* (Munich, 2014); Wierling, ed., *Heimat finden*, 243–252; Klaus J. Bade and Jochen Oltmer, "Einführung: Aussiedlerzuwanderung und Aussiedlerintegration: Historische Entwicklung und aktuelle Probleme," in Klaus J. Bade and Jochen Oltmer, eds., *Aussiedler: Deutsche Einwanderer aus Osteuropa* (Osnabrück, 1999), 9–51.
8. See Krieger, *Kolonisten, Sowjetdeutsche, Aussiedler*, 105–107.
9. Ibid., 109.
10. Ibid., 12.
11. I have reconstructed this history on the basis of Peter Oliver Loew, *Wir Unsichtbaren: Geschichte der Polen in Deutschland* (Munich, 2014); Detlef Haberland, Heinke Kalinke, Matthias Weber, and Tobias Weger, "Schlesien," in *Online-Lexikon zur Kultur und Geschichte der Deutschen im östlichen Europa* (2011) (https://ome-lexikon.uni-oldenburg.de/regionen/sch lesien) (accessed November 4, 2022).
12. Roland Borchers, "Deutsche Volksliste," in *Online-Lexikon zur Kultur und Geschichte der Deutschen im östlichen Europa* (2014) (http://ome-lexikon.uni-oldenburg.de/p32838) (accessed November 19, 2014).
13. See Gerhard Wolf, *Ideologie und Herrschaftsrationalität: Nationalsozialistische Germanisierungspolitik in Polen* (Hamburg, 2012).
14. This history is based on Cristian Cercel, "Rumänien," in *Online-Lexikon zur Kultur und Geschichte der Deutschen im östlichen Europa* (2013) (https://ome-lexikon.uni-oldenburg.de/laender/rumaenien) (accessed November 4, 2022).
15. See Joachim Baur, "Grenzdurchgangslager Friedland," in *Online-Lexikon zur Kultur und Geschichte der Deutschen im östlichen Europa* (2014) (https://ome-lexikon.uni-oldenburg.de/begriffe/grenzdurchgangslager-friedland) (accessed November 4, 2022).
16. See Christian Fuchs, "Informant Migrant," *taz* (March 25, 2009); https://dserver.bundestag.de/btd/16/020/1602059.pdf; https://dserver.bundestag.de/btd/16/022/1602225.pdf. More generally, see Sascha Schießl, *"Das Tor zur Freiheit": Kriegsfolgen, Erinnerungspolitik und humanitärer Anspruch im Lager Friedland (1945–1970)* (Göttingen, 2016), 365–368. On Western secret services in the Berlin-Marienfelde transit camp see Bettina Effner, "Das Notaufnahmelager Marienfelde in Berlin. Ein historischer und aktueller Ort der Migration," *APuZ* (May 8, 2017).
17. Quoted in Loew, *Wir Unsichtbaren*, 215.

18. See Wierling, ed., *Heimat finden*, 44.
19. Ibid., 99, 176–177 (Viktor Petri and Nikolaj Kuzelev in Hamburg container ships); Ulla Lachauer, *Ritas Leute: Eine deutsch-russische Familiengeschichte* (Reinbek, 2002), 233 (Osnabrück gym); Emilia Smechowski, *Wir Strebermigranten* (Munich, 2017), 43 (homeless shelter in Berlin-Neukölln).
20. Smechowski, *Wir Strebermigranten*, 46–47.
21. Wierling, ed., *Heimat finden*, 99–100.
22. Ibid., 101.
23. Ibid., 102.
24. Ibid., 90.
25. Ibid., 95.
26. Ibid., 56.
27. Gisela Székely, *Laßt sie selber sprechen: Berichte rußlanddeutscher Aussiedler* (Frankfurt am Main, 1990), 28.
28. Ibid., 29.
29. Ibid., 50. Many autobiographical documents note how Soviet Second World War propaganda's depiction of fascists as devils influenced ordinary people's perception of the Volga Germans. See for example Elena Denisova-Schmidt, *Russlanddeutsche Geschichte und Gegenwart: Zeitzeugen erzählen über Heimat, Migration und Engagement* (Stuttgart, 2015), 70.
30. Wierling, ed., *Heimat finden*, 115.
31. See Krieger, *Kolonisten, Sowjetdeutsche, Aussiedler*, 156–166; Viktor Krieger, *Bundesbürger russlanddeutscher Herkunft: Historische Schlüsselerfahrungen und kollektives Gedächtnis* (Berlin, 2013), 123–140; Kerstin Armborst, *Ablösung von der Sowjetunion: Die Emigrationsbewegung der Juden und Deutschen vor 1987* (Münster, 2001); www.russlanddeutschegeschichte.de/geschichte/tei l4/nach1956/aktionen.htm.
32. Wierling, ed., *Heimat finden*, 118.
33. Ibid., 120.
34. Ibid., 120–121.
35. Ibid., 122.
36. Gabriele Rosenthal, Viola Stephan, and Niklas Radenbach, *Brüchige Zugehörigkeiten: Wie sich Familien von Russlanddeutschen ihre Geschichte erzählen* (Frankfurt am Main, 2011), 142–143.
37. Karl-Markus Gauß, *Die versprengten Deutschen: Unterwegs in Litauen, durch die Zips und am Schwarzen Meer* (Bonn, 2005), 178.
38. Smechowski, *Wir Strebermigranten*, 35.
39. Ibid.
40. See interview with Ilka Scheidgen, *Fünfuhrgespräche: Ilka Scheidgen zu Gast bei Günter Grass, Peter Härtling, Herta Müller, Peter Rühmkorf, Dorothee Sölle, Arnold Stadler, Martin Walser, Gabriele Wohmann, Eva Zeller* (Lahr, 2008), 57–74.
41. On the complex statistics of Russian speakers in Germany see Jannis Panagiotidis, "Postsowjetische Migranten in Deutschland. Perspektiven auf eine heterogene 'Diaspora,'" *APuZ* 67, nos. 11–12 (2017), 23.

42. See Alice Schürmann, *Aussiedler mit Suchterkrankungen: Ursachen und Wirkung* (Saarbrücken, 2007); Barbara Dietz and Heike Roll, *Jugendliche Aussiedler – Porträt einer Zuwanderergeneration* (Frankfurt am Main, 1998); Katrin Vogel, *Psychosoziale Schwierigkeiten im Integrationsprozess von russlanddeutschen Spätaussiedlern: Qualitative Fallanalysen* (Stuttgart, 2008); Waldemar Vogelgesang, *Jugendliche Aussiedler: Zwischen Entwurzelung, Ausgrenzung und Integration* (Weinheim, 2008); Olga Blatz, *Beratung? – Nein, danke! Eine Untersuchung zur niedrigen Inanspruchnahme psychosozialer Versorgungsangebote seitens russlanddeutscher Aussiedler* (Saarbrücken, 2015).
43. Michael Wolffsohn, "Die Bundeswehr ist eine Unterschichtenarmee," *Die Welt* (August 21, 2009).
44. Wierling, ed., *Heimat finden*, 42.
45. Ibid., 58.
46. Ibid., 142.
47. Székely, *Laßt sie selber sprechen*, 34.
48. See Elke Windisch, "Russland nutzt 'Fall Lisa' für Retourkutsche am Westen," *Der Tagesspiegel* (January 30, 2016).
49. The micro census of 2017 found that 390,000 of 2.854 million *Spätaussiedler* and *Aussiedler* had dual citizenship. The real number including unreported cases is estimated to be higher, but not as high as the figure that the last full census (as opposed to the micro census) of 2011 produced.
50. See Anett Schmitz, *Transnational leben: Bildungserfolgreiche (Spät-)Aussiedler zwischen Deutschland und Russland* (Bielefeld, 2013).
51. See Sabine Ipsen-Peitzmeier and Markus Kaiser, *Zuhause fremd – Russlanddeutsche zwischen Russland und Deutschland* (Bielefeld, 2005). Also see Simon Goebel, "Weder Da- noch Dortsein. Wie die Hegemonie des Nationalen eine sinnvolle Bedeutung von 'Heimat' verhindert," in Hartmut Koschyk and Lothar de Maizière, eds., *Wie viel Heimat braucht der Mensch? Auf der Suche nach einer Identität zwischen Russland und Deutschland. Ein studentischer Essaywettbewerb* (Berlin, 2014), 46–50.
52. My translation. Quoted in http://polit.ru/article/2015/10/09/russian_world/#sdfootnote28sym. See also Nicolas Schupp, "Die 'Russische Welt.' Eine antiwestliche Ideologie als politische Ressource im heutigen Russland," Master's Thesis, University of Tübingen, 2017; Jan Plamper, "Brauchen wir deutsche Medien auf russisch?," *Frankfurter Allgemeine Zeitung* (February 3, 2018).
53. Smechowski, *Wir Strebermigranten*, 32.

7 Jewish *Germaniya*

1. Alice Lanzke, "'Ich habe so viel Lampenlicht,'" *Jüdische Allgemeine* (May 28, 2009). Also see Annika Schönstädt, "Daniel Donskoy – Vom Glauben keine Ahnung," *Berliner Morgenpost* (January 23, 2018); www.bild.de/bild-plus/unterhaltung/tv/tatort/moerder-daniel-donskoy-im-bild-interview-55762206.bild.html.

2. See for example Jess Smee, "A Belated Victory against the Nazis," *Guardian* (November 3, 2006); www.haaretz.com/jewish/news/1.584490; www.wshu.org/culture/2016-06-07/why-jewish-israelis-are-moving-back-to-germany; Patrick Saint-Paul, "En Allemagne, la communauté juive connaît une renaissance," *Le Figaro* (January 20, 2012).
3. More precisely, 97,791 in 2017. See https://zwst.org/sites/default/files/2022-05/ZWST-Mitgliederstatistik-2021-Kurzversion.pdf. Registered members of Jewish communities pay a religious tax.
4. Quoted in Almuth Berger, "Ein Tabu der Nachkriegsgeschichte wird gebrochen. Aufnahme russisch-jüdischer Emigranten in der DDR. Ein Zeitzeugenbericht," in Dmitrij Belkin and Raphael Gross, eds., *Ausgerechnet Deutschland! Jüdisch-russische Einwanderung in die Bundesrepublik* (Berlin, 2010), 56. For a more extended history see Ljudmila Belkin, "Verantwortung und Asylpolitik. Zur Vorgeschichte der jüdischen Kontingentflüchtlinge," in Marek Mazurkiewicz, Annemarie Franke, Tadeusz Siwek, and Magdalena Moj, eds., *Polska – Czechy – Niemcy wobec wyzwania migracji i integracji* (Opole, 2017), 230–250.
5. Quoted in Jeffrey Herf, "Post-totalitarian Narratives in Germany: Reflections on Two Dictatorships after 1945 and 1989," in Anatoly M. Khazanov and Stanley Payne, eds., *Perpetrators, Accomplices and Victims in Twentieth-Century Politics: Reckoning with the Past* (New York, 2009), 15.
6. Quoted in Helmut Eschwege, "The Churches and the Jews in the German Democratic Republic," *The Leo Baeck Institute Year Book* 37, no. 1 (1992), 511.
7. Quoted in ibid., 57.
8. See Dmitrij Belkin, *Germanija: Wie ich in Deutschland jüdisch und erwachsen wurde* (Frankfurt am Main, 2016), 17; Anne Gemeinhardt, "Eine Erneuerung des Judentums in Deutschland. Heinz Galinski und die jüdisch-russische Einwanderung," in Belkin and Gross, eds., *Ausgerechnet Deutschland!*, 61.
9. See Katja Iken, "Gestrandete der Apokalypse," *Spiegel Online* (December 1, 2008); Frank Bösch, "Engagement für Flüchtlinge. Die Aufnahme vietnamesischer 'Boat People' in der Bundesrepublik," *Zeithistorische Forschungen/Studies in Contemporary History* 14, no. 1 (2017), 13–40; Rupert Neudeck, *In uns allen steckt ein Flüchtling: Ein Vermächtnis* (Munich, 2016).
10. See Julius H. Schoeps, "Das Land der Täter als Ziel," *Die Welt* (October 21, 2003).
11. http://www.bamf.de/SharedDocs/Anlagen/DE/Downloads/Infothek/JuedischeZuwanderer/merkblatt-aufnahmeverfahren-deutsch.pdf?__blob=publicationFile
12. See Alina Gromova, *Generation "koscher light": Urbane Räume und Praxen junger russischsprachiger Juden in Berlin* (Bielefeld, 2013), 76.
13. Mischa Gabowitsch, "Pogromgerüchte in der UdSSR der Perestroika-Zeit," in Belkin and Gross, eds., *Ausgerechnet Deutschland!*, 42.
14. Dmitrij Kapitelman, *Das Lächeln meines unsichtbaren Vaters* (Munich, 2016), 114.
15. Belkin, *Germanija*, 15.

16. Ibid., 17.
17. Ibid., 18.
18. Ibid.
19. See https://ec.europa.eu/migrant-integration/news/ingrian-finns-could-lose-right-return-finland_en; https://yle.fi/uutiset/osasto/news/ingrian_finns_repatriation_queue_closing/5382006; Jannis Panagiotidis, *The Unchosen Ones: Diaspora, Nation, and Migration in Israel and Germany* (Bloomington, 2019).
20. See Eftihia Voutira, "Post Soviet Greeks. A Resourceful Diaspora," in Waltraud Kokot, Christian Giordano, and Mijal Gandelsman-Trier, eds., *Diaspora as a Resource: Comparative Studies in Strategies, Networks and Urban Space* (Münster, 2013), 130.
21. Belkin, *Germanija*, 30.
22. Kapitelman, *Das Lächeln meines unsichtbaren Vaters*, 28–29.
23. See Shahak Shapira, *Das wird man ja wohl noch schreiben dürfen: Wie ich der deutscheste Jude der Welt wurde* (Reinbek, 2016), 86, 180–182, 199–201. Also see Frank Jansen, "Eine Tragödie aus Deutschland," *Der Tagesspiegel* (January 6, 2015); Susanne Spülbeck, *Ordnung und Angst: Russische Juden aus der Sicht eines ostdeutschen Dorfes nach der Wende. Eine ethnologische Studie* (Frankfurt am Main, 1997).
24. Kapitelman, *Das Lächeln meines unsichtbaren Vaters*, 121.
25. Consider Uffa Jensen, a historian of antisemitism: "One criterion is whether a distinction is made between Israelis and Jews. There are about 14 million Jews in the world and fewer than half of them live in Israel. The rule of thumb is: the more someone blurs this distinction, the more antisemitic what they are saying is." Interview with Dominik Peters, "Hass kann man nicht mit Gesetzen abschaffen," *Spiegel Online* (December 14, 2017); www.nordbayern.de/politik/was-darf-ich-sagen-ohne-ein-antisemit-zu-sein-forscher-versucht-sich-an-einer-antwort-1.11078201.
26. Sasha Marianna Salzmann, *Außer sich* (Berlin, 2017), 100.
27. See Evgenia Gostrer, "Ihrer Oma geht es gut," in Dmitrij Belkin, Lara Hensch, and Eva Lezzi, eds., *Neues Judentum – altes Erinnern?* (Berlin, 2017), 75–77.
28. Anastassia Pletoukhina quoted in Anastassia Pletoukhina and Valentin Lutset, "Eine Frage der Selbstverwirklichung," in Dmitrij Belkin, ed., *#Babel 21. Migration und jüdische Gemeinschaft* (Berlin, 2017), 36–37.
29. Belkin, *Germanija*, 141.
30. Olga Grjasnowa, *All Russians Love Birth Trees*, trans. Eva Beacon (New York, 2014), 65.
31. Ibid., 36.
32. See Martin Krauss's interview with Volker Beck, "Zuwanderer gleich behandeln," *Jüdische Allgemeine* (December 14, 2015); Sergey Lagodinsky, "Eine Schande namens Armut," *Jüdische Allgemeine* (June 15, 2017); Martin Krauss, "Für gerechte Rente," *Jüdische Allgemeine* (June 15, 2017).
33. See Sun Diego in collaboration with Dennis Sand, *Yellow Bar Mitzvah: Die sieben Pforten vom Moloch zum Ruhm* (Munich, 2018); Dani Kranz, "Bruchstücke eines jüdischen Mosaiks aus scharfkantigen Steinen," *Jalta. Positionen zur jüdischen Gegenwart* no. 1 (2017), 150–155. This novel by

a male Jewish quota refugee is the exception to the rule: Jan Himmelfarb, *Sterndeutung* (Munich, 2015).

34. See Max Czollek, *Desintegriert euch!* (Munich, 2018). Also see Lena Gorelik, *"Sie können aber gut Deutsch!" Warum ich nicht mehr dankbar sein will, dass ich hier leben darf, und Toleranz nicht weiterhilft* (Munich, 2012).
35. See www.bvre.de/home.html.
36. Stephan Beetz, "Zündstoff Wohnheim. Spätaussiedler und jüdische Flüchtlinge in Potsdam," in Ingrid Oswald and Victor Voronkov, eds., *Postsowjetische Ethnizitäten: Ethnische Gemeinden in St. Petersburg und Berlin/Potsdam* (Berlin, 1997), 270–271, quoted in Gromova, *Generation "koscher light,"* 57.
37. Yuri Slezkine, *The Jewish Century* (Princeton, 2004), 1.
38. Digital Archive Research and Information Center Memorial "Fond Iofe" (St. Petersburg), fond B-1, op. 1, file Dik, Gerkhard Gerkhardovich (http://arch.iofe.center/showObject/63238875).
39. Video interview with Meytal Rozental, exhibition #BABEL 21. Migration und jüdische Gemeinschaft, Ernst Ludwig Ehrlich Studienwerk and Centrum Judaicum (Berlin, 2017).
40. For example the bestselling British Russianist historian Orlando Figes: see Michael Hesse's interview with Orlando Figes, "Als Deutsche können wir in Europa leben," *Berliner Zeitung* (April 19, 2017).
41. "They are taking the last things we have away from us," Dmitrij Belkin's parents say about the refugees. "The state is going to care even less about our medical and social wellbeing." Belkin, *Germanija*, 184.
42. Interview by Katrin Richter with Dmitrij Kapitelman, "Fast ein Sehnsuchtsort," *Jüdische Allgemeine* (August 25, 2016).
43. Video interview with Akiva Weingarten, exhibition #BABEL 21. Migration und jüdische Gemeinschaft, Ernst Ludwig Ehrlich Studienwerk and Centrum Judaicum (Berlin, 2017).
44. Interview by Maria Fiedler with Josef Schuster, "Es könnte sehr wohl auch Juden treffen," *Der Tagesspiegel* (September 24, 2017).
45. Quoted in Olga Goldenberg, *Neubeginn in der Fremde: Lebenssituation und Identitätskonstruktionen jüdischer Migranten aus der ehemaligen UdSSR* (Stuttgart, 2011), 9.
46. See www.youtube.com/watch?v=OfC8zsYYFs0.
47. See Karl Schlögel, "Berlin: 'Stiefmutter unter den russischen Städten,'" in Karl Schlögel, ed., *Der große Exodus: Die russische Emigration und ihre Zentren 1917 bis 1941* (Munich, 1994), 234–259.
48. For the United States and Europe, respectively, see Alan M. Dershowitz, *The Vanishing American Jew: In Search of Jewish Identity for the Next Century* (Boston, 1997) and Bernard Wasserstein, *Vanishing Diaspora: The Jews in Europe since 1945* (Cambridge, MA, 1996).
49. Belkin, *Germanija*, 137.

50. www.youtube.com/watch?v=8zuoBzRktAE. Concerning *Weihnachtszauberwahnsinn* (Christmas magic madness) see also https://52schabbatot.wordpress.com/2016/12/11/ich-will-meinen-tannenbaum.
51. See Jens Rosbach, "Shoah-Verfolgte auf Grundsicherung angewiesen," *Deutschlandfunk Kultur* (May 5, 2017) (www.deutschlandfunkkultur.de/juden-aus-der-ex-sowjetunion-in-sozialnot-erst-arzt-dann-100.html).
52. Lea Simon, "Ich komme aus Berlin," in Belkin, ed., *#Babel 21*, 23.

8 Welcoming Culture

1. Corresponding to 8,904,210 persons in 2015 and 9,837,730 in 2016. I arrived at these numbers by comparison with population figures for 2015 and 2016. See Petra-Angela Ahrens, *Skepsis und Zuversicht – Wie blickt Deutschland auf Flüchtlinge?* (Hannover, 2017), 7.
2. For the 19 percent figure see Allensbach polls cited in Bundesministerium für Familie, Senioren, Frauen und Jugend, ed., *Engagement in der Flüchtlingshilfe: Ergebnisbericht einer Untersuchung des Instituts für Demoskopie Allensbach*, November 2017, 8 (www.bmfsfj.de/resource/blob/122010/d35ec9bf4a940ea49283485db4625aaf/engagement-in-der-fluechlingshilfe-data.pdf). Also see Ahrens, *Skepsis und Zuversicht*; Bertelsmann Stiftung, ed., *Willkommenskultur im "Stresstest": Einstellungen in der Bevölkerung 2017 und Entwicklungen und Trends seit 2011/2012* (April 2017) (www.bertelsmann-stiftung.de/de/publikationen/publikation/did/willkommenskultur-im-stresstest).
3. See for example Christine Ulrich's interview with Oskar Fischer, "Interview mit Soziologen. Darum engagieren wir uns politisch," *Merkur* (April 18, 2017) (www.merkur.de/lokales/muenchen/stadt-muenchen/interview-mit-soziologen-ueber-soziale-bewegungen-wunsch-etwas-zu-veraendern-8144920.html); Ulrike Hamann, *Eine neue soziale Bewegung?* (May 2017) (www.rosalux.de/publikation/id/14864/eine-neue-soziale-bewegung).
4. See Sabine Hess, Bernd Kasparek, Stefanie Kron, Mathias Rodatz, Maria Schwertl, and Simon Sontowski, eds., *Der lange Sommer der Migration* (Hamburg, 2016).
5. Two addenda. First, the criterion of 8 years of legal residence in Germany was satisfied by having had a residence permit for 8 years or a permanent residence permit for 3 years. Second, a transitional rule (until December 31, 2000) applied to children. If they were born in Germany and had not yet turned 11 on January 1, 2000, they too became eligible for German citizenship.
6. *Zuwanderung gestalten, Integration fördern: Bericht der Unabhängigen Kommission "Zuwanderung"* (July 4, 2001), 3.
7. Marieluise Beck quoted in Lukas Wallraff, "Frost im Frühling der Zuwanderung," *taz* (February 14, 2002).
8. *Zuwanderung gestalten, Integration fördern*, 9.
9. Ibid., 9, 5.
10. Ibid., 12.
11. Ibid., 8.
12. Friedrich Merz, "Einwanderung und Identität," *Die Welt* (October 25, 2000).

13. www.queer.de/detail.php?article_id=19964; www.spiegel.de/politik/deutschland/cdu-will-integrationspflicht-fuer-migranten-beschliessen-a-1064918.html.
14. See Susann Sitzler, "Oh, du schöner deutscher Döner!," *Die Zeit* (December 1, 2011).
15. See *Zuwanderung gestalten, Integration fördern*, 9; www.documentarchiv.de/brd/2002/zuwanderungsgesetz.html.
16. Meier-Braun, *Einwanderung und Asyl*, 102.
17. Amounting to 4.9 million or 11.7 percent unemployed in 2005, the absolute maximum figure since 1990.
18. Ludwig Siegele, "Germany on the Mend," *The Economist* (November 17, 2004) ("the sick man of Europe, as Germany is now regularly called").
19. Roger Cohen, "Germany and the Cup. A Liberating Normality," *New York Times* (June 17, 2006); Laura Smith-Spark, "We All Love the Germans!" (June 18, 2006) (www.bbc.co.uk/blogs/worldcup/2006/06/we_all_love_the_germans.html).
20. See Michael Meng, "Silences about Sarrazin's Racism in Contemporary Germany," *Journal of Modern History* 87, no. 1 (2015), 114.
21. Thilo Sarrazin, *Deutschland schafft sich ab: Wie wir unser Land aufs Spiel setzen* (Munich, 2010), 100.
22. Ibid., 93.
23. Ibid., 424, endnote 64. In the body of the book's text Sarrazin also cites Stern on pages 188 and 221.
24. Elsbeth Stern, "Was heißt hier erblich?," *Die Zeit* (September 2, 2010).
25. Ibid. Here is one of many Sarrazin quotations regarding allegedly equal starting chances (as usual, he weaponizes a person of immigrant background to support his thesis): "In 1984 firefighter Ceyhun Heptaygun was the first Turk in Berlin's fire department: 'I graduated from [vocational] *Hauptschule* and became an electronic equipment mechanic. But I was determined. You can achieve something if you really want to. But you have to want it yourself.'" Sarrazin, *Deutschland schafft sich ab*, 307.
26. Sarrazin, *Deutschland schafft sich ab*, 259.
27. See for example Thomas Bauer and Klaus F. Zimmermann, "Gastarbeiter und Wirtschaftsentwicklung im Nachkriegsdeutschland," *Jahrbuch für Wirtschaftsgeschichte* 37, no. 2 (1996), 73–108.
28. Sarrazin, *Deutschland schafft sich ab*, 300.
29. See, for example, this 2017 study: https://interaktiv.br.de/hanna-und-ismail/english/index.html.
30. Sarrazin, *Deutschland schafft sich ab*, 294.
31. Ibid., 308 (emphasis in original).
32. Ibid., 313.
33. See Carolin Emcke, *Against Hate*, trans. Tony Crawford (Cambridge, 2019).
34. Sarrazin, *Deutschland schafft sich ab*, 326. A more hybridic concept of culture does occasionally surface, yet never with reference to Germans of immigrant background. For example, "What is essential is the correct preservation and further development of the identity of peoples and states. Boundaries are blurred here: Alemannic Swabians in many ways are similar to German

Swiss. Alsace is never going to renounce its German roots, just as one is always going to notice in Nice that it used to be Italian. The architectural styles and built urban environments of the European Plain from Bruges to Tallin, the former Reval, exhibit common cultural roots." Ibid., 392.

35. For racial (*völkisch*) see for example Micha Brumlik at www.tagesspiegel.de/kultur/radikalismus-der-mitte-8115622.html (September 3, 2010). For neo-Nazi see for example Wolfgang Lieb at www.nachdenkseiten.de/?p=6572 (August 24, 2010) and www.bz-berlin.de/archiv-artikel/sarrazin-wehrt-sich-gegen-beleidigungen (April 29, 2011).
36. See especially Sarrazin's mobilization of *The Bell Curve* on the purportedly lower intelligence of African Americans: "This very successful book triggered a fierce debate and was met with a wave of public criticism. However, that criticism focused on fundamental and ideological issues. No one ever published successful alternative attempts to measure intelligence." Sarrazin, *Deutschland schafft sich ab*, 425, endnote 78.
37. For example, "I am quite happy that I can quote Necla Kelek." Ibid., 306. Or: "To many do-gooders [*Gutmenschen*] in the German media, women like Necla Kelek, Seyran Ates, or Hirsi Ali are a nuisance because they will not fit into their liberal, lukewarm worldview that has been purged of uncomfortable contradictions. After all it is hard to label a German Turk [*Deutschtürkin*] as a German nationalist, yet they still try to do just that." Ibid., 307. Sarrazin uses the same strategy for white minority men like Walter Laqueur, Paul Scheffer, and Christopher Caldwell: "The first is an Israeli Jew, raised in Breslau, the second is Dutch, and the third US American. All three come from very polyglot states and are polyglots themselves. All three are liberal. They and their concerns can hardly be branded nationalist, *völkisch*, or even 'Islamophobic,' as is often done." Ibid., 288.
38. Ibid., 34. Sarrazin's best-known Islamophobic neologism is "headscarf girls" [*Kopftuchmädchen*], which is from as early as 2009: "I don't have to accept anyone who lives at the expense of the state, rejects that state, doesn't really care about the education of their children, and constantly produces new little headscarf girls [*neue kleine Kopftuchmädchen produziert*]." Sarrazin interviewed by Franz Berberich, "Klasse statt Masse. Thilo Sarrazin im Gespräch," *Lettre International*, no. 86 (2009), 199.
39. In the words of a teacher from Nuremberg, "My students bought the Sarrazin book, highlighted the passages where he rails against foreigners in yellow, and distributed photocopies in school." Birgit Mair, "Mit Pädagogik gegen Neonazismus und Rassismus," in Birgit Mair, ed., *Strategien gegen Neonazismus und Rassismus unter besonderer Berücksichtigung der Jugendarbeit* (Nuremberg, 2012), 18.
40. Cited in *Der Spiegel*, no. 31 (2018), 23.
41. Sarrazin, *Deutschland schafft sich ab*, 18.
42. The following passage came right before this sentence: "A notion of Germany that does not reduce belonging to a passport, a family biography or a faith, but is conceived more broadly. Christianity undoubtedly belongs to Germany. Judaism undoubtedly belongs to Germany. That is our Christo-Judean

history." www.bundespraesident.de/SharedDocs/Reden/DE/Christian-Wulff/Reden/2010/10/20101003_Rede.html.
43. Rainer Haubrich, "Wilders wirft Merkel Feigheit vor Islamisierung vor," *Die Welt* (October 2, 2010); Frank Jansen, "Geert Wilders unterstützt Wahlkampf in Berlin," *Die Zeit* (September 3, 2011).
44. www.youtube.com/watch?v=7_0s3uCIMmE (at 5:56–6:00) (October 14, 2017). Also see Thomas Wagner, *Die Angstmacher: 1968 und die Neuen Rechten* (Berlin, 2017).
45. The phrase "Döner murders" first appeared on August 31, 2005 in the *Nürnberger Zeitung*, by 2006 it could be found in the *Frankfurter Allgemeine Zeitung*, the *Neue Zürcher Zeitung*, *Bild*, and even the left-wing *taz*. See Christian Fuchs, "Wie der Begriff 'Döner-Morde' entstand," *Spiegel Online* (July 4, 2012).
46. See Christian Jakob, *Die Bleibenden: Wie Flüchtlinge Deutschland seit 20 Jahren verändern* (Berlin, 2016).
47. Ibid., 85–87.
48. Ibid., 149, 180; Madjiguène Cissé, *Papiere für alle: Die Bewegung der Sans Papiers in Frankreich* (Berlin, 2002); PICUM, PRO ASYL, and Freudenberg Stiftung, eds., *Book of Solidarity: Unterstützung für Menschen ohne Papiere in Deutschland, Belgien, den Niederlanden und Großbritannien* (Karlsruhe, 2004).
49. Özlem Topçu, Alice Bota, and Khuê Phạm, *Wir neuen Deutschen: Wer wir sind, was wir wollen* (Reinbek, 2012), 162.
50. Jakob, *Die Bleibenden*, 106; Dokumentationsstelle der Antirassistischen Initiative Berlin, ed., *Bundesdeutsche Flüchtlingspolitik und ihre tödlichen Folgen*, Hefte I–III, 24. Auflage, 305 ("rams a ball pen refill into his trachea"). For the twenty-third edition see www.ari-berlin.org/doku/titel.htm.
51. Quoted in Jakob, *Die Bleibenden*, 109.
52. Ibid., 117.
53. Ibid., 126.
54. Ibid., 128.
55. Ibid., 131.
56. Quoted in ibid., 135.
57. See Frank Bösch, "Engagement für Flüchtlinge. Die Aufnahme vietnamesischer 'Boat People' in der Bundesrepublik," *Zeithistorische Forschungen/Studies in Contemporary History* 14, no. 1 (2017), 13–40.
58. Jenny Marrenbach, "Die Odyssee der Familie Hammoudeh," *taz* (November 10, 2008); Torsten Hampel, "Die Heilig-Kreuz-Kirche – ein moralischer Multifunktionsraum," *Tagesspiegel* (November 19, 2013).
59. Jürgen Quandt quoted in Wolf-Dieter Just, "20 Jahre Kirchenasylbewegung," in idem, Beate Sträter, *Kirchenasyl: Ein Handbuch* (Karlsruhe, 2003), 142.
60. PRO ASYL, ed., *Aufnehmen statt abwehren: Flucht, Asyl und zivilgesellschaftliches Engagement* (Karlsruhe, 2011).
61. See Frank Jansen, Heike Kleffner, Johannes Radke, and Toralf Staud, "Interaktive Karte Todesopfer rechter Gewalt in Deutschland seit der Wiedervereinigung," *Tagesspiegel* (September 27, 2018) (https://www

.tagesspiegel.de/politik/interaktive-karte-todesopfer-rechter-gewalt-in-deutschland-seit-der-wiedervereinigung/23117414.html).

62. Jochen Stahnke's interview with António Guterres, "Ohne deutschen Beitrag hätten wir eine katastrophale Lage," *Frankfurter Allgemeine Zeitung* (November 29, 2015). Also see Harriet Grant, "UN Agencies 'Broke and Failing' in Face of Ever-Growing Refugee Crisis," *Guardian* (September 6, 2015); Steven Erlanger and Kimiko de Freytas-Tamura, "U.N. Funding Shortfalls and Cuts in Refugee Aid Fuel Exodus to Europe," *New York Times* (September 19, 2015).
63. See www.bmi.bund.de/SharedDocs/pressemitteilungen/DE/2016/01/asylantraege-dezember-2015.html.
64. Robert Roßmann, "Was Merkel meidet," *Süddeutsche Zeitung* (April 13, 2015).
65. Quoted in Robin Alexander, *Die Getriebenen: Merkel und die Flüchtlingspolitik: Report aus dem Innern der Macht*, revised edition (Munich, 2018), 33.
66. Quoted in ibid., 41.
67. Ibid., 26.
68. https://dserver.bundestag.de/btd/18/073/1807311.pdf.
69. Jakob, *Die Bleibenden*, 12. The other examples are in ibid., 11–12, 171.
70. Quoted in Robin Alexander, "Nicht in unserer Macht, wie viele nach Deutschland kommen," *Die Welt* (October 8, 2017).
71. www.spiegel.de/politik/deutschland/fluechtlinge-angela-merkel-spricht-von-historischer-bewaehrungsprobe-fuer-europa-a-1067685.html (December 14, 2015).
72. Alexander, *Die Getriebenen*, 76. Looking back, many have described 2015's welcoming culture as "intoxication" (*Rausch*) or "euphoria." See for example Alexander, *Die Getriebenen*, 63 ("German *Rausch*"). Or Markus Ackeret, "Schnelles Ende der Euphorie," *Neue Zürcher Zeitung* (September 5, 2016) ("naive euphoria").
73. See the cover of *Stern*, no. 30 (July 16, 2015) and the cover of *Der Spiegel*, no. 39 (September 19, 2015).
74. The CDU politician Jens Spahn on September 13, 2015 in a newspaper interview retorted to the statement "but according to the Politbarometer poll two-thirds of Germans consider the immigration correct" made by a journalist that "The mood is changing by the hour." Robert Roßmann interview with Jens Spahn, "Spahn kritisiert deutsche Flüchtlingspolitik," *Süddeutsche Zeitung* (September 13, 2015).
75. Roßmann interview with Spahn, "Spahn kritisiert deutsche Flüchtlingspolitik."
76. Jörg Baberowski, "Europa ist gar keine Wertegemeinschaft," *Frankfurter Allgemeine Zeitung* (September 14, 2015); Peter Sloterdijk, "Die Machtwandlerin," *Handelsblatt* (September 18, 2015); Safranski quoted in Matthias Matussek, "Deutschland fluten? Da möchte ich gefragt werden," *Die Welt* (September 28, 2015).
77. Friederike Beck, *Die geheime Migrationsagenda* (Rottenburg, 2016); Katja Schneidt, *Wir schaffen es nicht: Eine Flüchtlingshelferin erklärt, warum die Flüchtlingskrise Deutschland überfordert* (Munich, 2016); Ali Sperling,

Merkels Flüchtlinge: Die schonungslose Wahrheit über den deutschen Asyl-Irrsinn! (North Charleston, 2016); Rolf Peter Sieferle, *Das Migrationsproblem: Über die Unvereinbarkeit von Sozialstaat und Masseneinwanderung* (Waltrop, 2017); Petra Paulsen and Thorsten Schulte, *Deutschland außer Rand und Band: Zwischen Werteverfall, Political (In)Correctness und illegaler Migration* (Zühlsdorf, 2018); Michael Berlach, *Deutschland im Jahr 2030: Ein Land konvertiert zum Islam* (2016); Mehrak Shirkhanloo, *Ist Deutschland verloren? Der Islam, Deutschland und eine Iranerin: Wie wir die Islamisierung stoppen und die Flüchtlingskrise angehen müssen!* (2017); Douglas Murray, *The Strange Death of Europe: Immigration, Identity, Islam* (London, 2017).

78. Roßmann interview with Spahn, "Spahn kritisiert deutsche Flüchtlingspolitik."
79. Alexander, *Die Getriebenen*, 76.
80. "Bono: Europe Needs to Become a 'Feeling' Not Just a 'Thought'" (August 29, 2018), www.faz.net/aktuell/politik/ausland/u2-singer-bono-europe-is-a-thought-that-needs-to-become-a-feeling-15758113.html.
81. This debate revolves around two poles. The cosmopolitan pole emphasizes the bonds between all humans and hence the invalidity of national borders. The communitarian pole, by contrast, stresses belonging to smaller collectives, such as the nation, and hence the right of the nation-state to reserve the blessings of the welfare state for its own citizens. For cosmopolitanism see for example Seyla Benhabib, *The Rights of Others: Aliens, Residents, and Citizens* (Cambridge, 2004). For communitarianism see for example David Miller, *Strangers in Our Midst: The Political Philosophy of Immigration* (Cambridge, MA, 2016). For an overview see Frank Dietrich, ed., *Ethik der Migration: Philosophische Schlüsseltexte* (Berlin, 2017). Some observers associate cosmopolitanism with Max Weber's ethic of conviction (*Gesinnungsethik*), and by contrast associate communitarianism with the ethic of responsibility (*Verantwortungsethik*). On this see Konrad Ott, *Zuwanderung und Moral* (Stuttgart, 2016).
82. See for example Paul Collier, *Exodus: How Migration Is Changing Our World* (New York, 2013); Alexander Betts and Paul Collier, *Refuge: Rethinking Refugee Policy in a Changing World* (New York, 2017); Julian Nida-Rümelin, *Über Grenzen denken: Eine Ethik der Migration* (Hamburg, 2017).
83. Nida-Rümelin, *Über Grenzen denken*, 13.
84. See Deutsches Historisches Museum (Berlin), *Deutscher Kolonialismus: Fragmente seiner Geschichte und Gegenwart* (Darmstadt, 2016), 228–229.
85. See Jürgen Zimmerer, *Von Windhuk nach Auschwitz? Beiträge zum Verhältnis von Kolonialismus und Holocaust* (Münster, 2011); David Olusoga and Casper Erichsen, *The Kaiser's Holocaust: Germany's Forgotten Genocide and the Colonial Roots of Nazism* (London, 2010); Isabel V. Hull, *Absolute Destruction: Military Culture and the Practices of War in Imperial Germany* (Ithaca, 2005); Benjamin Madley, "From Africa to Auschwitz: How German South West Africa Incubated Ideas and Methods Adopted and Developed by the Nazis in Eastern Europe," *European History Quarterly* 35, no. 3 (2005), 429–464.

86. See for example Jürgen Zimmerer, "Völkermord? Nicht zuständig," *taz* (January 24, 2018).

Conclusion

1. Oscar Handlin, *The Uprooted: The Epic Story of the Great Migrations That Made the American People* (Boston, 1951), 3 (emphasis in original).
2. Sternberger coined the term in 1979 when the Federal Republic turned 30. Key texts include Dolf Sternberger, *Verfassungspatriotismus* (Frankfurt am Main, 1990); Jürgen Habermas, "Citizenship and National Identity," in Jürgen Habermas, *Between Facts and Norms: Contributions to a Discourse Theory of Law and Democracy*, trans. William Rehg (Cambridge, 1996), 491–515; Jan-Werner Müller, *Constitutional Patriotism* (Princeton, 2007).
3. Herfried Münkler and Marina Münkler, *Die neuen Deutschen: Ein Land vor seiner Zukunft* (Reinbek, 2016), 287.
4. See ibid., 287–289.
5. Habermas seems to be moving toward a similar position, arguing that "'constitutional patriotism' is often misunderstood; in reality it implies that citizens do not just absorb the principles of a constitution abstractly, but do so concretely from the historical context of their own respective national histories." Jürgen Habermas, "Vorpolitische Grundlagen des demokratischen Rechtsstaates?," in Jürgen Habermas and Joseph Ratzinger, *Dialektik der Säkularisierung: Über Vernunft und Religion* (Freiburg im Breisgau, 2005), 25.
6. See Robert Habeck, *Patriotismus: Ein linkes Plädoyer* (Gütersloh, 2010). Also see Thomas Lindemann, "Grüner verlangt 'Patriotismus ohne Deutschland,'" *Die Welt* (April 9, 2010).
7. Thea Dorn, *deutsch, nicht dumpf: Ein Leitfaden für aufgeklärte Patrioten* (Munich, 2018). The concept of a *Kulturnation* is also invoked by Matthias Matussek, *Wir Deutschen: Warum die anderen uns gern haben können* (Frankfurt am Main, 2006). Unlike Dorn, however, Matussek plays down the population's broad support for Nazism, calling Hitler a "freak accident of the Germans." Matussek, *Wir Deutschen*, 14.
8. See Bernhard Schlink, *Heimat als Utopie* (Frankfurt am Main, 2000); Christoph Türcke, *Heimat: Eine Rehabilitierung* (Springe, 2006); Eberhard Rathgeb, *Am Anfang war Heimat: Auf den Spuren eines deutschen Gefühls* (Munich, 2016); Christian Schüle, *Heimat: Ein Phantomschmerz* (Munich, 2017).
9. See Friedrich Merz, "Einwanderung und Identität," *Die Welt* (October 25, 2000).
10. www.zeit.de/politik/deutschland/2017-04/thomas-demaiziere-innenminister-leitkultur/komplettansicht.
11. Jakob Augstein, "Wir brauchen eine Leitkultur," *Spiegel Online* (September 3, 2015); Raed Saleh, "Wir brauchen eine neue deutsche Leitkultur," *Der Tagesspiegel* (October 19, 2015). Many others could be adduced here; see for example, from a pan-European perspective, Ivan Krastev, "Central Europe is a Lesson to Liberals: Don't Be Anti-nationalist," *Guardian* (July 11, 2018).

12. For Saleh "the felt German Leitkultur" includes rituals like Christmas, certain kinds of food, family vacations in Germany (on the Baltic Sea in the case of the Saleh family), generosity and a willingness to make donations, environmentalism, pacifism, direct, democratic civil society involvement and popular culture (TV series). See Raed Saleh, *Ich deutsch: Die neue Leitkultur* (Hamburg, 2017), 129–151.
13. See www.berlin.de/ba-steglitz-zehlendorf/politik-und-verwaltung/aemter/amt-fuer-buergerdienste/einbuergerung.
14. See Bernd Ulrich, "Der große Sprung nach vorn," *Die Zeit* (October 18, 2010).
15. "The routine exclusion of noncitizens from modern systems of 'universal' suffrage is exemplary in this respect." Rogers Brubaker, *Citizenship and Nationhood in France and Germany* (Cambridge, MA, 1992), 28.
16. See Ayelet Shachar, *The Birthright Lottery: Citizenship and Global Inequality* (Cambridge, MA, 2009).

Index

For EU product safety concerns, contact us at Calle de José Abascal, 56–1°, 28003 Madrid, Spain or eugpsr@cambridge.org.

www.ingramcontent.com/pod-product-compliance
Ingram Content Group UK Ltd.
Pitfield, Milton Keynes, MK11 3LW, UK
UKHW020356140625
459647UK00020B/2498

* 9 7 8 1 0 0 9 2 4 2 2 5 7 *